Crime, Law, and Justice

First Edition

Edited by Desiré J. M. Anastasia,
Mark M. Lanier, and Douglas Klutz

San Diego State University/Metropolitan State University of Denver
University of Alabama, Tuscaloosa

cognella
academic publishing

Bassim Hamadeh, CEO and Publisher
Michael Simpson, Vice President of Acquisitions
Jamie Giganti, Managing Editor
Jess Busch, Graphic Design Supervisor
Seidy Cruz, Acquisitions Editor
Sarah Wheeler, Senior Project Editor
Natalie Lakosil, Licensing Manager

First published in the United States of America in 2014 by Cognella, Inc.

Trademark Notice: Product or corporate names may be trademarks or registered trademarks, and are used only for identification and explanation without intent to infringe.

Printed in the United States of America

ISBN: 978-1-62661-754-4 (pbk)/ 978-1-62661-755-1 (br)

www.cognella.com   800-200-3908

Contents

Introduction   1
    Desiré J.M. Anastasia and Stuart Henry

Section I: The Study of Crime and Criminal Justice

1. What is Crime?   9
    Douglas Klutz and Mark M. Lanier

2. The Definition and Theories of Crime   11
    Mark M. Lanier and Stuart Henry

3. Crime in Society   17
    Joycelyn M. Pollock

4. Why Do People Commit Crime?   37
    Joycelyn M. Pollock

Section II: Introduction to Criminology

5. Defining Criminology   59
    Douglas Klutz and Mark M. Lanier

6. The Criminal Man   61
    Cesare Lombroso with Gina Lombroso-Ferrero

7. What is Criminology? The Study of Crime, Criminals, and
Victims in a Global Context   63
    Mark M. Lanier and Stuart Henry

8. The Scope of Victimology   77
    William G. Doerner and Steven P. Lab

SECTION III: RESEARCH AND POLICY IN CRIMINAL JUSTICE

9. Understanding Criminals and Crime: Theory and Research   95
   Doris Layton MacKenzie

10. Ethics and Criminal Justice Research   101
    Belinda R. McCarthy and Robin J. King

11. Diversity and the Policy Agenda in Criminal Justice   117
    Mark Mitchell

12. Ethical Issues in Crime Control Policy and Research   129
    Michael C. Braswell, Belinda R. McCarthy, and Bernard J. McCarthy

SECTION IV: POLICING AND LAW ENFORCEMENT

13. Overview of Policing and Law Enforcement in the United States   133
    Douglas Klutz and Mark M. Lanier

14. The Idea of Community Policing   137
    Victor E. Kappeler and Larry K. Gaines

15. The Police: Historical and Contemporary Perspectives   163
    Geoffrey P. Alpert and Roger G. Dunham

16. Ethics and Police in a Time of Change   177
    John P. Crank and Michael A. Caldero

SECTION V: COURTS AND JUDICIAL PROCESS

17. Overview of Courts and Judicial Process in the United States   181
    Douglas Klutz and Mark M. Lanier

18. Due Process of Law   183
    Bruce E. Altschuler, Celia A. Sgroi, and Margaret Ryniker

19. Justice Delayed or Justice Denied? A Contemporary Review of
   Capital Habeas Corpus   211
   Jon B. Gould

Section VI: Corrections

20. Overview of Corrections in the United States   225
   Douglas Klutz and Mark M. Lanier

21. The Scale of Imprisonment in the United States:
   Twentieth Century Patterns and Twenty-First Century Prospects   229
   Franklin E. Zimring

22. Prison   241
   Peter B. Wood

23. Community Corrections   255
   Leanne Fiftal Alarid

INTRODUCTION

*Desiré J.M.
Anastasia and
Stuart Henry*

C*rime, Law and Justice* provides criminology and criminal justice students with an essential understanding of the criminal justice system in the United States based on criminological research and theoretical analysis. This book is designed to introduce students to the complete field of criminal justice from definitions, types, and extent of crime; the role of criminal and constitutional law; law enforcement, justice, and functions at state and local level; and federal agencies, such as the Federal Bureau of Investigation (FBI); Drug Enforcement Administration (DEA); Bureau of Alcohol, Tobacco, Firearms and Explosives (ATF); and U.S. Immigrations and Customs Enforcement (ICE) and to outline corrections, probation, parole, and alternatives to these formal methods of social control. Then, this book will lay the foundation for more in-depth examinations of each of these areas of study, and it does so by asking critical questions about why the system is the way it is and how it could be different. The overall approach that this book takes is that we can make a difference to improve the system and develop policies that reduce crime and the forces that the justice system tries to combat.

Section one, "The Study of Crime and Criminal Justice," begins by defining crime as the "commission or omission of a specific act punishable by the government" (Klutz and Lanier 2012, p. 4) and expands this to include "acts prohibited, prosecuted, and punished by criminal law" (Lanier and Henry 2010 [in Klutz and Lanier 2012], p. 8). Criminologists study different ways that societies define crime that expand the legal definition to include those that are based in harm creation that are not always criminally defined, such as white collar crime, corporate crime, environmental crime and state crime. A brief introduction to the criminal justice system is followed by an overview of theories that explain why people commit crimes (also called the "etiology" of crime). This overview lays the foundation for establishing the scope of this text, and provides an all-inclusive structure for more focused courses on crime causation, law creation, law enforcement, court processes, and correctional outcomes. The overview discusses "how society directs resources and implements policies in policing and law enforcement, the courts and judicial processes, and corrections" (Klutz and Lanier 2012, p. 4).

Section two, "Introduction to Criminology," focuses on defining and outlining the scope of criminology, as well as a sometimes overlooked dimension of criminology called "victimology." Criminology is the systematic study of the nature of crime, types of crime, and causes of crime and systems that societies use to control it. It is an applied social science that draws on multiple disciplines to inform its study and analysis. Indeed criminology is informed by biology, psychology, social psychology, social constructionism, geography, sociology, political science, anthropology, cultural studies and post-modernism. An illustration of this is found in school violence which involves micro-level examination of the biological, psychological and interactive causes that predispose certain students to become shooters; meso-level analyses involving families, peer-groups, neighborhoods and the institution of the school; to macro-level analysis that includes geographical and spatial factors affecting communities, societal level-causes including socio-economics, and the role of violence in the media, as well as political decisions resulting in policies such as zero-tolerance and access to guns, and cultural contexts that shape the school learning environment. "Drawing from different fields, including sociology, psychology, and law, criminology provides an interdisciplinary approach in order to better understand crime" (Klutz and Lanier 2012, p. 55). Criminology … is "an applied social science in which criminologists work to establish knowledge about crime and its control based on empirical research. This research forms the basis for understanding, explanation, prediction, prevention, and criminal justice policy" (Lanier and Henry 2010, p. 78).

Victimology is the mirror image of criminology, since it is "the scientific study of the physical, emotional, and financial harm people suffer because of illegal activities", as well as "the study of who becomes a victim, how victims are victimized, how much harm they suffer, and their role in the criminal act" (Karmen 2013, p. 2; Lanier and Henry, 2010, p. 19). A history of criminological theory and research is discussed in this section, in addition to an explanation of studying crime, criminals, and victims in a global context.

Section three, "Research and Policy in Criminal Justice," provides readers with an introduction to methods of criminal justice research, performing ethical research, the connection between criminological theories and criminal justice research, criminal justice policies, and ethical issues in crime control policy. However, criminal justice research is also considered scientific inquiry, "a method of inquiry—a way of learning and knowing things about the world around us" that has particular characteristics that make it systematic and controlled (Maxfield and Babbie 2011, p. 1). These characteristics distinguish scientific research from commonsense everyday research, hopefully with a lot fewer "errors" along the way. In addition, scientific research has to be ethical. That means it should not harm the subjects of the research (human subject protection) and the subjects have to voluntarily participate; they cannot be coerced, or forced to participate. Several groups of subjects are in protected categories as they are seen as vulnerable to exploitation or coercison and that incudes children, the mentally ill and prisoners. Voluntary participation is protected by a process known as "informed consent" in which researchers, intending to study a particular population of human subjects, have to provide their research protocol to a review board (known as an Institutional Review Board or IRB) explaining the purpose of the research and the intended use of any findings or results. Only after the "informed consent form" is signed by the potential research subject can the research begin.

Generally there are two broad areas of research in criminology and criminal justice. The first is research on the nature, extent, and causes of crime (i.e., criminal behavior). The second is research on the effectiveness of policies that deal with crime, in particular, the effectiveness of the police, courts, corrections and alternative programs within the criminal justice system. In conducting criminal justice research, a researcher can explore all aspects of crime; who becomes a criminal, what crimes are committed and why, who becomes a victim, why and how do these individuals experience victimization, who is employed in crime control, why and how these individuals decided on a criminal justice career, and myriad other questions? These are narrowed down to specific research questions such as "Are disgruntled employees more likely to steal from their employer than happy or respectful employees?"

"Are victims of child abuse more likely to themselves become violent offenders as adults?"

Research methodology is the process by which the researcher conducts the study. Put simply, there are two broad types of methods: quantitative and qualitative research. Quantitative research uses large sets of data gathered anonymously and using a random selection process, through surveys of victims or offenders, or that are compiled by criminal justice personnel, such as the police or corrections officers. When using the qualitative method, a researcher interviews subjects face-to-face, either in institutions or in their neighborhoods. Qualitative research can also involve studying the subjects in the act of crime, such as selling drugs in a neighborhood bar or while they are committing acts of shoplifting or embezzlement. This type of "participant observation" is similar to the ethnographical research methods used by anthropologists when they live in the societies they are studying to obtain a deeper understanding of the culture's customs and practices. This kind of research methodology also raises important and challenging ethical issues, particularly when the researcher is involved in the scene of crime. In addition to the possible legal ramifications of associating with subjects involved in illegal activities, the researcher must also consider the threat of violence often associated with this type of behavior. Which method should be used depends upon what research questions are trying to be answered (see Tewksbury 2009). Some researchers combine qualitative and quantitative methods, which is called "mixed method." Others may use case studies of one or two offenders, and yet others may conduct experimental research measuring, for example, whether the rate of re-arrest of offenders charged with substance abuse (called recidivism) is lower if they are sentenced by a drug court rather than a regular criminal court.

While there are many reasons to conduct research exploring why crimes occur, a major reason is to find ways to develop policies that prevent, reduce, or control crime. A policy is defined as:

The overall prescription for addressing law violation. ... It incorporates several elements. These include: 1. a correctional ideology that includes (a) philosophies that justify the use of state power against offenders ... and (b) strategies for action to be taken in relation to the offender ... 2. an administrative apparatus, the criminal justice system for processing offenders; and 3. Actions in the form of crime control techniques (e.g. punishment, treatment, reorganization of institutions) to be applied in conformity with the rules of the administrative system, to satisfy the goals of the philosophies and strategies previously specified." (Einstadter and Henry 2006, p. 21)

Thus, crime control policies explicitly refer to laws, regulations, and other governmental actions that are designed to reduce criminal acts. Data and results from criminal justice research may also drive the creation of crime control policies, as do specific criminal events such as found in Megan's Law and Chelsea's Law (both dealing with sex offenders), or the Polly Klaas murder that led to California's Three Strikes Law in 1994. Of course, whether research influences policy development as much as criminal justice researchers hope it does is an open question (see Garrison 2009).

Section four, "Policing and Law Enforcement," presents an overview of formal social control in the United States, with a specific focus on both community and ethical policing. Law enforcement is the general description of formal social control that operates at federal, state and local levels through a variety of policing agencies. These agencies maintain public order and enforce the law, and are charged with the powers of crime prevention, detection, and investigation apprehension of suspected offenders, using techniques of surveillance, tracking, investigating, and monitoring and the latest in crime analysis involving GIS mapping. (Bureau of Justice Statistics 2013; Manning 2008). Current trends in law enforcement, as well as the use of force by police officers, are also discussed in this section.

Section five, "Courts and Judicial Process," examines the court system in the United States and the judicial process within. Our court system consists of two types of courts: trial courts and appellate courts. Travis distinguishes between trial courts which "are fact-finding bodies whose job it is to determine the facts of a case" and appellate courts which "are law-interpreting bodies whose job it is to determine if the laws were correctly applied and followed" (Travis III 2012, p. 207). In other words trial courts deal with the substance of the law and whether it has been violated, whereas appellate courts deal with whether the correct principles and due process procedures were followed by the trial courts.

For the purpose of this text, courts are concerned with criminal law which "specifies the acts or omissions that constitute crime" (Lanier and Henry 2010 [in Klutz and Lanier 2012], p. 8). An overview of the courts and judicial process is provided along with a discussion of fair treatment (due process) within this process. Due process provides protection for the individual against state power, and was derived from the 13th Century English Magna Carta (1215) which states "No free man shall be seized or imprisoned, or stripped of his rights or possessions, or outlawed or exiled, or deprived of his standing in any other way, nor will we proceed with force against him, or send others to do so, except by the lawful judgment of his equals or by the law of the land." In contemporary America, due process includes the following four elements: 1. Equality between the parties, i.e. prosecution and defense; 2. Rules protecting the defendant against error; 3. Restraint of arbitrary power; and 4. The presumption of innocence. In contrast to this "due process" model is the model of "crime control," which: 1. Presumes guilt, 2. Disregards legal controls, and 3. Seeks efficiency at the expense of protecting rights (Packer 1968). Our examination of the courts also includes a discussion of how our court system *really* operates versus what is typically portrayed on television and in movies.

Section six, "Corrections," centers on the United States' corrections system. This section focuses on "the variety of programs, services, facilities, and organizations responsible for the management of individuals who have been accused or convicted of criminal offenses" (Klutz and Lanier 2012, p. 8). In this final section of the book, we explore the history and diverse forms of correctional styles and institutions, including institutional corrections and community corrections.

"Institutional corrections" refers to those people either convicted or charged with an offense. Institutional corrections consist of three basic types. First local jails operated by counties or cities designed to hold people convicted or a misdemeanor or awaiting trial who could not meet or who were denied bail. These people are typically held for periods of up to a year. Second, prisons consist of facilities designed for long-term incarceration of convicted offenders who have convicted a felony, and these are operated by states or by the federal government. Some states such as California have recently blurred this distinction through a process called "realignment," which means the courts can send various categories of offender, who normally would have been sent to prison, to jails for sentences longer than a year. This is to reduce the state's over-crowded prison situation and which was mandated for reduction under a federal court order. Third, there also increasingly exist private prisons run by different companies such as "The Corrections Corporation of America," which operate under contracts to house convicted offenders. Beyond these three types of prison are a variety of correctional facilities operated under special jurisdiction (Bureau of Justice Statistics, 2013b).

In contrast to prisons, "community corrections" refers to various practices used for supervising offenders in the community. Probation is one example that is familiar to most criminal justice students and involves close monitoring and supervision by probation officers to whom offenders have to report once a week. Another type is parole in which a person is given an early release date from a correctional facility in order to finish out the rest of his or her sentence under supervision in the community. More recently community corrections has also included restorative justice possibilities in which offenders are brought to account for their actions and share solutions in collaborative discussions with the victim and the community to compensate for the harm they have caused. These community restorative practices have the potential to prevent future crimes occurring by demonstrating the skills necessary to resolve minor conflict before they manifest into serious conflicts.

Finally, this book assumes the viewpoint of social constructionism (Sutton 2011). This is the theoretical approach that sees social institutions like the law, the courts, policing and corrections as the product of human interaction, negotiation and settlement. Social constructionism also argues that because things are the way they are, they do not have to be this way. They can be un-made and re-made. The challenge is to engage criminal justice critically, always suggesting ways it could improve, while not becoming bogged down in the minute detail of its daily operations, which cloud any ability to move forward.

In summary, this book introduces students to the critical cornerstones of the study of criminal justice—deviance, crime, law, research methods, criminal behavior, and criminal justice operations—and the interplay among them. The aim is to give students a fundamental understanding of how crime is defined to include certain behaviors and exclude others; how the law works to control the behavior of citizens and justice system professionals; why some people violate the law and others do not; the mechanisms employed to control crime and deal with criminal offenders; and the research techniques we use to discover what works, what does not, and what needs to change.

REFERENCES

Bureau of Justice Statistics. 2013a. "Law Enforcement." http://www.bjs.gov/index.cfm?ty=tpandtid=7

Bureau of Justice Statistics. 2013b. "Corrections." http://www.bjs.gov/index.cfm?ty=tpandtid=1

Einstadter, W. J., and S. Henry 2006. *Criminological Theory: An Analysis of its Underlying Assumptions*, 2nd ed. Boulder: Rowman and Littlefield.

Garrison, A. H. 2009. "The Influence of Research on Criminal Justice Policy Making." *Professional Issues in Criminal Justice* 4 (1): 9–21.

Karmen, A. 2013. *Crime Victims: An Introduction to Victimology*, 8th ed. Belmont: Wadsworth.

Klutz, D., and Lanier, M. M. 2012. *From the Crime to the Courts: An Overview of Criminology and Criminal Justice*. San Diego: Cognella.

Manning, P. K. 2008. *The Technology of Policing: Crime Mapping, Information Technology, and the Rationality of Crime Control*. New York: New York University Press.

Maxfield, M. G. and Babbie, E. R. 2011. *Research Methods for Criminal Justice and Criminology*, 6th ed. Belmont: Wadsworth Cengage.

Lanier, M. M., and Henry, S. 2010. *Essential Criminology*, 3rd ed. Boulder: Westview Press.

Packer, H. 1968. *The Limits of the Criminal Sanction*. Stanford: Stanford University Press.

Remington, F. J. 1960. "Criminal Justice Research," *Journal of Criminal Law, Criminology and Police Science* 51: 7–18.

Sutton, L. P. 2011. *Social Construction of Justice: A New Approach to Understanding Crime, Criminality and Criminal Justice*. San Diego: Cognella.

Tewksbury, R. 2009. "Qualitative versus Quantitative Methods: Understanding Why Qualitative Methods are Superior for Criminology and Criminal Justice. *Journal of Theoretical and Philosophical Criminology* 1 (1): 38–58.

Travis III, L. F. 2012. *Introduction to Criminal Justice*, 7th ed. Burlington: Anderson Publishing.

SECTION

I

The Study of Crime
and Criminal Justice

WHAT IS CRIME?

*Douglas Klutz and
Mark M. Lanier*

W hat comes to mind when you hear the word "crime"? Understanding the wide-ranging scope of crime is critically important as you begin your studies in criminal justice and criminology. Traditionally, when people hear the word crime, the immediate response is to think of violent crimes such as robbery, aggravated assault, and murder. Take for example your local news station. On any given night of the week, the first few news stories usually pertain to violent crimes such as local bank robberies, assaults, and murders. But crime is not simply limited to violent physical acts of force. Property crime for example, involves no threat of force or physical force against a victim. Conversely, violent crime involves direct force or threat of force against a victim.

Consider for instance the distinction between robbery and larceny-theft. Robbery is a violent crime defined by the Federal Bureau of Investigation (FBI) as the "taking or attempting to take anything of value from the care, custody, or control of a person or persons by force or threat of force or violence and/or by putting the victim in fear." The FBI defines larceny-theft as a property crime that involves the "unlawful taking, carrying, leading, or riding away of property from the possession or constructive possession of another." The important distinction between burglary and larceny-theft is that with a larceny-theft, there is no force or threat of force against a victim upon the taking of property. If in the taking of property force or the threat of force is employed, then the crime would be defined as a robbery.

White-collar crime is another example of a broad category of crime that does not involve physical force or the threat of force that traditional violent crimes involve. Instead, white-collar crime is usually hidden from the public's eye and occurs behind closed doors and computer monitors. White-collar crime generally involves complex and technical schemes designed to dupe victims due to the high positions of authority or trust white-collar criminals hold in society. Due to the complex nature of business in fields like finance and medicine, white-collar criminals can abuse their positions of authority to take advantage of the unsuspecting public. For instance, think about an average investor looking to make stable returns that outpace your traditional returns in a savings account. The investor goes with a well-respected financial advisor who promises a stable return for years to come. A few months later that same investor finds out that their financial advisor is really a con artist running an elaborate Ponzi scheme, and their original capital investment has been completely wiped out. Enron's phony accounting practices and subsequent bankruptcy, coupled with Bernie Madoff's elaborate Ponzi scheme resulting in "clients" being swindled out of billions of dollars, help underscore the fact that crime is not simply limited to traditional street crimes. While not publicized to the same extent as traditional street crime, white-collar crime has become increasingly expensive in the United States. At the very minimum, the FBI estimates white-collar crime costs the U.S. $300 billion annually.

Each year, the FBI produces a detailed inventory of crime statistics known as the Uniform Crime Reports, or the UCR. The UCR provides a comprehensive database of crimes reported by law enforcement agencies nationwide. Crimes reported in the UCR include violent and property crime defined as Part I offenses, along with less serious crimes under Part II offenses. Part II offenses include simple assaults, fraud, embezzlement, and driving under the influence, just to name a few. Cataloging and documenting crimes enables law enforcement agencies to better track and disseminate information relating to trends in crime. In general, crime can be defined as the commission or omission of a specific act punishable by the government. For example, omitting earned income to reduce your tax liability is a form of tax evasion and is considered a crime. Tax noncompliance is investigated and pursued by the Internal Revenue Service (IRS). While there is controversy surrounding the Sixteenth Amendment and the constitutionality of a federally mandated income tax, neglect to pay or accurately disclose your full tax liability and the IRS is likely to come knocking on your door.

Now that we have formulated a basic working definition of crime, what exactly is criminal justice? Criminal justice can simply be defined as the way society responds to crime. This includes how society directs resources and implements policies in policing and law enforcement, the courts and judicial processes, and corrections. In the United States, our criminal justice system faces unprecedented challenges in light of constantly advancing technologies. Social media outlets have revolutionized how society responds to crime. Twitter©, Facebook©, and YouTube© all allow instant access to information and real-time events. Social media enables users to instantly disseminate information to a large audience. Police departments have created Facebook© pages to post information targeting wanted persons, and have received numerous tips and sources of information that might not be available with other forms of media. Social media has also played a large role in keeping corruption and abuse of power in check. Information that is available through social media outlets might not be available through traditional mainstream outlets, and thus provides the public with a better depiction of what is really occurring directly at the scene of the crime. The following excerpt by Henry and Lanier (1998) expands on the definition and scope of crime and the criminal justice system.

The Definition and Theories of Crime

*Mark M. Lanier
and Stuart Henry*

Most definitions of crime have reflected particular disciplinary perspectives, with their tendency to amplify certain features of its nature, while diminishing the contribution of other factors and variables. For example, the legal approach to defining crime emphasizes the governmental definition of behavior as violations of its laws, while philosophers accentuate the moral dimension of harmful behavior. Sociologists focus their efforts on the consensus or conflict in society that the behavior represents, while anthropologists highlight crime's cultural relativity. Finally, historians focus on crime's temporal quality, and geographers accentuate the spatiality of crime.

An alternative approach uses the concept of a *prism of crime*. The prism of crime builds on Canadian criminologist John Hagan's concept of the "pyramid of crime" to develop an integrated definition. This approach is consistent with an interdisciplinary or integrated criminology that allows one to conceptualize crime holistically rather than partially, thus emphasizing its multiple dimensions. The prism idea simultaneously takes into account a variety of its constitutive dimensions, such as harm, morality, social reaction, deviance, and visibility. The prism of crime captures these multiple dimensions in one schematic conceptual framework.

Existing Definitions of Crime

In attempting to grapple with the array of different definitions of crime, criminologists have often simplified the problem by categorizing definitions dichotomizing between those theories emphasizing consensus and those emphasizing conflict. Consensus approaches argue that there is agreement about what constitutes crime but place a different weight on which dimension of consensus is most important. Conflict approaches argue that crime is a reflection of disagreements in society among people with various needs, agendas, and conceptions of harm that reflect their struggles over access to power and control.

Consensus Approaches

The most familiar consensus approach to crime is one that characterizes it as behavior that is a violation of law. A legal definition of *crime* refers to acts prohibited, prosecuted, and punished under the auspices of the written criminal legal code as defined by government.

The problem with the purely legal definition, from the perspective of historical and anthropological analysis, is that codes vary by culture, location, jurisdiction, and time. For example, consider laws regarding alcohol consumption. Drinking alcohol is legal in some locations but illegal in others; likewise, the legal age of consumption varies. Each of these elements also changes with time, as the U.S. Prohibition Amendment (1919–1933) and later raising the legal drinking age in the United States illustrate. A behavior considered illegal in the United States, such as marijuana smoking, may be legal in other countries.

Another consensus perspective comes from those who take a moral functionalist perspective toward defining crime. The French sociologist Émile Durkheim (1858–1917), for example, argued that crime is behavior that offends the common or collective conscience; the more the common conscience is shocked and indignant, the more criminal the behavior. This approach is problematic in that it leaves the definition of crime up to the changing moral sensibilities of groups.

Conflict Approaches

Conflict approaches see crime as the outcome of a struggle between people with competing interests. Sociologist Thorsten Sellin (1896–1994) presented one version of the conflict view in which he saw crime as an outcome of a clash over differences in primary and secondary cultures. Other scholars, taking a Marxist view, see the conflict over issues of social class and having the power to define some behavior as harm. From yet another perspective, American sociologist Edwin Sutherland (1883–1950) defined crime as behavior that is socially injurious, whether or not the law defines it as such, which was a radical position for his time. By this, he meant to include the harms by businesses that

officials saw as administrative irregularities but not criminal behaviors.

For some, the conflict over what the state defines as crime stems from the view that it is the outcome of an interactive process among people in different social positions. In this view, crime is seen as socially constructed by offenders, victims, bystanders, witnesses, social control agents, and so on and thus requires a convergence in time and place of these actors. Moreover, this convergence occurs in political situations and contexts, with various actors making "truth claims." The British left-realist criminologist Jock Young took an interactive approach to defining crime in his "square of crime." He saw crime as defined through an interaction among four elements, or sides of a square: (1) the offender, (2) the victim, (3) police agencies, and (4) the public, which must all be present and must interact socially. Furthermore, each element can change and can alter its relation to the other three based on situational contexts such as time, space, and social situations.

The role of power is crucial to conflict approaches. Powerful groups have the ability to shape legislation, to influence which laws are enforced, to determine which neighborhoods the police monitor, and to mandate penalties. For example, use of crack cocaine, which mostly attracts members of ethnic minority groups, is penalized much more severely than powder cocaine, which affluent whites are more likely to use. Some see the power to define crime as reflecting class interests and argue that, instead, the state should define crime by universal standards of violations of human rights, rather than by laws that reflect the interests of dominant elites. Others see a central role in defining crime in the hands of the mass media and those who control them. The media affect the visibility and seriousness with which the public sees harmful behavior and thereby the degree of consensus or conflict surrounding a behavior's criminality. Indeed, constitutive criminologists Stuart Henry and Dragan Milovanovic argue that power itself is the central element in defining crime, such that it is not harm defined by law that constitutes crime, but any instance of the use of power to deny others their humanity. This postmodern view suggests that law itself can be criminal, as can other institutions of society such as the media, corporations, organizations, and governments, where their actions or policies oppress others.

Integrative Approaches

To overcome the partiality of any one of these definitional approaches, a few criminologists have adopted an integrated approach that combines several of the dimensions into a holistic framework. Hagan defined crime in 1977 as a kind of deviance, which, in turn, consists of variation from a social norm that is proscribed by criminal law. He visually represented this synthesis in what he called the "pyramid of crime," whereby he combined three core dimensions into a single framework: (1) severity of the social harm, (2) severity of the societal response, and (3) the degree of agreement or disagreement about the significance of the norm violation. He also argued that assessments of behavior on any of these dimensions could change over time, as well as across different cultural contexts.

THE PRISM OF CRIME

Building on Hagan's approach, Mark Lanier and Stuart Henry developed the "crime prism" in 1998 (see Figure 1). They attempted to provide an inclusive definition of crime that accommodates the ideas of competing theorists beyond those identified by Hagan. The prism embodies the idea that "crime" varies historically, temporally, culturally, situationally, and by location. Moreover, what counts as crime is affected by the power of those defining it, which, in turn, can affect its visibility and the severity with which it is subject to penalty in law. Finally, people's prior experiences and views affect how they view an act. Two individuals may view the same act (sodomy, for example), and one defines it as criminal while the other does not.

The crime prism includes public awareness or "visibility." Some crimes, such as terrorist acts, are very visible; others, such as pollution, may remain out of public awareness for years. The prism also includes the degree of harm, but this is not just with respect to

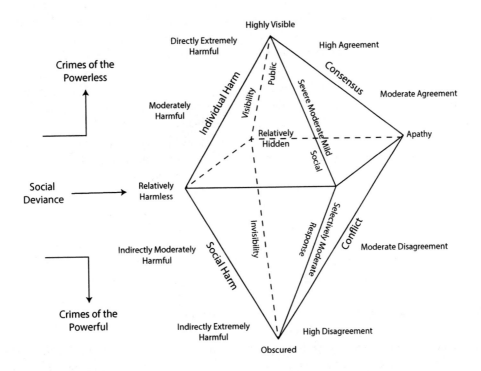

Figure 1 The Crime Prism

the greater or lesser severity for individual offenders; instead, it also involves a sense of collective or social harm, reflecting Sutherland's notion of social injury. The prism also considers the "extent of victimization." If only one person is harmed by a crime (for example, homicide), while certainly tragic and serious, such a crime is qualitatively and quantifiably different from a terrorist group murdering many people. The number of victims harmed influences a society's perception as to the seriousness of the crime, provided the victimization is visible. The "social response" to crime is also in the crime prism. The upper segment of the prism shows a high probability of severe sanctions (for instance, the death penalty or life in prison), followed by moderate sanctions (short prison terms, fines, or probation), to relatively mild sanctions (community service, public condemnation). The lower prism shows that severity of sanction can be selective, depending on the power of offenders to resist the law or to use legal resources to redefine their harms as less serious.

"Social agreement" about crime is included as a dimension of the prism, since individuals will disagree (that is, conflict) about the seriousness of different acts (for instance, pornography is more controversial than terrorism). As we move into the lower section of the prism, the obscurity of crime increases. Crime's effect becomes less direct and less visible. Conflict over its criminal definition increases and the seriousness of society's response becomes more selective. Acts that jurists have called mala prohibita crime are positioned here. Mala prohibita definitions of crime necessarily involve a social, ecological, and temporal context.

Crimes that do not reflect a consensus in society move toward the lower inverted part of the prism. At a lower level, crime is less apparent (hidden) and indirect, yet it may hurt many people over an extended period. Many white-collar crimes that involve insidious injury over time, such as pollution, would fit here. The impact of this type of crime is diffused and societal reactions diluted. Moreover, law enforcement is rarely equipped to handle it. In these situations, prison sentences are rarely given; the more common sanctions are fines, restitution, settlements, censure, and signs of disapproval. Regulatory agencies, rather than law enforcement, are responsible for law (or code) enforcement for many white-collar offenders. Unless the media publicize

the offense, corporations and their trade associations will likely handle these problems through their own disciplinary mechanisms.

At the very bottom, we find crimes that are so hidden that many may deny their existence, while others may argue the extent to which they are really crimes. For example, sexism is patriarchal, subdued, and so ingrained into the fabric of a society as to go unnoticed, yet its impact is widespread and harmful. The state rarely punishes hidden crimes. Those sanctions that occur generally involve social disapproval (though some groups will voice approval) and verbal admonishment,

The prism is easier to understand by placing actual examples of crimes on the prism schema. Consider, for example, a terrorist act. This crime is obvious, highly visible, extremely harmful, and noncontroversial with regard to the measure of consensus conflict, and the severity of societal reaction is typically the highest that society has, often the death penalty in those states that allow it. This crime would be placed at the very top of the prism. Slightly below the most serious crimes (mala in se) would be individual homicides, rapes, and so on, which, although extremely harmful, hurt few people with each individual act. Societal reaction is severe and involves little controversy. Sanctions may range from lengthy penal confinement to capital punishment. Below these come acts of robbery, burglary, larceny, and vandalism.

Apart from terrorism, which is viewed as a political crime, all the other examples considered were conventional crimes or "crimes of the powerless," reflecting the fact that persons in economically powerless positions in society tend to commit them. Each person committing such crimes uses excessive personal power to commit crime (such as guns, knives, or physical force), and their power does not come from their socioeconomic positions in society. Now consider "crimes of the powerful," committed by people in relatively strong legitimate economic and political positions in society, who use their structural rather than personal power to harm others. People in powerful occupational or political positions, such as business executives, professionals, lawyers, doctors, accountants, and politicians, commit these crimes (for example, insider trading, tax evasion, embezzlement, bribery and corruption, Medicare fraud, price-fixing, and pollution). These crimes would often be placed on the lower part of the prism, as they are often invisible and there are conflicting views about their criminality and their perpetrators' culpability, resulting in variable societal responses, yet they still can result in high levels of victimization. Overall, the upper half of the prism contains predominantly conventional crimes or "street crimes" while the lower half of the prism contains the greater preponderance of white-collar crimes, or "suite crimes," which are often obscured by conventional thinking about crime.

Having considered the location of crimes on the prism, it is apparent that the positioning of crimes in the prism varies over time, as society becomes more, or less, aware of them and recognizes them as more, or less, serious. For example, consider the changing positions of domestic violence, stalking, and sexual harassment, which have begun to move from the lower half to the upper half of the prism. Furthermore, consider the changing social consequences of cigarette smoking. It is also clear that by considering the multiple dimensions of crime, we are able more clearly to see behaviors that are harmful, regardless of their current legal standing, as well as the politics that suppresses their visibility from media attention and legal consequences. The implications of the prism approach suggest that a more integrative way of defining harm as crime would require a more comprehensive set of policies to protect society's members against both its visible and its invisible sources of victimization.

FURTHER READINGS

Barak, Gregg. (1996). *Integrating Criminologies*. Boston: Allyn and Bacon.

Canadian Law Commission. (2003). *What Is a Crime?* Ottawa: Author.

Gould, Leroy, Gary Kleck, and Mark Gertz. (2001). "Crime as Social Interaction." In *What Is Crime? Controversies over the Nature of Crime and What to Do about It*, edited by Stuart Henry and Mark Lanier. Boulder, CO: Rowman and Littlefield, 101–14.

Hagan, John. (1977). *The Disreputable Pleasures*. Toronto: McGraw-Hill.

Henry, Stuart, and Mark Lanier. (1998). "The Prism of Crime: The Arguments for an Integrated Definition of Crime." *Justice Quarterly* 15: 609–27.

Henry, Stuart, and Mark Lanier, eds. (2001). *What Is Crime? Controversies over the Nature of Crime and What to Do about It*. Boulder, CO: Rowman and Littlefield.

Henry, Stuart, and Dragan Milovanovic. (1996), *Constitutive Criminology: Beyond Postmodernism*. London: Sage.

Lanier, Mark, and Stuart Henry. (2004). *Essential Criminology*, 2d ed. Boulder, CO: Westview. (1st ed. 1998)

Michael, Jerome, and Mortimer, J. Adler. (1933). *Crime, Law, and Social Science*. New York: Harcourt Brace and Jovanovich.

Schnorr, Paul. (2001). "Defining Crime in a Community Setting: Negotiation and Legitimation of Community Claims." In *What Is Crime?* (supra), 115–38.

Schwendinger, Herman, and Julia Schwendinger. (2001). "Defenders of Order or Guardians of Human Rights." In *What Is Crime?* (supra), 65–100.

Surette, Ray, and Charles Otto. (2001). "The Media's Role in the Definition of Crime." In *What Is Crime?* (supra), 139–54.

CRIME IN SOCIETY

Joycelyn M. Pollock

What is crime? This seems like an easy question, and it is, in a way. However, the answer is not necessarily murder, robbery, or rape. Those may be examples of crime, but the definition of **crime** is simply "those actions that are prohibited by law." The definition exemplifies one of the fundamental problems of criminology. If criminology is the study of why people commit crime, then one can see why such a study may be difficult if the definition of crime changes. For instance, in past years abortion was a crime, and now it is not (at least in the first three months of a pregnancy), but it might be in the future. Gambling is usually illegal, unless it is buying a state lottery ticket or unless the state has legalized that specific form of gambling. So how does one construct an explanation for why people commit such "crimes" when sometimes they are and sometimes they are not crimes at all?

What is deviance? Crime and deviance may be considered synonyms, but they are definitely not. **Deviance** can be defined as behaviors that are contrary to the norm. Deviance has a negative connotation, but it simply means that the behavior is unusually infrequent. Most crime is deviant. There are very few serial killers (thank goodness!) and even relatively few burglars compared to the total population. On the other hand, some "crime" is not deviant at all. Can you think of some? (Hint: How many people break speeding laws?) Even simple assault is not really deviant. In fact, perhaps you have been a victim or perpetrator of simple assault and never realized it. The definition of simple assault in one state is:

1. intentionally, knowingly, or recklessly causes bodily injury to another, including the person's spouse;
2. intentionally or knowingly threatens another with imminent bodily injury, including the person's spouse; or
3. intentionally or knowingly causes physical contact with another when the person knows or should reasonably believe that the other will regard the contact as offensive or provocative.[1]

So, if you pushed or even hugged someone who you knew would consider it to be provocative or offensive, you have committed simple assault. This is a Class A misdemeanor unless some other conditions are met, therefore, it is not a very "serious" crime. Most simple assaults are not brought to the attention of the criminal justice system. However, many other, more serious crimes are also never reported. This creates what is known as the **dark figure** of crime, which is crime that does not find its way into official numbers. Crimes such as domestic violence, acquaintance rape, and even theft, are more likely than other crimes to be part of this dark figure of crime.

Because the dark figure of crime is so high, it makes any theorizing about criminals highly questionable. We do not know if the offenders who never come to the attention of authorities are similar to those who do. We do not know if these unknown offenders have similar motivations and patterns of criminal offending. Studies that are based only on known offenders may be faulty in that they are not able to base findings on all offenders—only those we know about.

DEFINING CRIMES

Crime is called a "constructed reality" because it is created based on the definitions and perceptions of the observers, formal system actors (such as police), victims, and the actions of the perpetrator. Box 3.1 illustrates the sequence of decision making. Person A shoves Person B. Is it simple assault? It would be only if Person A did it intentionally, believing it to be offensive to Person B. Is it a crime? It is only if it meets the legal definition as provided above. Is it prosecutable? It might be only if Person B reports it (unless a police officer happened to be standing nearby). Will it be prosecuted? A variety of factors affect the decision to prosecute, including the wishes of the victim, the resources of the prosecutor's office, the nature of the evidence, and, some say, perhaps the race and ethnicity of the offender and/or victim.

Definition of Crime by Legislators

Before we can punish any act as a crime, a law has to be created by legislation. As we learned in the last chapter, most of our laws come from common law; however, state and federal legislators are constantly fine-tuning our criminal codes and adding new laws or changing existing laws.

In most states, carrying a weapon onto state property, such as a university, is a crime, unless one is a licensed peace officer on duty. Since the tragedy at Virginia Tech University in 2007, when Seung-Hui Cho killed 32 students and professors and wounded dozens more, at least one state (South Carolina) has considered legislation that would make it legal to carry concealed weapons onto college campuses.[2] This illustrates the dynamic nature of law. Legal changes often occur in response to a specific event and some changes may take place before due consideration is given to their ramifications. Legislators typically pass legislation creating new laws in response to a news event and public attention toward a particular type of behavior. The public also has a great deal of influence when they want to increase

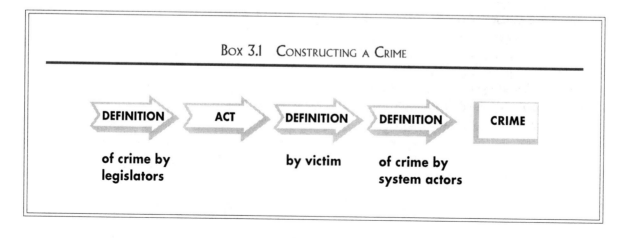

BOX 3.1 CONSTRUCTING A CRIME

DEFINITION → ACT → DEFINITION → DEFINITION → CRIME

of crime by legislators   by victim   of crime by system actors

the punishment for certain crimes. The perceptions and response to domestic violence, drunk driving, and drug use have undergone dramatic change in the last 30 years. Drug laws, especially, have changed in response to public sentiment and legislative initiatives.

Definition of Crime by Victim

Before a crime can be counted by officials, it must be reported by the victim. Why might someone *not* report a crime to authorities? The most common reason is that they believe police can't do anything about it, but they might also interpret the event as a private matter and not a crime. Domestic violence victims sometimes do not want the involvement of the police even though they are obviously victims of assault.

Rape victims also may not report their own victimization, sometimes because they do not want formal intervention, but sometimes because they do not interpret the event as a crime. Studies have shown that female victims who are raped in "date-rape" scenarios by someone they know in circumstances where the lack of consent may be somewhat ambiguous sometimes do not define what occurred as a crime. If the victim does not perceive the event as a crime, or does not want formal system intervention, then the event is never reported to police and cannot appear in our crime statistics.[3]

Definition of Crime by System Actors

Police do not arrest in a large percentage of cases where an arrest is legally justified; perhaps in as many as half of all cases. Although arrests are usually made in serious felony cases, or in situations in which victims demand an arrest, even assaults may be dealt with informally rather than by initiating a formal report or arrest.[4] Understanding when and why police choose to make arrests is a necessary part of understanding crime statistics. We forget that crime reports are simply the crimes that victims choose to report, and arrest statistics represent only the cases in which police officers made an arrest. Both are only a portion of the total number of criminal incidents.

One of the most important questions in the study of criminal justice is whether police enforce the law unfairly and are more likely to target minorities for formal system responses. There are many studies that explore the issue, but it is not an easy topic to analyze because it must involve the researcher being able to access information on each police-citizen interaction that might have resulted in an arrest to determine if certain factors, such as race, age, sex, or demeanor, affected the decision.

One of the reasons we use homicide, robbery, and burglary as indicators of crime is that they are less subject to the discretion of system actors. When these acts occur, it is more likely that everyone agrees that they are crimes, and system actors are more likely to begin formal processing. As we discussed above, even assault may be subject to individual definitions and interpretations of the offender, victim, and system actors, therefore fluctuations in assault rates may be real differences in such behavior, or differences in perception and/or enforcement of the behavior that can be defined as assault.

VICTIM-HARMING CRIMES

It might be helpful to consider crime as victim-harming or victimless. **Victim-harming crimes** are those where there is a specific victim who has been injured or suffered a loss. **Victimless crimes** are those where there is no direct victim. Thus, most drug laws are victimless crimes, as are gambling, underage drinking, and so on. These acts are prohibited because society has deemed them injurious to at least the perpetrator and, sometimes, others, but not in a direct way. Some might argue, in fact, that no crimes are truly victimless because such actions may harm, even if indirectly, family members or friends of the perpetrator.

Crimes such as assault, rape, robbery, burglary, larceny/theft and others are victim-harming crimes. Even theft from large corporations or income tax evasion would be considered victim-harming because there is a loss that is suffered directly from the action. What about computer hacking? Simply breaking into a computer security system on a dare and not doing any damage could still be considered an injury because it requires the company to bolster its defenses; therefore, one might place computer hacking into the victim-harming category.

What about prostitution? (Victimless?) Teen prostitution? (Victim-harming?) Pornography? (Victimless?) Child pornography? (Victim-harming?). If you disagree, what are the elements of your argument as to why it should be the other category? What are some other crimes that are victimless crimes? What are some that are victim-harming? There are several different drug-related crimes, including simple possession, possession with intent to sell, and smuggling. Are some victim-harming and some victimless crimes? The reason we may want to distinguish victim-harming and victimless crimes is that if we want to understand what motivates people to commit a crime, then there might be dramatically different answers depending on the crime. One can see, for instance, that different explanations might be applied to why someone uses drugs or gambles, from why someone rapes or robs another. On the other hand, there are some criminologists who would argue that the same underlying reason could explain both victim-harming and victimless crimes.[5]

Crime is not usually glamorous. Crime is not often committed by offenders who painstakingly plan their act and play cat-and-mouse games with determined detectives as we see in the movies or on television. Mostly, crimes are mundane, committed by individuals who are not necessarily committed to a criminal lifestyle, and result in relatively modest losses to the victim. Even homicide is rarely as it is depicted on television. On television, homicide is often committed by strangers; in reality, many homicides occur between people who know each other and happen as a result of a dispute or altercation.

Before we can ask the question "Why do people commit crime?" we need to be aware of the characteristics of crime. In other words, we need to know the "who, what, and where" of crime. To understand crime patterns, we use a number of sources of crime data. These are not perfect and each has inherent weaknesses, but they are the source of everything we think we know about crime in this country.

SOURCES OF CRIME DATA

The two most common sources of crime data are the Uniform Crime Reports and the National Crime Victimization Survey. It is important to note that everything that we think we know about crime is derived primarily from these sources; thus, if there is some bias (inaccuracy) present in the way they present the pattern of crime, then what we know is not necessarily accurate.

The Uniform Crime Reports

The most well-known and used source of crime statistics in this country is the **Uniform Crime Reports**. This collection of local crime reports and arrest data began in 1929 and is now produced by the Federal Bureau of Investigation. The numbers come either directly from local law enforcement agencies or from a state agency that collects the data from local agencies and delivers it in a centralized format. In 2004, according to *Crime in the United States, 2004*, the reports represented 94.2 percent of the total population of the country (the remaining locales did not participate).[6]

$$\text{Rate} = \frac{\text{\# crimes known to police}}{\text{\# total population}} \times 100,000$$

The Uniform Crime Reports presents crime in terms of **rates**. A rate is the number of crimes divided by the population and then multiplied to display by a standard number. Using the mathematical formula, one computes the number of crimes committed per every 100,000 people in the population.

The advantage of a rate is that it allows us to compare patterns of crime in very different populations. For instance, with rates, we can compare the same city in two different periods, even if the city has grown. We can also compare two different cities, even if one is very large and the other very small. Knowing, for instance, the raw number of burglaries in New York City, Portland, Oregon, and Detroit, Michigan, tells us something, but it doesn't tell us the relative risk of victimization in these cities because they do not have the same populations. The only way to compare the crime of two different populations is to compute the rate of each city, then compare the rates. In 2005, the *numbers* of reported burglaries and the *rates* for these cities looked like this:

CITY	POPULATION	NUMBER OF BURGLARIES	RATE
New York City	8,115,690	23,210	285
Portland	540,389	6,121	1,132
Detroit	900,932	15,304	1,698

Who would have thought that there were more burglaries per 100,000 people in Portland and Detroit than in New York? One might conclude that it was somehow connected with having a large population that made New York City's rate so low, but compare other big cities:

CITY	POPULATION	NUMBER OF BURGLARIES	RATE
Houston	2,045,732	27,541	1,346
Los Angeles	3,871,077	22,592	583
Boston	567,589	4,531	798

These cities also had higher rates than New York City. So, despite the stereotype of high crime in the Big Apple, these numbers indicate that maybe the city is not as unsafe as we might think.

It should also be noted, however, that the FBI cautions against anyone using these numbers to compare the crime risk between cities because there are so many variables that go into them, including reporting practices, urban density, the department's reporting practices, and so on. If a city extends its limits out into the suburbs, the crime rate will be lower because crime occurs less often in suburban than in urban areas. Thus, New York's city limits may be drawn in such a way that it brings down the rate of burglary, compared to other cities. Also, burglaries may not be recorded in the same manner, or people may be less inclined to report them in New York City.

It is very important to have an accurate population base for rates to mean anything. If the population base is inaccurate, then so, too, will be the rate. If, for instance, the population base is out of date and the actual population has grown considerably, then the crimes (which inevitably would increase with a larger population) will be divided by an artificially small population indicating that the rate of crime in that locale (the amount of crime per person) is higher than what it actually is. In contrast, if the population used is inaccurate in the other direction and shows a much larger population than what actually exists (perhaps because people have been moving away from that area), and crimes are divided by this inaccurately high population, then the crime rate will appear to be lower than it actually is. Usually, the FBI uses the most recent Census numbers for the area, but these numbers may be vulnerable to rapid fluctuations in population/migration.

You can look at the crime rates for your state or even your city by going to the FBI Web site or by looking in a library for their yearly report, titled *Crime in the United States*. Crimes are reported by state, region, and by city-rural categories.

These numbers are gathered from law enforcement agencies via a standard reporting form so that, for instance, larceny means the same thing in all states despite different state laws defining the dollar amount that would change larceny from a misdemeanor to a felony. Because these are standard definitions, they may or may not conform to the state's definition for that particular crime. Also, because of the index crime definitions, it is difficult to use this source to find out about certain crimes such as domestic violence or identity theft, because the reporting is not set up to identify them.

The UCR provides the total number of reported crimes for the seven index crimes: murder and nonnegligent manslaughter, forcible rape, robbery, aggravated assault, burglary, larceny-theft, motor vehicle theft, and arson. Box 3.2 shows how violent crime reports have decreased over the years, although the decreasing numbers seem to be leveling off. Box 3.3 shows property crimes.

The numbers of arrests are by no means a measure of crime, because they capture only the crimes in which a suspect was identified and a decision to arrest was made. It is interesting, however, that arrests also decreased during the period when we saw the large drop in reported crime. Arrest data is presented for 21 crime categories in Box 3.4. The table shows that arrests for most crimes have been decreasing over the last 15 years.

Many crimes go unsolved or are not cleared. Crimes are considered cleared when an arrest is made for an offense. The UCR reports the number of crimes cleared by arrest with a statistic called the **clearance rates**. The clearance rates vary greatly for different crimes. In 2004, The UCR showed national clearance rates. Homicide has the highest clearance rate (62.6%) while burglary has the lowest clearance rate (12.9%).[8]

One of the most often cited criticisms of the UCR is that it represents only reported crimes. If someone does not report a criminal victimization to the police, it does not get counted as a crime. Consequently, we note that there is a "dark" figure of crime that never appears in the UCR. The amount of unreported crime varies by the type of crime, but in general, it is estimated that about half of all crime does not appear in the UCR. This presents a distinct problem if one uses the UCR as a measure of crime. In fact, it is not a measure of crime, but only a measure of *reported* crime.

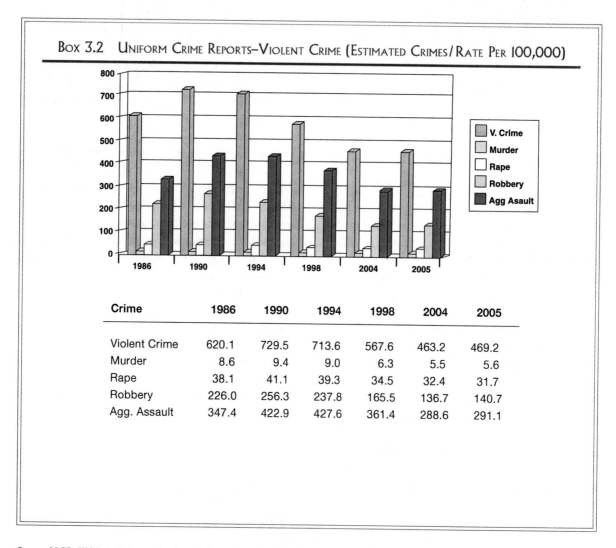

BOX 3.2   UNIFORM CRIME REPORTS–VIOLENT CRIME (ESTIMATED CRIMES/RATE PER 100,000)

Crime	1986	1990	1994	1998	2004	2005
Violent Crime	620.1	729.5	713.6	567.6	463.2	469.2
Murder	8.6	9.4	9.0	6.3	5.5	5.6
Rape	38.1	41.1	39.3	34.5	32.4	31.7
Robbery	226.0	256.3	237.8	165.5	136.7	140.7
Agg. Assault	347.4	422.9	427.6	361.4	288.6	291.1

Source: UCR, Table 1. *Crime in the United States.* By Volume and Rate, 1986–2005. Retrieved from: www.fbi.gov/ucr/05cius/data/table/_.01/html.

The FBI has also been collecting crime statistics in a different format. The National Incident Based Reporting System (NIBRS) gathers much more detailed information about each criminal incident. While the UCR reporting format is hierarchical, meaning that only the most serious crime is counted, NIBRS requires information to be submitted on each crime within a criminal transaction. Instead of reporting crimes via the eight index offenses, NIBRS will display information on Group A offense categories (22) and Group B offenses (11). More information is obtained about each offense, including information about the victim and offender. NIBRS reports are not comparable to the UCR because the way crimes are counted is different. For instance, a robbery, rape, and murder would only be reported as a murder in the UCR, but as three separate crimes under NIBRS. Law enforcement agencies have been slow to adopt the NIBRS reporting procedures, most probably because it is much more detailed, requiring more effort to enter the data.

Victimization Studies

Another source of crime statistics comes from victimization surveys. The Bureau of Justice Statistics presents findings from the **National Crime Victimization Survey**. Begun in 1973, the U.S. Bureau of the Census has been interviewing household members in a nationally representative sample. The items in the

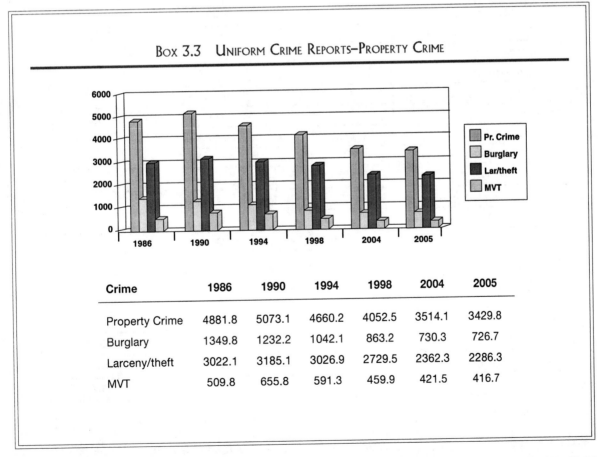

BOX 3.3   UNIFORM CRIME REPORTS–PROPERTY CRIME

Crime	1986	1990	1994	1998	2004	2005
Property Crime	4881.8	5073.1	4660.2	4052.5	3514.1	3429.8
Burglary	1349.8	1232.2	1042.1	863.2	730.3	726.7
Larceny/theft	3022.1	3185.1	3026.9	2729.5	2362.3	2286.3
MVT	509.8	655.8	591.3	459.9	421.5	416.7

Source: UCR, Table 1. *Crime in the United States.* By Volume and Rate, 1986–2005. Retrieved from: www.fbi.gov/ucr/05cius/data/table/_.01/html.

BOX 3.4   UNIFORM CRIME REPORT ARRESTS (BY RATE/PER 100,000)

CRIME	1995	2000	2005
Murder/non-negligent Manslaughter	8.5	4.8	4.7
Forcible rape	13.5	9.8	8.6
Robbery	70.2	39.7	39.2
Aggravated Assault	223.0	173.9	152.2
Burglary	148.8	104.0	101.2
Larceny/theft	592.7	429.5	392.6
MVT	75.9	54.2	49.7
Arson	7.6	5.9	5.5
Other assaults	496.5	471.4	440.2
Forgery and counterfeiting	46.8	39.1	40.0
Fraud	162.9	117.4	106.4
Embezzlement	5.9	6.9	6.5
Stolen Property	65.1	43.2	45.6
Vandalism	118.5	101.3	94.8
Weapons	95.3	57.9	65.6
Prostitution	41.3	33.7	28.8
Sex offenses	36.8	3.6	27.2
Drug abuse violations	582.5	572.4	496.8
Gambling	8.0	4.0	2.2
Offenses against family and children	53.4	50.1	55.3
DUI	526.0	508.6	328.2
Liquor laws	221.6	239.3	128.4
Drunkenness	268.4	232.5	80.1
Disorderly conduct	285.9	231.5	293.3
Vagrancy	10.4	12.1	10.4
All other (except traffic)	1,486.3	1,324.2	933.2
Curfew and loitering	58.5	58.0	86.1
Runaways	96.6	51.4	19.7

Source: UCR, Table 30. *Crime in the United States*, 1995, 2000, 2005: Number and Rate of Arrests. Retrieved from: http://www.fbi.gov/ucr/cius and http://www.fbi.gov/ucr/05cius/data/ table_30.html.

survey capture more information than what is available through the UCR. For instance, one question asks the respondent whether the crime was reported to the police. This is the source for our information about how much of crime goes unreported.

Questions cover information on the victim (i.e., age, sex, race, ethnicity, income, and educational level), and, if known, the offender (i.e., age, sex, race). It also reports findings on the victimization itself, including time and place and level of injury or loss. Findings from the National Crime Victimization Survey can be accessed most easily through the Bureau of Justice Statistics, an agency that also presents other forms of crime statistics.

These two sources of crime data may be compared, but it is important to note their differences. The NCVS excludes homicide, arson, commercial crimes, and crimes against children under age 12 (the UCR includes these crimes). The UCR only collects arrest data on simple assault and sexual assaults other than rape, not reported crimes in these areas. Further, the NCVS calculates rates on the basis of 1,000 *households* while the UCR calculates rates based on 100,000 *persons*. Thus, it would be a mistake to treat findings from the two sources as comparable statistically. In general, the UCR gives us a broad picture of crime patterns (as reported to police) in the United States while the NCVS gives us more information about the characteristics of victimizations and reporting trends by victims.

Because the NCVS is based on a random sampling of the population and does not collect reports of all victimizations, it is subject to all the potential problems of sampling and survey weaknesses. If any principles of random sampling are violated, then the applicability to the general population is in doubt. However, it is important to note that the NCVS also showed a decline of reported crime victimization in the last decade, thus the two sources of crime data were consistent in measuring a crime decline.

Self-Report Studies

Another source of crime data is simply to ask the offender. Self-report studies ask individuals to report the crimes they have committed. Obviously there are problems inherent in such an approach, such as whether the individual is answering honestly or not. Self-reports are generally only obtained from targeted groups, specifically juveniles (who are still in school), and offenders (who are incarcerated). We do not administer self-report surveys door-to-door to samples of citizens. Self-report studies provide interesting information, but the findings must be considered in light of the characteristics of the sample. For instance, self-report studies of juveniles often use measures of behavior that stretch the definition of "crime" to the breaking point by including minor deviances, such as truancy and other forms of juvenile misbehavior. The definitions of wrongdoing are expanded in such studies because most students have not committed any criminal acts. Therefore, in order to get sufficient numbers for statistical analysis, the definition of "offender" is expanded. It should be kept in mind when reading these studies that these "offenders" are not necessarily who we think of as criminals.

Part of the reason that student self-report studies have difficulty obtaining sufficient numbers of offenders for statistical analysis is that by the time they are administered in junior or senior years, many high-risk juveniles have already dropped out or are not in school the day the study is administered. Therefore, the group of young people most likely to have committed crimes are likely to be absent from the study and the reports of criminal activity are likely to underrepresent the true nature of juvenile crime.

Like school samples, prisoner samples are also relatively easy to obtain, but are also non-representative. Prisoners do not represent all offenders (only those who are caught and sentenced to prison). They also may not admit or may exaggerate their criminal activities. In addition, these surveys are subject to the potential inaccuracies of all surveys in that respondents may forget or mis-remember when events occurred.

Self-report studies give us more information about the offenders' patterns of criminal activity—if we can trust the data. One of the uses of self-report studies is to see if official statistics accurately represent who commits crime. We have found from self-reports of juveniles, for instance, that many more juveniles have committed crimes than official arrests indicate. This raises the question, "When do system actors (police) utilize formal methods of social control versus informal?"

Cohort Studies

One other source of crime data are **cohort studies**, which follow a group of subjects over a long period. For instance, one cohort study followed all males born in Philadelphia in 1948.[9] Another longitudinal study conducted by the Harvard Program on Human Development and Criminal Behavior collected data on a cohort sample.[10] Typically the follow-up period extends throughout childhood and into adulthood. Proponents of longitudinal research argue that this method of data collection can illuminate how factors work at various times in one's life. Longitudinal research identifies those correlates of delinquency that emerge during the lifetime of the cohort members. For instance, Farrington, Ohlin, and Wilson[11] identified the following as correlates of delinquency and crime:

> We know that the typical high-rate offender is a young male who began his aggressive or larcenous activities at an early age, well before the typical boy gets into serious trouble. We know that he comes from a troubled, discordant, low-income family in which one or both parents are likely to have criminal records themselves. We know that the boy has had trouble in school—he

created problems for his teachers and does not do well in his studies. On leaving school, often by dropping out, he works at regular jobs only intermittently. Most employers regard him as a poor risk. He experiments with a variety of drugs—alcohol, marijuana, speed, heroin—and becomes a frequent user of whatever drug is most readily available, often switch ing back and forth among different ones.[12]

Thus, individual differences, family influences, school influences, and peer influences were all identified as potential predictors of the onset of, continuation in, and desistance from crime.

PATTERNS OF CRIME

According to the Uniform Crime Reports and the National Crime Victimization Survey, crime has shown a steady overall decline since the early 1990s. In Box 3.5, we see that: (a) there is much more property crime than violent crime, and (b) that property crime has shown a more dramatic decline than violent crime. The long timeline in Box 3.5 does not show enough detail to see that violent crime actually declined quite substantially from a high of 758 crimes per 100,000 in 1991 to a low of 475 in 2003. The violent crime decline is shown in the second table.

The National Crime Victimization Survey also indicates that Americans have experienced a dramatically declining crime rate over the last decade. In Box 3.6, victimization survey data shows that, for violent crime and property crime, the decline is comparable to that recorded in the Uniform Crime Reports.

THE GREAT AMERICAN CRIME DECLINE

The biggest "story" in criminal justice in the last 20 years was the dramatic drop experienced through the

Box 3.5   UNIFORM CRIME RATE OVER TIME

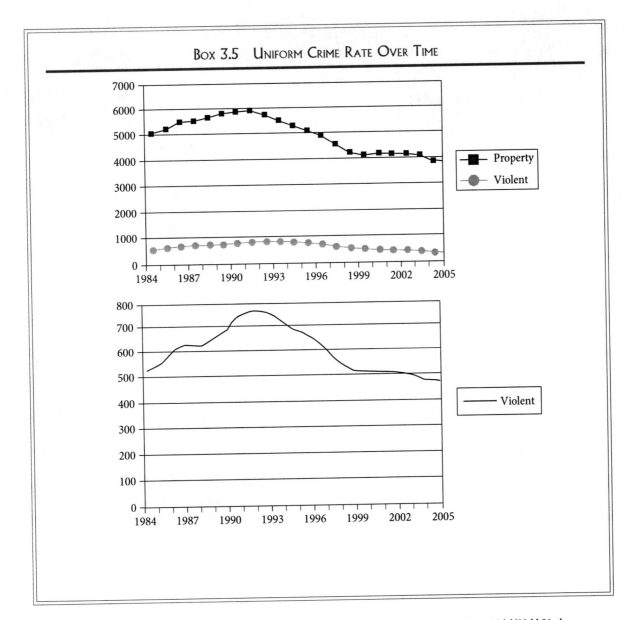

Source: Crime in the United States, 2003, Table 1. Retrieved November 11, 2007 from: www.fbi.gov/ucs/cius_03/xl/03tbl.01.xls.

latter half of the 1990s. Although the decrease has leveled off in some locales in recent years, we experienced truly amazing drops in all crime, including homicide and other violent crimes. Why? It could be any of the following factors:

+ aging birth cohort of baby boomers

+ stabilization of drug markets
+ higher incarceration rates
+ community policing
+ "zero tolerance" policing
+ home health care and pre- and post-natal health services
+ violence prevention programs in schools

BOX 3.6   BUREAU OF JUSTICE STATISTICS: PROPERTY AND VIOLENT CRIME VICTIMIZATION

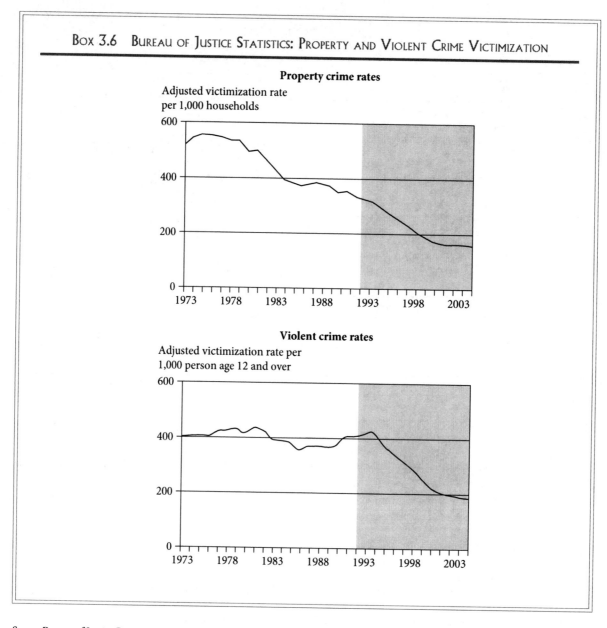

Source: Bureau of Justice Statistics. Retrieved April 1, 2007 from: http://www.ojp.usdoj.gov/bjs/glance/cv2.htm.

- increased numbers of abortions in the late 1970s and 1980s[13]

There is no consensus as to whether any of these factors, either alone or in combination, account for the dramatic decline of crime. One thing that hasn't happened as a result, however, is any decline in the size of criminal justice system.

It also appears that the great crime decline may be over. In Box 3.7, the introduction and summary of the 2006 Uniform Crime Reports is provided.

BOX 3.7   NEWS RELEASE (SEPTEMBER 2007): FBI RELEASES ITS 2006 CRIME STATISTICS

Washington, D.C.—For the second consecutive year, the estimated number of violent crimes in the nation increased, and for the fourth year in a row, the estimated number of property crimes decreased.

According to statistics released today by the FBI, the estimated volume of violent crime increased 1.9 percent, and the estimated volume of property crime decreased 1.9 percent in 2006 when compared with 2005 figures. The estimated rate of violent crime was 473.5 occurrences per 100,000 inhabitants (a 1.0-percent increase when the 2006 and 2005 rates were compared), and the estimated rate of property crime was 3,334.5 per 100,000 inhabitants (a 2.8-percent decline).

The FBI presented these data today in the 2006 edition of Crime in the United States, a statistical compilation of offense and arrest data as reported by law enforcement agencies throughout the nation. The FBI collected these data via the Uniform Crime Reporting (UCR) Program.

The UCR Program gathers offense data for violent and property crimes. Violent crimes are the offenses of murder and nonnegligent manslaughter, forcible rape, robbery, and aggravated assault; property crimes are the offenses of burglary, larceny-theft, motor vehicle theft, and arson. (Though the FBI classifies arson as a property crime, it does not estimate arson data because of variations in the level of participation at the agency level. Consequently, arson is not included in the estimated property crime total.) The Program also collects arrest data for violent and property crimes as well as 21 additional offenses that include all other offenses except traffic violations.

In 2006, more than 17,500 city, county, college and university, state, tribal, and federal agencies voluntarily participated in the UCR Program. These agencies represented 94.2 percent of the nation's population. A summary of the crime statistics presented in Crime in the United States, 2006, follows:

- Nationwide, there were an estimated 1,417,745 violent crimes reported in 2006.
- Of the violent crimes, the estimated number of murders and nonnegligent manslaughters increased 1.8 percent, and the estimated number of robberies increased 7.2 percent in 2006 when compared with 2005 data. The estimated number of aggravated assaults decreased 0.2 percent, and the estimated number of forcible rapes declined 2.0 percent.
- There were an estimated 9,983,568 property crimes, excluding arson, reported nationwide in 2006.
- Of the property crimes, burglary was the only offense to show an increase (1.3 percent) in volume when 2006 data were compared with the 2005 data. The estimated number of larceny-thefts decreased 2.6 percent, and the estimated number of motor vehicle thefts declined 3.5 percent.
- In 2006, excluding arson, victims of property crimes collectively lost an estimated $17.6 billion: thefts of motor vehicles resulted in losses of more than $7.9 billion, larceny-thefts resulted in losses of $5.6 billion, and burglaries, $4.0 billion.
- Slightly more than 44 percent (44.3) of violent crimes and 15.8 percent of property crimes were cleared by arrest or exceptional means by the nation's law enforcement agencies in 2006.
- A total of 13,943 law enforcement agencies reported 69,055 arson offenses to the UCR Program in 2006.

- The number of arsons reported in 2006 increased 2.1 percent when compared with the number of arsons reported in 2005.
- The average dollar loss for arson offenses was $13,325 per incident.
- The FBI estimated that law enforcement agencies nationwide made 14,380,370 arrests in 2006, excluding those for traffic offenses.
- Law enforcement agencies made 4,832.5 arrests for each 100,000 in population nationwide for the 29 offenses for which the UCR Program collects arrest data.
- The arrest rate for violent crime was 207.0 arrests per 100,000 inhabitants; for property crime, the rate was 524.5.
- The rate of arrests for murder and nonnegligent manslaughter in 2006 was 4.5 per 100,000 in population. The rate of arrests for forcible rape was 8.2; for robbery, 43.2; and for aggravated assault, 151.1.
- Of the property crimes, law enforcement made 102.5 arrests for burglary for each 100,000 in population, 370.0 for larceny-theft, 46.5 for motor vehicle theft, and 5.5 for arson.

Source: http://www.fbi.gov/pressrel/pressrel07/cius092407.htm.

BOX 3.8   TEN-YEAR ARREST TRENDS, BY SEX 1996–2005

	MALE		FEMALE	
OFFENSE	1996	2005	1996	2005
Total	6,773,900	6,261,672	1,845,799	1,982,649
Murder/mans	8,572	7,114	992	875
Rape	18,512	14,924	233	205
Robbery	73,192	60,096	7,788	7,745
Ag. Aslt	260,469	224,080	54,936	57,923
Burglary	195,124	153,888	25,674	27,085
Lar/Theft	595,297	421,828	310,666	270,765
MVT	86,405	67,522	13,913	14,638
Arson	9,972	8,114	1,628	1,602
Other Aslts	597,763	554,044	158,366	183,431
Forg/Ctf	45,250	43,068	26,853	27,670
Fraud	137,874	104,201	117,288	89,338
Embezz	5,545	5,979	4,607	6,108
Sex off	52,296	48,112	4,188	4,298
Drug Viol	688,006	832,707	142,678	202,137

Source: Crime in the United States, Table 33. Retrieved May 21, 2007 from: http://www.fbi.gov/ucr/05cius/data/table_33.html.

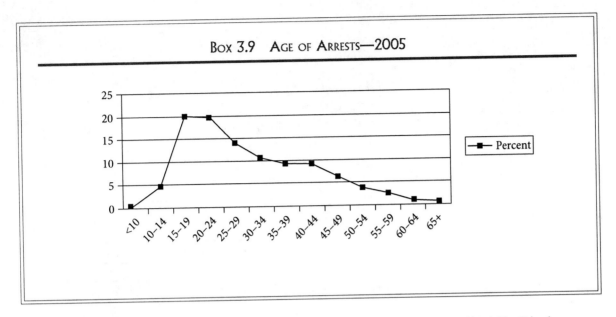

BOX 3.9   AGE OF ARRESTS—2005

Source: Crime in the United States, Table 38. Retrieved May 21, 2007 from: http://www.fbi.gov/ucr/05cius/data/table_38.html.

CORRELATES OF CRIME

Of course, these summary statistics of crime do not tell us much about who commits crime, when and where it is committed, or against whom. A **correlate** of crime is a factor that is associated statistically with the incidence of crime. In other words, it can be a predictor of crime. The three strongest predictors of crime seem to be sex, age, and race. We say "seem to be" because the information we have available is based on arrest statistics. We know who is arrested for crimes, and we assume that those arrested represent those who commit crimes, but we cannot be completely sure. For instance, the **chivalry theory** proposes the idea that women are less likely to be arrested than men in similar circumstances, and if arrested, are less likely to be tried and convicted. There has been a great deal of research testing whether or not this occurs, and the weight of evidence indicates that it occurred to some extent, for some women, for some crimes, in the past, but seems to be less likely to occur today.[14]

Generally, we are fairly certain that women are much less likely to commit violent crime than men, and somewhat less likely to commit property crimes. In Box 3.8 we see that for all crime categories the number of arrests of men exceeded that for women. For some crimes, the differential was quite extreme (homicide and rape); for others, it was marginal (fraud and embezzlement). It also seems to be the case that in the five-year period reported, women experienced an increase in arrests while men were less likely to be arrested in some crime categories (rape, aggravated assault, motor vehicle theft, other assaults, forgery/counterfeiting, and sex offenses/other than prostitution and rape). This could be the beginning of a long-range trend, or it could be a temporary pattern and not appear in the next reporting period.

Another clear correlate of crime is age. Crime is typically committed by those between the ages of 18 and 25. Box 3.9 illustrates this trend and shows how crime declines after age 30.

Race, a third correlate of crime, is not as predictable. The race of the offender varies quite a bit depending on the type of crime. Unfortunately, the FBI statistics

BOX 3.10   ARRESTS, BY RACE—2005

OFFENSE	PERCENT DISTRIBUTION		
	WHITE	BLACK	AM. INDIAN / ASIAN
Total	69.8	27.8	2.3
Murder/mans	49.1	48.6	2.3
Rape	65.1	32.7	2.2
Robbery	42.2	56.3	1.5
Ag. Aslt	63.3	34.3	2.4
Burglary	69.6	28.5	1.9
Lar/Theft	69.3	28.0	2.7
MVT	62.8	34.8	2.3
Assaults	65.1	32.3	2.5
Forg/Ctf	70.7	27.6	1.7
Fraud	68.7	30.1	1.2
Embezz	67.0	31.0	1.9
Sex off	73.6	24.3	2.1
Drug Viol	64.7	33.9	1.3

Source: Crime in the United States, Table 43. Retrieved May 21, 2007 from: http://www.fbi.gov/ ucr/05cius/data/table_43.html.

used to construct tables of those arrested does not include information on ethnicity; therefore, "whites" includes both whites and non-black Hispanic offenders. Box 3.10 shows that, considering their population percentage of about 13 percent, blacks are arrested at disproportionate rates, although for most crimes, not dramatically so. On the other hand, for some crimes, their arrest rates are highly disproportionate. Murder and robbery have very high rates of arrests for blacks and these two crimes are usually associated with black offenders in the public's mind. Although not displayed on the table, some of the more minor crimes have very high percentages of arrests for blacks as well. Almost 40 percent of the arrests for vagrancy were of blacks (38.4 percent), and an amazing 71.1 percent of arrests for gambling in 2005 were of blacks.[15] Because it is highly doubtful that 71 percent of those who engage in illegal gambling are black, we must look at whether other factors affect the arrest decision.

PUBLIC ATTITUDES TOWARD CRIME AND CRIMINALS

In Box 3.11, the public's views of crime and punishment are displayed. We see that public concern about crime was in a downward path until 2001. The terrorist attacks of September 11, 2001, no doubt contributed to the spike one sees in the number of people who believe crime has increased in the last several years, even though official statistics indicate that crime continues to decline.

The Gallup Poll indicates that the public has always favored social programs over more police and prisons. However, the Gallup poll also indicates that the public thinks courts don't deal harshly enough with offenders.

BOX 3.11   PUBLIC OPINION TOWARD CRIME AND PUNISHMENT

Public's Views on Crime

Question: Is there more crime in your area than there was a year ago, or less? (Deleted "same" answers)

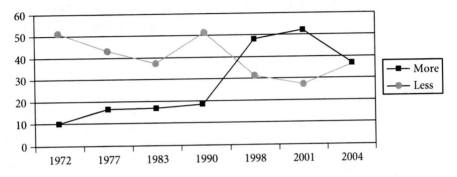

Public's Opinion on How to Address Crime Problems

Question: To lower the crime rate in the United States, some people think additional money and effort should go to attacking the social and economic problems that lead to crime through better education and job training. Others feel more money and effort should go to deterring crime by improving law enforcement with more prisons, police, and judges. Which comes closer to your view?

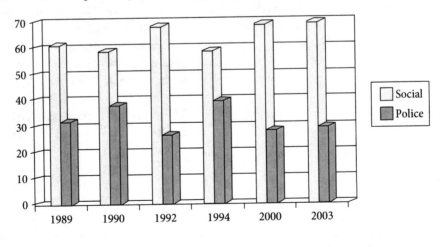

Source: Gallup Poll. Retrieved June 3, 2005 from: http://www.gallup.com/poll/1603/crime.aspx.

In 2003, only six percent of respondents thought the criminal justice system was "too tough," but 65 percent thought it wasn't "tough enough." This is quite a bit less than the 83 percent who thought the courts were not tough enough in 1992.[16] Other sources indicate that the public may be favorably inclined to community sanctions when they feel they are strictly managed. In one study, when asked about 25 crimes, only 27 percent of respondents chose prison as the appropriate sentence when offered a range of community alternatives.[17]

The Sentencing Project, a private non-profit policy body, offers statistical reports on sentencing practices and promotes alternatives to incarceration. This organization offers evidence that there are many myths that exist, such as the following:

1. **Crime is increasing.** The public is not generally aware of the official statistics that show crime has been declining for a decade. There is a widespread belief that crime continues to increase year after year and this misperception fuels the desire for harsh punishments.

2. **Criminals are not being sentenced to prison or not sentenced harshly enough.** Although the public believes that prison is used rarely, it is now the most frequent sentence handed down. The public is not aware that "truth in sentencing" statutes have drastically increased the percentage of the sentence that an average criminal serves. For instance, Florida residents, when polled, believed that offenders only served about 40 percent of their sentence, but, in reality, offenders in Florida are required to serve 85 percent of their sentence.

3. **The public is in favor of three-strikes laws and harsh sentences.** When asked, respondents indicate their approval of three-strikes laws; however, when presented with case scenarios that realistically portray criminal defendants, they favor alternative sanctions. This is so even though such offender profiles would be the types of offenders who would be subject to three-strikes sentences. Thus, it appears that the public favors the concept of three strikes, but not necessarily how it is likely to be implemented.

4. **The public supports "tough on criminal" platforms of politicians.** Again, the concept is different from reality. Politicians may be surprised to know that one study reported that policymakers estimated that only 12 percent of the public would be in support of alternative sanctions, but actually 66 percent of respondents indicated their support. As seen in Box 3.11 above, the majority of respondents favor social programs over police and prison responses to crime prevention.[18]

CONCLUSION

In this chapter, we have discussed the reality of crime; however, we first note that it is a "constructed reality" created by the perceptions of the victim and system actors. Only a portion of all crimes find their way into official statistics. Even the Uniform Crime Reports, our most commonly utilized source for crime statistics, only can report those crimes that are reported to the police. The "dark figure" of crime is that which is unreported. We do not know whether or not these offenders are similar or different from those who appear in official statistics.

In addition to the Uniform Crime Reports, we also have the National Crime Victimization Survey which provides additional information. We know more about victims' injuries and who is likely to report criminal victimization to the police because of victimization surveys. However, they also have some weaknesses and are not strictly comparable to the UCR in how crime is reported.

The biggest news is that crime declined dramatically during the last part of the 1990s and early 2000s. It now appears that the most dramatic decline has slowed and, in some crime categories, and in some locales, the trend has reversed itself. We must be alert to new crime reports to determine if crime will continue to rise, decline again, or remain stable. The strongest correlates of crime are sex, age and, to a much lesser degree, race. We know that most crime is committed by young men. Why this is so and what motivates individuals to commit crime is the subject of the next chapter.

REVIEW QUESTIONS

1. Why is the definition of crime problematic for the study of criminal justice and criminology?
2. Why is the dark figure of crime problematic for the study of criminal justice and criminology?
3. What do we mean when we say crime is a "constructed reality"?
4. Describe and provide examples for victim-harming and victimless crimes.
5. Describe the Uniform Crime Reports and crime "rates."
6. What are the most commonly committed crimes? What are the most infrequently committed crimes?
7. What are clearance rates?
8. What has been the pattern of crime in the last 30 years?
9. Describe the three correlates of crime.
10. Describe public opinion concerning what should be done about crime.

VOCABULARY

chivalry theory—proposes the idea that women are less likely to be arrested than men in similar circumstances, and, if arrested, less likely to be tried and convicted

clearance rates—the percent of crime solved by arrests

cohort studies—a group of subjects followed over a long period with data collected multiple times during the course of their lives

correlate (of crime)—a factor that is associated statistically with the incidence of crime

crime—actions that are prohibited by law

crime rate—the number of crimes divided by the population and then multiplied to display by a standard number (usually 100,000)

dark figure of crime—crime that does not find its way into official numbers

deviance—behaviors that are contrary to the norm

National Crime Victimization Survey—survey of a nationally representative sample about their criminal victimization

victim-harming crimes—crimes that harm specific victims (either physically or financially)

victimless crimes—crimes where there is no direct victim

Uniform Crime Reports—collection of local crime reports and arrest data begun in 1929 and now produced by the Federal Bureau of Investigation

FOR FURTHER READING

Alvarez, Alex and Ronet Bachman (2003). *Murder American Style*. Belmont, CA: Wadsworth/ITP.

Blumstein, Alfred and Joel Wallman (eds.) (2000). *The Crime Drop in America*. Cambridge, England: Cambridge University Press.

Pollock, Joycelyn (2005). *Women, Prison and Society*. Belmont, CA: Wadsworth, ITP.

Tonry, Michael, Lloyd Ohlin, and David Farrington (1991). *Human Development and Criminal Behavior: New Ways of Advancing Knowledge*. New York, NY: Springer-Verlag.

Zimring, Franklin (2006). *The Great American Crime Decline*. New York, NY: Oxford University Press.

NOTES

1. Texas Penal Code. Retrieved 4/10/07 from: http://tlo2.tlc.state.tx.us/statutes/docs/PE/content/htm/pe.005.00.000022.00.htm#22.01.00.
2. Retrieved 4/10/07 from "South Carolina Considers Gun Law" from: www.foxnews.com/story/10,2933,272974,00.html.
3. See Cleveland, H., M. Koss, and J. Lyons. 1999. "Rape Tactics From the Survivor's Perspective." *Journal of Interpersonal Violence* 14, 5: 532–548.
4. See Mendias, C. & E. Kobe (2006). "Engagement of Policing Ideals and the Relationship to the Exercise of

Discretionary Powers." *Criminal Justice and Behavior* 33, 1: 70–77.

5. See Gottfredson, M. & T. Hirschi (1990). *The General Theory of Crime*. Stanford, CA: Stanford University Press.

6. Federal Bureau of Investigation (2004). *Crime in the United States, 2004*. Washington, DC: FBI. Unfortunately the FBI did not publish this statistic for 2005 or 2006.

7. Federal Bureau of Investigation (2004). *Crime in the United States, 2005*. Table 8. Crime in the United States by State, by City, 2005. Washington, DC: FBI. Retrieved 9/5/2007 from www.fbi. gov/ucr/05cius/data/table_8.html.

8. Federal Bureau of Investigation. Retrieved 8/1/06 from: www.fbi.gov/ucr/cius_04/offenses_cleared/index.html.

9. Wolfgang, M., R. Figlio & T. Sellin (1978). *Delinquency in a Birth Cohort*. Chicago, IL: University of Chicago Press.

10. Tonry, M., L. Ohlin, & D. Farrington (1991). *Human Development and Criminal Behavior: New Ways of Advancing Knowledge*. New York, NY: Springer-Verlag.

11. Farrington, D., L. Ohlin & J. Wilson (1986). *Understanding and Controlling Crime: Toward a New Research Strategy*. New York: Springer-Verlag.

12. Farrington, D., L. Ohlin & J. Wilson (1986). *Understanding and Controlling Crime: Toward a New Research Strategy*. New York City: Springer Verlag., p. 2.

13. Steven Levitt's economic analysis indicated that the rising use of abortion by poor women after abortion became legal led to a reduced number of unwanted children who were at the highest risk for becoming delinquents and criminals.

14. See Pollock, J. (2005). *Women, Prison and Society*. Belmont, CA: Wadsworth/ITP.

15. From *Crime in the United States*, Table 43. Retrieved 5/21/07 from: http://www.fbi.gov/ucr/05cius/data/table_43.html.

16. Retrieved 6/2/05 from http://www.gallup.com/poll/1603/crime.aspx.

17. Bennett, L. 1991. The Public Wants Accountability. *Corrections Today* 53, 4: 92, 94–95.

18. The Sentencing Project (n.d.). "Crime, Punishment and Public Opinion: A Summary of Recent Studies and their Implications for Sentencing Policy." Available at: www.sentencingproject.org.

WHY DO PEOPLE COMMIT CRIME?

Joycelyn M. Pollock

Almost everyone thinks they know why people commit crimes. Their answers may include family factors (bad parents), individual/personality factors (bad kids), peer factors (bad friends), and societal factors (bad economy/neighborhood). For hundreds of years, researchers have attempted to understand why some people choose to commit crimes. **Criminology** is the study of crime and criminal motivation. It is usually a separate course in most college curriculums, and so, in this short chapter, we do not attempt to discuss all the various theories that have been proposed to answer this question. Instead, we will look at the types of theories that have been proposed and tested. Recall from the last chapter that the strongest predictors of crime are sex, age, and, to a lesser extent, race. Thus, any theory of crime should be able to explain why young men (and, for some crimes, young black men) are more likely than any other group to commit crimes (or perhaps only be arrested for them).

Another way to approach the study of criminology is to think of crime on a continuum of deviance, as displayed in Box 4.1. At one end are acts that are extremely rare. They are committed by very few people and happen infrequently, such as serial murder, sadistic killings, and serial rapes. At the other end of the continuum are acts that are committed by a large number of people quite frequently, such as speeding or perhaps minor income tax evasion (such as overstating the amount contributed to charity). All other crimes fall on the continuum in relation to how frequently they are committed and/or how many people commit the act. It seems reasonable that an explanation of why people commit crimes on the far left side of the continuum would more likely be individual theories, that is, explanations that are unique to the individual because they are so different from others. Therefore, psychoanalytic theories make more sense for these types of offenders. Crimes toward the right of the continuum may be explained by a wider range of criminological theories.

BOX 4.1 CONTINUUM OF DEVIANCE

"DEVIANT"   "NORMAL"

Serial Murder   Murder   Theft   Speeding

THE CLASSICAL SCHOOL VERSUS POSITIVISM

The **Classical School** is usually described by the contributions of Cesare Beccaria (1738-1794) and Jeremy Bentham (1748–1832).[1] Both theorists, writing in the 1700s, operated under a fundamental assumption that men were rational and operated with free will. Therefore, the elimination of crime could be achieved by promising punishment for offenses, which would act as a deterrent to crime. Philosophers during this period did not view women in the same manner as men and viewed their mental abilities to be more akin to children, therefore their discussions applied specifically to men.

Jeremy Bentham proposed that the justice system must employ punishment in such a way that it was slightly more punitive than the perceived profit of the crime contemplated (in order to deter individuals from attempting the crime). Bentham's "**hedonistic calculus**" called for punishment adjusted in this way for each offense. According to Bentham, punishment should be no more than necessary to deter. It should be adjusted upward in severity in relation to a decrease in certainty. Punishment that was swift, certain, and proportional to the potential profit or pleasure of the crime was most effective. The focus of these thinkers was on the legal system; the assumption was that everyone would respond to the legal system in a similar, rational manner. The Classical School is usually a historical preface to the theories of crime that developed after the rise of Positivism.

Positivism

Positivism can be described simply as "scientific method" or the search for causes using scientific method. It is typically associated with Cesare Lombroso,[2] who is often referred to as the "Grandfather of Criminology." With Lombroso, the focus shifted from the legal system to the offender. The cause of crime, in fact, was assumed to lie in the individual. Lombroso believed that a few "born criminals" were born with genetic defects that made them commit criminal acts. It should also be noted that over the course of his career, he developed a more sophisticated typology of criminals. He recognized other types in addition to the purely biological criminal, and these types represented some of the same explanations we use today, such as opportunity, influence, and passion. Later positivists in the early 1900s also looked at individual causes, and both biological and psychological factors were examined. According to positivists, criminals were different from non-criminals and criminologists merely needed to understand those differences.

Lombroso also wrote a book about criminal women.[3] Women were presumed to be biologically and psychologically different from men, which accounted for their lower crime rates. However, some women were evolutionary throwbacks, according to Lombroso, and these "primitive" women were criminal because, in his theory, all primitive women were more masculine and criminal than "modern" law-abiding women.

We can say that the field of criminology really began with the positivists because they initiated the search for differences between criminal men and women and law-abiding men and women. Their findings do not hold up over the passage of time, but their approach is still the basic approach of most criminologists today—that is, to seek out differences that motivate some people to choose crime.

BIOLOGICAL THEORIES OF CRIME

Recall that the three strongest predictors of crime—sex, age, and race—are biological constructs. Of the three, only race shows strongly different patterns cross-culturally. Furthermore, race is mediated by interracial mixing so that most people do not represent pure racial phenotypes. Contrary to the complications race presents, the other two strongest correlates are age and sex. Thus, it would seem that biology should be at least explored as a factor in crime causation. However, research on biological factors has been given little attention in most criminology textbooks. Part of the reason biological approaches in criminology have been so completely rejected is that there are serious policy implications for such theories. It is argued that such theories lead to **eugenics**, which is the idea of improving the human race through controlled procreation, and other forms of control repugnant to our democratic ideals.

Biological factors may be: (a) inherited genetic traits, or (b) biological, but not genetic. For instance, a brain tumor that puts pressure on the violence center of the brain and results in irrational violence is obviously a biological cause of crime, but tumors are not thought to be inherited. Chemicals or other environmental toxins can also affect the brain and are non-genetic biological factors that may influence criminal choice. More controversial, however, is the idea that criminality is inherited.

Is there a criminal gene? Of course not, but the argument of biological criminologists is that there are some inherited characteristics that predispose individuals to criminal choices. The methodological problem has always been trying to isolate genetic influences from socialization influences. If you are like your mother or father, is it because you have inherited traits from them or because they raised you? Trying to separate these influences is very difficult to do.

Twin studies identify and track twins (both monozygotic twins who share a single egg and dizygotic who have separate eggs but a single sperm) and look to see concordance or discordance in such things as intelligence, delinquency, alcoholism, and other behavioral indices. **Concordance** occurs if both twins possess the affliction (i.e., alcoholism). Discordance means that the twins do not share the trait. Higher rates of concordance among monozygotic twins than dizygotic twins lend support to biological explanations because monozygotic twins share the exact same genetic makeup. Several studies have found higher concordance rates, but the problem remains that such similarity could be because monozygotic twins are treated more alike than dizygotic twin pairs.[4]

Studies have also looked at the concordance between the criminality of children and their adoptive parents and biological parents. The best study would be of monozygotic twins separated from biological parents, and from each other, at birth, but obviously, such samples are extremely small.

Generally, it is difficult to get any large sample sizes to study the effects of genetic inheritance on criminality, mental illness, or other factors. However, we know that there are medical conditions that may be inherited. We also now know that certain forms of mental illness have a genetic component. It is also believed that a predisposition to alcoholism or addiction is inherited and scientists believe they have discovered the "addiction gene" on the DNA strand. Further, it may be that certain personality traits, such as impulsivity and poor conditionability (or ability to learn), are also inherited. Personality traits have long been associated with delinquency/criminality. Such traits as impulsiveness, aggressiveness, extroversion, and other traits have played a role in very early studies as well as more recent ones. These traits do not inevitably lead to criminal choices, but they predispose the individual to such choices, especially when the individual grows up in criminogenic environmental conditions.

Hormones and Brain Chemistry

When a personality trait is believed to be inherited, scientists look for the actual physical components of the trait. These origins lie in the neural structures of the brain, brain chemistry, and hormones. For instance, if aggressive tendencies are inherited, it is possible that what is actually inherited is a higher-than-average level of testosterone, which has long been associated with aggression. There has developed a fairly impressive body of knowledge regarding the correlation between testosterone and aggression, although such research has also been subject to heavy criticism. Although both men and women have testosterone in the body, men have about 10 to 15 times more testosterone than women. Therefore, many argue that when we observe male aggression, we are observing the effects of testosterone. Basic problems with such research include accurate measurements of testosterone; a valid definition and operationalization of the construct of aggression; and understanding the interactive effect of testosterone production, aggressive behavior, and environmental cues. Testosterone production seems to be moderated by environmental factors, and obviously the translation of aggressiveness to behavior is subject to social control, self-control, meanings ascribed to behavior, and learning, which may account for the ambiguous findings in this area.[5]

Brain chemicals may also affect personality traits. A chemical found in the brain has intriguing qualities that may be linked to a predisposition to delinquency. Researchers have found that a low level of monoamine oxidase (MAO) is linked to psychopathy, alcoholism, sensation-seeking, impulsivity, extraversion, schizophrenia, and criminal behavior.[6] Men, on average, have about 20 percent less MAO than women, and this difference exists at all ages. Studies have reported findings that MAO levels are linked to delinquency. Boys with low MAO levels were found to be more impulsive and sensation-seeking than other boys and were more likely to have drug and alcohol problems.[7] Associations are consistently found between low MAO activity and various correlates of criminal behavior, such as impulsiveness, childhood hyperactivity, learning disabilities,

sensation-seeking, substance abuse, and extroversion. MAO activity seems to be correlated with age, sex, and race. Testosterone evidently depresses MAO levels. In fact, testosterone levels are at their highest and MAO levels are at their lowest during the second decade of life (10–20, roughly corresponding with the crime-prone age years).[8]

Other research shows interesting connections between serotonin levels and negative emotionality and impulsivity.[9] Serotonin also seems to be linked with norepinephrine levels and, together, they may play a role in conditionability or the ability to learn.[10] There is evidence to indicate that individuals differ at a cellular level in their response to outside stimuli. Those with low levels of arousal tend toward behaviors that are risk-taking and sensation-seeking because these behaviors increase the cortical level of arousal. Risky behaviors are not necessarily antisocial. They could be sport-related activities or daredevil stunts. However, some individuals might be predisposed toward antisocial behaviors because these behaviors are exciting and produce the level of cortical arousal that extroverts seek. Thus, aggressive interactions, fast driving, shoplifting, robbery, and so on are risky and result in a thrilling rush of adrenalin that is much more pleasant for thrill-seekers than thrill-avoiders. Because thrill-seekers need a greater level of stimuli to respond, they do not learn as well, and do not absorb societal lessons that lead to law-abiding behavior.[11]

One model that incorporated physiological processes and learning theory postulates that traits that have been linked to delinquency; specifically, impulsivity, hyperactivity, sensation-seeking, risk-taking, and low self-control, are linked to neurophysiological mechanisms. Risky activities may release more endorphins in certain individuals than others because of brain chemistry. The differential experience of endorphins means that such behaviors become more internally rewarded for some than others, with the corollary prediction that they will continue to engage in such behavior.[12] Sex differences exist in cortical arousal levels, and men, in general, are more likely to have low cortical arousal.[13]

ADD, Hyperactivity, and Intelligence

There is consistent evidence that hyperactivity and Attention Deficit Disorder (ADD) are correlated with delinquency. It has been reported that those diagnosed with hyperactivity as children were 25 times more likely to exhibit later delinquency.[14] Deborah Denno[15] also reports that delinquency is linked to over-activity, perceptual-motor impairments, impulsivity, emotional lability, attention deficits, minor disturbances of speech, intellectual defects (learning disabilities), clumsiness, neuro-developmental lag, psychogenic factors, and minor physical anomalies. These features may be the result of genetic transmission, poor living environment, prenatal or birth trauma, or a combination of the above. It has been found that delinquents have significantly lower verbal skills, auditory verbal memory, interspatial analysis, and visual-motor integration in elementary school.

Such early evidence of cognitive deficits indicates that it is not simply a delinquent "lifestyle" and/or drug use that causes subsequent lower cognitive abilities; but, rather, there may be problems at birth that affect the child's performance in school. Evidence indicates that many children outgrow predisposing factors, but those who do not are more likely to become delinquent.

It is interesting to note that ADD and hyperactivity tend to be more common for boys than girls. Boys and men experience a higher incidence of prenatal and perinatal mortality and complications, reading and learning disorders, and mental retardation, as well as left hemisphere deficits.[16] In general, male children are more prone to learning dysfunctions due to brain differences.[17] Is it possible that the greater tendency of young men to engage in risky and/or violent behavior is not only culturally induced, but also may have a biological component?

There are numerous, hotly debated issues involved in the research concerning intelligence. The first is whether intelligence can even be defined and/ or measured. The next point of controversy, assuming that we can agree upon some definition of intelligence, is whether intelligence is inherited. Again, while some researchers maintain that the evidence is clear and convincing, others argue that the correlation in IQ scores between parents and children, between twins, or between siblings is simply the product of family environment or other social factors (such as poverty), rather than a product of inheritance. Finally, there is the issue of the relationship between intelligence and delinquency or criminality.

Most researchers accept that there is a correlation between intelligence scores and delinquency/criminality. Some researchers argue that the relationship is purely spurious, because both are affected by some other factors, i.e., poverty, family dysfunction, or something else. Other researchers, however, believe that the relationship exists even after controlling for all other factors.[18] The relationship between intelligence and delinquency may be that intelligence affects school performance, which, in turn, affects delinquency because of opportunity (kids who drop out have more time to get into trouble). It could also be a direct relationship in that poor conditionability would lead to poor school performance and poor conditionability would lead to poor socialization to law-abiding norms. Intelligence may be related to family and environmental variables as well as genetic inheritance.

Summary

Theorists who support the idea of a biological predisposition to choose criminal behavior argue that personality differences do not inevitably lead to delinquency, no more than social factors inevitably lead to delinquency. The traits of impulsivity and thrill-seeking are due to biological differences, such as MAO and serotonin levels, as well as low cortical arousal. However, these biological differences merely predispose individuals to certain behavior patterns. The choice of crime versus other types of behaviors is influenced by social, familial, and environmental factors.

Biological theories can help explain the sex and age differential in criminality. There are sex differences in the relative levels of brain chemicals and hormones associated with delinquency. Furthermore, these chemicals and hormones fluctuate over the life course, therefore explaining why younger people are more impulsive and thrill-seeking than older individuals. These predispositions don't necessarily translate into delinquency, but there is a higher probability of such behavior when such biological predispositions exist.

PSYCHOLOGICAL THEORIES OF CRIME

Criminology has largely ignored psychological theories of deviance and crime.[19] This is largely because criminology has emerged as a discipline from the field of sociology, not psychology. Psychological theories can be categorized into psychoanalytic theories, developmental theories, and learning theories. Of these, both developmental theories and learning theories have their correlates in sociological criminology, so to say that psychology is ignored in criminology textbooks is perhaps a misstatement of facts. Perhaps we could say that psychological theories are merely sociologized.

Psychoanalytic Theories

Neither Sigmund Freud nor many of his followers had a great deal to say about crime. The psychoanalytic tradition would assume, however, that crime was the result of a weak superego or ego.[20] According to psychoanalytic theory, one does not develop in a normal manner when childhood trauma occurs or there is deficient parenting. Crime may occur because of unresolved feelings of guilt and a subconscious wish to be punished, or, more likely, because of weak superego controls over id impulses; that is, the individual cannot control impulses and pursues immediate gratification.

Generally, when a criminal commits very unusual or extreme acts, psychological explanations are utilized. The FBI has been instrumental in the growing use of "profilers" who construct psychological profiles of offenders based on the small sample of offenders who have been caught and interviewed. The book and movie *Silence of the Lambs* and many similar movies and television shows dramatize the work of psychological profilers. "Forensic psychologists" are used by many police departments for a variety of tasks, including offender profiling. As information is collected from these offenders, profiles are constructed and refined based on similarities and differences between them

and how they commit their crimes. It should be noted, however, that the work of profilers is typically used for unusual criminals (such as serial or mass murderers, serial arsonists or serial rapists). Furthermore, profiles are not infallible. Recall that the predicted profile of the Washington sniper case was a white male 20 to 30 years of age, with a military background. John Malvo and John Mohammed did not fit the profile, but profiles are constructed from prior examples of such criminals, and the smaller the sample size, the greater the possibility of error.[21]

The most obvious contribution of psychological theory to an understanding of criminality is the concept of **sociopathy** or **psychopathy**. The psychopath has been differentiated from the sociopath in the following way: "[the psychopath is] an individual in whom the normal processes of socialization have failed to produce the mechanisms of conscience and habits of law-abidingness that normally constrain antisocial impulses" and the sociopath as "persons whose unsocialized character is due primarily to parental failures rather than to inherent peculiarities of temperament."[22] The Diagnostic and Statistical Manual (DSM-IV), used as the dictionary by mental health workers to diagnose and categorize all mental health problems, has replaced the terms "psychopathy" and "sociopathy" with the term "antisocial personality disorder." Regardless, these definitions describe an individual who is without a conscience and unable to form sincere, affectionate bonds with others. This describes many, but not all, of those who engage in criminal behavior.

Psychological explanations for crime do address sex differences and incorporate biological traits, but not all in a manner that most would agree with today. For instance, in an early theory of female delinquency, Cowie, Cowie, and Slater[23] wrote that social and psychological factors, such as poverty or broken and/or poor home environments, seemed to be stronger factors in predicting female delinquents than male delinquency. Comparing delinquent girls with delinquent boys, the girls were found to come from lower income homes, with a higher level of mental health problems in the family, "worse" moral standards and worse discipline. Additionally, the girls more often came from a broken home, experienced more frequent changes of home, more conflict at home, and more disturbed intra-familial relations. These researchers were psychological/biological theorists in that they argued that biology ordinarily played a part in restraining women from criminal choices, so that it was only in situations of extreme stress that women were not controlled by these biological predispositions. Research on the different paths and childhoods of female and male delinquents continues today, but rarely ascribes criminal differences to biology, nor do many theorists believe that delinquent girls are more psychologically distressed than delinquent boys. Interestingly, there is some evidence to indicate that girls do follow a different path to delinquency.

Developmental Theories

Theories of development address both cognitive development and social development. The general hypothesis is that all individuals progress through similar stages of understanding and maturity regarding the world around them. Those who engage in criminal behavior have, for some reason, become "stuck" at lower stages of development. They are immature, either in their response to the world, their interactions with others around them, and/or in their putting self above others.

Piaget[24] and Kohlberg[25] are most commonly identified with the cognitive development field. Those who subscribe to the stage theory of cognitive development assume that the infant goes through qualitatively different stages of understanding. Only gradually does the child come to understand that others have needs and desires similar to him- or herself. Higher levels of maturity are necessary to understand such abstract concepts as altruism and compassion. Kohlberg carried Piaget's work into moral development, arguing that cognitive development was necessary in order to develop a moral conscience, and understandings of right and wrong varied depending on what cognitive level one had reached. For instance, very young children understand that stealing is wrong only because parents have told them so. It is much later that they come to understand more abstract reasons for why stealing is wrong.

Later, Carole Gilligan,[26] a student of Kohlberg's, concluded that women tended to cluster at lower stages in Kohlberg's stage sequence than did men. Although controversial, her theory was that women followed a "different" morality and were more likely to continue to utilize themes of relationships and caring, while men moved on to principles and law-based models of morality.

This work has seldom been applied directly in criminology to the question of why people choose criminality. One of the problems seems to be that one's ability to understand the moral implications of one's acts does not necessarily translate into behavior. That is, many people know something is wrong, but do it anyway. The research on moral stages, however, has been utilized in corrections and it has been found that offenders can improve their moral reasoning given appropriate learning environments.[27]

Learning Theory and Behaviorism

Basically, learning theory proposes that individuals act and believe the way they do because they have learned to do so. Learning takes place through modeling or reinforcement. **Modeling** stems from the desire to be like others, especially those whom one admires; therefore, children will act as they see their parents or peers act. The other form of learning is through **reinforcement**. That is, one will continue behaviors and beliefs for which one has been rewarded, and eliminate behaviors and beliefs that have been punished or not rewarded. Ban-dura,[28] for instance, argues that individuals are not necessarily inherently aggressive, but rather learn aggression. He and others also point out that learning is mediated by intelligence and temperament. Personality traits such as impulsivity, activity, and emotionality affect one's ability to absorb learning.

One of the most enduring explanations of why women commit less crime, by both laypeople and criminologists, is the idea that they learn to be law-abiding and that the social sanctions against deviance for women and girls are much stronger than what boys or men would experience. If true, learning theory is perfectly consistent with the lower crime rates observed for women. Further, it also explains why women tend to cluster in consumer crimes, because women may be more likely to learn how to commit credit card fraud or check forgery than armed robbery. It might also explain why younger people commit more crime—we might suppose they haven't yet absorbed societal messages that condemn such behaviors.

Summary

Psychological theories concentrate on individual factors of criminal choice. More sophisticated theories also refer to environmental factors. So, for instance, Andrews and Bonta[29] developed a psychological theory of crime that includes the characteristics of the immediate environment and individual characteristics to explain crime choices. They point to the attitudes, values, beliefs, and rationalizations held by the person with regard to antisocial behavior, social support for antisocial behavior (perceived support from others), a history of having engaged in antisocial behavior, self-management and problem-solving skills, and other stable personality characteristics conducive to antisocial conduct. Then they relate these to a behavioral explanation of criminality where rewards and costs of crime are mediated by these individual differences.

Such theories can only explain why women commit less crime if we presuppose that women learn different messages from society (learning theory) or develop different moral definitions (developmental theory). The theories are somewhat consistent with the age differential because it can be assumed that one continues to develop and learn through young adulthood and that maturity changes one's inclination to commit criminal acts. Also, it might be assumed that reward structures change during the life course and criminal choices may result in greater rewards for young people than for those with family and career responsibilities.

SOCIOLOGICAL THEORIES OF CRIME

If the focus of the Classical School was the legal system, and the focus of the Positivists was the individual, then the focus of early sociology was society itself. Societal factors were determined to be the causes of crime. However, while the Classical School assumed all men would respond rationally to the deterrence of punishment, sociological theories offer more complicated assumptions.

Adolphe Quetelet (1796–1874) and Emile Durkheim (1858–1917) are credited as early sociologists who established the foundations of sociological criminology. Quetelet discovered that crime occurred in reasonably predictable patterns in society, thus supporting the notion that there was something about society that caused crime rather than crime occurring at random or because of individual causes. Emile Durkheim offered the principle that crime was normal and present in all societies. The absence of deviance or crime, in fact, was evidence of cultural stagnation.

Sociological theories can be further divided into social structure theories and social process theories. Societal factors that influence criminality may come from the social structure (i.e., elements of society that induce criminality), or the social process (i.e., the interactions between the individual and society that influence criminal choices). Both approaches reject the idea of the "criminal as different." In these theories, it is assumed that anyone who happens to be exposed to these factors would become criminal; thus, the approach is similar to the Classical School (which assumed sameness among individuals).

Social Structure Theories

Social structure theories identify some aspects of society as leading to criminal choices. The so-called Chicago School in the 1930s and 1940s truly began the study of societal influences on criminality when sociologists at the University of Chicago observed that crime occurred more often in **mixed zones** of the city. In these zones, residential, commercial, and industrial activity could be observed. The zones were also characterized by low home ownership, property damage, graffiti, and high rates of alcoholism, domestic violence, and mental health problems. Early sociologists discovered that these mixed zones always had higher crime rates, even though different demographic groups moved in and out of them over the decades. For instance, in the nineteenth century, Irish immigrants were the population that lived in the zones, but they eventually moved out, to be replaced by Eastern and Southern Europeans, and then blacks moving up from the South. Thus, it seemed that there was something about the zone, rather than the people who lived within it, that generated crime. Observers noted that subcultures existed in the mixed zone and these subcultures promoted values and beliefs that were different from the dominant culture and encouraged criminal behavior (such as prostitution, gambling, and other forms of deviance).

Subculture theories and cultural deviance theories, first developed in the 1950s, observed that there are some groups in society that teach antisocial behaviors (instead of socialize its members to follow the norms of the dominant culture). If one lives in these areas of the city, then one will most likely become delinquent because the subculture defines such behavior as acceptable.[30] **Cultural deviance theory** identifies cultures that clash when individuals migrate to a new culture; i.e., immigrants from India who sell their daughters into marriage in the United States are committing a crime, but in their culture, this behavior is not wrong. **Subcultural theories** look at subcultures that exist within the dominant culture but have different values and belief systems. Gangs are an example of a subculture, although this stretches the classic definition of a subculture, because members of any gang also participate and are socialized, to some extent, by the dominant culture as well. Women were largely ignored in early subcultural theories even though they obviously lived in the mixed zones alongside the boys and men who were being socialized to criminality. More recently, gang research has identified female gang members and female gangs, but there are mixed findings as to whether girls are increasing their participation in gangs.[31]

Another factor observed in the mixed zones was lack of opportunity. The individuals who lived in these neighborhoods had very little hope of economic success. **Strain or opportunity theory**, popularized in the 1960s, argued that lack of opportunity is the cause of crime. Individuals who are blocked from legitimate means of economic success, such as employment, family, or education, will choose crime.[32] A later application of the theory enlarged it to groups, so that those who were blocked from opportunities would form groups (gangs) distinct from those who had legitimate opportunities.[33] Because everyone is socialized to believe that they can and should achieve material success, those who do not have the means feel particular stress. In other cultures that are more static, i.e., where the poor have no expectations or hope that they will achieve wealth, there is less pressure or inclination to use illegitimate means to get ahead.

If the strain/opportunity thesis was perfectly able to explain crime, then one would think that women should be more criminal than men because, arguably, they have had fewer opportunities to achieve financial success and, therefore, should experience more strain. On the other hand, if women's goals are different, for instance, to get married and to have children, rather than achieve economic success, then the theory would adequately explain the sex differential in crime. Whether this has ever been true, or whether it is true today, is a subject that many researchers have addressed. The results indicate that there are differences between men and women and strain may predict to some extent the criminal choices of both groups, but economic strain does not completely explain why some people commit crime, or why men are more likely to make criminal choices.

Radical, Critical, or Marxist Criminology was somewhat popular in the 1970s. This type of theory can also be considered a social structure theory because it identifies an element of society as criminogenic. Radical or critical criminology challenges the "science" of criminology and the nature of the exercise, concentrating as it does on the individual "deviant." Critical or radical criminology addressed the process of defining crimes and the nature of law as a method of social control by those in power. Under a Marxist theory of crime, crime exists in the capitalist society as "work." It is an essential element of capitalism. Typical criminal activity represents false consciousness; the "lumpenproletariat" does not know who their true oppressors are, thus they steal from and hurt each other. This approach would expand the definition of crime to activities engaged in by government and business; for instance, the death of workers because of unsafe working conditions should be defined as homicide.

Elements of **critical criminology** include an identification of class-based definitions of crime, a challenge to the ideology of equality, and the lack of objectivity in law.[34] Critics of these theories contend that their view of society is oversimplified and that power coalitions are more complicated and diverse than can be represented by such theories. Another criticism that can be made is that these types of theories are unable to explain the sex differential.

More recently, the ideas of the Chicago School have been revived with **social support theory** and **social disorganization theory**. Basically, both point to the community as a prime factor in crime causation. These theories tend to look solely at macro-level factors that are correlated with crime causation. They are similar in that social support theory identifies elements of the society that provide emotional and practical support to the individual and proposes that the more support there is in a community, the less crime occurs.[35] Social disorganization theory states a similar assumption, arguing that communities that exhibit signs of disorganization and lack of cohesion are more likely to experience delinquency and criminality.[36] Thus, in both theories, crime is predicted in the neighborhoods and for the people who have few resources such as church, friendly neighbors, clubs, and other social organizations.

Social Process Theories

Social process theories focus on the individual's interaction with the world around him or her. Thus, relationships become a central feature of these theories. Social process theories have more in common in this respect with psychological theories and, in fact, many could be described as social-psychological.

Differential association theory, introduced originally by Edwin Sutherland in 1939, is very similar to learning theory.[37] Differential association assumes that delinquency and criminality develop because of an excess of definitions favorable to crime offered by one's close associates. That is, if family and friends are criminal, profess criminal values, and teach criminal methods, one will become criminal. This theory assumes that learning takes place most importantly within intimate personal groups and that learning includes techniques of crime, as well as motives, drives, rationalizations, and attitudes. Later, others applied social learning principles to the theory to make it even more similar to learning theory.[38]

In order for this theory to be consistent with the sex differential in crime, one must assume that girls and boys receive different societal messages, with girls less likely to be reinforced for delinquent behavior. Burgess and Akers argued that: "From infancy, girls are taught that they must be nice, while boys are taught that they must be rough and tough ... Girls are schooled in 'anti-criminal behavior patterns.'"[39] Evidently all girls are taught from birth to conform to one model of female normality that is homogeneous across social, economic, and subcultural categories, while boys are exposed to a variety of different definitions of normality depending on class, race, and neighborhood. These factors predict delinquency for boys, but not for girls under this theory. Further, the theory doesn't explain why crime is more common among young people and drops off after young adulthood because, if one learned criminal definitions, there is no reason to assume they would change after maturity.

Labeling theory relies on symbolic interactionism. The theory is unique from those discussed above in that, like radical criminology, it focuses attention on the official labeler as well as the deviant. This theory assumes even though almost all of us have engaged in "primary deviance," only certain individuals are labeled as deviant. This results in their accepting and absorbing the deviant role and committing further delinquency because of the label.[40] Criticisms of labeling theory include the observation that no explanation for primary deviance is offered. Also, whether secondary deviance would not exist except for the labeling is probably untestable.[41] Labeling does not explain persistent criminality when offenders are not subject to labeling (such as hidden corporate criminality) and ignores the fact that official intervention (such as prosecution and punishment) might deter individuals from future criminality.

Recall that the Classical School assumptions disappeared with the rise of positivism in the 1800s. However, the premises of the Classical School have been revived with **rational choice theory**. This modern-day theory presumes that criminals rationally choose criminal action because the immediate rewards outweigh uncertain punishments.[42] Burglars, for instance, are influenced by such facts as the affluence of the neighborhood, the presence of bushes, nosy neighbors, alarms, dogs, placement on the street, access to major traffic arteries, and other factors. They identify and target the houses where they have the best chance of success. Although the theory makes sense with burglars, and other purely economic crimes, it is more difficult to apply to other criminals.

Routine activities theory is slightly different from rational choice, and might even be placed in the social structure category because it ignores criminal motivation, assuming a motivated offender exists all the time.[43] According to these theorists, for a crime to happen, there must be a motivated offender, suitable targets of criminal victimization, and the absence of guardians of persons or property. Any changes in routine activities lead to changing opportunities for crime. For instance, the increase in the number of working women after WWII meant that more homes were left unattended during the day, and this created the opportunity for burglaries to occur. Most sociological theories look at the motivation of the offender, and these authors argue that it is also fruitful to look at changes in opportunities or guardianship. Tests of this theory focus on demographic, macro-level changes in society. However, it is difficult to identify any societal changes that occurred in the last decade that might have accounted for the dramatic drop in crime. Critics argue that, by not looking at the criminal motivations of the offender, this theory is incomplete.

Control theory, as presented by Travis Hirschi in 1969,[44] stated that the delinquent or criminal is one who is not controlled by bonds to society—specifically attachment, commitment, involvement, and belief. Attachment involves relationships; commitment involves the dedication to legitimate work and leisure activities; involvement measures actual time engaged in such activities; and belief refers to the agreement and acceptance of goals and rules of society. In the research that supported the development of control theory, Hirschi used self-report surveys of large numbers of young people and analyzed self-reported delinquency (validated by comparison to official records) and whether delinquency was correlated with the bonds to society described above. Control theory postulates that conformity occurs because of ties to society; deviance occurs when those ties are weak or nonexistent. Conformity is associated with good school performance, strong family ties, liking school, conventional aspirations, and respect for law.

Control theory provides a relatively adequate explanation for the sex differential in crime rates if we can assume that girls have more attachments and other bonds than boys. It is generally found that girls profess stronger ties to friends, family, and school, and they tend to possess more pro-social belief systems than boys.

Hirschi's control theory generated a wealth of theoretical and analytical response in criminology in the 1970s. A couple of decades later, in 1990, he and Michael Gottfredson[45] published a book describing the **General Theory of Crime**, which resulted in another flood of tests and applications from the 1990s through the 2000s. Actually, the two are not all that different. While control theory postulates that various bonds to society (attachment, commitment, belief, and involvement) control the individual and prevent delinquency, the general theory of crime proposes, simply, that individuals are born with and/or are raised to have different levels of self-control.

These authors propose that there are no real differences between serious and non-serious crimes, and disagree with the proposition that criminals are different from each other in their criminal orientation (i.e., career criminals versus occasional criminals). They propose that one variable explains all criminal offending and that variable is *self-control*. Gottfredson and Hirschi propose that people with low self-control commit criminal acts and a host of other dangerous and impulsive behaviors; people with more self-control do not. Low self-control types are also engaged in other activities indicative of low self-control, such as smoking, drinking, using drugs, gambling, having illegitimate children, and engaging in illicit sex.[46]

White-collar criminality is a problem for this theory. The authors explained that white-collar criminals, like embezzlers, simply have less self-control than their professional colleagues who do not commit crimes. However, their argument that white-collar crime by professionals is relatively rare flies in the face of evidence that graft, fraud, and other forms of corporate criminality are widespread.

The major cause of a lack of self-control, according to these authors, is ineffective parenting. They argue that the conditions necessary to teach self-control include monitoring behavior, recognizing deviant behavior, and punishing such behavior.[47] Applications and tests of this theory of crime typically explore associations between other indications of low self-control and criminality. Not surprisingly, such associations exist, although some researchers argue that self-control adds nothing new to existing facts that have identified the association between crime and impulsivity and risk-seeking.[48]

A major weakness of the theory is that it does not adequately explain the sex differential in crime unless one was to assume that women generally have more self-control than men.[49] Another criticism of the theory is that it does not include any concept of the meaning of actions and how personal meaning interacts with and influences self-control. Values, motivations, and meanings interact with individual self-control, explaining why some people show a great deal of self-control in some areas and none in others. Further, there is a qualitative difference, it seems, in the acts labeled "criminal" and those merely injurious to one's health. Many people drink and smoke but relatively few commit victim-harming crimes. In other words, there are many more "weak" people than there are "harming" people, thus, even if we find that most criminals have low self-control, it does not follow that most people with low self-control are criminals.

Robert Agnew[50] reformulated strain/opportunity theory (which was a social structure theory) into a social process theory by reinterpreting strain as an individual construct rather than an experience shared by the group or due to societal factors such as poverty. His **General Strain theory** proposes that individuals who commit crime experience strain from not getting what they want, losing something that was important, or in other ways being in a situation that is experienced as noxious. In this theory, negative relationships that generate negative emotions, such as disappointment, fear, depression, and anger cause delinquency and individuals commit delinquent acts in order to relieve the strain of the negative emotions.

Summary

Sociological theories are more common in criminology because the beginning of criminology in this country occurred with the Chicago School of the 1930s. These theories identify elements of society or the interaction of the individual with his or her environment as the reason people become criminal. These elements range from poverty and subcultures (in structural theories) to social bonds and negative emotions (in social process theories). While virtually none of these theories directly explains the sex or age differential in crime rates, later researchers have attempted to apply them in such a way as to explain these crime patterns. Some seem better able to explain these crime correlates than others.

INTEGRATED THEORIES OF CRIMINOLOGY

Integrated theories combine elements of psychological theories and sociological theories, and even accept some elements of biological criminology in a more complicated and comprehensive approach to explaining criminal choices. The methodology typically associated with integrated theories is the cohort study, also called longitudinal research because it involves following a sample of individuals for a long period.

One finding of the longitudinal research studies is that there seem to be two separate groups of delinquents/criminals. The first group begins committing delinquent acts very early and these individuals are chronic and serious criminal offenders; however, the second "late onset" group drifts into delinquency during their teenage years and matures out fairly quickly. Their delinquency seems to be episodic and peer-influenced.

The following traits or characteristics seem to be correlated with the group who begin delinquency very early: low intelligence; high impulsiveness; child abuse victimization; harsh and erratic parental discipline; cold and rejecting parents; poor parental supervision; parental disharmony, separation, and divorce; one-parent female-headed households; convicted parents or siblings; alcoholic or drug-using parents or siblings; non-white race membership, low occupational

BOX 4.2

Sampson and Laub's Development Theory

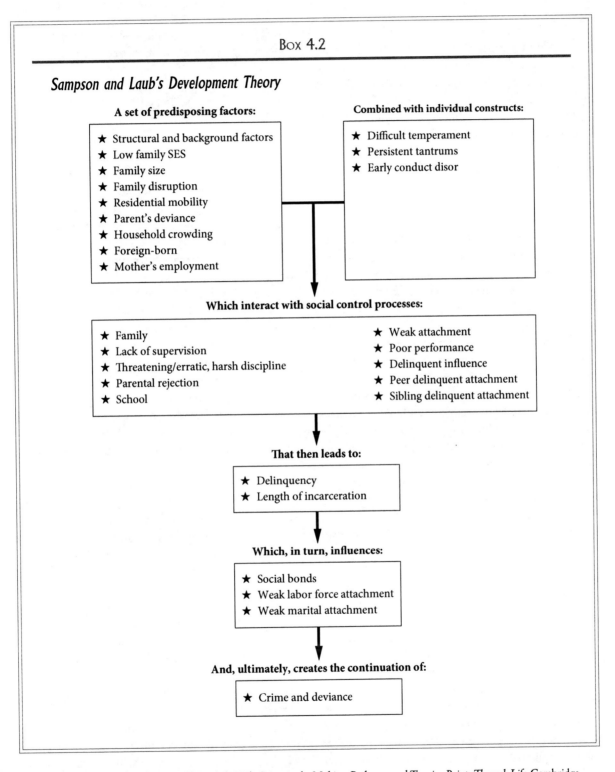

A set of predisposing factors:

- ★ Structural and background factors
- ★ Low family SES
- ★ Family size
- ★ Family disruption
- ★ Residential mobility
- ★ Parent's deviance
- ★ Household crowding
- ★ Foreign-born
- ★ Mother's employment

Combined with individual constructs:

- ★ Difficult temperament
- ★ Persistent tantrums
- ★ Early conduct disor

Which interact with social control processes:

- ★ Family
- ★ Lack of supervision
- ★ Threatening/erratic, harsh discipline
- ★ Parental rejection
- ★ School
- ★ Weak attachment
- ★ Poor performance
- ★ Delinquent influence
- ★ Peer delinquent attachment
- ★ Sibling delinquent attachment

That then leads to:

- ★ Delinquency
- ★ Length of incarceration

Which, in turn, influences:

- ★ Social bonds
- ★ Weak labor force attachment
- ★ Weak marital attachment

And, ultimately, creates the continuation of:

- ★ Crime and deviance

Source: Adapted from Sampson, R. and J. Laub (1993). *Crime in the Making: Pathways and Turning Points Through Life.* Cambridge, MA: Harvard University Press, p. 244.

prestige of parents; low educational level of parents; low family income; large family size; poor housing; low educational attainment of the child; attendance at a high delinquency school; delinquent friends; and high-crime area of residence.[51]

Unfortunately, cohort samples for longitudinal studies often exclude women. This is especially unfortunate because the studies consistently identify correlates of delinquency such as Attention Deficit Disorder (ADD) and hyperactivity, which are more prevalent among boys. Sex/gender differences may also be present in other factors related to criminal choices, such as sensation-seeking, low physiological arousal, intelligence, poor supervision and erratic discipline, and delinquent peers. By excluding women from the cohort sample, these studies are unable to determine the relative effects of these factors on male and female delinquency and criminality.

Denno[52] utilized biological and sociological factors in an integrated explanation of criminality and delinquency. She identified predisposing factors (that increase the likelihood of criminality), facilitating variables (that, in combination with predisposing, increase the likelihood of delinquency), and inhibiting variables (that counteract predisposing factors and decrease the probability of delinquency). At birth, individuals are already affected by such factors as culture, gender, prenatal maternal conditions, pregnancy and delivery complications, socioeconomic status, and family stability. By age seven, other factors, such as cerebral dominance, intelligence, and physical and health development have influenced their predisposition to delinquency, and during the pre-teen and teen years, school behavior, achievement, and learning disabilities are affected by intelligence and influence, in turn, the likelihood of delinquency and, eventually, adult crime. In Box 4.2, Sampson and Laub's integrated theory is presented.

Integrated studies are comprehensive in that they include precursors and facilitators of delinquency. In fact, most of the elements identified by all previous theories are incorporated into these integrated theories. While some may say that is the strength of these theories, others argue that it is a weakness because it makes the theory more complicated and by using every explanation, in effect, there is no explanation that easily explains crime choice. On the other hand, it is probably unrealistic to assume that there is a simple answer to criminal behavior—or any human behavior, for that matter.

CONCLUSION

Courses in criminology cover a multitude of theories that have been created and tested to attempt to answer the question, "Why do people commit crime?" This chapter barely skims the surface of this material, but it provides some general descriptions of the types of theories that have been developed. Any good theory should be able to explain the sex and age differential, as well as why minorities are overrepresented in street and violent crimes.

Generally the field of criminology has deemphasized biological and psychological factors of crime causation and focused solely on sociological causes of crime. More recent theories, such as the general theory of crime and general strain theory, bring the focus back to the individual and, thus, one can argue that the pendulum of scientific/criminological thought has swung from the legal system (classical) to the individual (positivist), to the society and neighborhood (Chicago School), and back to the individual (General theory). Integrated theories incorporate aspects of all three types of theories—biological, psychological, and sociological—and, arguably, provide the most complete answer to why people commit crime. In Box 4.3, there are very brief descriptions of the theories discussed in this chapter.

The quest for reasons why people make criminal choices is ultimately for a practical purpose. We want them to stop. All criminology serves the practical purpose of developing policies and societal interventions that reduce crime. Thus, another way to discuss the theories presented in this chapter is to figure out the policy implications that follow from each theory. It seems clear that most theories support the idea of full employment and strengthening the family unit to ensure that all children grow up in stable homes where parents are able to discipline and monitor their behavior through strong, loving attachments. Whether this can ever be accomplished is a difficult

---

Box 4.3

Theories of Crime

Biological
Non-genetic: idiopathic tumors, brain injuries, toxins
Genetic: testosterone, brain chemicals, neural conditionability, other inherited personality traits, such as impulsiveness

Psychological
Psychoanalytic: individual suffers trauma in childhood
Developmental: individual does not progress to mature social-interpersonal levels
Learning: individual is rewarded for criminal behavior

Sociological Theories
Social Structure Theories
Chicago School—individual lives in the mixed zone of a city where crime occurs
Cultural Deviance—individual is socialized to deviant norms
Strain—individual is blocked from achieving societal goals
Radical/Critical—individual is oppressed by capitalistic economic system
Social Support—individual lives in area with low social support
Social Disorganization—individual lives in area with indices of social disorganization

Social Process Theories
Differential Association—individual learns to be criminal
Labeling—individual is labeled a deviant and so lives up to the label
Rational choice—individual weighs options and chooses crime
Routine activities—crime occurs when there is motivated offender and opportunity
Control (bonds)—individual has few bonds to society
General theory of crime—individual has low self-control
General strain theory—individual suffers strain, which leads to crime

Integrated Theories
Different aspects of the theories above explain crime at different periods in the life course

question. The answer to why people commit crime and how we can reduce crime, in fact, goes far beyond the criminal justice system. But then we knew that, because the criminal justice system is the social control institution that steps in when others (family, church, school) fail. If those institutions could be made stronger, there would be less need for the criminal justice system components, because there would be less crime.

REVIEW QUESTIONS

1. What are the three strongest correlates of crime?
2. Differentiate between the classical school and the positivists.
3. What would be a way to study the relative effects of genetics and socialization?
4. What personality traits have been associated with criminality?
5. Distinguish between developmental theories and learning theories.
6. Distinguish social structure theories from social process theories.
7. Provide some examples of social structure theories and their policy implications.
8. What are the elements of critical or radical criminology?
9. Provide some examples of social process theories and their policy implications.
10. What are integrated theories? Describe.

VOCABULARY

classical School—includes the contributions of Cesare Beccaria and Jeremy Bentham and the ideas that men were rational, operated with free will, and could be deterred from criminal acts

concordance—measure of genetic influence; if one twin has an affliction (i.e., alcoholism), then so does the other twin. Discordance means that the twins are different

control theory—Hirschi's theory that delinquents are not controlled by bonds to society, specifically attachment, commitment, involvement, and belief

criminology—the study of crime and criminal motivation

critical criminology—rejects definitions of crime and includes the idea that the legal system is a tool of the powerful

cultural deviance theory—identifies crime as occurring when cultures clash, i.e., when individuals migrate to a new culture

differential association theory—Sutherland's theory that delinquency develops because of an excess of definitions favorable to crime

eugenics—the idea of improving the human race through controlled procreation

General Strain theory—Agnew's theory that delinquency occurs because of strain from negative emotions that are caused by a number of "strains"

General Theory of crime—Gottfredson and Hirschi's theory that crime results from low self-control

"hedonistic calculus"—Bentham's idea that punishment should be adjusted to slightly outweigh the perceived pleasure or profit from crime in order to deter people

integrated theories—combine elements of psychological, biological, and sociological theories and explain crime over the life course

labeling theory—focuses attention on the official labeler as well as the deviant and assumes that labeling creates secondary deviance

mixed zones—zones where residential, commercial, and industrial activity are mixed and characterized by crime and other forms of disorder

modeling—form of behavior change that occurs when one desires to be like others, especially those whom one admires

positivism—"scientific method" or the search for causes using scientific method

psychopathy—an individual without a conscience or habits of law-abidingness that normally constrain antisocial impulses

rational choice theory—theory that criminals rationally choose criminal action because of immediate rewards

reinforcement—form of learning in which behaviors and beliefs that are rewarded continue and behaviors and beliefs that are punished disappear

routine activities theory—theory that for a crime to happen, there must be a motivated offender, suitable targets of criminal victimization, and the absence of guardians of persons or property

sociopathy—persons whose unsocialized character is due primarily to parental failures rather than to inherent peculiarities of temperament

social process theories—theories of crime that focus on the individual's interaction with the world around them

social disorganization theory—theory that crime occurs in neighborhoods where there is no cohesion, transitory populations, and few indices of social support

social support theory—theory that assumes crime occurs where social supports (both emotional and concrete) are absent

strain or opportunity theory—theory that assumes that lack of economic opportunity causes crime

subcultural theories—theory that deviant subcultures with different values and belief systems socialize individuals to crime

For Further Reading

Agnew, Robert (2007). *Pressured into Crime: An Overview of General Strain Theory*. New York, NY: Oxford University Press.

Andrews, Don and James Bonta (2006). *The Psychology of Criminal Conduct*, Fourth Edition. Newark, NJ: LexisNexis/Matthew Bender.

Brown, Stephen E., Finn-Aage Esbensen, and Gilbert Geis (2007). *Criminology: Explaining Crime and Its Context*, Sixth Edition. Newark, NJ: LexisNexis/Matthew Bender.

Tonry, Michael, Lloyd Ohlin, and David Farrington (1991). *Human Development and Criminal Behavior: New Ways of Advancing Knowledge*. New York, NY: Springer-Verlag.

Vold, George, Thomas Bernard, and Jeffrey Snipes (2002). *Theoretical Criminology*, Fifth Edition. New York, NY: Oxford University Press.

Walsh, Anthony (1995). *Biosociology: An Emerging Paradigm*. Westport, CT: Praeger.

Notes

1. Bentham, J. (1843/1970). "The Rationale of Punishment." In R. Beck and J. Orr (eds.), *Ethical Choices: A Case Study Approach*. New York, NY: Free Press, pp. 326–340.

2. Lombroso, C. & W. Ferrero (1895/1972). *The Criminal Man*. Montclair, NJ: Patterson Smith.

3. Lombroso, C. & W. Ferrero (1894/1958. *The Female Offender*. New York, NY: Philosophical Library.

4. Andrews, D. & J. Bonta. 2006. *The Psychology of Criminal Conduct*, Fourth Edition. Newark, NJ: LexisNexis/Matthew Bender, p. 128-129.

5. Maccoby, E. & C. Jacklin (1974). *The Psychology of Sex Differences*. Stanford, CA: Stanford University Press. See also Tedeschi, J. & R. Felson (1994). *Violence, Aggression and Coercive Actions*. Washington, DC: American Psychological Association; Mednick, S. & K. Christiansen. 1977. *Biosocial Bases for Criminal Behavior*. New York, NY: Gardner; Mednick, S., T. Moffitt, & S. Stack (eds.) (1987). *The Causes of Crime*. New York, NY: Cambridge University Press; Walsh, A. (1991). *Intellectual Imbalance, Love Deprivation and Violent Delinquency: A Biosocial Perspective*. Springfield, IL: Charles C Thomas.

6. Eysenck, H. & G. Gudjonsson (1989). *The Causes and Cures of Criminality*. New York, NY: Plenum, p. 135. See also Walsh, A. (1991). *Intellectual Imbalance, Love Deprivation and Violent Delinquency: A Biosocial Perspective*. Springfield, IL: Charles C Thomas, p. 140.

7. Walsh, A. (1991). *Intellectual Imbalance, Love Deprivation and Violent Delinquency: A Biosocial Perspective*. Springfield, IL: Charles C Thomas, p. 127.

8. Walsh, A. (1995). *Biosociology: An Emerging Paradigm*. Westport, CT: Praeger, p. 50–54. See also Ellis, L. (1991). "Monoamine Oxidase and Criminality: Identifying an Apparent Biological Marker for Antisocial Behavior."

Journal of Research in Crime and Delinquency 28: 227–251.

9. Caspi, A., T. Moffitt, P. Silva, M. Stouthamer-Loeber, R. Krueger, & P. Schmutte (1994). "Are Some People Crime Prone? Replications of the Personality-Crime Relationship across Countries, Genders, Races, and Methods." *Criminology* 32: 163–195.

10. Raine, A. (1993). *The Psychopathology of Crime: Criminal Behavior as a Clinical Disorder.* San Diego, CA: Academic Press, p. 93.

11. Eysenck, H. & G. Gudjonsson (1989). *The Causes and Cures of Criminality.* New York, NY: Plenum, p. 55.

12. Wood, P., B. Pfefferbaum & B. Arneklev (1993). "Risk-Taking and Self-Control: Social Psychological Correlates of Delinquency." *Journal of Crime and Justice* 16, 1: 111–130.

13. Eysenck, H. & G. Gudjonsson (1989). *The Causes and Cures of Criminality.* New York, NY: Plenum, p. 126.

14. Sandhu, H. & H. Satterfield (1987). "Childhood Diagnostic and Neurophysiological Predictors of Teenage Arrest Rates." In S. Mednick, T. Moffitt and S. Stack (eds.), *The Causes of Crime.* New York, NY: Cambridge University Press, pp. 146–168.

15. Denno, D. (1990). *Biology and Violence: From Birth to Adulthood.* New York, NY: Cambridge University Press, p. 15.

16. Denno, D. (1990). *Biology and Violence: From Birth to Adulthood.* New York, NY: Cambridge University Press, p. 17.

17. Moffitt, T. (1990). "The Neuropsychology of Juvenile Delinquency: A Critical Review." In M. Tonry & N. Morris, *Crime and Justice: A Review of Research,* Vol. 12. Chicago, IL: University of Chicago Press, pp. 99–171.

18. See Moffitt (1990), "The Neuropsychology of Juvenile Delinquency: A Critical Review." In M. Tonry and N. Morris, *Crime and Justice: A Review of Research,* Vol. 12. Chicago, IL: University of Chicago Press, pp. 99–171, p. 112. See also Andrews, D. & J. Bonta (2006). *The Psychology of Criminal Conduct,* Fourth Edition. Newark, NJ: LexisNexis/Matthew Bender, p. 128–129; and Raine, A. (1993). *The Psychopathology of Crime: Criminal Behavior as a Clinical Disorder.* San Diego, CA: Academic Press.

19. Andrews, D. and J. Bonta (2006). *The Psychology of Criminal Conduct,* Fourth Edition. Newark, NJ: LexisNexis/Matthew Bender.

20. Andrews, D. and J. Bonta (2006). *The Psychology of Criminal Conduct,* Fourth Edition. Newark, NJ: LexisNexis/Matthew Bender.

21. Holloway, J. (2003). *The Perils of Profiling for the Media.* Retrieved 5/24/07 from APA Online: http://www.apa.org/monitor/jan03/perils.html.

22. Lykken, D. (1995). *The Antisocial Personalities.* Hillsdale, NJ: Lawrence Erlbaum, p. 6–7.

23. Cowie, J., B. Cowie, & E. Slater (1968). *Delinquency in Girls.* London, England: Heinemann.

24. Piaget, J. (1965). *The Moral Judgment of a Child.* New York, NY: Free Press.

25. Kohlberg, L. (1981). *The Philosophy of Moral Judgment.* San Francisco, CA: Harper and Row.

26. Gilligan, C. (1982). *In a Different Voice: Psychological Theory and Women's Development.* Cambridge, MA: Harvard University Press.

27. For a review of research, see Pollock, J. (2007). *Ethics in Criminal Justice: Dilemmas and Decisions,* Fifth Edition. Belmont, CA: Wadsworth.

28. Bandura, A. (1977). *Social Learning Theory.* Englewood Cliffs, NJ: Prentice-Hall.

29. Andrews, D. & J. Bonta (1994). *The Psychology of Criminal Conduct,* Second Edition. Cincinnati, OH: Anderson, p. 111.

30. See, for instance, Shaw, C. & H. McKay (1934/1972). *Juvenile Delinquency and Urban Areas.* Chicago, IL: University of Chicago Press.

31. Pollock, J. (2002). *Women, Prison, and Crime.* Belmont, CA: Wadsworth.

32. Merton, R. (1938). "Social Structure and Anomie." *American Sociological Review* 3, 6: 672–682.

33. Cohen, A. (1955). *Delinquency in Boys: The Culture of the Gang.* New York, NY: Free Press. Also see Cloward, R. & L. Ohlin (1960). *Delinquency and Opportunity.* New York, NY: Free Press.

34. See, for instance, Taylor, I., P. Walton & J. Young (1998). *The New Criminology.* New York, NY: Harper and Row; and, Quinney, R. (1973). *Critique of the Legal Order.* Boston, MA: Little, Brown.

35. Bursik, R. & H. Grasmick (1993). *Neighborhoods and Crime: the Dimensions of Effective Community Control.*

New York, NY: Lexington Books. See also Cullen, F. (1994). "Social Support as an Organizing Concept for Criminology." *Justice Quarterly* 11, 4: 528–559.

36. Reiss, A. & M. Tonry (1986). *Communities and Crime*. Chicago, IL: University of Chicago Press. See also Sampson, R. & W. Groves (1989). "Community Structure and Crime: Testing Social Disorganization Theory." *American Journal of Sociology* 94: 774–802.

37. Sutherland, E. & D. Cressey (1960/1966). *Principles of Criminology*. Philadelphia, PA: Lippincott.

38. Akers, R. (1973). *Deviant Behavior: A Social Learning Approach*. Belmont, CA: Wadsworth. Burgess, R. & R. Akers. (1966). "A Differential Association-Reinforcement Theory of Criminal Behavior." *Social Problems* 14: 128–47.

39. Burgess, R. & R. Akers (1966). "A Differential Association-Reinforcement Theory of Criminal Behavior." *Social Problems* 14: 142.

40. See, for instance, Lemert, E. (1951). *Social Pathology: A Systematic Approach to the Theory of Socio pathic Behavior*. New York, NY: McGraw-Hill.

41. Akers, R. (1973). *Deviant Behavior: A Social Learning Approach*. Belmont, CA: Wadsworth

42. Cornish, D. and R. Clarke (1986). *The Reasoning Criminal: Rational Choice Perspectives on Offending*. New York, NY: Springer-Verlag.

43. Cohen, L. and M. Felson (1979). "Social Change and Crime Trends: A Routine Activities Approach." *American Sociological Review* 44: 588–608.

44. Hirschi, T. (1969). *Causes of Delinquency*. Berkeley, CA: University of California Press.

45. Gottfredson, M. & T. Hirschi (1990). *A General Theory of Crime*. Stanford, CA: Stanford University Press.

46. Gottfredson, M. &d T. Hirschi (1990). *A General Theory of Crime*. Stanford, CA: Stanford University Press, p. 90.

47. Gottfredson, M. & T. Hirschi (1990). *A General Theory of Crime*. Stanford, CA: Stanford University Press, p. 97.

48. Longshore, D., S. Turner, & J. Stein (1996). "Self Control in a Criminal Sample: An Examination of Construct Validity." *Criminology* 34, 2: 209–227.

49. Miller, S. & C. Burack (1993). "A Critique of Gottfredson and Hirschi's General Theory of Crime: Selective (In) Attention to Gender and Power Positions." *Women & Criminal Justice* 4, 2: 115–134.

50. Agnew, R. (2007). *Pressured into Crime: An Overview of General Strain Theory*. New York, NY: Oxford University Press.

51. Tonry, M., L. Ohlin, & D. Farrington (1991). *Human Development and Criminal Behavior: New Ways of Advancing Knowledge*. New York, NY: Springer-Verlag, p. 142.

52. Denno, D. (1990). *Biology and Violence: From Birth to Adulthood*. New York, NY: Cambridge University Press.

SECTION II

Introduction to Criminology

DEFINING CRIMINOLOGY

Douglas Klutz and Mark M. Lanier

W hy do individuals engage in criminal behavior? The scientific study of criminology seeks to answer this very question. Drawing from different fields including sociology, psychology, and law, criminology provides an interdisciplinary approach in order to better understand crime. Criminological theories that provide a comprehensive explanation of why individuals engage in criminal behavior serve to help shape and guide more efficient public policies structured to deter and prevent crime as a whole. But what actually constitutes a comprehensive criminological theory? As you will soon discover, criminologists are still grappling with this same question today.

Criminology has evolved a great deal over the course of the past few centuries. In fact, prior to the late 1700s, crime was explained as a product of being possessed by evil spirits. The demonic perspective of crime centered on religion as the primary explanation as to why individuals engaged in delinquent or criminal acts. Individuals accused of committing delinquent acts would be physically beaten or tortured in an attempt to rid the body of the evil spirits. Often the individual being physically tortured would die as a result of the intense physical abuse. Keep in mind all of this occurred before the protections against cruel and unusual punishments established in the Eighth Amendment of the Bill of Rights.

The Age of Enlightenment ushered in an entirely new viewpoint regarding criminal behavior. Throughout the 1700s, a secular push for increased rational thought grounded in scientific reasoning continued to gain strength. Superstitions rooted in a religious context, including crime being explained as a product of evil spirits, were thrown out in favor of establishing scientifically testable and measurable theories. The demonic perspective of crime failed to provide any form of quantifiable or testable evidence as to why individuals engaged in delinquent acts. However, Cesare Beccaria would change this by providing the first modern criminological theory rooted in science in his seminal work, *On Crimes and Punishments*.

Cesare Beccaria is credited as being the first and most well-known Classical Criminologist. Classical Criminology differs from the demonic perspective not only in secular terms, but also due to the fact the classical school seeks to explain crime as a product of free will.[1] Classical Criminology emphasizes that individuals are rational people making rational choices. The focus on the rational decision-making process in the classical school draws from the larger context of rational decision-making processes found throughout the Age of Enlightenment. Explaining crime as a product of rational choice was a significant departure from explaining crime solely as a product of evil spirits. Instead of being compelled to commit crimes through evil forces, classical criminologists suggested that rational individuals base their decision on whether or not to engage in a delinquent act through a simple cost-benefit analysis. Since all individuals are said to be rational under the classical school, people want to maximize their pleasure while minimizing their pain. Thus, if a rational individual views the benefit of the potential delinquent act to outweigh the cost, the individual will choose to engage in the delinquent act. Conversely, if the perceived cost outweighs the perceived benefit, the individual will make the rational choice to forego committing the delinquent act.

The deterrent effect is important to note within Classical Criminology. In order for crime to be prevented, the threat of a punishment as an absolute certainty must exist.[2] Without the threat of an effective punishment present, rational individuals will choose to engage in criminal activity because of the absence of a specific deterrent to crime. Classical Criminology was the first modern school of criminology to focus on observable secular forces. More specifically, they argue that the absence of effective punishments will result in a greater amount of crime.[3] Classical Criminology has significant limitations, though. For one, the classical school assumed that all individuals are rational, and all can formulate and execute a cogent rational decision-making process. But are all individuals really capable of generating such a process? Take for example juveniles. Is an 8-year-old is capable of the same rational decision

making as someone in their thirties? Similarly, the juvenile might also not be able to conceptualize the full scope of the prescribed deterrent, or the swift and certain punishments suggested under the classical school.

Due to these limitations with Classical Criminology, and coupled with the fact that crime rates were increasing under a criminal justice system structured largely around Classical Criminology, the classical school of criminology started to lose favor in the late 1800s. Cesare Lombroso and the Positive School of Criminology, which was based on scientific principles, were the main challengers in the criminology arena. Lombroso and members of the Positive School formulated the first biological approach to explaining criminal behavior, drawing heavily from Darwin's theory of evolution. Under positivism, criminals were viewed differently than non-criminals, even from a literal physical sense, according to Lombroso. This was in direct opposition to Classical Criminology, where criminals and non-criminals are viewed to be inherently the same. Cesare Lombroso wrote about these perceived biological and evolutionary differences in criminals versus non-criminals in *The Criminal Man*.

NOTES

1. Akers, R. and Sellers, C. (2009). *Criminological Theories: Introduction, Evaluation, and Application.* (5th ed.). Oxford, NY: Oxford University Press. (p. 18).
2. Beccaria, Cesare. 1983 [1775]. *An Essay on Crimes and Punishments.* Brookline Village, MA: Branden Press. (pp. 4–8).
3. Cullen, F. and Agnew, R. (2011). *Criminological Theory: Past to Present.* (4th ed.). Oxford, NY: Oxford University Press. (p. 23).

THE CRIMINAL MAN

*Cesare Lombroso
with Gina
Lombroso-Ferrero*

The Classical School [of criminology] based its doctrines on the assumption that all criminals, except in a few extreme cases, are endowed with intelligence and feelings like normal individuals, and that they commit misdeeds consciously, being prompted thereto by their unrestrained desire for evil. The offense alone was considered, and on it the whole existing penal system has been founded, the severity of the sentence meted out to the offender being regulated by the gravity of his misdeed.

The Modern, or Positive, School of Penal Jurisprudence, on the contrary, maintains that the anti-social tendencies of criminals are the result of their physical and psychic organization, which differs essentially from that of normal individuals; and it aims at studying the morphology and various functional phenomena of the criminal with the object of curing, instead of punishing him. ...

If we examine a number of criminals, we shall find that they exhibit numerous anomalies in the face, skeleton, and various psychic and sensitive functions, so that they strongly resemble primitive races. It was these anomalies that first drew my father's attention to the close relationship between the criminal and the savage and made him suspect that criminal tendencies are of atavistic origin.

When a young doctor at the Asylum in Pavia, he was requested to make a postmortem examination on a criminal named Vilella, an Italian Jack the Ripper, who by atrocious crimes had spread terror in the Province of Lombardy. ... "At the sight of that skull," says my father, "I seemed to see all at once, standing out clearly illumined as in a vast plain under a flaming sky, the problem of the nature of the criminal, who reproduces in civilized times characteristics, not only of primitive savages, but of still lower types as far back as the carnivora."

Thus was explained the origin of the enormous jaws, strong canines, prominent zygomae, and strongly developed orbital arches which he had so frequently remarked in criminals, for these peculiarities are common to carnivores and savages, who tear and devour raw flesh. Thus also it was easy to understand why the span of the arms in criminals so often exceeds the height, for this is a characteristic of apes, whose fore-limbs are used in walking and climbing. The other anomalies exhibited by criminals—the scanty beard as opposed to the general hairiness of the body, prehensile foot, diminished number of lines in the palm of the hand, cheek-pouches, enormous development of the middle incisors and frequent absence of the lateral ones, flattened nose and angular or sugar-loaf form of the skull, common to criminals and apes; the excessive size of the orbits, which, combined with hooked nose, so often imparts to criminals the aspect of birds of prey, the projection of the lower part of the face and jaws (prognathism) found in negroes and animals, and supernumerary teeth (amounting in some cases to a double row as in snakes) and cranial bones (epactal bone as in the Peruvian Indians): all these characteristics pointed to one conclusion, the atavistic origin of the criminal, who reproduces physical, psychic, and functional qualities of remote ancestors.

Subsequent research on the part of my father and his disciples showed that other factors besides atavism come into play in determining the criminal type. These are: disease and environment. Later on, the study of innumerable offenders led them to the conclusion that all law-breakers cannot be classed in a single species, for their ranks include very diversified types, who differ not only in their bent towards a particular form of crime, but also in the degree of tenacity and intensity displayed by them in their perverse propensities, so that, in reality, they form a graduated scale leading from the born criminal to the normal individual.

Born criminals form about one third of the mass of offenders, but, though inferior in numbers, they constitute the most important part of the whole criminal army, partly because they are constantly appearing before the public and also because the crimes committed by them are of a peculiarly monstrous character; the other two thirds are composed of criminaloids (minor offenders), occasional and habitual criminals, etc., who do not show such a marked degree of diversity from normal persons.

DISCUSSION QUESTIONS

1. Lombroso argues that crime is not the result of free will; rather, it is due to factors over which the individual often has little or no control. This deterministic view focuses less on punishment of the offender and more on "curing" the offending. To what extent do you think crime is an act of free will or one caused by forces beyond the individual's control?

2. What policy recommendations might an adherent of Lombroso's theory make for controlling crime? (A consideration of these recommendations will help you understand one of the reasons why the theory was later attacked.)

3. List those factors said to distinguish "born criminals" from others. How would one go about providing a good test of Lombroso's theory?

WHAT IS CRIMINOLOGY?

The Study of Crime, Criminals, and Victims in a Global Context

Mark M. Lanier
and Stuart Henry

The horrendous events of September 11, 2001, in which the World Trade Center in New York was totally destroyed, and the Pentagon in Washington substantially damaged, by hijacked commercial airliners that were flown into them, killing 2,982 people, have proved to be the defining point of this decade. The United States was horrified, unified, motivated, and eager to apply its superior military might immediately and unequivocally against the aggressors. However, unlike the Japanese attack on Pearl Harbor on December 7, 1941, this time it was not clear who to strike or what effect a strike would have. For the first time in its history the United States did not have a well-defined nation-state enemy. Clearly, the nature of war, the American way of life, what counts as "crime," and how a society responds to harms, internal or external, changed on that day. This act of terrorism was undoubtedly aimed at the American people. The terrorist organization al-Qaeda claimed responsibility. From a geopolitical perspective, the major consequence of 9/11 was that an explicitly hostile Islamic state, Iraq, was soon invaded/liberated/occupied on the rationale that it was storing weapons of mass destruction that could be targeted at Western interests. (We purposefully say "invaded/liberated/occupied," as one's worldview, political beliefs, and context determine which word is most appropriate.) The logic was that a preemptive attack was necessary to prevent a catastrophe worse than 9/11 (a concept known as the Bush Doctrine). Yet the 9/11 attackers were predominantly from Saudi Arabia, and al-Qaeda was substantially based in Afghanistan; seven years later the 2008 presidential debate was dominated by discussions about whether Iraq or Afghanistan was the best place to fight against those who perpetrated this and other acts of terrorism. The purpose of this introductory chapter is to show how the changing geopolitical landscape and other factors shape our renewed discussion of crime and its causes, as well as possible policy responses.

Six fundamental changes can be identified that demonstrate the changed nature of our world. These changes all move toward increasing interconnection and interdependence. They are: (1) globalization; (2) the communications revolution, particularly the Internet; (3) privatization and individualization; (4) the global spread of disease; (5) changing perceptions of conflict and national security; and (6) the internationalization of terrorism.

GLOBALIZATION

Globalization is the process whereby people react to issues in terms of reference points that transcend their own locality, society, or region. These reference points include material, political, social, and cultural concerns that affect the planet, such as environmental challenges (e.g., global warming or overpopulation) and commercial matters (e.g., fast food, in particular so-called McDonaldization, which describes the spread of McDonald's restaurants throughout the world's economies). Globalization is a process of unification in which differences in economic, technological, political, and social institutions are transformed from a local or national network into a single system. Globalization also relates to an international universalism, whereby events happening in one part of the world affect those in another, none more dramatic than the collapse of world financial markets (Stiglitz 2002, 2006), which went global in September 2008. Indeed, the emergence of worldwide financial markets and under- or unregulated foreign exchange and speculative markets resulted in the vulnerability of national economies. In short, "'Globalization' refers to all those processes by which peoples of the world are incorporated into a single world society, global society" (Albrow 1990, 9). Conversely, while globalization relates to the way people in different societies identify with values that cut across nations and cultures, it also relates to the recognition of different cultures' diversity of experience and the formation of new identities. As globalization integrates us, these new identities and our sense of belonging to differentiated cultures are also driving many of us apart (Croucher 2004, 3).

The greatest effect of the global society is the global economy as it relates to the increasing multinationalization of corporations that produce on the "global assembly line" (Ehrenreich and Fuentes 1994). The result is that "economic goods, services, and personnel flow back and forth across national, hemispheric

and continental boundaries" such that "economic, social, political and environmental events in one part of the world have significant impacts in other parts of the world ... beyond the ability of any one society to control" (Soroka and Bryjak 1999, 176). Indeed, both advocates and critics of globalization agree that it has resulted in the circumvention of both national boundaries and state controls over economic trade and production processes. Further, ethnic identities and religious affiliations transcend both political and geographic boundaries. As Frank Schmalleger says:

> On a global scale, there appears to be a shared agreement that society is experiencing a period of unprecedented change. Both the substance and the pace of change are fundamentally different from what has occurred in past decades and centuries. No longer are sequences of events occurring in relative isolation over longer patterns of time. No longer are discrete groups of people affected by each change; rather, there is a greater simultaneity of occurrence, swifter interpenetration, and increased feedback of one set of changes upon another. ([1999] 2002, 480)

A classic example of the interconnection and inability of individual societies to influence and control the crime and harm created by globalization is the case of one of the worst industrial accidents in the world: In 1984, in Bhopal, India, Union Carbide's insecticide plant leaked toxic gas, resulting in between 4,000 and 15,000 deaths and injuries to as many as 600,000 people (Beirne and Messerschmidt 2000, 494–495).

> What is most frightening about Bhopal is ... the way people are routinely treated by corporations. ... Cancer-causing pesticides banned in the West are freely sold to farmers in Latin America, Eastern Europe and Asia. Native American Nations are bribed to accept nuclear waste. ... Malaysian hill people are killed or run off their land so Japanese companies can cut down their forests to make chopsticks. Leaded gasoline, banned

in the West because of its devastating health effects on children, is sold to Thailand, Mexico and India. This kind of corporate violence is repeated in every corner of the Earth. (Cohen 1998, 3, cited in Beirne and Messerschmidt 2000, 494–495)

Some critics of globalization, known as the anti-globalization movement, such as Nikos Passas (2000), have argued that the process of globalization, including the spread of capital, labor, management, news, and information across national borders, is itself "criminogenic," because it provides motivation and opportunities for corporate deviance at the same time that it leads to less effective control systems (M. Robinson 2004). Other critics, such as Noam Chomsky, argue that it is not so much the existence of global integration they oppose but the way in which it occurs, in that it benefits the rich nations at the expense of the poor and polarizes and accentuates inequality within societies.

The Globalization of Communications

Prior to 1985 global communication was largely restricted to the affluent. The advent of the personal computer and the development of the Internet transformed the way we communicate. Now people connect daily with others all over the world at little or no expense. They exchange ideas, performances, propaganda, ideologies, and technical information; through Internet search engines they can draw on knowledge from any part of the globe. Members of any society can read newspapers and opinions, engage in chat-room discussions, and take university courses via the Internet.

They can also share the most intimate details of their daily lives through Web blogs and social-networking sites such as YouTube, Facebook, and MySpace, communication mechanisms that have become global. No longer are people limited to what their own government's or society's ideology and culture feed them, which paradoxically can lead to expanded knowledge and perspectives or reinforcement for any idea or view, however strange or outrageous it may seem. This means

that we are increasingly interconnected with the world in both positive and negative ways. What affects people in one part of the globe can affect others in another.

At the same time, the development in global communications has led to a massive shift of jobs from manufacturing into service, communications, and information (called the postindustrial society), and because the latter jobs require higher education and training, increasing numbers of people the world over are underemployed or unemployed. The result has been to increase worker anxiety and job stress among those who have "not yet been 'bumped,' 'deselected,' 'surplussed,' 'vocationally relocated,' 'de-hired,' 'decruited' or otherwise done away with" (Soroka and Bryjak 1999, 180). Work-related stress leads to increased competition, "backstabbing," isolation, detachment, and alienation as well as increased family and workplace violence.

Increased global communication has also brought a rush of new crimes that are perpetrated on and via the Internet, such as fraud and identity theft, drug smuggling, and bomb making. The growing dependence on global communications has also made national infrastructures and governments vulnerable to Internet terrorism through hacking and computer viruses.

Privatization and Individualization

Related to globalization and global unemployment are two trends that, in spite of our being connected to ever-greater numbers of people, have produced a reduction in our concern for others. We have already mentioned the increased competition in the workplace, the attitude of everyone looking out for themselves. This is in contrast to the shared movement around trades and professions that culminated in unionization and collective action during the middle of the twentieth century, when people banded together for strength and solidarity.

More and more we are seeing the "death of society," that is, the decline in collective action and social policy requiring some to give up part of their wealth to help the less fortunate or to increase the public good. Instead, partly because of government fiscal crises and partly because of conservative ideology, the twenty-first century has witnessed a growing privatization of government, particularly in the areas of welfare and social programs. Privatization reinforces the individualization of human actions, as well as allowing major policy decisions to be made not in terms of a society's public or social interests but in terms of what maximizes profit for corporate shareholders. Thus, the 1980s and 1990s saw massive deregulation and privatization, from transportation, communications, and energy to finance, welfare, and even law enforcement.

We have also seen the increasing tendency for family members to stay at home, not as families but as appendages to technology, such as televisions, computers, and video games. The result is an impersonal society, one where we are living in isolation from other real people, "bowling alone" (Putnam 1995), where media images and game characters become interspersed with real people who are seen as superficial, object-like caricatures.

Moreover, because of the impact of globalization on the economic structures of societies, there has been a polarization of rich and poor, with numerous groups excluded from opportunities (J. Young 1999). In their relatively impoverished state, they are vulnerable to violence, both in their homes and in their neighborhoods.

Globalization of Disease

Although the black death, or plague, smallpox, and polio have demonstrated that throughout human history, disease can be a global phenomenon, the systemic use of hygienic practices, including clean water and effective sanitation and sewerage, and the discovery and use of antibiotics, vaccines, and other drugs meant that for much of the twentieth century the global spread of disease was seen as a thing of the past, or at least occurring only in underdeveloped countries. But by the end of the twentieth century, through the advent of increased global travel, the terror of disease on a global scale was given new meaning, first with HIV/AIDS, then with mad cow disease, West Nile virus, SARS (severe acute respiratory syndrome), and resistant strains of tuberculosis. Worse was the fact that, unlike times past, groups could potentially introduce disease, such as smallpox or anthrax, on a global scale as part of a

terrorist operation against individuals or governments. Like the previous developments, the dual effect was, on the one hand, to render people increasingly fearful of contact, especially intimate contact with strangers, tending to undermine interpersonal relations, while, on the other, demonstrating just how interconnected we have become.

This area of change has led to the development of an emerging semiparadigm in criminology. Timothy Akers and Mark Lanier (2009) founded the Virtual Center for Epidemiological Criminology (VCEC) to address the correlates and causes of crime and health issues. Public health and criminal justice issues are closely related and often inseparable. Many diverse entities are now acknowledging the connections between crime and health variables. For example, recent data sets released by the Centers for Disease Control and Prevention (CDC) include crime statistics. On January 8, 2008, the CDC made the following announcement: "The CDC Behavioral Surveillance Branch (BSB) is pleased to announce the release of a county-level data set [that] will allow users to compare health behaviors with … core health outcomes and risk factors such as cardiovascular disease (CVD), diabetes, asthma, physical activity, obesity, and smoking. … These variables include health care delivery information, health and vital statistics indicators, environmental measures, *crime statistics*, business indicators, and poverty/income figures" (emphasis added).

Moving beyond what the CDC and others have accomplished, VCEC seeks to theoretically and empirically link and examine the two disciplines of crime and public health. VCEC's primary function is to research specific strategies that integrate long-tested public health and criminological theories to produce practical interventions that will improve the well-being of communities. The objective is to isolate interventions that simultaneously impact the co-occurrence of crime and public health problems. VCEC and the related online journal *Epidemiological Criminology* clearly suggest the linkages between the issues.

The Changing Nature of Global Conflict

During the twentieth century, until the end of the cold war, each generation faced a significant war or warlike threats to its survival. Examples include the two world wars, Korean War, Vietnam War, and cold war. In these twentieth-century global conflicts it was possible to clearly identify the enemy posing the threat, and to come together as nations to wage war to defeat that threat. In contrast, in the twenty-first century it is becoming ever more apparent that for many nations, "the enemy" is multiple, diffuse, and interwoven into the very fabric of society.

Globalization is not simply an economic process but, rather, the term for the technological movement away from the dyadic analysis of "independent events" toward complex, interdependent "systems analysis." The most fundamental questions for peace researchers at the present time include: "What is the general quality of peace and is it improving, stagnating, or deteriorating?" "Where, and under what conditions, is organized violence most likely to occur?" "How do we understand the quality of peace in its many systemic variations, both successes and failures?" (CSP 2009).

Nations in the continent of Africa, for example, face very serious threats on several fronts, including starvation, the spread of HIV/AIDS, and numerous civil wars. For example, civil wars in Sierra Leone, Rwanda, Ethiopia, and Mozambique have resulted in the deaths of millions of innocent people over the past two decades. But as the Center for Systemic Peace (CSP) indicates, although "the level of societal warfare increased dramatically and continuously through the Cold War period," it was a result of "the protractedness of societal wars during this period and not from a substantial increase in the numbers of new wars" (ibid.). In the twentieth century former colonial powers would step in during such times of civil conflict, while multinational peacekeeping forces, such as the United Nations, NATO, and the "Coalition of the Willing," appeared, at least on the surface, to provide both clarity and stability. Since the 1990s, however, these bodies seem reluctant to intervene everywhere that violence occurs. Part of the explanation may be that the "international community is increasingly reluctant to provide peacekeeping forces for difficult, expensive and politically unrewarding operations" (Brayton 2002, 304).

Another part of the explanation is the changing nature of war and conflict. The two superpowers of the cold war, the United States and the Soviet Union, no longer square off since the latter's breakup in 1991, and so far Russia has presented a limited challenge to America. The United States has emerged as the world's dominant military power, and as a result, "America has reduced the military role of its European allies in NATO to that of its strategic reserve, to be used where the job is relatively easy, requires less capable forces, and where such tasks require long-term commitment of troops and peace building rather than fighting duties" (Cilliers 2003, 112). The role of allies and multinational organizations, such as NATO and the United Nations, is changing. Consequently, the nature of war is also changing. Today, "to an extent unprecedented in modern times, entities other than nation-states wage war across multiple physical and ideological boundaries. The Cold War's clear dichotomies and array of proxy wars have devolved into myriad intrastate conflicts and cross-border wars of uncertain and shifting ideological foundation" (Brayton 2002, 305).

The incidence of both societal and interstate warfare has declined dramatically since the 1990s, and this trend continues in the early 2000s, falling more than 60 percent from its peak level. For example, there were twenty-five major armed conflicts (societal warfare) in 2000, yet only two were between nation-states (interstate warfare), according to a 2001 report by the Stockholm International Peace Research Institute (cited in Brayton 2002). If nation-states are not waging war with each other, and if major powers are not intervening in conflict resolution or conflict promotion (except, of course, when oil is involved), how are the conflicts that do occur resolved, and why are their numbers declining? Part of the answer is the withdrawal of superpowers supporting civil unrest, particularly since the end of the cold war.

In the poorest of countries and regions, conflicts do continue, albeit at a lesser rate. According to the CSP:

In late 2007, there are 24 states directly affected by ongoing wars (28 wars total, up from 26 at the end of 2006). Of these 24 states, half (12) are affected by protracted wars, that is, armed conflicts persisting for more than ten years. These protracted societal conflicts include Afghanistan (30 years), Colombia (24), D. R. Congo (16), India (56), Iraq (28), Israel (43), Myanmar (60), Nigeria (11), Philippines (36), Somalia (20), Sri Lanka (25), Sudan (25), Turkey (24), and Uganda (37). These wars continue to defy concerted efforts to gain settlement or resolution. (CSP 2009)

Moreover, the end of the cold war saw the rise of numerous ethnic wars: "Ethnic wars, which had previously paralleled the trend of revolutionary war, continue to rise through the late 1980s and early 1990s as separatists and other political entrepreneurs attempt to take advantage of the vast changes in political arrangements that accompanied the transformation of the post—Cold War world system" (ibid.).

One way the conflicts that do occur are being resolved is through the use of armies for hire, that is, mercenaries who fight for pay. Increasingly, small countries, and some large ones, are finding themselves unable to "protect the political, military, economic social and cultural life of their citizens" (Brayton 2002, 303). Papua New Guinea provides an illustrative example. In 1997, the Bougainville Revolutionary Army was seriously threatening the regime of Prime Minister Julius Chan. As a result of this conflict the Panguan copper mine was closed—the source of 30 percent of the country's export income. Chan hired the mercenary force Sandline International for $36 million. Sandline recognized the economic advantages of opening and protecting the mine, and Chan was able to obtain the military assistance he needed.

What's wrong with using private security firms? Some argue that "in proffering security to collapsing, mineral-rich states … multinational corporations accentuate the international exploitation and marginalization of the states in question" (ibid., 310). The proliferation of these large, well-organized private armies also alarms the United Nations, which views them as a threat to "sovereign equality, political independence and territorial integrity" (ibid., 304). There are dozens of these huge corporate armies for hire around the world. Their "peacekeeping" role is based solely on profit and armed conflict.

Large, well-funded nation-states, such as the United States, are also increasingly using mercenaries. In fact, the best-known example of a private army served primarily at the discretion of the second Bush administration. Founded in 1997, Blackwater Worldwide is an American company that provides military private-sector solutions to both government and nongovernment clients. A former Navy Seal, Erik Prince, started the company as a basic-training operation to help support the needs of local and regional law enforcement. Its main headquarters is in Moyock, North Carolina, where its 7,000-acre training facility is the largest private training center in the United States. The company claims to be the world's most successful security-service corporation, having designed and manufactured remotely piloted airships, IED safe-armored personnel carriers, and training support systems. It operates in nine countries, delivering critical assistance to clients focused on postconflict and postdisaster stabilization efforts (Blackwater, USA 2008).

Through its contract with the U.S. Defense Department, Blackwater Worldwide and two other security companies had an estimated 137,000 employees working in Iraq as of 2007. The U.S. government pays these private firms to supply armed guards to protect people and buildings and furnish transportation in hostile areas. The security contractors also provide protective services for diplomats and for companies working on reconstruction projects, including escorting people to and from meetings and job sites.

On September 16, 2007, Blackwater employees were on a mission to evacuate senior American officials after a nearby explosion. (Some question the need for the evacuation because the officials were already in a secure compound.) After the explosion at 11:50 A.M., the diplomats were escorted via a Blackwater convoy to a Green (safe) Zone. To get to the Green Zone they had to go through Nisour Square, in Baghdad. Another convoy went to Nisour first to block off traffic so the convoy could get through without delay. At least four SUVs blocked lanes entering the square, and some guards got out of their vehicles and took positions on the street. At 12:08 P.M. at least one guard began to fire in the direction of a car, killing its driver. The same guard walked toward the car, firing more shots, killing a woman and an infant.

There are several different versions explaining how the shooting began. The Blackwater guards said they believed they were fired upon first. An Iraqi preliminary investigation concluded that there was no enemy fire, but some Iraqi witnesses said that Iraqi commandos in nearby guard towers could have been shooting. Ultimately, eight civilians were killed and fourteen others injured.

Whereas national conflicts have become decentralized, global conflicts have become dispersed. Rather than nations facing off, we now have terrorist tactics, once limited to anarchists and fringe radical groups, becoming a method of war for a variety of causes, from antiabortionists to Muslim extremists.

Global Terrorism

The single most feared event, and according to surveys of public opinion the "crime" considered most serious, is a terrorist attack. Events such as the September 11, 2001, suicide airliner bombings and the Mumbai hotel takeover in December 2008 illustrate that the threat of terrorism on a global scale has become part of the daily fear of populations around the world, not least because of the ways these events are instantly communicated to everyone, everywhere, as they happen. No longer restricted to the tactics of a few extreme radical or fringe groups in certain nations, terrorism has become the method of war for any ethnic or religious group that does not have the power to succeed politically. It has been facilitated by developments in communication, transportation, and technology that have enabled explosives and other weapons to become smaller and more lethal. Whether there is an interconnected web of terrorism around fundamentalist Muslim religious extremism (such as that claimed by followers of Osama Bin Laden and al-Qaeda), an Arab-led terrorist movement opposed to Western culture, more specific

actions such as those in Northern Ireland by the IRA and splinter groups against Protestants and the British government, or in Indonesia or Bali against supporters of the West, it is clear that terrorism has become a global threat. Data assembled by the Center for Systemic Peace show that since 2001, both the number and the severity of terrorist incidents have increased.

What is significant about the way terrorist tactics are used is that they exploit the very systems of interconnection that globalization has spawned, whether these are via transportation, communication, energy, or immigration and democracy. Theories based on particular assumptions of biology, or psychology, or those based on the sociology of particular societies are inadequate to deal with the global dimensions of twentyfirst-century crime.

So how do societies reconfigure their vision of crime to deal with its global dimensions? Should acts of terrorism and acts of war be considered crimes? What about the actions of states that abuse human rights? Are there new criminologies that are able to confront these more integrated global-level forms of harm creation?

In part due to these changes, in the early twenty-first century we have witnessed some surprising and shocking changes in the study of crime. Theoretically, the most significant change is the increased attention given to defining crime (which we address in the next chapter), not least because global terrorism has caused us to question the connection among politics, harm creation, and what kinds of actions should count as crime. There is also greater attention being focused on crimes of the powerful, from governments to corporations, more generally known as white-collar crime.

In practical terms the increase in severity and frequency of terrorism has altered our belief in the amount of freedom that individuals are prepared to sacrifice to the government in exchange for state protection. Instead of security in the home to protect our private property, we are now more interested in "homeland security," to protect our energy resources, health network, water supply, communications system, and mass transportation facilities, including ports, airports, and trains. We are also strengthening public safety services: police, firefighting, emergency medical services, and the National Guard. We are moving from decentralized and fragmented protective services to an integrated national system of security designed to protect "the homeland" of America. Fear in the minds of Western populations has shifted from burglars in the night to low-flying aircraft and bombs at movie theaters and sporting events. The perceived vulnerability of Western civilizations stemming from the combination of openness and large concentrations of population has reached a national crisis.

As a result of these changes, criminology is itself undergoing major changes. What historically has been a discipline focused on explaining individual criminal motivations in relation to domestic institutions and social processes has become a multifaceted examination that links genetic disposition to political and global forces. What is this discipline, this study of crime? To contemporary criminologists, the scope of crime is much broader than media portrayals of inner-city gang violence, child abductions, carjackings, drive-by shootings, serial murders, workplace homicides, and drug wars. Crime also includes a variety of misdeeds by governments, political corruption, corporate fraud, employee theft, and offenses committed by "ordinary" Americans.

Ever since the watershed of Watergate in the early 1970s when it was reluctantly realized that even a president could be a "crook," there has been accelerating media coverage of crimes by those in positions of power. Former president Bill Clinton reinforced this realization. The incredibly bad intelligence—or, worse, outright lies—that led to the hunt for weapons of mass destruction in Iraq provides yet another presidential example of abuse of power. Also consider the harm caused by U.S. government radiation experiments on unknowing citizens who subsequently developed cancer. Consider also the 1930s syphilis experiments that were conducted on African American men in Tuskegee, Alabama. These infected men were diagnosed with syphilis but deliberately not treated, even when penicillin was discovered as a cure, in order for government doctors to study the long-term effects of syphilis. False advertising and price-fixing by corporate giants like the Archer Daniels Midland Company (forcing consumers to pay more than the market price by undermining competition) are just some of the crimes committed

by corporations. Other crimes of the powerful involve corporate executives deceiving investors, as in the Enron, WorldCom, and Arthur Andersen scandals; even Martha Stewart has made *insider trading* a household phrase. Corporate crime can also include manufacturers and hazardous-waste companies that pollute the environment; the knowing manufacture of defective products, as in the case of the Ford Pinto gas tank that exploded on low-speed rear-end impact or the use of dangerous Firestone tires on Ford Motor Company automobiles, particularly its SUVs; and unsafe food-handling practices by meat-processing companies resulting in E. coli contamination.

Also falling within the scope of criminology are the unsafe production practices that result in death and injury in the workplace, such as the case of the Imperial chicken plant in Hamlet, North Carolina, where twenty-five deaths occurred when the factory caught fire. Imperial's owners had padlocked the plant's fire exits to stop petty pilfering of chicken; each of the owners received a ten-year prison sentence for non-negligent manslaughter. Contemporary criminologists also study employees who steal from their bosses, bosses who employ workers "off the books" to evade taxes, and professionals such as doctors who defraud the government and rob the public purse through Medicare and Medicaid fraud.

Finally, and most glaring, the United States has become the target of terrorist groups, as evidenced by the 9/11 suicide hijackings and the attacks on American interests abroad, including the USS *Cole* and the U.S. Embassy in Nairobi. What light can criminology shed on the political movements that lead humans to commit suicide bombings in furtherance of their cause? What global forces congeal to produce such widespread human suffering, and what can we learn about the forces that prevent these devastating consequences?

Criminologists study not only the nature of this harmful behavior but also its causes and the systemic practices that produce patterns of harms in a variety of social contexts. Take something as seemingly innocent as a recreational activity like surfing. This may seem to be a crime-free activity, and generally it is. But in September 1995 at Laguna Beach, California, two surfers were videotaped beating another surfer who had ventured into their designated contest area. The two surfers were arrested and charged with felony assault. In court on December 20, 1995, the two surfers had their charges reduced through a plea bargain, and each was released on three years' probation. The videotape played a vital role in the case. Media coverage was vast, and the case was featured on *Court TV*. Since we first provided this example, there has been a flurry of similar cases involving surfers and violence. A September 2, 2002, *People* article on the problem may have further influenced the prosecution of these territorial violent surfers, or it may have increased the violence. Indeed, the media play a significant role in shaping our conception of what crime is, especially through such infamous cases as the police beating in Inglewood, California, of a young teen, the Clarence Thomas-Anita Hill sexual harassment hearings, and the murder and kidnapping trials of O. J. Simpson and Michael Skakel (Barak 1994, 1996). The movie *Point Break* (1991) with Keanu Reeves even focused on territorially violent surfers.

BOX 7.1. CRIME, RISK, AND THE CHANGING WORLD ORDER

Christiaan Bezuidenhout, University of Pretoria

As perceived risks increase, spurred on by the global spread of crime, particularly terrorism, many countries around the world are having to pay excessive prices for freedom, liberty, and equality. The global terrorist attacks on innocent people to convey a specific message in an attempt to achieve political and ideological objectives illustrate the extent of the problem. Following the 9/11 attacks on the United States, the United Kingdom and Spain were also targeted. The attacks in Spain (2004) and in the UK (2005) highlighted the change in global risk and challenged our conception of crime. India has also been the target of several terrorist attacks on hotels in which many innocent people were killed, most recently in December 2008. These criminal attacks have impacted the global community on several levels. For the members of any specific country, death, destruction, financial loss, as well as psychological and physical suffering are some of the direct, blatant aftereffects of such an attack. However, the impact on confidence and security in the global community is more indirect but perhaps more pervasive in its long-term implications. Consider how global air travel has changed in the past few years. Travelers face security delays and invasive screening, are required to remove shoes and clothing at the security and customs areas at airports, and are not allowed to carry any liquids or knives on board the airplane. The risks and resultant security measures have become very apparent and present challenges for newly formed, struggling democracies.

Consider South Africa as an example. The changes within the "new" South Africa as well as the adoption of a Bill of Human Rights and Constitution have resulted in drastic changes being made to the way in which accused offenders are being processed and treated in this country. More restorative justice programs and less incarceration are being utilized. In addition, the freedoms that have come with South African democracy have been accompanied by extraordinarily high crime and homicide rates. Serious crimes in any country cause fear and insecurity, and dramatic increases in crime rates intensify the perceived personal risk of victimization. Risk is part of any society and does not discriminate with regard to social class, level of development, or the size of law enforcement or defense budgets. Risk is real and very relevant to the study of criminology. In this context it could be assumed that many governments have lost their monopoly on crime control, and this predicament has forced them to adapt to the changing landscape of crime, order, and control. Increasingly, law enforcement is being contracted out to private security organizations.

Taking this argument to the next level, some criminologists (e.g., Garland 2001) have proposed that because crime and risk have become part of everyday life, and because governments in general have lost their ability to control crime over the past thirty years, societal adjustments, particularly in the manner of governance, have become obligatory for survival. The new global hum in governance is "risk," "actuarial thinking," and "early intervention"—also known as proactive prevention. The logic of risk is inherently political, stimulates action, and triggers communication (Loader and Sparks 2002). The term *risk society* is used to describe a society that is organized in response to risk. According to sociologist Anthony Giddens, a risk society is "a society increasingly preoccupied with the future (and also with safety), which generates the notion of risk" (1999, 3). Risk here can be defined as a systematic way of dealing with hazards and insecurities induced and introduced by modernization itself. Risk becomes a way of thinking in all spheres of day-to-day life. We live in a world of manufactured uncertainty (crime, terrorist attacks, school and hotel shootings) and external risks (hurricanes, tsunamis, earthquakes). Risk management—in other words, how to identify and manage risk—has become the focus of the new actuarial criminology (Beck 1992; Giddens 1999).

Garland refers to the changing landscape of the global crime canvas in his theory on social control and governance through crime as the "new predicament" (2001, 110). In his view, the government's capacity to deliver security is being questioned. Globally, police and criminal justice officials are finding it more and more difficult to control crime. A managerial or value-for-money approach in crime prevention is becoming increasingly evident in a global context. Local-level crime-prevention partnerships between the police and the citizens are being formed, and citizens are increasingly expected to take responsibility for their own safety. They should install safety mechanisms such as alarms in their homes and electric fences around their properties, or consider moving to a gated community. In addition, policing and security have become commodities for the so-called haves. The middle and upper classes can afford private security, armed-response protection, and closed-circuit television monitoring. Security companies categorize citizens as high or low risk and adapt their policies and payouts based on age, gender, and level of risk. This commodity (security) and the false belief in safety do not take the lower classes and the poorest of the poor into consideration (e.g., the majority of citizens in South Africa). Think too of a country like Zimbabwe, where daily survival is a huge challenge. It is probably the country with the poorest citizens in the world; food is its most valuable commodity. Thus, the safety commodity is of little value to them (although they really are in need of safety and protection), as they have to struggle on a daily basis to get food to see the next day.

The changing world order and the crime phenomenon have changed significantly in the new millennium. Criminology as a science is therefore challenged in many new ways to provide answers to these changes. It is becoming apparent that criminology not only offers theoretical insights but also serves a practical function in society.

References

Beck, Ulrick. 1992. *Risk Society: Towards a New Modernity*. London: Sage.

Garland, David. 2001. *The Culture of Control: Crime and Social Order in Contemporary Society*. Oxford: Oxford University Press.

Giddens, Anthony. 1999. "Risk and Responsibility." *Modern Law Review* 62, no. 1: 1–10.

Loader, Ian, and Richard Sparks. 2002. "Contemporary Landscapes of Crime, Order, and Control: Governance, Risk, and Globalization." In *The Oxford Handbook of Criminology*, edited by M. Maguire, R. Morgan, and R. Reiner, 83–111. 3d ed. Oxford: Oxford University Press.

What do these various crimes have in common? What kinds of cases grab media attention? Which do people consider more criminal? Which elicit the most concern? How does the social context affect the kind of crime and the harms suffered by its victims? How are technology and the media changing the face of crime? What do these events have to do with criminology? After reading this book, you should have a better understanding of these issues, if not clear answers.

WHAT IS CRIMINOLOGY?

At its simplest, criminology can be defined as the systematic study of the nature, extent, cause, and control of lawbreaking behavior. Criminology is an applied social science in which criminologists work to establish knowledge about crime and its control based on empirical research. This research forms the basis for understanding, explanation, prediction, prevention, and criminal justice policy.

Ever since the term *criminology* was coined in 1885 by Raffaele Garofalo (1914), the content and scope of the field have been controversial. Critics and commentators have raised several questions about its academic standing. Some of the more common questions include the following: Is criminology truly a science? Does its applied approach, driven predominantly by the desire to control crime, inherently undermine the value-neutral stance generally considered essential for scientific inquiry? Is criminology an autonomous discipline, or does it rely on the insights, theory, and research of other natural and social science disciplines, and increasingly the media and public opinion? Which of the several theories of criminology offers the best explanation for crime? Answers to these questions are complex, and they are further complicated by criminology's multidisciplinary nature, its relative failure to recommend policy that reduces crime, and its heavy reliance on government funding for research. The complexity of these issues has been further compounded by increasing globalization, which has spawned crimes across national boundaries, and the failure of national enforcement agencies to prevent crime's global effects.

Criminology's subject matter is elastic. Unquestionable core components include: (1) the definition and nature of crime as harm-causing behavior; (2) different types of criminal activity, ranging from individual spontaneous offending to collective organized criminal enterprises; (3) profiles of typical offenders and victims, including organizational and corporate law violators; (4) statistical analysis of the extent, incidence, patterning, and cost of crimes, including estimates of the "dark figure" of hidden or unreported crime, based on surveys of victims and self-report studies of offenders; and (5) analysis of crime causation. Less agreement exists about whether the scope of criminology should be broadened to include society's response to crime, the formulation of criminal laws, the role of victims in these processes, and the extent to which criminology needs to adopt a comparative global perspective.

In the United States, the inclusive term *criminal justice* generally refers to crime-control practices, philosophies, and policies used by the police, courts, and system of corrections (in Europe it is called penology). Those who study such matters are as likely to identify themselves, or be identified by others, as criminologists, however, as are those who study criminal behavior and its causes. Criminology, by contrast, concerns itself with the theoretical and empirical study of the causes of crime. The two areas are obviously closely related, but a distinction is necessary.

Is Criminology Scientific?

Criminology requires that criminologists strictly adhere to the scientific method. What distinguishes science from nonscience is the insistence on testable hypotheses whose support or refutation through empirical research forms the basis of what is accepted among scientific criminologists as valid knowledge. Science, then, requires criminologists to build criminological knowledge from logically interrelated, theoretically grounded, and empirically tested hypotheses that are subject to retesting. These theoretical statements hold true as long as they are not falsified by further research (Popper 1959).

Theory testing can be done using either qualitative or quantitative methods. Qualitative methods (Berg [1989] 2000) may involve systematic ethnographic techniques, such as participant observation and in-depth interviews. These methods are designed to enable the researcher to understand the meaning of criminal activity to the participants. In participant observation, the researcher takes a role in the crime scene or in the justice system and describes what goes on between the participants. Criminologists using this technique study crime and its social context as an anthropologist would study a nonindustrial society. These methods have produced some of criminology's richest studies, such as Laud Humphries's study of homosexuality in public restrooms, *Tearoom Trade* (1970), and Howard Becker's study of jazz musicians and marijuana smoking in his book *Outsiders* ([1963] 1973).

Quantitative methods involve numbers, counts, and measures that are arrived at via a variety of re-search techniques. These include survey research based on representative random samples and the analysis of secondary data gathered for other purposes, such as homicide rates or corporate convictions for health and safety violations. Criminologists using quantitative techniques make up the mainstream of academic crimi-nology. Perhaps one of the most illustrative examples of quantitative research is the series of longitudinal stud-ies of a cohort of 10,000 boys born in Philadelphia in 1945 and followed through age eighteen with respect to their arrests for criminal offenses (Wolfgang, Figlio, and Sellin 1972) and a second cohort of 27,000 boys and girls born in 1958 (Tracy, Wolfgang, and Figlio 1990). Each study seemed to indicate that a small pro-portion of offenders (6 percent), called "chronic offend-ers," accounted for more than half of all offenses. Other quantitative research methods include the use of his-torical records, comparative analysis, and experimental research. Unfortunately, most quantitative research is not theory driven; in other words, it does not involve theory testing. A survey conducted in 1992 revealed that only 27 percent of the articles published over a period of twenty-eight years in the journal *Criminology* tested theory (Stitt and Giacopassi 1992). Thus, ap-parently, theoretically grounded research is lacking. This begs the question: Is criminology scientific?

Disciplinary Diversity

Although strongly influenced by sociology, criminol-ogy also has roots in a number of other disciplines, including anthropology, biology, economics, geogra-phy, history, philosophy, political science, psychiatry, psychology, and sociology (Einstadter and Henry 2006). Each of these disciplines contributes its own assumptions about human nature and society, its own definitions of crime and the role of law, its own preference of methods for the study of crime, and its own analysis of crime causation with differing policy implications. This diversity presents a major chal-lenge to criminology's disciplinary integrity. Do these diverse theoretical perspectives, taken together when applied to crime, constitute an independent academic discipline? Are these contributing fields of knowledge merely subfields, or special applications of established disciplines? Alternatively, is criminology interdisciplin-ary? If criminology is to be considered interdisciplinary, what does that mean? Is interdisciplinarity understood as the integration of knowledge into a distinct whole? If so, then criminology is not yet interdisciplinary. Only a few criminologists have attempted such integration (see Messner, Krohn, and Liska 1989; Barak 1998; and M. Robinson 2004). There is sufficient independence of the subject from its constituent disciplines and an acceptance of their diversity, however, to prevent criminology from being subsumed under any one of them. For this reason, criminology is best defined as multi-disciplinary. Put simply, crime can be viewed though many lenses. This is well illustrated through an overview of its component theories, discussions of which form the bases of subsequent chapters. There is, however, a caveat that suggests a question: Because globalization makes us interdependent, is integrated theory more necessary in the future to capture this complexity?

Comparative and Global Criminology

Comparative criminology has been defined as the system-atic study of crime, law, and social control of two or more cultures (Beirne and Hill 1991). As Winslow has argued,

"The global approach to the study of crimes recognizes its growing international nature and, in time, may become the primary focus of criminology in a world rapidly being unified by technological improvements in transportation and communication" (1998, 6). Winslow and Zhang's *Criminology: A Global Perspective* (2007) includes a Web site that provides a window on global crime (http://www-rohan.sdsu.edu/faculty/rwinslow/index.html). Beirne and Messerschmidt have argued that comparative analysis of crime enables criminologists to overcome their ethnocentric tendencies and sharpen their understanding of key questions: "Indeed, one reason why the United States has experienced such relatively high crime rates is that policy makers have relied on limited parochial theories regarding the causes of crime" (2000, 478). They show the value of looking at cross-national data on crime and victimization and countries and cities with low crime rates. Increasingly important also is the ability of corporations to evade the regulatory policies of one country by moving their operations to other countries. Clearly, this applies to regulatory attempts to control environmental pollution. However, it also applies to the ways that deliberately contaminated food, such as the Chinese production of milk products containing melamine that injured many babies, can be distributed globally.

WHAT IS VICTIMOLOGY?

The scientific study of victimology is a relatively recent field, founded by Hans von Hentig (1948) and Benjamin Mendelsohn (1963), who claims to have coined the term in 1947. It is almost the mirror image or "reverse of criminology" (Schafer 1977, 35). Criminology is concerned mainly with criminals and criminal acts and the criminal justice system's response to them. Victimology is the study of who becomes a victim, how victims are victimized, how much harm they suffer, and their role in the criminal act. It also looks at victims' rights and their role in the criminal justice system.

Victimology has been defined as "the scientific study of the physical, emotional, and financial harm people suffer because of criminal activities" (Karmen 2001, 9). This interrelationship has a long history. Prior to the development of formal social control mechanisms, society relied on individualized informal justice. Individuals, families, and clans sought justice for harms caused by others. Endless feuding and persistent physical confrontation led to what has been called the "Golden Age" (Karmen 2001), when restitution became the focus of crime control (see Chapter 5). With the advent of the social contract, individuals gave up the right to retaliation, and crimes became crimes against the state—not the individual. The classicist social contract, simply put, says that individuals must give up some personal liberties in exchange for a greater social good. Thus, individuals forfeited the right to individualized justice, revenge, and vigilantism. This creed is still practiced today. For that reason, O. J. Simpson's first criminal trial for murder was *The State of California v. Orenthal J. Simpson*, not *Goldman and Brown-Simpson v. Orenthal J. Simpson*, which was the realm of the civil trial. Advanced societies relying on systems of justice based on the social contract increasingly, though inadvertently, neglected the victims of crime. In the United States, "Public prosecutors … took over powers and responsibilities formerly assumed by victims. … Attorneys decided whether or not to press charges, what indictments to file, and what sanctions to ask judges to invoke. … When the overwhelming majority of cases came to be resolved through confessions of guilt elicited in negotiated settlements, most victims lost their last opportunity to actively participate" (Karmen 1990, 17).

Since the founding of victimology, there has been controversy between the broad view (Mendelsohn 1963) that victimology should be the study of all victims and the narrow view that it should include only crime victims. Clearly, if a broad definition is taken of crime as a violation of human rights (Schwendinger and Schwendinger 1970; S. Cohen 1993; Tifft and Sullivan 2001), this is more consistent with the broad view of victimology.

It is only since the early 1970s that victimization has been included in mainstream criminology. This followed studies by Stephen Schafer (1968, 1977) and a flurry of victimization studies culminating in the U.S. Department of Justice's annual National Crime Victimization Survey, begun in 1972. There are numerous texts on the field (see Elias 1986; Walklate 1989; and Karmen [2001] 2006).

Victimology has also been criticized for the missionary zeal of its reform policy (Fattah 1992; Weed 1995) and for its focus on victims of individual crimes rather than socially harmful crimes, although there are rare exceptions to this in French victimology studies (Joutsen 1994). The more recent comprehensive approach considers the victim in the total societal context of crime in the life domains of family, work, and leisure as these realms are shaped by the media, lawmakers, and interest groups (Sacco and Kennedy 1996).

SUMMARY

We began this chapter by showing how the "world" has changed and how criminology has had to change with it. We looked at six major changes that have impacted the ways that we see crime and the way that we think about its causes: (1) globalization and its impact on economic, social, and political institutions; (2) the globalization of communications, particularly the advent of the Internet; (3) privatization and individualization and the decline of group and class solidarity; (4) the global spread of disease and the development of epidemiological criminology; (5) changing perceptions of conflict and national security since the end of the cold war; and (6) the internationalization of terrorism. Criminology has evolved and will continue to expand to provide improved methods of study and more comprehensive explanatory theories for understanding crime. The current direction is moving toward a more inclusive and expansive criminology that considers crime as deprivation and harm—regardless of legislated law. It also is beginning, through comparative and global criminology, to move toward recognizing the interconnectedness of people across countries and cultures, and so needs to be both integrated and comparative in its approach.

We have also seen that criminology has a much broader scope than simply studying criminals. If nothing else, the reader should have developed a sense that there are few definitive "truths" in the study of crime. Controversy and diverse views abound. This is not without good reason. Criminology is perhaps the most widely examined (by the public, media, and policy makers) of the social sciences. As a result of the nightly news, talk shows, newsmagazine programs, and popular television dramas, such as *Law and Order, CSI,* and *Criminal Minds,* crime and its control are topics in which everyone's interest is engaged and everyone has an opinion.

Criminology is clearly also policy oriented. The criminal justice system that implements the law and policy of governments itself is a significant source of employment and expenditure. Considering only corrections, twenty years ago the combined states spent $10.6 billion from their general funds on corrections. In 2007, they spent more than $49 billion—a 362 percent increase. By comparison, inflation-adjusted prison spending increased 127 percent, while the budget for higher education increased only 21 percent nationwide (Pew Charitable Trusts 2008). In 2008 the states spent a record $51.7 billion on corrections, 6.7 percent of state budgets, which rises to $68 billion when local, federal, and other funding is included. Moreover, in 2008, 7.3 million, or 1 in 31, Americans were under some supervision by the U.S. corrections system, including people on probation and parole (Pew Charitable Trusts 2009). The long-term implications of this decreased emphasis on education and increased focus on punishment and incarceration are disturbing and the subject of much debate. Several states have taken steps to reduce prison expenses. California has taken the lead, reducing its prison population by 4,068 in 2007 (Pew Charitable Trusts 2008). However, thirty-six states and the Federal Bureau of Prisons experienced increases in 2007. Similar debate was lacking, however, following the terrorist attacks against the United States. Government powers were increased dramatically following the events of September 11, 2001, with little or no debate.

Regardless of one's theoretical inclinations, preferred research tools, or policy preferences, dissension demands a clear articulation of one's position. Such articulation requires considerable thought in order to make convincing arguments and the insight to appreciate other positions. The end result is that criminology as a whole is strengthened.

The Scope of Victimology

William G. Doerner and Steven P. Lab

Introduction

Something not very funny happened on the way to a formal system of justice. The victim got left out. As strange as it may sound, the bulk of history has seen crime victims become further removed as an integral part of dealing with criminals. Fortunately, this trend is beginning to reverse itself. Recent years have seen an increased interest in the plight of crime victims and a movement toward reintegrating the victim into the criminal justice system. This chapter will look at the role of the victim throughout history and will trace the elimination of the victim from social processing of criminal acts. We will see how victimology emerged and we will investigate the resurgence of interest in the victim.

The Victim Throughout History

Most people take the existence of the formal criminal justice system for granted. They do not realize that this method of handling deviant activity has not been the norm throughout history. Indeed, the modern version of criminal justice is a relatively new phenomenon. In days gone by, responsibility for dealing with offenders fell to the victim and the victim's kin. There were no "authorities" to turn to for help in "enforcing the law." Victims were expected to fend for themselves, and society acceded to this arrangement.

This state of affairs was not outlined in any set of laws or legal code. With rare exceptions, written laws did not exist. Codes of behavior reflected prevailing social norms. Society recognized murder and other serious affronts as *mala in se* (totally unacceptable behavior). However, it was up to victims or their survivors to decide what action to take against the offender. Victims who wished to respond to offenses could not turn to judges for assistance or to jails for punishment. These institutions did not exist yet. Instead, victims had to take matters into their own hands.

This depiction does not imply there were no provisions for victims to follow. Society recognized a basic system of retribution and restitution for offenders. In simplest terms, *retribution* meant the offender would suffer in proportion to the degree of harm caused by his or her actions. Often times, retribution took the form of *restitution*, or making payment in an amount sufficient to render the victim whole again. If the offender was unable to make restitution, his or her kin were forced to assume the liability.

This response system emphasized the principle known as *lex talionis*—an eye for an eye, a tooth for a tooth. Punishment was commensurate with the harm inflicted upon the victim. Perhaps the most important feature of this system was that victims and their relatives handled the problem and were the beneficiaries of any payments. This arrangement was truly a "victim justice system."

This basic system of dealing with offensive behavior found its way into early codified laws. The Law of Moses, the Code of Hammurabi (2200 B.C.E.), and Roman law all entailed strong elements of individual responsibility for harmscommitted against others. Restitution and retribution were specific ingredients in many of these early codes. Part of the rationale behind this response was to deter such behavior in the future.

The major goal of *deterrence* is to prevent future transgressions. The thinking is that the lack of any enrichment or gain from criminal activity would make these acts unattractive. Retribution and restitution attempt to reestablish the status quo that existed before the initial action of the offender. Thus, removing financial incentives would make it not profitable to commit crimes.

This basic system of dealing with offensive behavior remained intact throughout the Middle Ages. Eventually, though, it fell into disuse. Two factors signaled the end of this victim justice system. The first change was the move by feudal barons to lay a claim to any compensation offenders paid their victims (Schafer, 1968). These rulers saw this money as a lucrative way to increase their own riches. The barons accomplished this goal by redefining criminal acts as violations against the state, instead of the victim. This strategy recast the state (the barons being the heads of the state) as the aggrieved party. The victim diminished in stature and was relegated to the status of witness

for the state. Now the state could step in and reap the benefits of restitution.

A second factor that reduced the victim's position was the enormous upheaval that was transforming society. Up until this time, society was predominantly rural and agrarian. People lived in small groups, eking out an existence from daily labor in the fields. Life was a rustic struggle to meet day-to-day needs.

People, for the most part, were self-sufficient and relied heavily upon their families for assistance. Families often lived in relative isolation from other people. Whenever a crime took place, it brought physical and economic harm not only to the individual victim, but also to the entire family network. This simple *gemeinschaft* society (Toennies, 1957) could rely on the individual to handle his or her own problems.

As the Middle Ages drew to a close, the Industrial Revolution created a demand for larger urbanized communities. People took jobs in the new industries, leaving the rural areas and relocating to the cities. They settled into cramped quarters, surrounded by strangers. Neighbors no longer knew the people living next door. As faces blended into crowds, relationships grew more depersonalized. The interpersonal ties that once bound people together had vanished.

As this *gesellschaft* type of society continued to grow, the old victim justice practices crumbled even further. Crime began to threaten the delicate social fabric that now linked people together. At the same time, concern shifted away from making the victim whole to dealing with the criminal. Gradually, the *victim* justice system withered and the criminal justice system became its replacement. In fact, some observers would contend that the victim *injustice* system would be a more apt description.

Today, crime victims remain nothing more than witnesses for the state. Victims no longer take matters into their own hands to extract retribution and restitution from their offenders. The victim must call upon society to act. The development of formal law enforcement, courts, and correctional systems in the past few centuries has reflected an interest in protecting the state. For the most part, the criminal justice system simply forgot about victims and their best interests. Instead, the focus shifted to protecting the rights of the accused.

THE REEMERGENCE OF THE VICTIM

The criminal justice system spends the bulk of its time and energy trying to control criminals. It was within this preoccupation of understanding criminal activity and identifying the causes of criminal behavior that the victim was "rediscovered" in the 1940s. Interestingly, the victim emerged not as an individual worthy of sympathy or compassion but as a possible partner or contributor to his or her own demise. Students of criminal behavior began to look at the relationship between the victim and the offender in the hopes of better understanding the genesis of the criminal act.

As interest in victims began to sprout and attract more scholarly attention, writers began to grapple with a very basic issue. What exactly was victimology? Some people believed victimology was a specialty area or a subfield within criminology. After all, every criminal event had to include a criminal and a victim by definition. Others countered that because victimology was so broad and encompassing, it deserved to stand as a separate field or discipline in its own right. They foresaw the day when college catalogs would list victimology as a major area of study along with such pursuits as biology, criminology, psychology, mathematics, political science, and other subjects.

Early scholarly work in victimology focused considerable energy upon creating victim typologies. A *typology* is an effort to categorize observations into logical groupings to reach a better understanding of our social world (McKinney, 1950; McKinney, 1969). As we shall see in the following sections, these early theoretical reflections pushed the field in a direction that eventually created an explosive and haunting reaction, nearly crippling this fledgling enterprise.

THE WORK OF HANS VON HENTIG: *THE CRIMINAL AND HIS VICTIM*

An early pioneer in victimology was a German scholar, Hans von Hentig. As a criminologist, von Hentig spent much time trying to discover what made a criminal predisposed to being a criminal. As he focused on crime victims, von Hentig began to wonder what it was that made the victim a victim. The key ingredient, according to von Hentig, was the *criminal-victim dyad*.

In an early publication, von Hentig (1941) claimed the victim was often a contributing cause to the criminal act. One example would be an incident in which the ultimate victim began as the aggressor. However, for some reason, this person wound up becoming the loser in the confrontation. Von Hentig's message was clear. Simply examining the outcome of a criminal event sometimes presents a distorted image of who the real victim is and who the real offender is. A closer inspection of the dynamics underlying the situation might reveal the victim was a major contributor to his or her own victimization.

Von Hentig expanded upon the notion of the victim as an *agent provocateur* in a later book called *The Criminal and His Victim*. He explained that "increased attention should be paid to the crime-provocative function of the victim. ... With a thorough knowledge of the interrelations between doer and sufferer new approaches to the detection of crime will be opened" (1948: 450).

Von Hentig was not naive enough to believe that all victim contribution to crime was active. Much victim contribution results from characteristics or social positions beyond the control of the individual. As a result, von Hentig classified victims into 13 categories depending upon their propensity for victimization.

Many of von Hentig's victim types reflect the inability to resist a perpetrator due to physical, social, or psychological disadvantages. For example, very young people, females, and elderly persons are more likely to lack the physical power to resist offenders. Immigrants and minorities, because of cultural differences, may feel they are outside the mainstream of society. This lack of familiarity may lead them into situations in which criminals prey upon them. Individuals who are mentally defective or deranged, "dull normal," depressed, lonesome, or blocked may not understand what is occurring around them or may be unable to resist. The acquisitive person and the tormentor are individuals who, due to their own desires, are either directly involved in the criminal act or place themselves in situations in which there is a clear potential for victimization.

Figure 8.1   Hans von Hentig's Victim Typology

Type	Example
1. The Young	children and infants
2. The Female	all women
3. The Old	elderly persons
4. The Mentally Defective and Deranged	the feeble-minded, the insane, drug addicts, alcoholics
5. Immigrants	foreigners unfamiliar with the culture
6. Minorities	racially disadvantaged persons
7. Dull Normals	simple-minded persons
8. The Depressed	persons with various psychological maladies
9. The Acquisitive	the greedy, those looking for quick gains
10. The Wanton	promiscuous persons
11. The Lonesome and the Heartbroken	widows, widowers, and those in mourning
12. The Tormentor	an abusive parent
13. The Blocked, Exempted, or Fighting	victims of blackmail, extortion, confidence games

Source: Adapted from von Hentig, H. (1948). *The Criminal and His Victim: Studies in the Sociobiology of Crime.* New Haven: Yale University Press, pp. 404–438.

The typology that von Hentig created does not imply the victim is always the primary cause of the criminal act. What he does suggest is that victim characteristics may contribute to the victimization episode. According to von Hentig (1948: iii), we must realize "the victim is taken as one of the determinants, and that a nefarious symbiosis is often established between doer and sufferer. ..."

The Work of Beniamin Mendelsohn: Further Reflections

Some observers credit Beniamin Mendelsohn, a practicing attorney, with being the "father" of victimology. Mendelsohn, like von Hentig, was intrigued by the dynamics that take place between victims and offenders. Before preparing a case, he would ask victims, witnesses and bystanders in the situation to complete a detailed and probing questionnaire. After examining these responses, Mendelsohn discovered that usually there was a strong interpersonal relationship between victims and offenders. Using these data, Mendelsohn (1956) outlined a six-step classification of victims based on legal considerations of the degree of the victim's blame.

The first type was the "completely innocent victim." This victim type exhibited no provocative or facilitating behavior prior to the offender's attack. The second grouping contained "victims with minor guilt" or "victims due to ignorance." These unfortunate people inadvertently did something that placed themselves in a compromising position before the victimization episode.

Mendelsohn reserved the third category for the "victim as guilty as the offender" and the "voluntary victim." Suicide cases and parties injured while engaging in vice crimes and other victimless offenses were listed here.

The next two categories address some of von Hentig's earlier concerns. Mendelsohn's fourth type, "victim more guilty than the offender," represents the situation in which the victim instigates or provokes the criminal act. A person who comes out on the losing end of a punch after making an abusive remark or goading the other party would fit here. Similarly, a victim who entered the situation as the offender and, because of circumstances beyond his or her control, ended up the victim is considered the "most guilty victim." An example of this category would be the burglar whom the home owner shoots during the intrusion.

Figure 8.2 The Vocabulary of Victimology

Victimhood	the state of being a victim
Victimizable	capable of being victimized
Victimization	the act of victimizing, or fact of being victimized, in various senses
Victimize	to make a victim of; to cause to suffer inconvenience, discomfort, annoyance, etc., either deliberately or by misdirected attentions; to cheat, swindle, or defraud; to put to death as, or in the manner of, a sacrificial victim; to slaughter; to destroy or spoil completely
Victimizer	one who victimizes another or others
Victimless	the absence of a clearly identifiable victim other than the doer, for example, in a criminal situation

Source: Viano, E.C. (1976b). "From the Editor: Victimology: The Study of the Victim." *Victimology* 1:1–7. Reprinted by permission from *Victimology: An International Journal*, Victimology, Inc. All rights reserved.

The last category is the "simulating or imaginary victim." Mendelsohn reserves this niche for those persons who pretend they have been victimized. The person who claims to have been mugged, rather than admitting to gambling his or her paycheck away, would be an example.

Mendelsohn's classification is useful primarily for identifying the relative culpability of the victim in the criminal act. Besides developing this typology, Mendelsohn also coined the term "victimology" and proposed the terms "penal-couple" (a criminal-victim relationship), "victimal" and "victimity" (as opposed to criminal and criminality), and "potential of victimal receptivity" (an individual's propensity for being victimized). Figure 8.2 lists some common terms that victimologists use.

THE WORK OF STEPHEN SCHAFER: *THE VICTIM AND HIS CRIMINAL*

Scholarly interest in victims and the role they played in their own demise evoked little interest throughout the 1950s and 1960s. Stephen Schafer, in a playful twist on Hans von Hentig's seminal work, revisited the victim's role in his book *The Victim and His Criminal*. The key

Figure 8.3 Schafer's Victim Precipitation Typology

1. Unrelated Victims (no victim responsibility)	Instances in which the victim is simply the unfortunate target of the offender.
2. Provocative Victims (victim shares responsibility)	The offender is reacting to some action or behavior of the victim.
3. Precipitative Victims (some degree of victim responsibility)	Victims leave themselves open for victimization by placing themselves in dangerous places or times, dressing inappropriately, acting, or saying the wrong things, etc.
4. Biologically Weak Victims (no victim responsibility)	The aged, young, infirmed, and others who, due to their physical conditions, are appealing targets for offenders.
5. Socially Weak Victims (no victim responsibility)	Immigrants, minorities, and others who are not adequately integrated into society and are seen as easy targets by offenders.
6. Self-Victimizing (total victim responsibility)	Individuals who are involved in such crimes as drug use, prostitution, gambling, and other activities in which the victim and the criminal act in concert with one another.
7. Political Victims (no victim responsibility)	Individuals who are victimized because they oppose those in power or are made victims in order to be kept in a subservient social position.

Source: Adapted from Schafer, S. (1968). *The Victim and His Criminal: A Study in Functional Responsibility.* New York: Random House.

concept that undergirded Schafer's thinking was what he termed "functional responsibility." Once again, the victim-offender relationship came under scrutiny.

As Figure 8.3 shows, Schafer (1968) provided a typology that builds upon victim responsibility for the crime. In many respects, Schafer's groupings are a variation of those proposed by von Hentig (1948). The difference between the two schemes is primarily one of emphasis on the culpability of the victim. Where von Hentig's listing identifies varying risk factors, Schafer explicitly sets forth the responsibility of different victims.

Other Scholarly Efforts

Von Hentig, Mendelsohn, and Schafer were not the only persons to produce significant analyses regarding victims during this time. Most assuredly, some other scholars began recognizing the importance of a victim-based orientation. These early attempts probing the victim-offender relationship signaled the beginning of a renewed academic interest in the victim.

This concern, however, was lopsided. The early victimologists generally failed to look at the damage offenders inflicted upon their victims, ignored victim recuperative or rehabilitative efforts, and bypassed a host of other concerns. In an attempt to understand the causes of crime, they concentrated on how the victim contributed to his or her demise. Eventually, the idea of victim precipitation emerged from this preoccupation with "blaming the victim." As we shall see later in this chapter, the assumption that somehow the victim shared responsibility for or instigated the criminal episode would spark a major ideological confrontation.

EMPIRICAL STUDIES OF VICTIM PRECIPITATION

Victim precipitation deals with the degree to which the victim is responsible for his or her own victimization. That involvement can be either passive (as much of von Hentig's typology suggests) or active (as seen in Mendelsohn's classification). Each typology presented

in this chapter implicates victim contribution as a causative factor in the commission of crime. However, none present any empirical evidence to support that point of view. The first systematic attempt to overcome this objection was Wolfgang's (1958) analysis of police homicide records. A few years later, one of Wolfgang's students, Menachem Amir, applied this framework to forcible rape cases. His formulation and interpretation quickly met with a barrage of stinging criticism.

THE WORK OF MARVIN E. WOLFGANG: *PATTERNS IN CRIMINAL HOMICIDE*

Using homicide data from the city of Philadelphia, Wolfgang reported that 26 percent of the homicides that occurred from 1948 through 1952 resulted from victim precipitation. Wolfgang (1958: 252) defined victim-precipitated homicide as those instances in which the ultimate victim was:

> the first in the homicide drama to use physical force directed against his subsequent slayer. The victim-precipitated cases are those in which the victim was the first to show and use a deadly weapon, to strike a blow in an altercation—in short, the first to commence the interplay of resort to physical violence.

Wolfgang identified several factors as typical of victim-precipitated homicides. First, the victim and the offender usually had some prior interpersonal relationship. Typical examples include relationships of spouses, boyfriends-girlfriends, family members, and close friends or acquaintances. In other words, victims were more likely to die at the hands of someone they knew rather than from the actions of a complete stranger.

Second, the homicide act is often the product of a small disagreement that escalates until the situation bursts out of control. That change in degree could be either short-term or may be the result of a longer, drawn-out confrontation. For instance:

> A husband had beaten his wife on several previous occasions. In the present instance,

she insisted that he take her to the hospital. He refused, and a violent quarrel followed, during which he slapped her several times, and she concluded by stabbing him (Wolfgang, 1958: 253).

Third, alcohol consumed by the victim is a common ingredient in many victim-precipitated homicides. Several possibilities surface here. It may be that as intoxicated persons lose their inhibitions, they vocalize their feelings more readily. Eventually, these inebriated parties grow more obnoxious and belligerent, and unwittingly provoke their assailants into a deadly confrontation. Another alternative is that alcohol consumption renders these people so impaired that they lose the physical ability to defend themselves in a skirmish. In any event, Wolfgang (1958: 265) points out that "connotations of a victim as a weak and passive individual, seeking to withdraw from an assaultive situation, and of an offender as a brutal, strong, and overly aggressive person seeking out his victim, are not always correct."

The Work of Menachem Amir: *Patterns in Forcible Rape*

Several years later, Menachem Amir undertook what perhaps became the most controversial empirical analysis of rape. Amir (1971) gathered information from police records on rape incidents that took place in Philadelphia between 1958 and 1960. Based on details contained in the files, he claimed that 19 percent of all forcible rapes were victim-precipitated.

According to Amir (1971: 266), victim-precipitated rape referred to those situations in which:

> the victim actually, or so it was deemed, agreed to sexual relations but retracted before the actual act or did not react strongly enough when the suggestion was made by the offender. The term applies also to cases in risky situations marred with sexuality, especially when she uses what could be interpreted as indecency in language and

gestures, or constitutes what could be taken as an invitation to sexual relations.

Amir proceeded to list a variety of factors that helped precipitate the criminal act. Similar to Wolfgang's homicide findings, alcohol use—particularly by the victim—was a major factor in a precipitated rape. The risk of sexual victimization intensified if both parties had been drinking.

Other important factors include seductive actions by the victim, wearing revealing clothing, using risqué language, having a "bad" reputation, and being in the wrong place at the wrong time. According to Amir, such behaviors could tantalize the offender to the point that he simply "misread" the victim's overtures. At one point, Amir (1971) even suggested that some victims may have an unconscious need to be sexually controlled through rape.

In the concluding remarks of the section on victim precipitation, Amir (1971: 275–276) commented:

> These results point to the fact that the offender should not be viewed as the sole "cause" and reason for the offense, and that the "virtuous" victim is not always the innocent and passive party. Thus, the role played by the victim and its contribution to the perpetration of the offense becomes one of the main interests of the emerging discipline of victimology.

Criticisms and Reactions

The notion of victim precipitation, particularly regarding Amir's claims about rape, came under swift attack. Weis and Borges (1973, 1976), for example, attributed Amir's conclusions to faults implicit in relying upon police accounts, to a host of procedural errors, as well as to ill-conceived theoretical notions. For example, Amir suggested victims may *psychologically* prompt or desire the rape as a means of rebelling against accepted standards of behavior. In contrast, though, the male is simply responding to *social* cues from the female.

Despite these different origins of behavior, Amir does not provide any justification for why female behavior stems from psychological factors while male actions derive from social variables. Amir's study attracted blistering rebuttals from academic quarters, along with enraged reactions from women's groups and victim advocates. This reception made many victimologists very uncomfortable with the precipitation argument as it had developed to that point.

Cooler heads soon prevailed. Rather than abandoning the idea of victim precipitation, some scholars began a more sensitive probing. Curtis (1974), for one, suggested that what was needed was a more accurate definition of victim precipitation. For example, one set of researchers might define hitchhiking as a precipitating factor. Other studies may not make such a blanket assumption or may view hitch-hiking as substantively different from other precipitating actions.

A more productive approach came from a critical examination of the underpinnings of the victim-precipitation argument. Franklin and Franklin (1976) exposed four major assumptions behind this victimological approach. First, victim precipitation assumes that the behavior of the victim can explain the criminal act. However, some factors often identified as precipitous also appear in instances where no criminal act takes place. For example, many people go to bars at night. Sometimes they drink excessively and then stagger home alone without becoming victimized. Thus, supposedly precipitating acts are not enough, in and of themselves, to cause criminal behavior.

Second, victim precipitation assumes the offender becomes activated only when the victim emits certain signals. This belief ignores the fact that many offenders plan their offenses ahead of time and do not simply react to another person's behavior. For these criminals, crime is a rational, planned enterprise.

Third, Franklin and Franklin (1976) disagree with the assumption that a victim's behavior is necessary and sufficient to trigger the commission of a criminal act. In fact, the opposite is probably closer to the truth. Many offenders commit crimes despite any specific action by the victim. Others will not seize the opportunity to commit a crime, for whatever reason, although a potential victim presents himself or herself.

Finally, victim precipitation arguments assume the intent of the victim can be gauged by the victimization incident. Unfortunately, if intent is equivalent to action, there would be no need for criminal court proceedings beyond the infallible identification of the person who perpetrated the crime. Our criminal justice system, however, explicitly assumes possible variation in intent, regardless of the action.

Although each of these assumptions shows how the victim precipitation argument falters, there is a much larger issue requiring attention. Studies of victim involvement tend to be myopic. That is, they do not address the offender. Instead, they imply all offenders are equal in their drive and desire to engage in deviant activity. This assumption, however, is untenable. Some offenders may actively hunt for the right situation, while others display little or no prior intent. What was needed was an integrated approach that would take both the victim and the offender into account.

Curtis (1974) attempted to do just this when he sketched a simple grid that allows the degree of victim precipitation to vary. As Figure 8.4 shows, Curtis (1974) merged victim provocation with offender intent. This strategy results in recognizing five degrees of precipitation, ranging from pure victim precipitation to total offender responsibility. This presentation shows that even in the position of clear outright provocation by the victim, the offender may still be an equally responsible partner in the final outcome. What is important to remember here is that, at best, one should conceive of victim precipitation as a contributing factor and, certainly, not as the predominant force.

A NEW APPROACH: GENERAL VICTIMOLOGY

The preoccupation with victim precipitation, along with its divisiveness and ensuing fragmentation, threatened to stagnate this fledgling area of interest. The lack of theoretical advances brought genuine worries from some quarters that victimology was bogging down in an academic quagmire (Bruinsma and Fiselier, 1982; Levine, 1978). However, an antidote emerged from the discussions held at an international conference in Bellagio, Italy, during the summer of 1975 (Viano, 1976a). It was the concept of "general victimology."

The remedy proposed by Beniamin Mendelsohn called for victimology to move out of the provincial backwaters of criminology and into its own rightful

Figure 8.4 The Precipitation Grid Outlining the Relative Responsibility of Both Victim and Offender

	Degree of Victim Involvement		
Degree of Offender Intent	Clear Provocation	Some Involvement	Little or No Involvement
Deliberate Premeditation	Equal	More Offender	Total Offender Responsibility
Some Intent	More Victim	Equal	More Offender
Little or No Intent	Pure Victim Precipitation	More Victim	Equal

Source: Adapted from Curtis, L.A., *Criminal Violence: National Patterns and Behavior*, p. 95, Copyright © 1974 Jossey-Bass Inc., Publishers. First published by Lexington Books. Reprinted with permission. All rights reserved.

domain. As mentioned earlier, some scholars wondered whether victimology was a discipline in its own right or if it was merely an attractive subfield of criminology. Mendelsohn attempted to assure victimology of its independence from criminology by devising the term "general victimology."

According to Mendelsohn (1982: 59), victimologists aim to "investigate the causes of victimization in search of effective remedies." Because human beings suffer from many causal factors, focusing on criminal victimization is too narrow a perspective. A more global term, like general victimology, is needed to convey the true meaning of the field.

According to Mendelsohn (1976), *general victimology* subsumes five types of victims. They include victims of:

+ one's self
+ a criminal
+ the social environment
+ technology
+ the natural environment.

The first category (crime victims) is self-explanatory. It refers to the traditional subject matter that victimologists have grown accustomed to studying. Self-victimization would include suicide, as well as any other suffering induced by victims themselves. The term "victims of the social environment" incorporates individual, class, or group oppression. Some common examples here would include racial discrimination, caste relations, genocide, and war atrocities. Technological victims are people who fall prey to society's reliance upon scientific innovations. Nuclear accidents, improperly tested medicines, industrial pollution, and transportation mishaps provide fodder for this category. Finally, victims of the natural environment would embrace those persons affected by such events as floods, earthquakes, hurricanes, famine, and the like.

In line with Mendelsohn's formulations, Smith and Weis (1976) proposed a broad overview of the areas encompassed by general victimology. As Figure 8.5 illustrates, there are four major areas of concern. They include the creation of definitions of victims, the application of these definitions, victim reactions during the post-victimization period, and societal reactions to victims.

When viewed in this context, general victimology becomes a very broad enterprise with extensive implications. As Mendelsohn (1976: 21) explains:

> Just as medicine treats all patients and all diseases, just as criminology concerns itself with all criminals and all forms of crime, so victimology must concern itself with all victims and all aspects of victimity in which society takes an interest.

CRITICAL VICTIMOLOGY

One recent trend in victimology is the call to shift the focus from the more general approach outlined above to what some people call *critical victimology*. Proponents of this move maintain that victimology fails to question the basic foundations of what crime is, overlooks the question of why certain acts are sanctioned, and, consequently, has developed in the wrong direction. Mawby and Walklate (1994: 21) define critical victimology as:

Figure 8.5   General Model of the Areas of Research and Application in the Field of Victimology

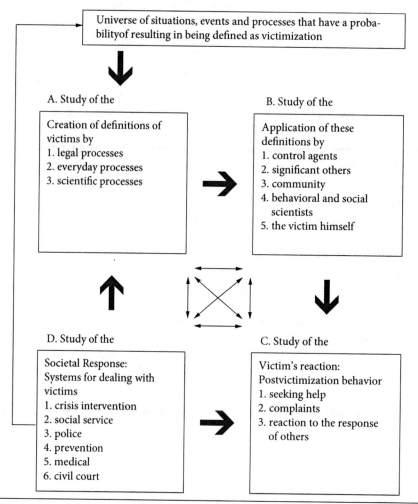

Source: Smith, D.L., and K. Weis (1976). "Toward an Open-System Approach to Studies in the Field of Victimology." In E.C. Viano (ed.), *Victims & Society*. Washington, DC: Visage Press, Inc., p. 45.

an attempt to examine the wider social context in which some versions of victimology have become more dominant than others and also to understand how those versions of victimology are interwoven with questions of policy response and service delivery to victims of crime.

Central to critical victimology, therefore, is the issue of how and why certain actions are defined as criminal and, as a result, how the entire field of victimology becomes focused on one set of actions instead of another. This notion is not entirely different from Mendelsohn's category of "victim of the social environment" outlined previously under the rubric of general victimology. Mawby and Walklate (1994) point out that many crimes committed by the powerful in society are not subjected to the criminal code. Some writers point to the neglect of criminological attention to genocide (Day and Van-diver, 2000; Friedrichs, 2000; Yacoubian, 2000), war crimes (Hoffman, 2000), political campaign law violations (Levine, 1997; Liddick, 2000; Taylor, 2000), clandestine arms sales and weapons of mass destruction (Berryman, 2000; Phythian, 2000; Whitby, 2001), smuggling (Beare, 2002; Bruinsma and Bernasco, 2004; Naylor, 2004; van Duyne, 2003), the human slave trade (Mameli, 2002; Schloenhardt, 1999; Shelley, 2003; Taylor and Jamieson, 1999), deportation (Chan, 2005), investment and consumer fraud (Holtfretter, 2004; Holtfreter, van Slyke, and Blomberg, 2005; Naylor, 2007; Pontell, 2005) as evidence of the overly conservative nature of the field. Consequently, the victims of those crimes do not enter into the typical discussion of victimological concerns.

Under critical victimology, most victim-oriented initiatives tend to perpetuate the existing definitions of crime by failing to question the supportive social factors that give rise to the action and the response (Elias, 1990). The reason for this failure is multifaceted. One contributing factor is the reliance on official definitions and data in most analyses of victim issues. This subjugation inevitably leads to solutions that do not question the underlying social setting. Another factor is the ability of existing agencies to co-opt and incorporate emerging movements (such as children's rights) into existing social control systems. A more radical argument posits that the control of criminal justice and victimology rests in the hands of a powerful few who would view a critical approach as a threat to the status quo.

While critical victimology offers an interesting viewpoint and carries much potential for victimology, debating its merits is beyond the scope of this text. Various points throughout this book, however, will raise issues which are relevant to a critical approach. Examples of this include sociocultural discussions of why violence occurs and investigations of impediments to victim programs. A deeper and more intense examination of critical victimology will be left for other forums.

THE VICTIM MOVEMENT

While academicians were debating the victim-precipitation argument, practitioners had pinpointed the victim as someone who deserved assistance from society and the criminal justice system. To some extent, this grass-roots concern for the victim's well-being was a reaction to the charges of victim complicity in the offense. Several different movements occurred simultaneously and contributed to the renewed interest in the plight of the victim. Among them were (1) the women's movement, (2) efforts to establish children's rights, (3) concerns over the growing crime problem, (4) the advocacy of victim compensation, (5) legal reforms, and (6) some other factors.

THE WOMEN'S MOVEMENT

The women's movement, especially in the mid- to late-1960s, included a large component dealing with victims. Victim-blaming arguments often dealt with rape and sexual assault. The female victim found herself and her lifestyle on trial whenever an offender was apprehended. Reformers complained the system dealt with sexual assault victims as if they themselves were the offenders. Advocates pushed for equal treatment. They found the actions of the criminal justice system to be strong ammunition for their arguments. Beyond simply calling for changes in the formal system of justice, the women's movement made many gains. A short list would include the development of rape crisis centers, shelters for battered women, counseling for abused women and their children, and other forms of assistance. As women demanded an equal place in society, they worked to overcome the disadvantages of the criminal justice system.

CHILDREN'S RIGHTS

A growing concern over the needs and rights of youths blossomed during this period. Many writers point to the mid-1960s as the time when child abuse was "discovered." It was around this time that society decided to define abuse against children as a social problem. However, that does not mean child abuse was a new phenomenon. Child abuse is an age-old practice and, by many accounts, may have been much worse in the past than today. The difference in the 1960s, however, was that many physical and psychological actions used with children began to be questioned and labeled as abuse. States enacted legislation outlining the limits to which a child could be physically "disciplined." Specific children's bureaus within criminal justice agencies were either established or expanded to deal with the growing recognition of child maltreatment. Shelters were created to house children from abusive situations.

Runaways also gained publicity as a serious problem in the late 1960s. The general rebellion of youths in the United States enticed many juveniles to seek freedom from authority. Consequently, runaway shelters appeared in most large cities for the purpose of assisting the youths rather than returning them to their homes. Children were emerging as a new class of victims—both of abuse at home and of society in general.

THE GROWING CRIME PROBLEM

The level of crime in the United States began to register giant strides in the 1960s and throughout the 1970s. According to Uniform Crime Reports (UCR) data, crime in the United States more than doubled from 1960 to 1980. Along with concern over the Vietnam War, crime was the most important issue of the day. Presidential and local elections targeted the problem of law and order as a major concern. In an attempt to identify the causes of the growing problem and possible solutions, President Johnson appointed a commission to examine crime and the criminal justice system. Victim issues were a major focus of the President's Commission (1967) report. Among the victim components of the report were the beginnings of systematic victimization surveys, suggestions for the means of alleviating the pain and loss of victims, ideas for community programs aimed at providing victim services, and calls for involving victims further in the criminal justice system.

Some 15 years after this report was aired, another national task force concluded that victims still had substantial needs that were going unfilled. Many of the identified problems were similar to those noted by the earlier commission.

VICTIM COMPENSATION

One suggestion made by the President's Commission (1967) was the establishment of methods for compensating crime victims for their losses. Among these techniques were restitution and *victim compensation*. Neither of these ideas, however, originated with the Commission. As was mentioned earlier in this chapter, restitution was the common method for dealing with crime throughout most of history. Victim compensation (state payments made to crime victims) was first introduced in Great Britain by Margery Fry in 1957. Although that early attempt failed, victim compensation fast became a major issue around the world.

New Zealand passed the first compensation legislation in 1963, closely followed by England in 1964. In the United States, California established victim compensation in 1965, New York in 1966, Hawaii in 1967, and Massachusetts in 1968. The federal government enacted legislation in 1984 that outlined compensation in instances in which federal crimes were committed. The statute also provided for monetary assistance to states with compensation programs. By 1989, 45 states had enacted compensation statutes. Other countries, such as Australia and Finland, also have established compensation programs. While each program may differ in its particulars, the basic premise of assisting crime victims remains the same.

LEGAL REFORMS

In addition to the establishment of compensation legislation, a variety of legal reforms aimed at protecting and helping crime victims have appeared since the 1960s. Among the changes that have emerged are statutes that protect the rape victim's background and character in court proceedings. New laws were designed to protect battered spouses and their children. Legislation mandating doctors and teachers to report suspected cases of child abuse represented a bold initiative. Guidelines for informing victims about court proceedings and the legal system, as well as provisions that allow victim impact statements in sentencing and parole decisions, began to surface. In some instances, states passed a

Figure 8.6   Examples of Landmark Federal Victims' Rights Legislation Enacted in the Twenty-first Century

2000	*Trafficking Victims Protection Act* Strengthens criminal enforcement, prosecution, and penalties against human traffickers; provides new protections to victims; and enables victims of severe forms of trafficking to seek benefits and services available to other crime victims.
2001	*Air Transportation Safety and System Stabilization Act* Creates a new federal victim compensation program specifically for the victims of September 11. The program includes many types of damages normally available only through civil actions, such as payment for pain and suffering, lifetime lost earnings, and loss of enjoyment of life.
2003	*PROTECT Act ("Amber Alert" Law)* Creates a national AMBER network to facilitate rapid law enforcement and community response to kidnapped or abducted children.
2003	*Prison Rape Elimination Act* Develops national standards aimed at reducing prison rape.
2003	*Fair and Accurate Credit Transactions Act* Provides new protections against identity theft and help victims of identity theft recover their financial losses.
2004	*Justice for All Act* Provides mechanisms at the federal level to enforce the rights of crime victims, giving victims and prosecutors legal standing to assert victims' rights, authorizing the filing of writs of mandamus to assert a victim's right, and requiring the Attorney General to establish a victims' rights compliance program within the Department of Justice.
2006	*Adam Walsh Child Protection and Safety Act* Increases supervision of sex offenders; also extends the federal Crime Victims' Rights Act to federal habeas corpus proceedings arising out of state convictions, eliminates the statute of limitations for federal prosecution of sexual offenses or child abduction, and extends the civil remedy for child sex crime victims to persons victimized as children, even if their injuries did not surface until the person became an adult.

Source: Compiled from Department of Justice (2006). *National Crime Victims' Rights Week Resource Guide, Crime Victims' Rights in America: A Historical Overview.* Washington, DC: National Center for Victims of Crime. Retrieved on August 17, 2007, from http://www.ojp.usdoj.gov/ovc/ncvrw/2007/pdf/overview.pdf

"Victims' Bill of Rights." These provisions outline the rights of the victim in a manner similar to those appearing in the U.S. Bill of Rights, which focuses on protections for the accused.

As Figure 8.6 illustrates, Congress has continued its legislative efforts to soften the plight of victims and to bring them back into the criminal justice system. Back in 1981, President Ronald Reagan issued a proclamation, seen in Figure 8.7, establishing victims' rights week. Since then, every sitting President has followed this tradition dutifully.

OTHER FACTORS

Other factors have played either a direct or indirect role in emphasizing victim issues. One such source of influence has been the mass media. Rarely a week goes by in which a "crime of the week" does not appear in a special movie or as part of an ongoing series. Shows such as "America's Most Wanted" portray not only the offender but the harm to the victim, often relying on interviews with the victim or victim's family. Such media attention and interest in the victim naturally influences viewers in the audience.

Another factor not to be overlooked is the increasing interest in victims among academics. Four decades ago, there were virtually no books specifically focusing on victims. The publication of Schafer's (1968) *The Victim and His Criminal* signaled an era of increasing interest in victimology. Many texts have appeared since then. They range from general victim topics to specific discussions of compensation, intimate partner violence, child abuse, victim services, and other areas of interest.

Figure 8.7   President Reagan's Proclamation Establishing the First Victims' Rights Week in the United States

_____

April 8, 1981
By the President of the United States of America
A Proclamation

For too long, the victims of crime have been the forgotten persons of our criminal justice system. Rarely do we give victims the help they need or the attention they deserve. Yet the protection of our citizens—to guard them from becoming victims—is the primary purpose of our penal laws. Thus, each new victim personally represents an instance in which our system has failed to prevent crime. Lack of concern for victims compounds that failure.

Statistics reported by the Federal Bureau of Investigation and other law enforcement agencies indicate that crime continues to be a very serious national problem. But statistics cannot express the human tragedy of crime felt by those who are its victims. Only victims truly know the trauma crime can produce. They have lived it and will not soon forget it. At times, whole families are entirely disrupted—physically, financially and emotionally. Lengthy and complex judicial processes add to the victim's burden. Such experiences foster disillusionment and, ultimately, the belief that our system cannot protect us. As a Nation, we can ill afford this loss of faith on the part of innocent citizens who have been victimized by crimes.

We need a renewed emphasis on, and an enhanced sensitivity to, the rights of victims. These rights should be a central concern of those who participate in the criminal justice system, and it is time all of us paid greater heed to the plight of victims.

Now, Therefore, I, Ronald Reagan, President of the United States of America, do hereby proclaim the week beginning April 19, 1981, as Victims Rights Week. I urge all Federal, state and local officials involved in the criminal justice system to devote special attention to the needs of victims of crime, and to redouble their efforts to make our system responsive to those needs. I urge all other elected and appointed officials to join in this effort to make our justice system more helpful to those whom it was designed to protect. And I urge all citizens, from all walks of life, to remember that the personal tragedy of the victim is their own tragedy as well.

In Witness Whereof, I have hereunto set my hand this eighth day of April, in the year of our Lord nineteen hundred and eighty-one, and of the Independence of the United States of America the two hundred and fifth.

   Ronald Reagan

_____

Source: U.S. National Archives and Records Administration. *The Ronald Reagan Presidential Library, Proclamation 4831—Victims Rights Week, 1981.* Retrieved on August 16, 2007, from http://www.reagan.utexas.edu/archives/speeches/1981/40881a.htm

The first International Symposium on Victimology was held in Jerusalem in 1973. Since then, there have been several more world-wide gatherings and an uncounted number of national, state, and local meetings of academics and professionals working with crime victims. These efforts culminated in the establishment of the American Society of Victimology in 2003. The spurt in college courses devoted to victimology or topical victim issues is encouraging. Some cam puses (i.e., California State University–Fresno, Sam Houston State University, University of New Haven) now offer specialized programs in victim services. As Figure 8.8 shows, a variety of specialty journals devoted to victim issues now exist. In short, the victim movement has made strides over a relatively short period and continues to gain momentum.

SUMMARY AND OVERVIEW OF THIS BOOK

As you have read, Mendelsohn (1976) saw general victimology as addressing five distinct types of victims. In addition to crime victims, he saw self-victimization, social victims, technological victims, and victims of the natural environment as legitimate focal concerns. All these victims suffer some degree

Figure 8.8   Selected Journals Devoted to Victim Issues

Child Abuse & Neglect
Child Maltreatment
Homicide Studies
International Review of Victimology
Journal of Child Sexual Abuse
Journal of Elder Abuse & Neglect
Journal of Family Violence
Journal of Interpersonal Violence
Violence Against Women
Violence & Abuse Abstracts
Violence and Victims

of social or physical pain or loss. Each deserves assistance to offset the devastating effects of the victimization episode.

While Mendelsohn's vision of general victimology is quite impressive, it does cover a huge territory. Because Mendelsohn's approach is such a large undertaking, we will confine ourselves to a more manageable task. For that reason, this text must restrict itself to only the first category—crime victims. By the time you finish this book, we think you will agree with us. Victimology is so broad and complex that it makes sense to look at it in slices.

WEBSITE

American Society of Victimology
http://www.american-society-victimology.us

Amnesty International
http://www.amnesty.org

International Victimology Web Site
http://www.victimology.nl

National Center for Victims of Crime
http://www.ncvc.org

National Crime Victims Research and Treatment Center
http://colleges.musc.edu/ncvc/index.htm

National Criminal Justice Reference Service
http://www.ncjrs.org

National Organization for Victim Assistance
http://www.try-nova.org

United Nations
http://www.un.org

U.S. Department of Justice, Office for Victims of Crime
http://www.ojp.usdoj.gov/ovc/welcovc/welcome.html

World Society of Victimology
http://www.ce.ucf.edu/asp/wsv/default.asp

SECTION III

Research and Policy in Criminal Justice

UNDERSTANDING CRIMINALS AND CRIME

Theory and Research

Doris Layton MacKenzie

Why do people commit crimes? Why does one person commit a certain type of crime and another person commit another? In this book we examine different types of crimes and criminals. As is evident, no one classification system or theoretical perspective adequately describes all types of crimes and criminals. Our task in this book is to examine these different types of crimes and criminals. For each, we discuss the characteristics of the offenders, theories dominating the current research on the offender or offense, and provide a critical analysis of the research. Effective methods for identifying, classifying, managing, preventing, and treating the diverse types of offenders differ dramatically. The contributing authors examine the effectiveness of various prevention strategies and treatment options for the different types of crimes and criminals. Theories, research, and classification schemes differ widely for the different offenses and offenders. That is the reason for the title of this book; it is in recognition of the many differences that exist among offenders and their crimes.

A Multidisciplinary Perspective: Sociology, Psychology, and Biology

For years, the academic discipline of criminology looked towards the social and physical environment to try to understand criminal behavior. This was, in part, a result of the domination of criminology by sociologists. Sociologists studying crime attempted to propose one theory that would explain all types of crimes. Currently, criminologists have begun to realize that these explanations for crime are not adequate to understand all of the different types of crimes and criminals. The person who commits infanticide differs greatly from the serial murderer and the arsonist who, in turn, differ from each other. Criminologists recognize that individual differences in cognitions and biology are important in understanding criminal behavior.

The students [of a graduate course on the topic of "Psychology and Crime"] were asked to select one type of crime or criminal, and examine the literature. They were asked specifically to: (1) discuss the characteristics of the offender who commits this type of crime; (2) report on the theoretical perspective that is most helpful in understanding this type of offender; (3) review the research on prevention and/or treatment of this type of offender, and (4) evaluate research on effectiveness of treatment and prevention programs. The papers submitted by the students were so outstanding that we decided to combine them in this book. Each chapter discusses the above topics in regard to a different type of crime or criminal. Chapters were reviewed by experts in the field, to ensure pertinent information was included.

A review of the different theoretical perspectives presented in the chapters clearly demonstrates that no one overall theory is adequate to describe all these offenders. Traditionally, criminologists have been trained in the field of sociology and most criminology theories have been based of this perspective. However, sociological theories do not appear adequate to explain all of these crimes. Many sociological theorists search for a general theory of crime. Indeed, one general theory of criminal behavior does not seem sufficient to understand these criminals.

Many of the chapters discuss the importance of biological perspectives in promoting our understanding of the crimes. For example, in her chapter, Jaclyn Smith presents some of the biological explanations that could, in part, explain infanticide. Jennifer Gibbs presents biological theories as one possible explanation for domestic violence. Yet, there is little scientific evidence for how biology directly affects the person who commits infanticide or domestic violence. We are still at a point where these theoretical perspectives appear to present viable possibilities for increasing our understanding of why these offenders commit their crimes, but as yet there is little hard evidence of exactly how this might occur.

Many of the contributing authors to this book refer to psychological theories to help us understand the behavior of these offenders. For example, Summer Acevedo believes stalkers can best be understood using the American Psychiatric Association DSM IV categories of personality disorders, including those who have antisocial, narcissistic, borderline, and histrionic personality disorders (American Psychiatric Association, 1994). Danielle Harris, in the chapter on child molestation, reviews behavioral and cognitive behavior theories that view child abuse as a learned behavior.

The importance of multidisciplinary theoretical perspectives and multiple theories to help us understand the different offenders is demonstrated in many of the chapters. For instance, in Ashlee Parker's words: "Because rapists comprise such a heterogeneous sample of offenders, it is difficult to develop theories and paradigms that envelope all types and patterns of rape." Jennifer Gibbs makes a similar point in discussing treatment and theory: "Unfortunately, one theory cannot encompass all forms of battering behavior, and batterer intervention programs currently follow a 'one size fits all' approach for those involved in treatment, despite emerging evidence that all batterers are not the same." Another example comes from the chapter by Elizabeth Smith and Wendy Povitsky," Individual differences between adolescents may make any blanket explanation of juvenile drug use nearly impossible. There are a variety of sociological, biological, and psychological factors that influence children in different ways and contribute to illegal behavior and drug use." Thus, for many of the criminals examined, multidisciplinary theoretical perspectives or multiple theories are proposed to assist us in understanding their behavior.

TREATMENT PERSPECTIVES

Some crimes are so heinous that no one would expect the offender to be returned to the community; treatment is not considered a viable option. A good example of this type of criminal is the serial murderer. Once such offenders are convicted, they are usually incarcerated for the rest of their lives. They will have no opportunity to return to the community; therefore, little thought is given to what treatment programs would be effective in changing or rehabilitating them. There is some interest in identifying prevention techniques so that children will not grow into the kind of people who commit such crimes. However, although there is interest in preventing serial murderers from committing their crimes, as Raven Korte and Susan Fahey point out in their chapter, we know little about how to this might be done.

Most crimes are not as monstrous as serial murder. And, most convicted criminals do not spend the rest of their lives in prison. Most return to the community. For these offenders, effective treatment that will reduce their later recidivism is critical. Contributing authors to this book were asked to review and report on the treatment and prevention programs available for the types of offender discussed. Furthermore, they were asked to examine research studies of treatment and prevention, and report on the effectiveness of the programs.

Another consistency among chapters is the search for treatment programs guided by specific theoretical perspectives. Some theories do not lend themselves easily to treatment applications. "Psychodynamic approaches have failed to yield empirical support that would help in developing treatment or prevention"(Chapter 5). Perhaps the most consistent perspective for treatment is cognitive behavior or social learning theory. Most of the chapters report on treatment based on some type of cognitive behavior programming.

Evidence-Based Corrections

Contributing authors were asked to evaluate the effectiveness of prevention strategies and treatment programs from an evidence-based perspective. As prison populations continue to grow nationally, and corrections takes up an increasing proportion of state and local budgets, many jurisdictions are seeking to determine if their funds are being spent effectively. They want to know if the money they are putting into prevention strategies and treatment programs is being used most effectively. I argue that these questions can be best answered using scientific knowledge. I refer to this practice as evidence-based corrections or the use of scientific evidence to determine policies and practices. Such evidence-based corrections would implement guidelines and evaluate the performance of agencies and programs. Evidence-based decisionmaking would use research to guide practice. In the words of Larry Sherman (1999), evidence-based practice would "use

the best evidence to shape the best practice . . . in a systematic effort to parse out and codify unsystematic 'experience' as the basis for decision-making."

The use of evaluation results is often the missing link in correctional decisionmaking. The basic premise of "evidence-based practice is that we are all entitled to our own opinions but not to our own facts"(Sherman, 1999:4). Without help, practitioners come up with their own "facts," which often turn out to be very wrong. The goal then is to use scientific evidence to hold officials accountable for the outcome of their programs. As is evident throughout this book, we have little scientific evidence to tell whether particular types of interventions are effective in reducing the recidivism of delinquents and offenders, or in preventing youth from becoming involved in certain types of crime. For example, we know little about the effectiveness of different gang intervention strategies, whether sex offender treatment is equally as effective for rapists and pedophiles, or what treatment might be effective in treating violent offenders with schizophrenia.

Determining What Works

All of the chapters in this book review prevention, management, and/or treatment programs for the offenders. The authors discuss the quality of the research and the outcomes in order to determine if the programs are effective. Many authors have based their discussion on the University of Maryland scoring system used in the "What Works Report," while others report on the results of meta-analyses.

What Works Report. University of Maryland researchers developed an innovative technique for answering the question of the effectiveness of various programs. Their work was completed in response to a request by the U.S. Congress for a "comprehensive evaluation of the effectiveness of more than $3 billion annually in Department of Justice (DOJ) grants to assist state and local criminal justice and community efforts to prevent crime" (Sherman et al., 1997). Congress required that the research included in the evaluation be independent, and that it employ rigorous and scientifically recognized standards and methods (MacKenzie,

2000). The culmination of the work was a report to the U.S. Congress, *Preventing Crime: What Works, What Doesn't, What's Promising* (Sherman et al., 1997). In the report, the researchers reported on the results of more than 500 studies of various crime prevention programs. For each study, they assessed the quality of the research methods as well as the direction and significance of the research results. They used this information to draw conclusions about the effectiveness of various crime prevention programs. Later work made use of the technique they developed; it permits scientifically based conclusions about the effectiveness of various treatment programs and management strategies (Sherman et al., 2002; MacKenzie & Hickman, 1998).

One of the goals of this book is to provide a critical analysis of the research examining the effectiveness of prevention strategies and treatment options for the various criminals. Where appropriate, the authors use the University of Maryland scientific methods score to evaluate the quality of the research. If there are sufficient studies in an area, the authors use the decision-making system developed by the University of Maryland researchers.

The University of Maryland decision-making system is a two-stage process to assist in drawing conclusions about what works. The first step involves locating and assessing each individual study for the quality of the research design and methodology and the direction and significance of the outcomes. The second step involves examining each topic area for research quality and the direction and significance of the results. The results of the second step are used to draw conclusions about what works, what doesn't, what is promising, and what we do not know.

The scientific methods scores determined in the first step can vary from 1 to 5, with 5 being the most rigorous experimental designs. Studies with scores of 1 are used to determine some correlation between the program and the outcome but these studies are considered so low in scientific quality that they are not used in decisionmaking. Scores of 2 can be used to determine a temporal sequence between the program and the outcome but are still considered low in scientific quality. University of Maryland researchers reported on studies with scores of 2 but they did not use them

for the step two decisionmaking. Studies scoring 3 on the scientific methods score used a comparison group design, those scoring 4 used a comparison group design but also controlled for other factors. Studies scoring 5 were the "gold standard," these experimental designs used random assignment to conditions. This scoring system is helpful because it permits an easy assessment of the quality of the research design in a study. Many of the chapters in this book use this scoring system to determine the quality of the research in the area they are examining.

Step 2 of the decision-making process developed at the University of Maryland involved drawing conclusions about whether the program areas were effective in reducing crime. The researchers developed decision-making rules to classify each program area into one of the following categories: (1) program works, (2) program doesn't work, (3) program is promising, and (4) there are too few studies to determine whether or not the program works.

A very good example of the two-stage process is shown in Lauren O'Neill's chapter on Gangs. She begins by identifying four studies of treatment and prevention of youth gang problems. She identifies four studies that were scored 2 or above on the methods score. Two of the studies scored 3 and one scored 4. She does not draw conclusions about the overall effectiveness of the programs because the programs were extremely varied in the focus and the components so it is not appropriate to group them together to draw a conclusion about effectiveness. Several other contributing authors report on studies that used the scientific methods scoring system. For instance, in the Rape chapter, Ashlee Parker reports on the review Polizzi et al. (1999) completed in which they used the two-stage decision-making system to examine sex offender treatment in prison and in the community.

Campbell Collaboration. Subsequent to the University of Maryland report, a second development occurred in the field of evidence-based public policy: the Campbell Collaboration (http://www.campbellcollaboration.org/). The collaboration is designed to facilitate the preparation, maintenance, and accessibility of systematic reviews and meta-analyses of research on the effects of social science interventions. One section of the Collaboration, the Justice Group, focuses on crime and justice topics. Evidence-based correctional studies will fall under the purview of this group.

There is a growing consensus that systematic reviews and metaanalysis can be important in evidence-based decisionmaking. Researchers have long grappled with the problem of understanding how to interpret the results of separate but similar studies. The University of Maryland's two-step process was one attempt to develop a scientifically based method to assess the research in an area. Another method is the process of systematic review and meta-analysis. Meta-analysis provides a more precise way of determining the "success" of interventions. Systematic review is a term used to describe scientific syntheses using explicit methods for the review. Meta-analysis is a method of summarizing, integrating, and interpreting selected sets of empirical studies that produce quantitative findings. It is a method of encoding and analyzing the statistics that summarize research findings from research reports. The method requires a clear definition of which studies will be eligible for inclusion in the analysis. Once inclusion criteria are clearly identified, an intensive search is made for all studies that fit the criteria. Independent samples from the eligible studies are identified and the data are coded. An effect size statistic, a standardized measure of the difference between the treatment and comparison group, is calculated and analyzed for each study.

Some of the chapters in this book report on meta-analyses that have examined the effectiveness of treatment programs or management strategies. For example, in the chapter on Rape, Ashlee Parker reports on meta-analyses completed by my colleagues and myself (Gallagher et al., 1999), where we identified 25 independent studies evaluating the impact of various treatment programs for sex offenders. Parker reports also on another meta-analysis by Hansen et al. (2002), examining the effectiveness of treatment for sex offenders. Both studies found treatment reduces the recidivism of sex offenders. However, these meta-analyses combined all sex offenders in the analyses so we do not know if the effects of treatment are similar for different types of sex offenders. Thus, we do not know if treatment is effective for rapists. However, in the future, Hansen et al. (2002) plan to examine the effectiveness of treatment programs for different types of sex offenders.

REFERENCES

American Psychiatric Association (1994). *Diagnostic and Statistical Manual of Mental Disorders*, Fourth Edition. Washington, DC: American Psychiatric Press.

Campbell Collaboration (2005). http://www.campbell-collaboration.org/

Gallagher, C.A., D.B. Wilson, P. Hirschfield, M.B. Coggeshall, and D.L. MacKenzie (1999). "The Effects of Sex Offender Treatment on Sexual Reoffending." *Corrections Management Quarterly*, 9(4):19–29.

Hanson, K., A. Gordon, A. Harris, J. Marques, W. Murphy, V. Quinsey, and M. Seto (2002). "First Report of the Collaborative Outcome Data Project on the Effectiveness of Psychological Treatment for Sex Offenders." *Sexual Abuse: A Journal of Research and Treatment*, 14(2):169–194.

MacKenzie, D.L. (2000). "Evidence-Based Corrections: Identifying What Works." *Crime & Delinquency*, 46(4):457–471.

Polizzi, D. M., D.L. MacKenzie, and L. Hickman (1999). "What Works in Adult Sex Offender Treatment?: A Review of Prison- and Non-Prison-Based Treatment Programs." *International Journal of Offender Therapy and Comparative Criminology*, 43(3):357–374.

Sherman, L.W., B.C. Welsh, B., D.P. Farrington, and D.L. MacKenzie (eds.) (2002). *Evidence-Based Crime Prevention*, London, UK: Harwood Academic Publishers.

Sherman, L.W. (1999). *Evidence-Based Policing: Ideas in American Policing*. Washington, DC. The Police Foundation

Sherman, L.W., D. Gottfredson, D. MacKenzie, J. Eck, P. Reuter, and S. Bushway (1997). *Preventing Crime: What Works, What Doesn't, What's Promising*. Washington, DC: A report to the U.S. Congress prepared by National Institute of Justice.

ETHICS AND CRIMINAL JUSTICE RESEARCH

Belinda R.
McCarthy and
Robin J. King

No area of life or work is free of ethical dilemmas, and the field of research is no exception. In recent years a number of scandals surrounding the professional behavior of academic researchers have made newspaper headlines and stirred government inquiries. Academic researchers have been charged with falsifying data to obtain additional research funding and to falsify publication of results.

Of a different nature, a conflict within a sociology department at Texas A&M University has left faculty choosing sides in a nasty dispute (*Chronicle of Higher Education*, 1999). Three professors have accused each other of plagiarism and theft of data. While no amicable resolutions have been made, the department has suffered a major public relations blow. The incident escalated to a degree requiring investigation by the university, the National Science Foundation, and the American Sociological Association (*Chronicle of Higher Education*, 1999).

A noted criminologist was investigated by the Florida Commission on Ethics when it was disclosed that he had been paid millions of dollars by private corrections firms while simultaneously being paid via a contract as an academic consultant (*Miami Herald*, 1999). The professor admitted that his involvement in both research projects was a conflict of interest (*Miami Herald*, 1999).

The issue of plagiarism in academic publication is an area that deserves much attention in the literature. Published research has the potential to influence the conduct of practitioners and policy within criminal justice and other social professions (Jones, 1999). Thus, it is imperative that criminal justice researchers are conscious of these potential pressures when disseminating results from research projects.

One might think that scientific endeavors, with their objective and unbiased approach to the world, would create fewer dilemmas than other occupational activities. Although most researchers are not faced with the same kind of corrupting influences confronting street-level criminal justice officials, the pressures of "grantsmanship" and publication provide significant motivations. The dilemmas of working with human subjects in a political environment are equally challenging. Moreover, the goal of scientific purity, of unbiased objectivity, may be corrupting as well, as researchers are tempted to put scientific objectives before their concern for the welfare of others.

In this chapter we will examine the nature of ethical dilemmas confronting the criminal justice researcher. To a large degree these problems are comparable to those difficulties faced by other social scientists. Additional problems arise as a result of the particular focus of research on deviance and law-breaking.

PROBLEMS INVOLVING WORK WITH HUMAN SUBJECTS

Stuart Cook (1976) lists the following ethical considerations surrounding research with human subjects:

1. Involving people in research without their knowledge or consent.
2. Coercing people to participate.
3. Withholding from the participant the true nature of the research.
4. Deceiving the research participant.
5. Leading the research participants to commit acts which diminish their self-respect.
6. Violating the right to self-determination: research on behavior control and character change.
7. Exposing the research participant to physical or mental stress.
8. Invading the privacy of the research participant.
9. Withholding benefits from participants in control groups.
10. Failing to treat research participants fairly and to show them consideration and respect (p. 202).

INVOLVING PEOPLE IN RESEARCH WITHOUT THEIR KNOWLEDGE OR CONSENT

Often the best way to study human behavior is to observe people in a natural setting without their knowledge. Self-reported descriptions of behavior may be unreliable because people forget or are uncertain about their actions. Although most people might tell you that they would attempt to return a lost wallet, a hidden camera focused on a wallet lying on the sidewalk might reveal very different behaviors. People who know they are being watched often act differently, especially when unethical, deviant, or criminal behaviors are involved. For these reasons, studies of deviance often involve direct observation, which involves listening as well as visual observation.

At times, the observer participates to some degree in the activities being studied. Whyte's (1955) study of street-corner society involved just this form of participant observation. Humphreys's (1970) examination of homosexual behavior in public restrooms, Short and Strodtbeck's (1965) study of delinquency in Chicago, and Cohen's (1980) observations of female prostitutes in New York all involved the observation of persons who never consented to become research subjects.

Studies of persons on the other side of the criminal justice process have also been undertaken without the consent of those participating in the research. Meltzer (1953), for example, studied jury deliberations through the use of hidden microphones. The importance of discretion in the criminal justice process and the hidden nature of most decisionmaking support the greater use of such techniques in efforts to understand how police, prosecutors, and correctional personnel carry out their duties.

The ethical dilemma, however, is a complicated one: Is the value of the research such that persons should be turned into study "subjects" without their permission? The conditions of the research are extremely important to this deliberation. If the behaviors being studied would have occurred without the researcher's intervention, the lack of consent seems less troubling. Such studies involve little personal cost to unknowing subjects. Unobtrusive research that involves only behaviors that occur in public view is also less questionable, because the invasion of personal privacy is not at issue.

But what about experiments that create situations to which subjects must react, such as those involving a

> "Human subjects have the right to full disclosure of the purposes of the research as early as it is appropriate to the research process, and they have the right to an opportunity to have their questions answered about the purpose and usage of the research" (Academy of Criminal Justice Sciences Code of Ethics, 2000:5).

"lost" wallet? Or a study of witness response to crime that involves an actor or actress screaming and running from an apparent assailant down a crowded street? Observation might be the only method of determining how citizens would really respond, but the personal cost of being studied might be considerable.

Not only may such research be troubling for the persons involved, but when sensitive activities that are normally considered private or confidential are the subject of study, additional problems may arise. Cook (1976) reports that Meltzer encountered such difficulties in his study of jury deliberations:

> Members of Congress reacted to the jury recording as a threat to fundamental institutions. When the news of the study came out, a congressional investigation resulted. Following the investigation legislation was passed establishing a fine of a thousand dollars and imprisonment for a year for whoever might attempt to record the proceedings of any jury in the United States while the jury is deliberating or voting (p. 205).

Although the response might be less severe, one can anticipate similar objections to the taping of discussions involving police, attorneys, judges, correctional officials, and probation and parole authorities.

COERCING PEOPLE TO PARTICIPATE

You have probably received a questionnaire in the mail at some time that offered you some small incentive for completing the form—perhaps a free pen or a dollar bill. This practice is a common one, reflecting the assumption that people who are compensated for their efforts may be more likely to participate in a research endeavor than those who receive nothing. Similarly, college students are often provided a grade incentive for participation in their instructor's research. When, though, does compensation become coercion? When is the researcher justified to compel participation? The issues here involve the freedom not to participate, and the nature and quantity of the incentives that can be ethically provided without creating an undue influence.

The person receiving the questionnaire in the mail is free to keep the compensation and toss away the form. Students may be similarly free not to participate in their instructor's research, but the instructor's power over the grading process may make students feel quite ill at ease doing so. Thus, the relationship between students and researcher as teacher can be particularly coercive. One example of the coercive nature of this relationship can be seen when researchers, acting as teachers, *require* student participation in a research project as part of their course grade (Moreno, 1998). Again, there is a discernable differential in power that would eliminate the students' ability to refuse to participate in the research project.

It might seem that the easiest way out of this dilemma is to simply rely on volunteers for research subjects. But volunteers are different from others simply by virtue of their willingness to participate. At a minimum they are more highly motivated than nonvolunteers. It is important to obtain a more representative sample of participants, a group that mirrors the actual

> "Criminologists must not coerce or deceive students into serving as research subjects" (American Society of Criminology Code of Ethics, 1999:6).

characteristics of those persons to whom study results will be applied.

This problem becomes especially critical when research subjects are vulnerable to coercion. Although students might be considered a captive population, jail and prison inmates are clearly the most vulnerable of research subjects.

The history of inmate involvement in research is not a very proud one. Prisoners have been used as "guinea pigs" by pharmaceutical companies that set up laboratories at correctional institutions. For minimal compensation, or the possibility that participation might assist in gaining parole, inmates have participated in a variety of medical research projects.

In the United States, the first use of correctional subjects for medical experiments took place at the Mississippi state prison in 1914, when researchers attempted to discover the relationship between diet and the disease pellagra. The Governor of Mississippi promised pardons to persons volunteering for the experiment. The situation may be contrasted to a more recent experiment in New York in which eight prisoners were inoculated with a venereal infection in order to test possible cures. In exchange for their voluntary participation, the subjects, in their own words, "got syphilis and a carton of cigarettes" (Geis, 1980:226). Today, prisoners are forbidden to engage in such research efforts, but inmates are frequently required to participate in efforts to evaluate the impact of correctional treatment, work, or education programs.

> Criminologists "should inform research participants about aspects of the research that might affect their willingness to participate, such as physical risks, discomfort, and/or unpleasant emotional experiences" (Academy of Criminal Justice Sciences Code of Ethics, 2000:5).

In the early 1990s, research on prisoners was allowed under federal regulations. In order to pass federal guidelines, research on prisoners had to take one of four forms: (1) studies of treatment or therapies that were implemented with the goal of helping prisoners, (2) low-risk research examining inmate behavior and inmate criminality, (3) studies of correctional institutions, and (4) research that examines inmates as a class or group (Moreno, 1998). Currently, the standards by which prisoner or prison research is determined to be ethical depends on the degree to which the research will ultimately benefit individual prisoners or prisoners as a class or group (Moreno, 1998).

The reason for requiring participation is the same as that stated above. Volunteers are sufficiently different from others that relying on their participation would probably produce more positive outcomes than the intervention alone would warrant. Freedom of choice is highly valued in this society, but how much freedom of choice should prisoners have? Before denying a subject the opportunity to refuse participation, it should be clear that the overall value of the research outweighs the harm of coercion. In this consideration, the nature of the participation must be carefully evaluated—coercion to participate in weekly group therapy is quite different from coercion to participate in eight weeks of paramilitary training. One must also assess whether coercion is the only or best means available to obtain research results. Confronting this dilemma requires a balancing of such matters with a concern for individual rights.

WITHHOLDING FROM THE PARTICIPANT THE TRUE NATURE OF THE RESEARCH

Informed consent requires that subjects know fully the nature of the research, its possible effects, and the uses to be made of the data collected. However, even in the most benign circumstances, written notification may deter further action. Full and complete notification has the added potential of prejudicing responses. Often more accurate assessments are achieved when the subject believes that one aspect of his or her behavior is the focus when research interest is really on something else.

Researchers are understandably reluctant to provide too much information in this regard, especially in the early stages of a project, when the need to develop rapport and a willingness to cooperate are especially important. From a research perspective, fully disclosing

> "Criminologists should not mislead respondents involved in a research project as to the purpose for which that research is being conducted" (American Society of Criminology Code of Ethics, 1999:3).

the purpose of the research could severely limit findings of the study. For example, a participant's mindfulness of being observed can seriously alter his or her behaviors. Specifically, research participants are typically less willing and likely to admit to undesirable attitudes or behaviors if they know they are being studied (Singleton & Straits, 1988). This *social desirability effect* can produce error in the data collected from the research. Ethically speaking, informed consent should precede involvement in the study, so that individuals are given a meaningful opportunity to decline further participation.

Balancing research interests and respect for human dignity requires that subjects be informed about all aspects of the research that might reasonably influence their willingness to participate. Any risks that the subjects may expect to face should be fully discussed. Geis (1980) recommends that researchers remember the example of Walter Reed, who participated as a subject in his own experiments on yellow fever because he could ask no one to undergo anything that he himself was not willing to suffer.

> "Members of the Academy should take culturally appropriate steps to secure informed consent and to avoid invasions of privacy" (Academy of Criminal Justice Sciences Code of Ethics, 1999:3).

DECEIVING THE RESEARCH PARTICIPANT

Perhaps the most flagrant example of deception in criminological research is provided by Humphreys's (1970) study, *Tearoom Trade*. Humphreys assumed the role of lookout in public restrooms so that strangers unaware of his research objective could engage uninterrupted in homosexual activity. He copied down the automobile license tags of the subjects and obtained their addresses. Later, he went to their homes, explaining that he was conducting a health survey. He asked the respondents many personal questions that became part of his research on public homosexual conduct.

The rationale for such deception emphasizes the importance of the research and the difficulties of obtaining accurate information through other means. All deceptive acts are not equal. There are differences between active lying and a conscious failure to provide all available information. Deception may be considered an affront to individual autonomy and self-respect or an occasionally legitimate means to be used in service of a higher value (Cook, 1976).

One alternative to deception is to provide only general information about the research project prior to the experiment and offer full disclosure after the research has been completed. Another technique relies on subjects to role-play their behavior after the nature of the research project has been explained. There is mixed evidence, however, on the effectiveness of this technique (Cook, 1976).

In regard to deception, the researcher must evaluate the nature of the research and weigh its value against the impact of the deception on the integrity of participants. The degree to which privacy is invaded and the sensitivity of the behaviors involved are important considerations. Finally, the possibility of harming the research participant should be considered before attempting to deceive the participant. If the nature of the research is potentially harmful, the research participant should be able to fully assess whether he or she wishes to risk participating in the study.

LEADING THE RESEARCH PARTICIPANTS TO COMMIT ACTS THAT DIMINISH THEIR SELF-RESPECT

Research subjects have been experimentally induced into states of extreme passivity and extreme aggression.

Efforts to provoke subjects to lie, cheat, steal, and harm have proven very effective. Cook (1976) describes a study in which students were recruited to participate in a theft of records from a business firm. The inducements described included an opportunity to perform a patriotic service for a department of federal government. A substantial number of students were significantly encouraged to take part in the theft, although ultimately the burglary was not carried out.

Research by Haney, Banks, and Zimbardo (1973) involved the simulation of prison conditions, with 21 subjects assuming the roles of prisoners and guards. After a very short time, the guards began behaving in an aggressive and physically threatening manner. Their use of power became self-aggrandizing and self-perpetuating. The prisoners quickly experienced a loss of personal identity, exhibiting flattened affect and dependency; eventually they were emotionally emasculated by the encounters.

Because of the extreme nature of the subjects' responses, the project was terminated after only six days. The debriefing sessions that followed the research yielded the following comments:

Guards:

"They (the prisoners) seemed to lose touch with the reality of the experiment—they took me so seriously."

". . . I didn't interfere with any of the guards' actions. Usually if what they were doing bothered me, I would walk out and take another duty."

". . . looking back, I am impressed by how little I felt for them . . ."

"They (the prisoners) didn't see it as an experiment. It was real, and they were fighting to keep their identity. But we were always there to show them just who was boss."

"I was tired of seeing the prisoners in their rags and smelling the strong odors of their bodies that filled the cells. I watched them tear at each other, on orders given by us."

". . . Acting authoritatively can be fun. Power can be a great pleasure."

". . . During the inspection, I went to cell 2 to mess up a bed which the prisoner had made and he grabbed me, screaming that he had just made it, and he wasn't going to let me mess it up. He grabbed my throat, and although he was laughing, I was pretty scared. I lashed out with my stick and hit him in the chin (although not very hard), and when I freed myself I became angry."

Prisoners:

". . . The way we were made to degrade ourselves really brought us down, and that's why we all sat docile towards the end of the experiment."

". . . I realize now (after it's over) that no matter how together I thought I was inside my head, my prison behavior was often less under my control than I realized. No matter how open, friendly and helpful I was with other prisoners I was still operating as an isolated, self-centered person, being rational rather than compassionate."

". . . I began to feel I was losing my identity, that the person I call _____, the person who volunteered to get me into this prison (because it was a prison to me, it still is a prison to me, I don't regard it as an experiment or a simulation . . .) was distant from me, was remote until finally I wasn't that person; I was 416. I was really my number, and 416 was really going to have to decide what to do."

"I learned that people can easily forget that others are human."

In Milgram's (1974) research, participants showed "blind obedience" to a white-coated "researcher" who ordered them to provide what appeared to be electric shocks of increasing severity to subjects who failed to respond correctly to a series of questions. Although they were emotionally upset, the subjects continued to follow their instructions as the "shocked" subjects screamed in agony.

Follow-up research revealed that Milgram's subjects experienced only minor and temporary disturbances (Ring, Wallston & Corey, 1970). One might argue that the subjects even benefited from the project as a result of their greater self-awareness, but the fact that the educational experience occurred without their initial understanding or consent raises ethical concerns.

To what degree should subjects be asked to unknowingly engage in activities that may damage their self-esteem? Again, the researcher is required to engage in a balancing act, reconciling research objectives and the availability of alternative methods with a concern for the integrity of subjects. At a minimum, such research efforts should provide means to address any possible harm to subjects, including debriefings at the conclusion of the research and follow-up counseling as needed.

VIOLATING THE RIGHT TO SELF-DETERMINATION: RESEARCH ON BEHAVIOR CONTROL AND CHARACTER CHANGE

The film *A Clockwork Orange* provides an excellent illustration of the dilemmas of behavior-modifying research. In the film, a thoroughly violent and irredeemable individual named Alex is subjected to therapy that requires him to observe violent acts on film at the same time that the chemicals he has ingested make him physically ill. After a while, the acts that he has observed make him sick as well, and he is changed from a violent individual to one who avoids violence at all cost, including that required for his own self-defense. At the end of the film, the "powers that be" decide to reverse his treatment for political reasons.

Although there is little possibility of behavior modification being used to exact such effect in the near future, the question remains: To what extent should experimental efforts be made to alter human behavior against the will of the participant? Remembering the vulnerability of the inmate to coercion (in the film, Alex only participated in the violence control project because he thought it would help him gain early release), it becomes clear that the greatest desire to use behavior control strategies will be evident in areas involving those persons most vulnerable to coercion—criminals and persons with problems of substance abuse. Although research on crime prevention and control generally has only the most laudable aims, it should be remembered that it is often well-intentioned actions that pose the greatest threat to individual freedoms.

EXPOSING THE RESEARCH PARTICIPANT TO PHYSICAL OR MENTAL STRESS

How would you evaluate the ethics of the following research project: an evaluation of a treatment program in which persons convicted of drunk driving are required to watch and listen to hours of films depicting gory automobile accidents, followed by horrifying emergency room visits and interviews with grieving relatives? Would it matter whether the actions of the drunk drivers had contributed to similar accidents? If your answer is yes, you are probably considering whether the viewers deserve the "punishment" of what they are forced to observe on film.

This not-so-hypothetical scenario raises a difficult issue. Is it acceptable for a research project to engage in activities that punish and perhaps harm the subject? To test various outcomes, subjects in different settings have been exposed to events provoking feelings of horror, shock, threatened sexual identity, personal failure, fear, and emotional shock (Cook, 1976). The subjects in Haney, Banks, and Zimbardo's research and Milgram's research were clearly stressed by their research experiences. To what extent is it acceptable to engage in these practices for the objective of scientific inquiry?

In most situations, it is impossible to observe human reactions such as those described above in their natural settings, so researchers feel justified in creating experiments that produce these reactions. The extent of possible harm raises ethical dilemmas, however, because theoretically there is no limit to what might be contrived to create a "researchable" reaction. The balancing of research objectives with a respect for human subjects is a delicate undertaking, requiring researchers to scrutinize their objectives and the value of their proposed studies dispassionately.

INVADING THE PRIVACY OF THE RESEARCH PARTICIPANT

The issues of privacy and confidentiality are related concerns. Ethical questions are raised by research that invades an individual's privacy without his or her consent. When information on subjects has been obtained for reasons other than research (e.g., the development of a criminal history file), there are questions about the extent to which data should be released to researchers. Some records are more sensitive than others in this regard, depending on how easily the offender's identity can be obtained, as well as the quantity and nature of the information recorded. Even when consent has been given and the information has been gathered expressly for research purposes, maintaining the confidentiality of responses may be a difficult matter when the responses contain information of a sensitive and/or illegal nature.

CONFIDENTIALITY

The issue of confidentiality is especially important in the study of crime and deviance. Subjects will generally not agree to provide information in this area unless their responses are to remain confidential. This may be a more difficult task than it appears. Generally, it is important to be able to identify a subject so that his or her responses

> "Subjects of research are entitled to rights of personal confidentiality unless they are waived" (Academy of Criminal Justice Sciences Code of Ethics, 2000:5).

can be linked to other sources of data on the individual. Institutionalized delinquents might be asked in confidence about their involvement in drug use and other forms of misconduct during confinement. An important part of the research would involve gathering background information from the offender's institutional files to determine what types of offenders are most likely to be involved in institutional misconduct. To do this, the individual's confidential responses need to be identifiable; therefore, complete anonymity is unfeasible.

As long as only dispassionate researchers have access to this information, there may be no problem. Difficulties arise when third parties, especially criminal justice authorities, become interested in the research responses. Then the issue becomes one of protecting the data (and the offender) from officials who have the power to invoke the criminal justice process.

One response to this dilemma is to store identifying information in a remote place; some researchers have even recommended sending sensitive information out of the country. Because the relationship between the researcher and his or her informants is not privileged, researchers can be called upon to provide information to the courts.

Lewis Yablonsky, a criminologist/practitioner, while testifying in defense of Gridley White, one of Yablonsky's main informants in his hippie study, was asked by the judge nine times if he had witnessed Gridley smoking marijuana. Yablonsky refused to answer because of the rights guaranteed him in the Fifth Amendment of the U.S. Constitution. Although he was not legally sanctioned, he said the incident was humiliating and suggested that researchers should have guarantees of immunity (Wolfgang, 1982:396).

It is also important that researchers prepare their presentation of research findings in a manner that ensures that the particular responses of an individual cannot be discerned. Presentation of only aggregate findings was especially important for Marvin Wolfgang (1982) when he reinterviewed persons included in his earlier study of delinquency in a birth cohort. His follow-up consisted of hour-long interviews with about 600 youths. The subjects were asked many personal questions, including many about their involvement in delinquency and crime. Four of his respondents admitted committing criminal homicide, and 75 admitted to forcible rape. Many other serious crimes were also described, for which none of the participants had been arrested.

At the time of the research, all of the respondents were orally assured that the results of the research would remain confidential, but Wolfgang raises a number of ethical questions surrounding this practice. Should written consent forms have been provided to the subjects, detailing the nature of the research? Wolfgang concludes that such forms would have raised more questions than they answered. Could a court order impound the records? Could persons attempting to protect the data be prosecuted for their actions? Could the data be successfully concealed?

The general willingness to protect subjects who admit to serious crimes also requires close ethical scrutiny. Wolfgang (1982) takes the traditional scientific stance on this issue, proposing that such information belongs to science. Because the information would have not been discovered without the research effort, its protection neither helps nor hinders police. The ethical judgment here requires a weighing of interests—the importance of scientific research balanced against society's interest in capturing a particular individual.

It should be noted that if researchers began to inform on their subjects routinely, all future research relying on self-reports would be jeopardized. Thus, the issue at hand is not simply that of the value of a particular study, but the value of all research utilizing subject disclosures. Researchers are generally advised not to undertake such research unless they feel comfortable about protecting their sources. This requires that all research involving the use of confidential information provide for controlled access to sensitive data and protect the information from unauthorized searches, inadvertent access, and the compulsory legal process (Cook, 1976).

WITHHOLDING BENEFITS TO PARTICIPANTS IN CONTROL GROUPS

The necessity of excluding some potential beneficiaries from initial program participation arises whenever a classical experimental design is to be used to evaluate the program. This research design requires the random assignment of subjects to experimental and control groups. Subjects in the control group are excluded from the program and/or receive "standard" rather than "experimental" treatment.

In a program evaluation, it is important that some subjects receive the benefits of the program while others do not, to ensure that the outcomes observed are the direct result of the experimental intervention and not something else (subject enthusiasm or background characteristics, for example). It is imperative that those who receive the intervention (the experimental group) and those who do not (the control group) be as identical in the aggregate as possible, so that a clear assessment of program impact, untainted by variation in the nature of subjects, can be obtained. Though randomization is important from a methodological point of view, the participants who, by chance, end up in the control group are often denied treatment, or possibly services, that could be of the utmost importance to their lives. The Minneapolis Domestic Violence Experiment is a classic example of how those persons involved the control group were denied potential law enforcement interventions that could have benefited them. Figure 10.1 is a description of Sherman and Berk's (1984) study that looked at various responses to domestic violence.

The best way to ensure that experimental and control subjects are identical is randomization. Randomization is to be distinguished from arbitrariness. Randomization requires that every subject have an equal chance to be assigned to either the experimental or control group; arbitrariness involves no such equality of opportunity.

In many ways, randomization may be more fair than standard practice based on good intentions. Geis (1980) reports:

> For most of us, it would be unthinkable that a sample of armed robbers be divided into two groups on the basis of random assignment—one group to spend 10 years in prison, the second to receive a sentence of 2 years on probation. Nonetheless, at a federal judicial conference, after examining an elaborate presentence report concerning a

---

Figure 10.1   The Minneapolis Domestic Violence Experiment

Domestic violence was beginning to be recognized as a major public affairs and criminal justice problem. Victim advocates were demanding the automatic arrest for domestic violence offenders. However, there was no empirical research that showed that arresting domestic violence offenders deterred future acts of domestic violence. Thus, Sherman and Berk, sponsored by funding from the National Institute of Justice, designed a randomized experiment that looked at the effects of arrest on domestic violence.

Sherman and Berk enlisted the help of the Minneapolis Police Department. When on misdemeanor domestic violence calls, the police were to respond to the call depending on the random call response they were assigned. There were three responses with which the police could respond to the misdemeanor domestic violence call: arrest, removal of batterer from the premises without an arrest, or counsel the batterer and leave the premises. While the initial findings of this research indicated that arresting domestic violence offenders reduced the incidence of future incidents, the methodology and ethics of this experiment have been heavily scrutinized. The victims of the misdemeanor domestic violence certainly did not consent to the randomized assignment of response to the situation. Thus, not only were potential benefits withheld from the certain women, some victims could have been placed at greater risk as a result of the random treatment. While the benevolent intentions behind this research agenda were admirable, the implementation of the experiment and the variable being randomized (i.e., type of response to domestic violence) should have been further considered before implementation of the research.

Based on Sherman L.W. & R.A. Berk (1984). "The Specific Deterrent Effects of Arrest for Domestic Assault." *American Sociological Review*, 49(2):261–272.

---

bank robber, 17 judges said they would have imprisoned the man, while 10 indicated they favored probation. Those voting for imprisonment set sentences ranging from 6 months to 15 years (p. 221).

Randomization is also acceptable under law, because its use is reasonably related to a governmental objective, that is, testing the effectiveness of a program intervention (Erez, 1986).

Although randomization is inherently fair, it often appears less so to the subjects involved. Surveys of prisoners have indicated that need, merit, and "first come, first served" are more acceptable criteria than a method that the offenders equated with gambler's luck (Erez, 1986). Consider Morris's (1966) description of "the burglar's nightmare":

If eighty burglars alike in all relevant particulars were assigned randomly to experimental and control groups, forty each, with the experimentals to be released six months or a year earlier than they ordinarily would be and the control released at their regularly appointed time, how would the burglar assigned to the control group respond? It is unfair, unjust, unethical, he could say, for me to be put into the control group. If people like me, he might complain, are being released early, I too deserve the same treatment (cited in Erez, 1986:394).

Program staff are also frequently unhappy with randomization because it fails to utilize their clinical skills in the selection of appropriate candidates for intervention. Extending this line of thought, consider the likely response of judges requested to sentence burglary offenders randomly to prison or probation. While this might be the best method of determining the effectiveness of these sanctions, the judicial response (and perhaps community response as well) would probably be less than enthusiastic. This is because it is assumed, often without any evidence, that standard practice is achieving some reasonable objective, such as individualizing justice or preventing crime.

Randomization does produce winners and losers. Of critical importance in weighing the consequences of randomization are the differences in treatment experienced by the experimental and control groups. Six factors are relevant here:

1. *Significance of the interest affected.* Early release is of much greater consequence than a change of institutional diet.
2. *Extent of difference.* Six months early release is of greater significance than one week's early release.
3. *Comparison of the disparity with standard treatment.* If both experimental and control group treatment is an improvement over standard treatment, then the discrepancy between the experimental and control group is of less concern.
4. *Whether disparity reflects differences in qualifications of subjects.* If the disparity is reasonably related to some characteristic of the subjects, the denial of benefits to the control group is less significant.
5. *Whether the experimental treatment is harmful or beneficial to subjects compared with the treatment they would otherwise receive.* A program that assigns members of the experimental group to six weeks of "boot camp" may be more demanding of inmates than the standard treatment of six months' incarceration.
6. *Whether participation is mandatory or voluntary.* Voluntary participation mitigates the concern of denial of benefit, while coercion exacerbates the dilemma (Federal Judicial Center, 1981:31–40).

Similar to the management of other ethical dilemmas, an effort is required to balance values of human decency and justice with the need for accurate information on intervention effectiveness. Problems arise not in the extreme cases of disparity but in more routine circumstances. Consider the following example: How do we judge a situation in which a foundation grant permits attorneys to be supplied for all cases being heard by a juvenile court in which attorneys have previously appeared only in rare instances? A fundamental study hypothesis may be that the presence of an attorney tends to result in a more favorable disposition for the client. This idea may be tested by comparing dispositions prior to the beginning of the experiment with those ensuing subsequently, though it would be more satisfactory to supply attorneys to a sample of the cases and withhold them from the remainder, in order to calculate in a more experimentally uncontaminated manner the differences between the outcomes in the two situations.

The matter takes on additional complexity if the researchers desire to determine what particular attorney role is the most efficacious in the juvenile court. They may suspect that an attorney who acts as a friend of the court, knowingly taking its viewpoint as *parens patriae*, and attempting to interpret the court's interest to his or her client, will produce more desirable results than one who doggedly challenges the courtroom procedure and the judge's interpretation of fact, picks at the probation report, raises constant objections, and fights for his or her client as he would in a criminal court. But what results are "more desirable" (Geis, 1980:222-223)?

It could be contended that little is really known about how attorney roles influence dispositions and that, without the project, no one would have any kind of representation. Over the long term, all juveniles stand to benefit. On the other hand, it could be argued that it is wrong to deprive anyone of the best judgment of his or her attorney by requiring a particular legal approach. What if there are only enough funds to supply one-half of the juveniles with attorneys anyway? Is randomization more or less fair than trying to decide which cases "need" representation the most?

Randomization imposes a special ethical burden because it purposefully counters efforts to determine the best course of action with the element of chance. The practice is justifiable because the pursuit of knowledge is a desirable objective—as long as the overall benefits outweigh the risks. The balancing of risks and benefits is complicated by the fact that judgments must often be made in a context of ambiguity, attempting to predict the benefits of an intervention that is being tested precisely because its impact is unknown.

The Federal Judicial Center (1981) recommends that program evaluations should only be considered when certain threshold conditions are met:

> First, the status quo warrants substantial improvements or is of doubtful effectiveness.
>
> Second, there must be significant uncertainty about the value or effectiveness of the innovation.
>
> Third, information needed to clarify the uncertainty must be feasibly obtainable by the program experimentation but not readily obtainable by other means.
>
> And fourth, the information sought must pertain directly to the decision whether or not to adopt the proposed innovation on a general, non-experimental basis (p. 7).

Several conditions lessen the ethical burdens of evaluative research. Random assignment is especially acceptable when resources are scarce and demand for the benefit is high. Denying benefits to the control group is quite acceptable when members of the control group can participate at a later date. Finally, discrepancies between the treatment of experimental and control groups are decreased when the groups are geographically separated (Federal Judicial Center, 1981).

FAILING TO TREAT RESEARCH PARTICIPANTS FAIRLY AND TO SHOW THEM CONSIDERATION AND RESPECT

The basic tenets of professionalism require that researchers treat subjects with courtesy and fulfill the variety of commitments they make to subjects. In an effort to obtain cooperation, subjects are often promised a follow-up report on the findings of the research; such reports may be forgotten once the study

has been completed. Subjects are often led to believe that they will achieve some personal benefit from the research. This may be one of the more difficult obligations to fulfill.

Researchers need to treat their human subjects with constant recognition of their integrity and their contribution to the research endeavor. This is especially important when subjects are powerless and vulnerable. Although such treatment may be a time-consuming chore, it is the only ethical way to practice scientific research.

BALANCING SCIENTIFIC AND ETHICAL CONCERNS

This discussion has emphasized the importance of balancing a concern for subjects against the potential benefits of the research. Cook (1976) identifies the following potential benefits of a research project:

1. Advances in scientific theory that contribute to a general understanding of human behavior.
2. Advances in knowledge of practical value to society.
3. Gains for the research participant, such as increased understanding, satisfaction in making a contribution to science or to the solution of social problems, needed money or special privileges, knowledge of social science or of research methods, and so on (p. 235).

The potential costs to subjects are considerable, however, and it is often difficult for the researcher to be objective in assessing the issues. For this reason, many professional associations have established guidelines and procedures for ethical research conduct. Generally, because little active monitoring occurs, the professional is honor-bound to follow these guidelines.

INSTITUTIONAL REVIEW BOARDS AND SETTING ETHICAL STANDARDS

To ensure that their faculty follow acceptable procedures (and to protect themselves from liability), universities have established institutional review boards to scrutinize each research project that involves the use of human subjects. These review boards serve a valuable function in that they review the specifications of each research project prior to implementation. They are generally incapable of providing direct monitoring of projects so, again, the responsibility for ethical conduct falls on the researcher.

How are the ethical standards being set within the criminal justice community, and how and to what degree are ethics being taught in criminology and criminal justice academic settings? McSkimming, Sever, and King (2000) analyzed 11 research methods textbooks that are frequently used in criminal justice and criminology courses. The authors looked at the extent to which ethical issues were addressed within the criminal justice texts and the type of ethical issues that were covered within the texts. The authors found that there was no collective format being utilized in the major criminal justice texts regarding ethics in criminal justice. Furthermore, the significance and positive functions of institutional review boards were rarely mentioned.

Of further concern was the noticeable absence of some important ethical topics in these criminal justice research methods texts. These topic areas concerned ethics related to the dissemination of information into the criminal justice audience. These areas concerned "plagiarism, fabrication of data, Institutional Review Boards, authorship rank, and ethical considerations in journal editing and grant-writing" (p. 58).

Institutional review boards are often the only source for ethical guidance and standards for the criminal justice academic researcher (McSkimming, Sever & King, 2000). It is imperative that graduate students, publishing professors, and other disseminators of information within the criminal justice discipline have some guideline or gauge with which to measure ethical standards.

ETHICAL CODES

In order to address some of these key ethical considerations, two predominant criminal justice associations have developed and make known a standard or code of ethics. The Academy of Criminal Justice Sciences (ACJS) and the American Society of Criminology (ASC) have each advanced a standard for those persons researching and writing within the criminal justice discipline. The two codes of ethics are similar; they address the ethical standards of conducting social science research as well as the dissemination of information within the criminal justice discipline. Specifically, these codes provide criminologists with ethical standards concerning fair treatment; the use of students in research; objectivity and integrity in the conduct of research; confidentiality, disclosure, and respect for research populations; publication and authorship standards; and employment practices (ACJS Code of Ethics, 2000; ASC Code of Ethics, 1999).

ETHICAL / POLITICAL CONSIDERATIONS

Applied social research, that is, research that examines the effectiveness of social policies and programs, carries with it additional ethical responsibilities. Such research influences the course of human events in a direct fashion—often work, education, future opportunities, and deeply held values and beliefs are affected by the outcomes. Researchers must be prepared to deal with a variety of pressures and demands as they undertake the practice and dissemination of research.

It is generally acknowledged that organizations asked to measure their own effectiveness often produce biased results. Crime statistics provide a notorious example of data that tend to be used to show either an effective police department (falling crime figures) or a need for more resources (rising crime figures). Criminal justice researchers are often asked to study matters that are equally sensitive. A correctional treatment program found to be ineffective may lose its funding. A study that reveals extensive use of plea bargaining may cost a prosecutor his or her election.

Often the truth is complicated. A survey that reveals that drug use is declining in the general population may prove troublesome for those trying to lobby for the establishment of more drug treatment facilities. The survey results may lead the public to believe that there is no problem at the same time that the need for treatment facilities for the indigent is substantial.

Such research has been known to produce unintended consequences. The publication of selected results of a study on the effectiveness of correctional treatment programs (Martinson, 1974) was used by many persons to justify limiting funds for education and treatment programs in correctional institutions. The research revealed that there was little evidence that correctional treatment programs were effective means of reducing recidivism (a finding that has been widely challenged). Rather than stimulating the development of more theoretically sound programs and rigorous evaluations of these efforts, the apparent product of the research was a decrease in the humaneness of conditions of confinement.

Sometimes research results conflict with cherished beliefs. Studies of preventive police patrol (Kelling et al., 1974) and detective investigations (Chaiken, Greenwood & Petersilia, 1977) both revealed that these practices, long assumed to be essential elements of effective law enforcement, were of little value. Researchers can expect findings such as these to meet with considerable resistance.

Researchers may be asked to utilize their skills and their aura of objectivity to provide an organization or agency with what it wants. When the group that pays the bills has a direct interest in the nature of the outcome, the pressures can be considerable. Marvin Wolfgang (1982) reports:

> I was once invited to do research by an organization whose views are almost completely antithetical to mine on the issue of gun control. Complete freedom and a considerable amount of money to explore the relationship between gun control legislation and robbery were promised. I would not perform the research under those auspices. But the real clincher in the decision was that if the research produced conclusions opposite from that the organization wanted, the agency would not publish the results nor allow me to publish them. Perhaps their behavior, within their ideological framework, was not unethical. But within my framework, as a scientist who values freedom of publication as well as of scientific inquiry, I would have engaged in an unethical act of prostituting my integrity had I accepted those conditions. (p. 395)

In-house researchers, who are employed by the organization for which the research is being conducted, face special problems in this regard, because they lack the freedom to pick and choose their research topic. These problems must balance their concern for rigorous scientific inquiry with their need for continued employment.

Generally, the issues confronted are subtle and complex. Although researchers may be directly told to conceal or falsify results, more often they are subtly encouraged to design their research with an eye toward the desired results. The greatest barrier to such pressures is the development of a truly independent professional research unit within the organization. Such independence protects the researcher from political pressures and at the same time promotes the credibility of the research being conducted. Without this protection, the individual is left to his or her own devices and standards of ethical conduct.

THE PURITY OF SCIENTIFIC RESEARCH

The ideal of scientific inquiry is the pure, objective examination of the empirical world, untainted by personal prejudice. However, research is carried out by human beings, not automatons, and they have a variety of motivations for undertaking the research that they do. Topics may be selected because of curiosity or a perceived need to address a specific social problem, but the availability of grants in a particular field may also encourage researchers to direct their attention to these areas. This is critical if one is working for a research organization dependent upon "soft" money. The need for university faculty to publish and establish a name for themselves in a particular area may encourage them to seek "hot" topics for their research, or to identify an extremely narrow research focus in which they can become identified as an expert.

There is some evidence that the nature of one's research findings influences the likelihood of publication (*Chronicle of Higher Education*, 1989d). A curious author submitted almost identical articles to a number of journals. The manuscripts differed only in one respect—the nature of the conclusions. One version of the article showed that the experiment had no effect; the other described a positive result. His experiment produced some interesting findings—the article with positive outcomes was more likely to be accepted for publication than the other manuscript.

If research that concludes that "the experiment didn't work" or that "differences between Groups A and B were insignificant" are indeed less likely to see the light of day, then pressures to revise one's research focus or rewrite one's hypotheses to match the results produced can be anticipated.

None of the practices described above involve scandalous violations of ethical conduct. Their presentation should function, however, to remind us that actions justified in the name of scientific inquiry may be motivated by factors far less "pure" than the objective they serve.

PUBLIC POLICY PRONOUNCEMENTS AND TEACHING CRIMINAL JUSTICE

When is a researcher speaking from the facts and when is he or she promoting personal ideology? If there were any fully conclusive and definitive studies in the social sciences, this question would not arise. However, research findings are always tentative, and statements describing them invariably require conditional language. On the other hand, researchers have values and beliefs like everyone else, and few of us want to employ the same conditional language required to discuss research when we state our views on matters of public policy and morality. Researchers thus have a special obligation to carefully evaluate their remarks and clearly distinguish between opinion and apparent empirical fact. This is not always an easy task, but it is the only way to safeguard the objectivity that is critically important to scientific inquiry. Furthermore, criminal justice researchers acting as teachers and mentors have a responsibility to their students, due to the influence their position has over the lives of the students (ACJS, 2000). Specifically, a researcher's influence and authority used inappropriately has the potential to mislead and distort the perspectives of their students

by disseminating information that was merely personal ideology as opposed to scientific findings.

CONCLUSION

Conducting scientific research in criminal justice and criminology in an ethical fashion is a difficult task. It requires a constant weighing and balancing of objectives and motivations. It would be nice to conclude that the best research is that which is undertaken in an ethical fashion, but such a statement would skirt the dilemma. This is the exact nature of the problem: those actions required to meet the demands of scientific rigor sometimes run counter to ethical behavior.

Evaluating rather than avoiding ethical dilemmas does provide a learning experience, though, the benefits of which can be expected to spill over into all aspects of human endeavor. Thinking and doing in an ethical fashion requires practice, and conducting research provides considerable opportunity for the development of experience.

REFERENCES

ACJS (2000). "Academy of Criminal Justice Sciences: Code of Ethics."

ASC (1999). "American Society of Criminology: Code of Ethics."

Chaiken, J., P. Greenwood & J. Petersilia (1977). "The Criminal Investigation Process: A Summary Report." *Policy Analysis* 3:187–217.

Chronicle of Higher Education (1989a), January 25:A44.

Chronicle of Higher Education (1989b), June 14:A44.

Chronicle of Higher Education (1989c), July 19:A4.

Chronicle of Higher Education (1989d), August 2:A5.

Chronicle of Higher Education (1999), November 46:A18.

Cohen, B. (1980). *Deviant Street Networks: Prostitution in New York City.* Cambridge, MA: Lexington Books.

Cook, S.W. (1976). "Ethical Issues in the Conduct of Research in Social Relations." In *Research Methods in Social Relations*, 3rd ed., Claire Sellitz, Lawrence Rightsman & Stuart Cook (eds.). New York: Holt, Rinehart and Winston.

Driscoll, A. (1999). "UF Prof Who Touted Privatized Prisons Admits Firm Paid Him." *Miami Herald*, April 21:A1.

Erez, E. (1986). "Randomized Experiments in Correctional Context: Legal, Ethical and Practical Concerns." *Journal of Criminal Justice*, 14: 389–400.

Federal Judicial Center (1981). *Experimentation in the Law. Report of the Federal Judicial Center Advisory Committee on Experimentation in the Law.* Washington, DC: Federal Judicial Center.

Geis, G. (1980). "Ethical and Legal Issues in Experiments with Offender Populations." In *Criminal Justice Research: Approaches, Problems & Policy*, S. Talarico (ed.). Cincinnati: Anderson.

Haney, C., C. Banks & P. Zimbardo (1973). "Interpersonal Dynamics in a Simulated Prison." *International Journal of Criminology and Penology*, 1:69–97.

Humphreys, L. (1970). *Tearoom Trade: Impersonal Sex in Public Places.* Chicago: Aldine.

Jones, K.D. (1999). "Ethics in Publication." *Counseling and Values*, 43:99–106.

Kelling, G.L., T. Page, D. Dieckman & C.E. Browne (1974). *The Kansas City Preventive Patrol Experiment.* Washington, DC: The Police Foundation.

Martinson, R. (1974). "What Works?—Questions and Answers About Prison Reform." *Public Interest*, 35:25–54.

McSkimming, M.J., B. Sever & R.S. King (2000). "The Coverage of Ethics in Research Methods Textbooks." *Journal of Criminal Justice Education*, 11:51–63.

Meltzer, B.A. (1953). "A Projected Study of the Jury as a Working Institution." *The Annals of the American Academy of Political and Social Sciences*, 287:97–102.

Milgram, S. (1974). *Obedience to Authority: An Experimental View.* New York: Harper and Row.

Moreno, J.D. (1998). "Convenient and Captive Populations." In J.P. Kahn, A.C. Mastroianni & J. Sugarman (eds.), *Beyond Consent: Seeking Justice in Research* (pp. 111–130). New York: Oxford University Press, pp. 111–130.

Morris, N. (1966). "Impediments to Penal Reform." *Chicago Law Review*, 33:646–653.

The New York Times (1983). February 26, 1983: 7.

Ring, K., K. Wallston & M. Corey (1970). "Mode of Debriefing as a Factor Affecting Subjective Reaction to a Milgram Type Obedience Experience: An Ethical Inquiry." *Representative Research in Social Psychology*, 1:67–88.

Sherman, L.W. & R.A. Berk (1984). "The Specific Deterrent Effects of Arrest for Domestic Assault." *American Sociological Review*, 49:261–272.

Short, J.F., Jr. & F. Strodtbeck (1965). *Group Processes and Gang Delinquency.* Chicago: University of Chicago Press.

Singleton, Jr., R.A. & B.C. Straits (1988). *Approaches to Social Research*, 3rd ed. New York: Oxford University Press.

Whyte, W.F. (1955). *Streetcorner Society.* Chicago: University of Chicago Press.

Wolfgang, M. (1982). "Ethics and Research." In *Ethics, Public Policy and Criminal Justice*, F. Elliston & N. Bowie (eds.). Cambridge, MA: Oelgeschlager, Gunn and Hain.

Diversity and the Policy Agenda in Criminal Justice

Mark Mitchell

Introduction

Rather like a wet bar of soap, 'diversity' is a slippery concept—one that is almost impossible to grasp. Yet in recent years it has become one of those words that, like 'democracy' and 'freedom', are cheered every time they get a mention. How did diversity achieve such high prominence across the public policy terrain; what has been its impact within the criminal justice sector in particular; what difficulties face organisations that seek to devise and implement diversity plans; and has diversity been a help or a hindrance in furthering the kind of multi-agency partnership working that is essential if rates of reoffending are to be reduced and more offenders are to be rehabilitated? These questions provide the core concerns that will be addressed in this chapter.

Diversity—A Brief History

For anyone with a longstanding interest in policies designed to combat discrimination in the UK, the recent rise and rise of the concept of 'diversity' must have come as a surprise. The standard literature on equality of opportunity from the 1970s and 1980s makes hardly any mention of the term (see, for example, EOC, 1985; Gregory, 1987); and the reawakening of interest in the issue of human rights, associated with rising levels of migration and asylum across the European Union (EU), was not accompanied by any significant discussions of diversity, choosing rather to focus on the issue of multiculturalism as a possible basis for a new form of citizenship. (Mitchell and Russell, 1998; Sassen, 1999). Yet over the past 10 years, diversity policies have become standard fare across most of the public sector and many public sector organisations have appointed diversity advisors to oversee the implementation of these policies. So how did this happen? How did a term that was not widely used in discussions and debates about how to increase fairness and equality in society rise to the predominant position it now occupies?

To answer this question, we need to recognise that for well over 30 years, from the early 1960s onwards, the campaign for legislation to support the attainment of equality of opportunity in the UK drew much of its inspiration and most of its key ideas from the US, particularly from the US 1963 Equal Pay Act and the US 1964 Civil Rights Act. It was these pioneering pieces of legislation that became the inspiration for equal opportunity campaigners in the UK. Thus, the somewhat timid efforts to combat race discrimination through the 1965 and 1968 Race Relations Acts and the much more radical attempts to address more structural causes of inequality by tackling direct and indirect discrimination in the 1975 Sex Discrimination Act and the 1976 Race Relations Act all drew their inspiration from across the Atlantic.

Diversity as a policy driver in the UK owes its origins to two interrelated developments that began to shape public policy in the late 1990s. The first of these was the response by the Labour government to the publication of the Macpherson report into the murder of Stephen Lawrence (Macpherson, 1999). This will be discussed in more detail in the next section of this chapter. But the second development took place at the level of the EU. For the first time, the European Commission and the individual member states began to recognise that, in addition to sex discrimination, other forms of discrimination were having an adverse impact on the operation of the European labour market. In retrospect, we can see that the UK's longstanding, relatively progressive and US-influenced anti-discrimination legislation had a significant impact in shaping the development of European initiatives in this field. At the same time, the way in which the EU's anti-discrimination directives were rolled out as part of a broader ideological framework of 'valuing difference' helped to shape the way in which these directives were implemented in the UK.

Following the signing of the Amsterdam Treaty in 1997, EU member states began to take the issue of discrimination much more seriously, particularly in relation to the operation of the labour market. The Treaty committed the EU to issue appropriate directives to ensure that member states introduced national legislation to combat discrimination in five new areas of social life and at the same time to strengthen the previous directives relating to equal pay and sex discrimination. As a result, new laws to protect people against discrimination on the grounds of racial or ethnic origin, religion or belief, disability, age and sexual orientation were agreed by all EU countries in 2000 and were harmonised with a new directive covering sex discrimination.

> Anti-discrimination laws to protect people against being discriminated against on the grounds of racial or ethnic origin, religion or belief, disability, age and sexual orientations were agreed by all EU countries in 2000. This means that all 27 countries in the EU today are required to incorporate these rules into their national laws. As well as making sure that these laws are respected, the European Commission works to inform citizens of their rights and responsibilities, to raise awareness of discrimination, and to promote the benefits of diversity. (www. stop-discrimination.info/27.0.html)

It is clear that the development of these European directives was strongly influenced by countries like the UK, which had had considerable experience of the operation of anti-discriminatory legislation. The distinction between direct and indirect discrimination and the provision for positive action, for example, were strikingly similar principles that had shaped the laws in the UK since the mid-1970s, as can be seen in the following:

> The directives recognise explicitly that outlawing discrimination will not necessarily be enough by itself to ensure genuine equality of opportunity for everyone in society. Specific measures might be called for to compensate for disadvantages arising from a person's racial or ethnic origin, age or other characteristics which might lead to them being treated unfairly.

For example, ethnic minorities may need special training and specific help to have a reasonable chance of finding a job. Putting on training courses or making different arrangements especially for them are ways of improving their chances. The directives allow positive action of this kind to be undertaken and do not regard it as infringing the principle of equal treatment. (www.stop-discrimination.info/84.0.html)

One of the principal ways in which the Commission has promoted diversity is through the 'For Diversity, Against Discrimination' campaign, which commenced in 2003. The campaign strap line demonstrates clearly the thinking behind the campaign and the concern that an over-emphasis on 'banning discrimination' is likely to be perceived as portraying what the EU is against rather than what it stands for. The European directives outlawing discrimination on the grounds of sex, race/ethnicity, disability, age, religion and sexual orientation are seen as a means by which member states can foster and encourage greater levels of tolerance and mutual self-respect between individuals who are 'different'. Valuing difference is the goal and anti-discrimination legislation is a prerequisite for achieving this. In contrast to the 1960s and 1970s, the link between discrimination and the denial of civil/human rights has been decoupled and the emphasis on rights has been downplayed in favour of diversity.

DIVERSITY AND CRIMINAL JUSTICE IN ENGLAND AND WALES

The impact within the UK of this shift in emphasis towards valuing difference and diversity can be traced through a number of important initiatives that took place from the late 1990s onwards. Most importantly, the publication in 1999 of the report of the Macpherson Inquiry into the murder of Stephen Lawrence promoted a degree of soul searching within criminal justice agencies. Macpherson had concluded that the Metropolitan Police Service (MPS) was institutionally racist because its organisational culture was characterised by 'processes, attitudes and behaviour which amount to discrimination through unwitting prejudice, ignorance, thoughtlessness and racist stereotyping which disadvantage minority ethnic people'(Macpherson,1999:para 6.34). Because of institutional racism,the service provided by the MPS to London's black and minority ethnic communities was unprofessional and ineffective. The multiple failures that occurred during the investigation of the Stephen Lawrence murder were not just a consequence of the incompetence of individual police officers. Rather, because of commonsense racist assumptions and attitudes that were deeply embedded in the organisation, the murder had been investigated less competently than if a white teenager had been unlawfully killed. This of course implied that other criminal justice organisations might also be infested with routine, taken-for-granted ways of operating that disadvantaged individuals from the black and minority ethnic communities, whether as employees or as service users of these organisations.

The Labour government's response to the Macpherson Inquiry was to introduce the first significant modifications to the 1976 Race Relations Act for 25 years. The most important change was the requirement for public sector organisations to introduce race equality schemes designed to eliminate race discrimination,foster harmonious race relations and actively promote race equality. Under the 1976 Act, employers had been permitted to introduce a range of positive action measures to promote more equal access to scarce goods and services in society. But there was no duty to take positive action and it was only permitted if an organisation could demonstrate that there was existing under-representation of individuals from the black and minority ethnic communities in terms of access to recruitment, training and development, promotion and/or service provision. Following the passage of the 2000 Race Relations (Amendment) Act, positive action became a mandatory obligation for nearly all major public sector organisations.

Additional equalities legislation has been needed to implement the EU directives and ensure that the UK's anti-discrimination laws and employment regulations are fully aligned with the new European requirements. This has presented the Labour government with an opportunity to extend the principles enshrined in the 2000 Race Relations (Amendment) Act to other areas. Consequently, because of the 2005 Disability Discrimination Act and the 2006 Equality Act, major public organisations in the UK are now required to develop disability equality and gender equality schemes in addition to their existing race equality schemes. However, no such duties apply to the other areas covered by the European directives and, as a result, we now have in effect a two-tier system of legislation in the UK. On the one hand, most of the public sector, together with private sector organisations that deliver services that have been 'contracted out' by the public sector, are required actively to promote race, gender and disability equality through positive action measures. On the other hand, in the areas of religion/faith, age and sexual orientation, no such public duties to secure greater equality apply. While it is now unlawful to discriminate directly or indirectly in terms of employment or in the provision of goods and services on the basis of an individual's religion, age or sexual orientation, there is no requirement on the public sector to develop equality schemes in these areas.

The response of all the major criminal justice agencies to these legislative changes has, on the surface, been exemplary and it is no exaggeration to say that diversity came to occupy a centre-stage position in the strategic plans of most of these agencies in the early years of the new millennium. However, analysis of the ways in which these diversity policies have evolved over the last 10 years shows two clear trends. First, there has been growing focus on equality at the expense of diversity in strategic and business planning, exemplified by the emergence of what is known as the 'single equality policy'. This shift in emphasis from diversity to equality reflects both the implementation of the European directives and the merger of the Commission for Racial Equality, the Disability Rights Commission and the Equal Opportunities Commission to form the Equality and Human Rights Commission in October 2007. Second, there has been a growing trend to prioritise action planning—as well as the allocation of the resources to achieve targets—on those areas where agencies have a statutory duty to promote equality. As a result, across the criminal justice

system we have witnessed the emergence of a two-tier distinction between the areas of race, sex/gender and disability where this statutory duty exists and the areas of sexual orientation, age and religion where no such statutory duties apply. These trends will be illustrated by reference to the published plans of the MPS, the Crown Prosecution Service (CPS) and the Prison and Probation Services.

Perhaps unsurprisingly given the fact that the Macpherson report had labelled it an institutionally racist organisation, the MPS was first to grasp the diversity nettle. In November 1998, just as the Macpherson Inquiry was concluding its hearings, the MPS adopted its *Protect and Respect* diversity strategy (see Grieve and French, 2000:15). As the Metropolitan Police Authority reported in 2000 (MPA, 2000), this strategy was updated following the Inspector of Constabulary's report *Policing London: Winning Consent* (HMIC, 2000) and was subsequently replaced with a new *Diversity Strategy* in 2005 to reflect the changing legal terrain that has been outlined above (MPS, 2005). A Diversity Directorate (now the Diversity and Citizen Focus Directorate) was established to oversee a massive programme of training and development, internal performance monitoring and external community engagement. The current *Equalities Scheme 2006–10*, which was updated in 2008, sets out equality targets for each of the six areas now covered by anti-discrimination laws as a result of the European directives (MPS, 2008a).

In 2003, the Crown Prosecution Service (CPS) was aspiring to become 'a beacon organisation in terms of equality and diversity both as employer and prosecutor' (CPS, 2003:19). The same document refers explicitly to the CPS race equality scheme and to its work with the Commission for Racial Equality (see, for example, 2003:6) and the Disability Rights Commission (see, for example, 2003: 19). In 2006, the CPS published a comprehensive *Single Equality Scheme* (CPS, 2006), which was updated in 2008. This document also sets out equality action plans for all six areas that are now covered by legislation, although it is noticeable that the plans for disability, gender and race are far more comprehensive than those for sexuality, religion and age. The same difference of emphasis in relation to race, sex and disability equality can be found in the *Equalities Scheme* of the MPS, where the monitoring of actual performance against the targets set out in the MPS *Equalities Scheme* appears to be well established (see, for example, MPS, 2007, 2008b).

In 2001, the new National Probation Service made 'valuing and achieving diversity' one of the nine 'stretch objectives' that were at the core of its first corporate plan (NPS, 2001: 33–7). Likewise, the corporate and business plans of the Prison Service make similar commitments, with statements like: 'The Prison Service remains determined to promote diversity, eliminate racism and improve the representation of minority ethnic staff in its workforce' (HM Prison Service, 2003: 26).

Today, both the Probation and Prison Services' commitments to diversity are subsumed under the National Offender Management Service's (NOMS) *Single Equality Scheme* (Ministry of Justice, 2009b). However, the scheme is almost entirely devoted to the work of the Prison Service, both in the monitoring of past performance and in the setting of future targets as 'each of the 42 probation areas is separately responsible for developing an equality scheme which covers service delivery and employment functions across the range of equality issues' (Ministry of Justice, 2009b: 3).

The NOMS *Single Equality Scheme* also makes explicit reference to the 'business case' for diversity (Ministry of Justice, 2009b: iii), in line with the way that both the European Commission and the UK's Department for Trade and Industry have attempted to 'sell' diversity by emphasising its potential economic benefits in recent years (see, for example, DTI, 2005; European Commission, 2008). However, this business case is not reflected in the NOMS business plan itself (Ministry of Justice, 2009a). Here, diversity and equality are mentioned only briefly and in ways that restate in the most general way the values that should be expected of any organisation, public or private, that is responsible for delivering services to the public. For example, is anyone surprised that NOMS is committed to deliver its services 'with decency, valuing diversity and promoting equality' (Ministry of Justice, 2009a: 11)?

IMPLEMENTING DIVERSITY: CONCEPTUAL AND PRACTICAL DIFFICULTIES

The public sector's love affair with the concept of diversity began to cool after the publication of the report by the Community Cohesion Review Team into the riots that took place in Bradford, Burnley and Oldham in the summer of 2001 (Home Office, 2001). The report raised some disturbing questions about the extent to which black and minority ethnic communities in some parts of the UK were increasingly leading lives that were almost entirely separate from other communities.

> Whilst the physical segregation of housing estates and inner city areas came as no surprise, the team was particularly struck by the depth of polarisation of our towns and cities. The extent to which these physical divisions were compounded by so many other aspects of our daily lives was very evident. Separate educational arrangements, community and voluntary bodies, employment, places of worship, language, social and cultural networks, means that many communities operate on the basis of a series of parallel lives. These lives often do not seem to touch at any point, let alone overlap and promote any meaningful interchanges. (Home Office, 2001: 9)

The text of the report is replete with positive references to the importance of diversity and makes an impassioned plea for everyone to recognise that the days of a 'monoculturalist view of nationality' are no longer relevant to Britain in an increasingly globalised world (Home Office, 2001: 18). At the same time, the support for diversity is subject to an important caveat, namely that it should be underpinned by a shared commitment to citizenship, comprising common values, moral principles and codes of behaviour, together with support for political institutions and participation in politics (Home Office, 2001: 13).

> This needs a determined effort to gain consensus on the fundamental issue of 'cultural pluralism'. In other words, an acceptance, and even a celebration, of our diversity

and that within the concept of citizenship, different cultures can thrive, adding to the richness and experience of our nationality. (Home Office, 2001: 18)

The report appears to be saying that a commitment to valuing and achieving diversity will not in itself provide the 'glue' required to secure community cohesion. In other words, valuing diversity is a necessary rather than a sufficient condition for any society characterised by a wide range of sociocultural differences. Consequently, it follows that 'valuing difference' can never be unconditional. The extent to which we are able to feel at ease with, actively participate in and even enjoy life in a diverse society is dependent on deeper values and moral principles that comprise the basis of our civic culture and that sustain the mutual respect that is a prerequisite for, at the very least, the toleration of difference.

It is clear from the above discussion that no society or organisation can respect and value all differences unconditionally. Rather, there must be limits to difference and diversity. The problem is that there is nothing inherent in these concepts themselves to enable organisations or individuals to determine what these limits should be. Neither are these merely philosophical conundrums, of interest only to those who inhabit academic ivory towers. Professionals from across the public sector continue to face serious dilemmas over their approaches to certain cultural practices that many find abhorrent but that are deeply rooted in some of our minority communities, for example female circumcision, polygamy and the ritual slaughter of animals (see Parekh, 2000, especially chapters 8 and 9, for an interesting discussion of some of the dilemmas raised by these cultural differences). Most would agree that cultural relativism, the belief that white middle-class professionals should never act in ways that impose 'alien' Western values on minority ethnic communities or act in ways that undermine or marginalise their alternative cultural beliefs and practices, cannot provide a coherent basis for professional intervention. An unquestioning commitment to 'multiculturalism', where the traditions and practices of minority communities are always respected, is wrong in principle and unsustainable in practice. This is why social workers

are generally agreed that there must be limits to multiculturalism in relation to childcare/protection practice (see Cheetham, 1982: 143–6; Watson, this volume). The problem today is that a 'relativism of difference' threatens to replace cultural relativism because of the unquestioning acceptance of the principle of diversity. This in turn is disempowering for professionals since it provides no guidance on where to draw the line when it comes to valuing and respecting differences.

However, the problems with diversity are not solely conceptual; they are also practical, and raise significant issues for practitioners who work in a multi-agency context and particularly in relation to the community sector. All organisations have to make hard choices over the use of scarce resources and must therefore prioritise between competing interests when implementing their diversity policies. A broad commitment to valuing difference does not help when deciding precisely how the resources available to implement this commitment should be allocated. In view of this, it is perhaps unsurprising that most organisations prioritise those areas that have been legally designated as more important than others. Thus, as we have seen above, policies designed to address disadvantage and discrimination in the areas of race, sex/gender and disability tend to figure more prominently in action plans than those that focus on age, religion and sexual orientation because of the statutory disability, gender and race equality duties that recent legislation has imposed on many public sector organisations.

This should not be taken to mean that diversity/equality policies are a waste of time. Some of the plans and policies of criminal justice agencies that were

Imagine you are the manager of a hostel. A male offender wishes to display white supremacist posters and other far Right material in his room. When challenged by staff, he claims that he has the right to display this material because the local Probation Trust has a policy of valuing diversity. What is your decision on this matter and how will you justify this decision to your line manager?

discussed in the previous section should, if implemented fully, begin to address some of the deep-rooted institutional disadvantages within these agencies. The Accelerate programme, a two-year management development programme offered to middle managers with a disability and/or who are from one of the black and minority ethnic communities and who work in probation or youth justice, is a good example of how these agencies can translate fine words into actions. (For details of the Accelerate programme, see YJB, 2009.) But this and similar programmes across the public sector represent the specific ways in which these agencies have responded to meet what are now legal requirements, namely to take action to promote disability, gender and race equality in an active manner. The contribution that such programmes make to addressing institutional discrimination and disadvantage in these areas have come about as a result of legislative changes and not as a result of any general commitment to valuing and achieving diversity.

Of course, the six areas of difference now subject to legal regulation represent only a tiny fraction of those that can and sometimes do result in disadvantage. Take, for example, left-handedness. The writer of this chapter is often struck when lecturing to large groups of students in one of the many new and well-equipped lecture theatres across the campus where he works that many of the lecture theatres are very poorly equipped for those who write with their left hand. This is because the seats have retractable tables, all of which are designed for people who write with their right hand. The same is true of many of the computer rooms around the campus, where each computer is fitted with a right-handed mouse. This is a clear case of institutional discrimination against left-handed people and one which, in an ideal world, should be addressed by ensuring that at least 10% of the tables and computers are designed for those who are left-handed. But to rectify this disadvantage would require the commitment of additional resources involving hard choices between competing priorities. In the circumstances, it is not surprising that most organisations give greater weight to meeting their legal responsibilities and downplay other areas of institutional discrimination.

Think about the organisational context where you work and/or study. Can you identify areas of institutional discrimination that, while not unlawful, are disadvantageous and unfair to particular groups?

DIVERSITY AND PARTNERSHIP WORKING

This section will address the question: is diversity a help or a hindrance to multi-agency working? At first glance, the common commitment to valuing difference and respecting the diversity of people's lifestyles and choices might appear to provide a solid foundation for the partnership work that is essential if rates of offending and reoffending are to be reduced. Furthermore, the legislation that now applies to all the major criminal justice agencies requiring them to take positive action measures to meet their disability, gender and race equality duties, should in theory provide a common basis for the development of training and development programmes that, at the very least, are founded on a common approach to equal opportunity in employment and promotion. At a policy level, the information given above about the Accelerate programme provides an example of a positive action management development programme run for middle managers from both probation and youth justice designed to address the under-representation of staff at senior management level who have a disability and/or who are from one of the black and minority ethnic communities. For practitioners there are good examples of interventions developed by partnerships between relevant agencies, and which seek to develop an empowerment approach by utilising relevant community resources (see Hilder and also Goldhill, this volume).

However, the lack of definitional clarity over the concept of diversity inevitably makes it more complicated for staff from different agencies to work seamlessly together, particularly on practice-related matters. The conceptual/definitional muddle is further complicated by the use of alternative, perhaps complementary concepts, such as equality, which as we have seen is increasingly coupled together with diversity in the strategic and business plans of criminal justice agencies. Further, the continuing use of the term 'anti-discriminatory practice' across the probation service, which has its origins in attempts to reconceptualise social work theory and practice in the late 1970s and early 1980s, represents another complicating factor (see Thompson, 2006). This is an issue that the writer has experienced as a barrier to group learning in the training and development of multi-agency youth offending teams, where what was a core professional value to anyone from a professional social work background was a source of incomprehension and confusion to some of the police officers and health professionals present (see Pamment, this volume).

On a more practical level, there is another reason why diversity cannot provide a secure value. The message that has come across loud and clear to the writer, who has been responsible for delivering diversity training to trainee probation officers for the last six years, is one of suspicion and lack of receptivity to diversity training. Many of them complain of being in effect 'diversified to death', since diversity issues are continuously raised in every part of their training programme. At the same time, the trainees are acutely aware of the enormous gap between the rhetoric of diversity policy

---

The previous paragraph makes reference to the following concepts:

+ equality;
+ diversity;
+ anti-discriminatory practice.

What do you understand by these terms? Are they linked or do they refer to different things?

---

on the one hand and the reality of implementing this in ways that respect and value the vast array of offenders' individual differences on the other. The dissonance created complicates and muddies the link between the strategic commitment to diversity and day-to-day

---

Can you identify any 'diversity dilemmas' that have arisen in the organisation where you work and/or study? How might such dilemmas be resolved in ways that are compatible with the equality/diversity policies of your organisation?

---

probation practice. In part, this 'implementation gap' can be blamed on the lack of resources deployed to manage offenders in the community in ways that take full account of their individual differences and diverse needs. As we have seen in the previous section, faced with hard choices over how scarce resources are to be used, most agencies have taken the decision to prioritise those areas of difference that are covered under the UK's existing equalities legislation.

However, the difficulties encountered in transposing diversity policy to everyday professional practice cannot be explained entirely by reference to a lack of resources. It is important to recognise that many of the 'diversity dilemmas' that professionals across the criminal justice system face cannot be resolved or answered by appealing to the diversity policies of their agencies. Practice cannot be 'read off' from policy in this way. As a result of years of experience of anti-racist community work, the writer of this chapter has come to appreciate that anti-racist practice can rarely if ever be deduced logically from a more general commitment to anti-racism. In the same way, taking the right 'diversity' decision, one that gives concrete expression to an agency's policy of valuing and achieving diversity, is rarely an easy or straightforward matter for practitioners.

Such practice dilemmas are normally best resolved through informal discussion among team members, especially when those members are drawn from a variety of agencies with different professional/organisational cultures and values. But here, too, concerns about 'saying the wrong thing' in relation to diversity may undermine confidence in discussing and debating practice dilemmas that have a diversity dimension to them. To this extent, there may be a grain of truth in the popular myth that 'diversity disempowers' if practitioners are worried about what their colleagues will say or do should they express uncertainty about how to resolve a difficulty that has a diversity dimension to it. Successful multi-agency collaboration is bound to be undermined when there are residual concerns over issues related to 'political correctness' and a worry that using an 'inappropriate' phrase may be seen by some as problematic.

SUMMARY OF KEY POINTS

+ Recent legislation in the UK has been shaped by the EU anti-discrimination directives and the Macpherson Inquiry into the murder of Stephen Lawrence.
+ The response to these twin pressures has seen criminal justice agencies and the public sector generally embrace diversity over the subsequent 10 years.
+ The evolving equalities legislation has resulted in diversity policies becoming subsumed within more general equality/community cohesion policies.
+ These agency policies give expression to little more than the statutory duty to foster greater equality in the areas of sex/gender, race and disability.
+ There are serious doubts over whether a general commitment to valuing and achieving diversity is either morally defensible or practically attainable.
+ Many criminal justice practitioners feel confused and concerned over how to translate their agency's diversity policy into effective practice interventions.
+ A general commitment to 'valuing and achieving diversity' is not particularly helpful to resolving the practice dilemmas that face practitioners.
+ Because of the above, there is a danger that a shared commitment to diversity will offer little to facilitate partnership working between practitioners from different agencies.

CONCLUSION

This chapter has focused on the challenging problems relating to diversity policy and practice in the criminal justice system and more widely across the public sector. We have seen that shifting political and legislative sands in both the UK and the EU have had a direct impact on the rise—and perhaps partial demise—of diversity across the public sector. Most public sector agencies still make ritual obeisance towards diversity in the most general sense but today this is frequently located within a broader commitment to 'achieving equality' and/or 'promoting community cohesion'. The chapter has tried to show that, in spite of the fine words contained in strategic plans committing agencies to valuing difference and achieving diversity, in practice most of the diversity/equality action planning of these agencies focuses on differences that are covered by the UK's equality and anti-discrimination legislation, namely sex/gender, race, disability, age, religion and sexual orientation. Further, and again in line with the laws relating to equality duties, we have seen that agencies have tended to prioritise differences related to sex/gender, race and disability in their action plans and in the deployment of resources to achieve the targets set. Finally, it has been argued that the conceptual confusion that surrounds the concept of diversity, the unwillingness to focus on practice where the diversity issues are frequently complex and fractured, and an over-emphasis on the rhetorical appeal of the call to respect and value difference at the expense of a more hard-nosed discussion of issues related to priority and practice, have left frontline criminal justice professionals in a state of confusion over how to square the diversity circle.

FURTHER READING

Clements, P. and Jones, J. (2006) *The Diversity Training Handbook: A Practical Guide to Understanding and Changing Attitudes.* London: Kogan Page.

Gelsthorpe, L. and McIvor, G. (2007) 'Difference and diversity in probation', in Gelsthorpe, L. and Morgan,

R. (eds) *Handbook of Probation*. Cullompton: Willan Publishing.

Hudson, B. (2007) 'Diversity, crime and criminal justice', in Maguire, M., Morgan, R. and Reiner, R. (eds) *The Oxford Handbook of Criminology*. Oxford: Oxford University Press.

REFERENCES

Cheetham, J. (1982) 'Some thoughts on practice', in Cheetham, J. (ed) *Social Work and Ethnicity*. London: Allen and Unwin.

CPS (Crown Prosecution Service) (2006) *Single Equality Scheme 2006–10*. London: CPS. Available at www.cps.gov.uk/publications/docs/ses_2006_2010.pdf

DTI (Department for Trade and Industry) (2005) *Women in the IT Industry: Towards a Business Case for Diversity*. London: DTI. Available at www.berr.gov.uk/files/ file9334.pdf

EOC (Equal Opportunities Commission) (1985) *Code of Practice: Equal Opportunity Policies, Practices and Procedures in Employment*. London: HMSO.

European Commission (2008) *Continuing the Diversity Journey: Business Practices, Perspectives and Benefits*. Luxembourg: Office for Official Publications of the European Communities.

Gregory, J. (1987) *Sex, Race and the Law: Legislating for Equality*. London: Sage Publications.

Grieve, J. and French, J. (2000) 'Does institution racism exist in the Metropolitan Police Service?', in Green, D. (ed) *Institutional Racism and the Police: Fact or Fiction?* Trowbridge: Civitas.

HMIC (Her Majesty's Inspector of Constabulary) (2000) *Policing London: Winning Consent*. Available at www.nationalarchives.gov.uk/ERORecords/HO/421/2/hmic/pollondn.pdf

HM Prison Service (2003) *Corporate Plan 2003–2004 to 2005–2006:Business Plan 2003–2004*. London: HM Prison Service. Available at www.hmprisonservice.gov.uk/assets/documents/10000153corporateplan2003-2006businessplan03-04.pdf

Home Office (2001) *Community Cohesion: A Report of the Independent Review Team Chaired by Ted Cantle (Cantle Report)*. London: Home Office.

Macpherson, W. (1999) *The Stephen Lawrence Inquiry: Report of an Inquiry by Sir William Macpherson*. Cm 4262-1. London: The Stationery Office.

Ministry of Justice (2009a) *NOMS Strategic and Business Plans: 2009–10 and 2010–11*. London: Ministry of Justice. Available at www.justice.gov.uk/publications/docs/noms-strategic-and-business-plans-2009-2011.pdf

Ministry of Justice (2009b) *Promoting Equality in Prisons and Probation: The National Offender Management Service Single Equality Scheme 2009–2012*. London: Ministry of Justice. Available at www.justice.gov.uk/publications/docs/noms-singleequality-scheme.pdf

Mitchell, M. and Russell, D. (1998) 'Fortress Europe, national identity and citizenship', in Carr, F. (ed) *Europe: The Cold Divide*. Basingstoke: Macmillan.

MPA (Metropolitan Police Authority) *HMIC Report 'Winning Consent': Recommendations relating to Consultation and Diversity*. Available at www.mpa.gov.uk/committees/x-cdo/2000/000728/08/#appendix01

MPS (Metropolitan Police Service) (2005) *Diversity Strategy 2005 Consultation*. London: MPS. Available at http://cms.MPS.police.uk/news/policy_organisational_news_and_general_information/diversity/diversity_ strategy_2005_consultation

MPS (2007) *Disability Annual Report*. London: MPS. Available at www.MPS.police.uk/dcf/equality_stm.htm

MPS (2008a) *Equalities Scheme 2006–10* (updated version). London: MPS. Available at www.MPS.police.uk/dcf/files/equality_stm/MPSEqualitiesScheme_full_3. pdf

MPS (2008b) *Gender Annual Report*. London: MPS. Available at www.MPS.police. uk/dcf/index.htm

NPS (National Probation Service) (2001) *A New Choreography: Strategic Framework 2001–2004*. London: Home Office.

Parekh, B. (2000) *Rethinking Multiculturalism: Cultural Diversity and Political Theory*. Basingstoke: Palgrave Macmillan.

Sassen, S. (1999) *Guests and Aliens*. New York: New Press.

Thompson, N.(2006) *Anti-Discriminatory Practice* (4th ed).Basingstoke: Palgrave Macmillan.

YJB (Youth Justice Board) (2009) *Workforce Development: Accelerate*. London: YJB. Available at www.yjb.gov. uk/en-gb/practitioners/WorkforceDevelopment/ HRandLearning/Accelerate

ETHICAL ISSUES IN CRIME CONTROL POLICY AND RESEARCH

Michael C. Braswell, Belinda R. McCarthy, and Bernard J. McCarthy

How should we approach problems related to crime control? We are spending increasing sums of money in areas of law enforcement and corrections, and we have continued to pass new legislation with an eye toward developing more effective crime control policies. Still, violent crime continues to increase. In addition, we have to contend with public perceptions regarding crime and the justice system's response that are largely shaped by the media. Newspaper headlines, television programs, and films each try to attract readers or viewers. How much is fact and how much is fiction? Whether founded entirely on fact or not, our citizens' fear of crime is certainly real to them.

An increasing awareness of the scope and nature of corporate crime challenges the abilities and resources of our justice system on additional fronts. Our traditional approach to controlling crime seems more comfortable when addressing familiar criminal behavior in such areas as burglary, robbery, and assault. The "bad guys" are typically more clearly defined. This is not always the case with much of corporate crime. Problems involving consumer safety, pollution, and other related issues often involve business executives who are considered upstanding members of their communities, and with the rapid development of the computer, such crimes are increasingly difficult to track down. In some ways it seems that our traditional approach to administering justice is simply not adequate to resolve the more sophisticated problems of much of the corporate world. Still, the demands of culture can encourage and stimulate us to develop new ways of thinking about crime and, as a result, more innovative responses to crime-related problems.

There are also a variety of ethical concerns surrounding criminal justice research. The scientific life provides no barrier to unethical conduct. The problem of employing unethical means to an otherwise desirable end is ever present in the research setting, where scientists are sometimes tempted to sacrifice the well-being of their subjects for the sake of scientific knowledge. Subjects can easily come to be viewed as the means to an end when the products of scientific research are equated with the utilitarian's "greater good."

In the name of scientific research, subjects may experience invasions of privacy, unknowing participation in simulated research experiments, and physical and emotional stress. In experimental research designs, which systematically withhold an intervention from one group while exposing another, research subjects may be denied participation in programs offering medical, educational, or psychological treatment.

Although the nature of the research task poses many ethical dilemmas, additional problems involve the political context of the research. No one wants to hear bad news about a popular new law enforcement or correctional program, least of all the people who administer the program. Researchers can find themselves in very difficult circumstances when results indicate that the program is not achieving its goals. Is the correct response to redo the results until a more palatable outcome is achieved, or to report findings honestly? How is this decision affected when the people administering the program are the same ones paying the researcher's salary?

Researchers should police themselves, using standards of professional ethics and censure to provide appropriate guidance. It must be recognized, however, that there are significant pressures against the objective exercise of such standards. Competition for research funds is considerable—few universities or research centers are interested in forfeiting research funds on ethical grounds, and few scholars are interested in creating any more obstacles for their research efforts than necessary. It is therefore very important to establish a climate of high ethical standards in the graduate schools that produce researchers and in the organizations ultimately responsible for conducting research.

SECTION
IV

Policing and Law
Enforcement

Overview of Policing and Law Enforcement in the United States

*Douglas Klutz and
Mark M. Lanier*

Law enforcement officers, or as they are more commonly called, "police," are the most visible arm of government. "Government" itself is not something we often observe; as the most visible component of government, the police place an important symbolic role. As the agency vested with the power to take citizens' liberty and life without specific judicial approval, the police function is extremely powerful in the criminal justice system. *Despite* their visibility and power, or perhaps *because* of their visibility and power, law enforcement officials are often unpopular with large segments of society (we suspect CJ majors reading this text will probably have a more positive view of police).

It is easy to criticize the police. They have to make split-second decisions in extremely stressful situations. These decisions are generally correct; however, sometimes they are wrong. We often neglect to applaud the numerous correct choices police make on a daily basis, but society is quick to pounce on the few incorrect decisions. This is perhaps inevitable and may serve to create a positive check on police behavior. One of the best contemporary illustrations of checks on police behavior stems from the evolution of social media technologies in our digital world. YouTube© videos can be uploaded almost instantaneously from the scene of an event and disseminated across social media outlets like Facebook© to the tune of thousands of viewers within minutes. This form of instant news to a mass audience creates new challenges in policing. On one hand, it creates even better checks on police abuse of power and authority. Conversely, these videos might provide just a small segment of the entire event, and in turn distort the true rendition of the situation. Video documentation that is piecemealed together can create a negative bias in public perception to policing efforts even when proper procedures are being followed. The evolution in technology places even greater pressures on the police and coupled with their visibility, makes police the widely studied, critiqued, and displayed (think of the television shows and movies devoted to police) part of American Criminal Justice. This section explores the history of American police, the source of their power, the art and science that underlie police practice, and the inherent problems that exist with policing a free, democratic society.

There are differences in policing between the United States and the rest of the world. Some policing systems are similar (e.g., American policing can trace their roots to the English, as can the Canadians). Even within the U.S. there are significant differences in policing; these variations are based on the level of jurisdiction: local, state, or federal and on the specific mandate (e.g., traffic enforcement, firearms control, drug eradication, tax evasion, etc.).

The widespread discretion of the Progressive Era led to abuses of power and unequal treatment. Members of minority groups in particular were subjected to uneven policing. The Professionalization era developed in response to these problems. The Professional era was characterized by uniform treatment, higher standards (both for employment and day-to-day practice), and further militarization of the police with specialized units such as vice and SWAT. The number of arrests and things such as response time measured police success. Unfortunately, response time means the crime has already occurred and the police simply "react" or respond. Crime skyrocketed in the U.S. during the professional era. The police solution was proactive or community-oriented policing.

The Community Policing or Proactive Policing era is still occurring. Proponents of community policing argue that the community itself has some responsibility for crime control and the police must work closely within specific neighborhoods to solve problems *prior* to a crime occurring. Perhaps the seminal article that argued for Community Policing ironically did not appear in a peer-reviewed academic journal. Instead James Q. Wilson and George Kelling published "Broken Windows" in the March 1982 edition of *Atlantic Monthly*. Academics, mostly at Harvard University's Kennedy School of Government and the National Center for Community Policing at Michigan State University (the nation's oldest Criminal Justice program), seized on this philosophy and greatly expanded its use. Today virtually every law enforcement agency incorporates some aspect of proactive or community-oriented policing; however, none have reached the full potential suggested by advocates.

True, or pure, community policing has characteristics that are simply not compatible with contemporary American police. For example, the hierarchical rank-and-file military structure (Chief, Deputy Chiefs, Colonels, Majors, Captains, Lieutenants, Sergeants, Patrol, etc.) under pure community policing would be a flat structure—one chief and everyone else. Each office would be "chief" or in charge of their specific neighborhood. There are many problems and reasons that this will never happen—although the Aurora, Colorado, Police Department under Chief Jerry Sloan attempted it. First, since police have followed the military model, rank is necessary to convey orders; rank signifies seniority, experience, and higher pay; and police unions would bitterly oppose abolishing rank, as would any officer who had achieved rank. This is but one example of why the idealized version of community policing will not be fully implemented. However, many important aspects are compatible with modern American policing and have already reduced crime and proven successful.

For example, community policing seeks to replace the isolation that officers experience by simply patrolling and the responding—"reacting"—to call for service. Instead it advocates officers walking (or riding bicycles) in the form of foot patrols. Police officers conducting foot patrols informally and conversationally get to know community residents in specific areas, work with the community to solve problems that develop into serious crime, and work to improve the area in ways seemingly unrelated to crime. Both small and large cities with serious crime problems have experienced success when implementing these strategies (e.g., New York, NY, and Flint, MI). Regardless of the style of policing employed by an agency (professional or proactive), there are certain intangibles that will affect police success or failure.

INTANGIBLES

The first intangible is officer discretion, or lack thereof. The Professional era sought to remove or greatly reduce officer discretion. This was due to abuses, excessive force, and community demand. Laws also aim to limit an officer's discretion. However, proactive policing argues that discretion is needed and will occur regardless of legal mandates. What exactly is police officer discretion? Think about a time you were pulled over for speeding or failure to yield. If a police officer lets you off with just a warning instead of issuing a citation, this is a perfect example of the concept of discretion being employed. The police officer might see it as a better use of their time and resources to focus on apprehending more serious offenders. Discretion is a concept that permeates the entire criminal justice system due to the reality of strained resources.

The second intangible is acknowledgment that the police have the authority to deprive citizens of their liberties in specific circumstances. Police also have the right to use physical, chemical, electronic, and deadly force against citizens. This is area that has caused the most public outcry against police due to abuse of power. It is also the area that causes the most anxiety for police administrators and government officials. Because the police are charged with maintaining order in the community, they are called to oversee any form of public unrest and demonstration. This is where most visible problems occur.

Birmingham, Alabama, police Chief Bull Conner is infamous for his use of police dogs and fire hoses against non-violent African American Civil rights demonstrators in the 1960s. In 1968, the Chicago, Illinois, police department under Mayor Daley violently beat protestors at the Republican National Convention. Police officers were also captured on videotape violently beating Rodney King in Los Angeles, California, and replayed on national news outlets for millions to see. The Rodney King incident sparked the infamous LA Riots and led to an intense standoff between the police and the LA community. After Hurricane Katrina, New Orleans police and National Guard went door to door taking legal firearms from citizens under martial law, then New Orleans Police officers were caught shooting unarmed citizens on a freeway bridge where they sought safety from rising Katrina floodwaters. All of these events were anomalies, rare events that statistically hardly ever occur, yet they are seared into the American consciousness and reflect negatively on police. All involved the police exceeding their legally mandated use of force. They all illustrate the importance of proper police procedure.

The final factor is that crime control and criminal apprehension are considered prime police functions, yet many of the factors that cause, contribute to, or increase crime are beyond the control of the police. For example, the police cannot influence the economy. The police cannot be in every home of drunken and abusive parents. The police cannot, seemingly, even control the flow of illegal drugs into our country. What the police can do is provide a visible, reassuring, and 24-hour available presence.

ART OR SCIENCE?

We want to conclude this section, and introduce you to the selected police readings, by asking you to consider and try to answer some fundamental questions. Is good policing the result of *scientifically* verified practices, procedures, and policies? For example, has significant research demonstrated that community policing is effective at reducing crime? Have tasers reduced the use of lethal force by police? Or, have tasers increased the frequency of police use of force? Can you apply scientifically derived policy in every situation? Are all traffic stops the same, for instance?

Or, on the other hand, is the "best" police officer the one who never needs to make an arrest (or use a taser) since s/he addresses *artfully* or creatively addresses crime problems before they escalate into an event requiring arrest? How do you measure this type of officer success? In short, is good policing the result of science or immeasurable, intangible personal skills of individual officers? Which should it be?

We present these as questions rather than as definitive statements because we do not know the answers! We suspect that the best answer is "a little of each." Clearly science and research provide a vital role in all aspects of modern society, policing included. However, individual officer characteristics, traits, beliefs, and practices might ultimately determine what "good" policing is. This is why careful pre-employment screening, experience, and careful monitoring are all important. Consider this analogy. Do you have some professors whose class you really look forward to attending? Do you have others whom you really dislike? They probably all desire to be liked and all wish to convey important useful knowledge, and hope they all present you the necessary information to be successful. So why the difference? As you read this section, bear in mind that policing is much more varied and difficult than teaching.

THE IDEA OF COMMUNITY POLICING

Victor E. Kappeler and Larry K. Gaines

Community policing is the first substantive reform in the American police institution since it embraced the professional model nearly a century ago. It is a dramatic change in the philosophy that determines the way police agencies engage the public. It incorporates a philosophy that broadens the police mission from a narrow focus on crime and law enforcement to a mandate encouraging the exploration of creative solutions for a host of community concerns—including crime, fear of crime, perceptions of disorder, quality of life and neighborhood conditions. Community policing, in its ideal form, not only addresses community concerns, but it is a philosophy that turns traditional policing on its head by empowering the community rather than dictating to the community. In this sense, policing derives it role and agenda from the community rather than dictating to the community. Community policing rests on the belief that only by working together with people will the police be able to improve quality of life. This implies that the police must assume new roles and go about their business in a very different way. In addition to being law enforcers, they must also serve as advisors, facilitators, supporters and leaders of new community-based initiatives. The police must begin to see themselves as part of the community rather than separate from the community. In its ideal form, community policing is a grassroots form of participation, rather than a representative top-down approach to addressing contemporary community life. In this sense, police become active participants in a process that changes power configurations in communities. It empowers the police to bring real-life problems of communities to those governmental authorities with the capacity to develop meaningful public policy and provide needed services to their communities.

Community policing also embodies an organizational strategy that allows police departments to decentralize service and reorient patrol (Skogan & Hartnett, 1997). The focus is on the police officer who works closely with people and their problems. This Community Policing Officer (CPO) has responsibility for a specific beat or geographical area, and works as a generalist who considers making arrests as only one of many viable tools, if only temporarily, to address community problems. As the community's conduit for positive change, the CPO enlists people in the process of policing and improving the quality of life in a community. The CPO serves as the community's ombudsman to other public and private agencies that can offer help. If police officers are given stable assignments to geographical areas, they are able to focus not only on current problems, but also become directly involved in strategies that may forestall long-range problems. Also, by giving people the power to set local police agendas, community policing challenges both police officers and community members to cooperate in finding new and creative ways to accurately identify and solve problems in their communities.

What started as an experiment using foot patrols and problem solving in a few departments exploded into a national mandate. As a result of the Violent Crime Control and Law Enforcement Act of 1994 and its provision to fund 100,000 more CPOs, most police departments in the United States now say they ascribe to community policing. McEwen (1994), in a national survey of police departments, found that 80 percent of the responding departments stated that they were using community policing. In the 1990s, community policing became an institutionalized and publicly understood form of policing (NIJ, 1997; Gallup, 1996). Even the media presented a limited but very positive depiction of community policing (Mastrofski & Ritti, 1999; Chermak & Weiss, 2006). "Community policing, or variations of it, has become the national mantra of American policing. Throughout the United States, the language, symbolism, and programs of community policing have sprung up in urban, suburban, and even rural police departments" (Greene, 2000:301). Additionally, community policing became a standard in many other countries. Police departments all over the world embraced the language of community policing. It has become ingrained throughout departments as managers attempt to develop strategies and tactics to deal with day-to-day issues and community problems.

Despite this impressive progress, many people, both inside and outside police departments, still do not know precisely what "community policing" is and what it can do. Although most everyone has heard of community policing, and most police departments say that they have adopted the philosophy, few actually understand how it works and the possibilities it has

for police agencies and communities. Indeed, it is viewed from a number of different perspectives. Does community policing work in practice or is it just a pipe dream? Is community policing simply a new name for police-community relations? Is it foot patrol? Is it crime prevention? Is it problem solving? Is it a political gimmick, a fad, a promising trend, or is it a successful new way of policing? Perhaps, David Bayley (1988:225) best summarizes the confusion about community policing:

> Despite the benefits claimed for community policing, programmatic implementation of it has been very uneven. Although widely, almost universally, said to be important, it means different things to different people—public relations campaigns, shop fronts, and mini-stations, re-scaled patrol beats, liaisons with ethnic groups, permission for rank-and-file to speak to the press, Neighborhood Watch, foot patrols, patrol-detective teams, and door-to-door visits by police officers. Community policing on the ground often seems less a program than a set of aspirations wrapped in a slogan.

There is substantial confusion surrounding community policing (Colvin & Goh, 2006). It stems from a variety of factors that, if not attended to, can undermine a department's efforts to successfully implement community policing. The sources of confusion are:

• Community policing's introduction into American policing has been a long, complicated process. It is rooted in team policing, police-community relations, and crime prevention;
• Some police departments are using community policing as a cover for aggressive law enforcement tactics rather than serving the needs of their communities. When this happens, confusion arises about a police department's real commitment to the community;
• The movement continues to suffer because some police departments claim to have implemented community policing, but they violate the spirit

or the letter of what true community policing involves and demands;

+ Most police agencies have adopted the language of community policing, but have yet to change their organizational structures and value systems to bring them into line with the community policing philosophy;

+ Community policing threatens the status quo, which always generates resistance and spawns controversy within police organizations (Gaines, Worrall, Southerland & Angell, 2003). This is because community policing challenges basic beliefs, which have become the foundation for traditional policing. It requires substantive changes in the way police officers and commanders think, the organizational structure of police departments, and the very definition of police work;

+ Community policing may generate public expectations that go unfulfilled, thus creating a backlash against community policing and the department (Klockars, 1988; Manning, 1988);

+ Community policing is often confused with problem-oriented policing and community-oriented policing. Community policing is not merely problem-oriented policing or becoming "oriented" toward the community. While community policing does use problem-solving approaches, unlike problem-oriented policing community policing always engages the community in the identification of and solution to problems rather than seeing the police as the sole authority in this process.

THE PHILOSOPHICAL AND STRUCTURAL FACETS OF COMMUNITY POLICING

Although community policing has taken a number of directions, there is a common overarching logic and structure to it. Four major facets occur when community policing is implemented: (1) the philosophical facet, (2) the organizational and personnel facet, (3) the strategic facet, and (4) the programmatic facet. All four facets must exist if a department is indeed implementing community policing. The following section explains the philosophy and structure of community policing along these lines, which is displayed in Figure 14.1.

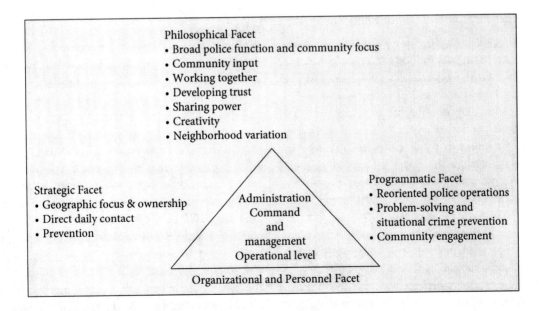

Figure 14.1 Applying Community Policing to a Department

The Philosophical Facet

Historically, even though there have been sporadic variations in the underpinnings or theme for American law enforcement, it has remained substantively a legal-bureaucratic organization focusing on professional law enforcement. Outputs such as numbers of arrests, reductions and increases in crime rates, volume of recovered property, numbers of citations issued, and a rapid response to calls have been more important than the end result of police work. This philosophy translated into a reactive police institution that does little to deal tangibly with social problems. A substantial body of research that began in the 1970s questions a number of the basic assumptions associated with the legal-bureaucratic model. Consequently, people began to search for a new philosophy and way to conduct police work.

Philosophically, community policing consists of a number of community-based elements that differentiate it from the traditional professional model. Some of community policing's core ideas are: (1) broad police function and community focus, (2) community input (3) concern for people, (4) developing trust (5) sharing power, (6) creativity, and (7) neighborhood variation.

Broad Police Function and Community Focus

Community policing is a philosophy of policing, based on the concept that police officers and people working together in creative ways can help solve contemporary community problems related to crime, fear of crime, quality of life, and neighborhood conditions. The philosophy is predicated on the belief that achieving these goals requires that police departments develop a new relationship with people by expanding their role in the community, allowing ordinary people the power to set local police priorities, and involving them in efforts to improve the overall quality of life in their neighborhoods. It shifts the focus of police work from responding to random crime calls to proactively addressing community concerns.

Community policing dictates that police departments move from law enforcement or crime fighting as the primary function. The police should have a broader function

that incorporates fear reduction, order maintenance, and community health. Indeed, fear reduction, order maintenance, and a community's overall health become the primary goals for the department supplanting crime reduction as the central organizing theme of police work.

This change in police philosophy emanates from three general observations. First, research examining police operations and crime statistics show that police are not effective, nor will they become effective, in controlling crime by law enforcement alone. Crime is a product of socio-economic conditions and poor public policy; therefore, it cannot be controlled through police action alone. Crime can be affected only through the control and manipulation of social conditions and public policy. The police can, at best, only manage and document most crime. Order maintenance and addressing the health of a community are legitimate police goals in themselves. For the police to have an impact on crime they must first impact social conditions and public policy.

Second, fear has a far greater debilitating effect on a community or individuals than does actual crime or crime rates. The fear of crime results in persons becoming virtual prisoners in their own homes; it inhibits commerce; and it imposes a subtle psychological cost to everyone (Hale, 1996). Fear destroys community because it isolates people and causes apprehension and suspicion. Research shows that oftentimes an individual's level of fear of crime bears no relationship to the actual amount of crime or victimization. The traditional approach to fear reduction, however, has been to attack crime, hoping that reducing crime will ultimately lessen fear. Because traditional policing relies primarily on motor patrol, which is basically reactive, there are obvious structural limitations that make it difficult to provide an effective means of confronting fear of crime separately and directly. The simple fact of the matter is that most crime in American society is not committed or solved on the streets, nor is it committed by strangers (Kappeler & Potter, 2005). Though crime prevention and police-community relations programs have helped broaden the traditional police role in ways that impinge on fear of crime, these peripheral attempts tended to chip away at problems that demand a bulldozer. Police-sponsored fear-reduction programs have the potential to yield positive results in a number of areas: community participation in crime prevention programs, increased crime reporting, and positive relations with people (see Zhao, Scheider & Thurman, 2002).

Community policing recognizes that fear of crime can be as much of a problem as crime itself. It is fear of crime that can trap the elderly in their homes or can make people afraid to venture out alone. Traditional policing efforts have had little, if any, ability to reduce fear. Fear was not even a consideration or objective in traditional policing. Periodically the police would make arrests that might have had a short-lived impact on fear, but for the most part, people sustained a fairly significant level of fear for which the police did little. This fear adversely affected people's daily lives. An important ingredient in community policing is active police involvement with people through a wide range of programs designed to reduce fear. Police must get people out of their homes and actively involved in their communities. This means police must become directly involved in community activities and become organizers of community. Police must also be careful not to promote unnecessary fear of crime to gain short-lived political and community support. Even more important, the police must address the sources that cause fear of crime—most often the politicization of crime and the media's construction of crime (Kappeler & Potter, 2005). Historically, political leaders and the media used fear of crime to promote their own interests and agendas. Today, they use terrorism for the same purposes.

Third, we have long debated the primary role of the police in society (Wilson, 1968; Manning, 1997), and over the past 30 years we have come to the point whereby everyone accepts that the police role has expanded well beyond law enforcement and "crook catching." In fact, reviews of police activities show that the majority of calls and the vast amount of time police spend on the job are of a non-crime nature (see, Gaines & Kappeler, 2008). The advent of community policing has resulted in a broader police mission evolving. Today, police should see crime, fear of crime, and the general quality of life all as being important parts of the police mission. Indeed, all of these societal factors are intertwined and interact with one another.

Community Input

The police have traditionally developed and implemented programs that involved community members. For the most part, however, these programs bordered on public relations schemes with little consideration given to community or human needs. Team policing programs of the 1970s and some of the police-community relations programs of earlier years never seriously involved and considered people, for the most part, the police were concerned with educating the public about their own needs rather than listening to the public about community needs. One of the most difficult aspects of community policing is determining the needs, concerns and desires of the community. Real community policing requires the police to set aside their own agendas to fairly and accurately measure the needs of the communities they serve. This requires not only listening to people but also acting on their concerns.

Community policing employs methods that cause the police to work more closely with people. To develop a better relationship, police departments have attempted to collect information about peoples' attitudes toward crime problems and the effectiveness of the police. For example, the police in Baltimore County, Reno, Atlanta, Newport News, St. Louis, and other cities have requested that community members complete surveys. Other departments have attempted to collect information by holding town or neighborhood meetings or by regularly meeting with minority and business groups. Gathering information from people allows the police to accomplish several tasks. Survey information can be used to evaluate the effectiveness of police programs in terms of fear reduction or attitudes toward the police. They also gauge behavior such as victimization or crime prevention efforts. Finally, they can also be used to collect data to assist the police in establishing community goals and priorities (Peak & Glensor, 1996). Community policing gets people involved in developing communities through two-way communication. Only by engaging the people and by collecting information from the public can the police begin to understand the needs and concerns of the community and begin to develop a community-based agenda.

Concern for People

The professional model of policing was institutionalized in the early 1900s. It dictated that police officers remain aloof and detached from the people they served. Police administrators believed that if officers were "professional" in their interactions with people, as defined by this aloofness and detachment, then there would be less possibility of police corruption and political intervention into police affairs, which were two significant problems at the time (Bracey, 1992).

This professional model, as represented in popular culture, was perhaps best typified by the popular 1950s television show that fictionalized real-life police situations—"Dragnet." The main character in the show was Sergeant Joe Friday, who always quipped, "Just the facts, ma'am," anytime a witness or victim became overly verbose or strayed from the facts. Sergeant Friday was portrayed as a professional, uncaring bureaucrat who cared only about making the arrest and little about the emotional or physical welfare of people with whom he came into contact. Police officers commanded respect and demanded answers; they were the persons holding all the power in any interaction with the public. Sergeant Friday's narrow mandate, to solve the crime, meant that he could not allow anything to interfere with achieving his goal. He had no time to listen to anyone's petty concerns, such as rowdy kids in the neighborhood, barking dogs, or potholes in the street. Sergeant Friday showed little sympathy or concern even for frightened victims, since their emotions simply got in the way of his opportunity to get the facts. Community policing drastically departs from the Joe Friday mind-set of policing. Today, community officers are concerned with health issues, zoning laws, barking dogs, or potholes, and it is just as important for officers to attend to victims' emotional needs, as it is to attend to their injuries.

Developing Trust

Community policing suggests that to get "the facts," the police must do more than attempt to impose their authority and sense of order on a community, that they must find new ways to promote cooperation between community members and the police. Information is the lifeblood of both traditional and community policing. Without information, police officers cannot solve crimes or social problems. The challenge the police face in getting information is that there must be some level of trust for people to cooperate with the police. Historically, the affluent and middle-class segments of a community had a great deal of trust for their police, but relationships with most poor and minorities left a great deal to be desired (Kappeler, Sluder & Alpert, 1998; Carter, 1985; Scaglion & Condon, 1980). In many instances, the police were seen as armed, uniformed strangers who could hurt you, but would not help you. The police were intimidating. For far too many in the community and for far too many years, contact with the police could lead to nothing good. Today, officers must continue fostering better relations with all segments of society. They must attempt to gain all community members' trust so that they can also gain their cooperation.

A prime example of the trust problem occurred in New Orleans in the mid-1990s. During that period, the police department was rife with corruption and the police were known for their brutality. The police essentially were out of control. The problem came to a culmination with the shooting of a police officer by another officer who was committing an armed robbery. During the period, people had good reason not to trust the police. Some people stated that when cases went to court, they would have more faith in the defendants' testimony than that of police officers. Not only was there a lack of trust of the police, people were afraid of them. After national attention and substantial public outcry, the city began a reform of the police department. History shows that it is a long and arduous process for a police department to reform itself and regain public support and trust (Kappeler, Sluder & Alpert, 1998).

In contrast, a central part of community policing is building trust. An important strategy is for community officers to directly communicate with as many individuals and groups of people as possible. CPOs not only portray themselves as friends and partners in the community—they must become friends and partners with the community. This philosophy ultimately fosters greater trust and cooperation.

Sharing Power

The third dramatic departure from the past is that a community policing agenda is influenced by the community's needs and desires, not just the dictates of the department. Historically, politicians and police administrators have set the agenda for policing, often without any regard or input from the people who were being policed. The police, from chief to line police officer, must recognize that people have a legitimate right to make demands on the police and control their agenda. Police departments, in addition to being law enforcement organizations, are service organizations, and as such, they should provide the best level of service possible. This means asking all community members, not just those supportive of the police or those with political power, about the kinds and levels of services they need and want. There is a wide divide in American society between those who have power and those who experience the victimization of crime—power sharing can close this divide.

Empowering a community requires an important adjustment in the line officer's thinking. Traditional officers who believe their authority should be sufficient to demand compliance may find it difficult to make the shift to sharing power as demanded by community policing. A traditional officer might find it difficult or unwieldy to chat with people about seemingly petty concerns, but this is an important part of community policing. It builds a bond between the police and community members, and it allows officers to gather information about what they should be doing. The best CPOs understand that people are not obstacles the officer must overcome to do the job, but a tremendous resource that can be tapped to make the community a safer, more harmonious environment. It also takes the sustained presence of a CPO to persuade people that the department now sees them in this new light, and that there is a real commitment to sharing power.

The community policing challenge includes involving people directly in efforts to identify and solve problems in the community. Community policing is not just a tactic to make people the eyes and ears of the department, it solicits their direct participation in identifying and solving problems. In this regard, community policing goes well beyond other programs such as foot patrol, neighborhood watch, crime prevention, or police-community relations. It might mean encouraging volunteers to help staff the local office. It could mean urging groups of parents to volunteer their time to coach summer athletic activities for kids. It often means asking businesses to donate goods, services, or expertise for neighborhood projects. Perhaps more importantly, it means organizing people to bring pressure on policy makers who have ignored community problems. The goal is for the CPO to recruit as many volunteers as possible and to organize them, so that the community has dozens of people working together to make a difference. Generating community involvement is one of the most difficult aspects of community policing (Skogan & Hartnett, 1997).

Creativity

The "Profiles in Community Policing," featured at the end of this book, demonstrate that community policing can work in any kind of police department, from large municipalities to small towns. Community policing can be successful because it is not a static program. It represents a philosophy whereby problems are identified and the community, not just the police, determines strategies and tactics. Community policing, in its ideal sense, is a form of accountable creativity whereby officers are allowed to experiment with a variety of tactics that directly involve people (Spelman, 2004). Community input and participation can be a rich source of innovation and creativity—it opens up possibilities that the police and political leaders may never consider. Since community members come from all walks of life, have a rich diversity of knowledge and occupational experience they can be a vital source of innovation. If police view people as know-nothings having little knowledge or nothing to contribute then innovation and creativity is not really possible. Accountability is interjected into the process because officers are forced not only to successfully address specific problems and community concerns but also to seek community involvement in possible solutions. This is a departure from traditional policing whereby a police department had a limited repertoire of enforcement-based programs, and all problems were essentially addressed using the same strategies and tactics. Also, officers in traditional policing were evaluated on response times, the numbers of arrests they made, and the numbers of citations they issued. These measures have little to do with community policing or the quality of police work (Stephens, 1996). Community police demands that the people become the judge of the quality of police service, rather than just relying on the cold crime accounting practices of the past.

Neighborhood Variation

Traditional, professional policing mandated that officers disavow the existence of discretion, and police every situation and neighborhood as if they were the same. That is, the police cultivated the image of full or uniform enforcement of the law. This, however, has never been a reality. There has always existed variation in law enforcement and service across communities, different neighborhoods and among people. Community policing, on the other hand, recognizes that a political jurisdiction is comprised of a number of communities or neighborhoods, each with its own set of problems and expectations. Suttles (1972) notes that people develop "cognitive maps" where they designate certain places as theirs, or their neighborhood. Stable neighborhoods have relative homogeneity of activity, people, and values. Because neighborhoods are defined by ethnic, religious, socioeconomic factors, and geographical boundaries differential expectations evolve within neighborhoods. Particular neighborhoods develop expectations not only about what the police should do, but about what types of behavior by residents and nonresidents is acceptable or unacceptable—police cannot afford to ignore these variations.

Community policing dictates that the police follow the "will of the community" when dealing with situations and enforcing the law. This means that police must first learn to accurately read the will of the community rather than projecting their will on the community. This requires the police to get out of their cars, engage the community, collect information and begin a dialog with the people living in the neighborhoods they police. It also requires the police to become more open minded and think outside their occupation filters and their own socialization. For the most part, there is little variation in how the police react to serious crimes or felonies. However, the police must be cognizant of community standards when policing minor infractions of the law and dealing with activities that may be acceptable in one neighborhood, but not another. For example, a person working on his car while parked on the street would not be acceptable in many upper- and middle-class neighborhoods, but it is a way of life for many people residing in poor neighborhoods. Police must begin to realize these variations and that the law is a tool that can be used to either build community or to cause conflict. Police officers must rely on community or neighborhood standards when encountering such situations. The police must maintain a balance between neighborhood values and overall legal goals and objectives. A poor person cited by the police for repairing his car on the street is not very likely to be either supportive of the police or to provide much needed information to solve a serious crime. In this situation police have not gained a partner but rather alienated a member of the community. The overall mission of the police should not be subordinated to the issuance of a traffic ticket or the enforcement of a petty violation of a city ordinance. Police must recognize variation in communities and use the law as a responsive tool rather than a tool of repression.

The Organizational and Personnel Facet

Community policing requires both a philosophical shift in the way that police think about their mission, as well as a commitment to the structural changes this form of policing demands. Police organizations must decentralize their organizations to be more responsive to the community. Community policing provides a new way for the police to provide decentralized and personalized service that offers every community member an opportunity to become active in the police process. In this way, people who have been isolated or disenfranchised, either because of economics or the lack of political power, can have both a voice in police activities and an interest in the development and health of their community. Community policing can help mitigate some of the harsh realities of modern life. Community policing is more than involving people in crime control, it is active involvement in enhancing the health of the community.

This helps explain why it is crucial to understand that community policing is a philosophy that offers a coherent strategy that departments can use to guide them in making the structural changes that allow the concept to become real. Community policing is not just a tactic that can be applied to solve a particular problem—one that can be abandoned once the goal is achieved. It implies a profound difference in the way the police view their role and their relationship with the community. Just adopting one or more tactics associated with community policing is not enough. Police must change their organizational structures, modify their personnel's orientation, and adjust their value systems to allow for community policing.

A police department's philosophy sets the stage for the development and implementation of strategies and specific tactics. A philosophical change, as required with the implementation of community policing, generally is enumerated in a department's mission statement. Mission statements should endorse the most essential aspect of the community policing philosophy: giving people the power to set the police agenda and developing people-based accountability of the police. Also a mission statement must find its expression in coherent strategies. That is, strategies must be employed that will further the overarching philosophy or mission of the department. The same can be said of the tactics that are used by officers as they attempt to attend to problems and concerns. A philosophy serves as the department's rudder, which helps guide the department as it serves the public.

Community officers answer calls and make arrests, just like any other police officer, but these activities actually are only a small part of the job. The community police officer acts as an innovator, looking beyond individual crime incidents for new ways to solve problems. They are the police department's direct link to the community, providing policing with a human touch as an officer who people know on a first-name basis and as a friend who can help. They act as catalysts, involving people in efforts to police themselves. They are minichiefs in beat areas, with the autonomy to do what it takes to solve problems. They are referral specialists, the community's ombudsman who can link people to the public and private services that can

help and who can jog reluctant bureaucracies to do the jobs they are supposed to do.

The hallmark of community policing is that policing is tailored to neighborhood needs. In some programs, the officers operate out of offices in schools, public housing, or even in shopping malls. Police service and access are decentralized so that the police are more approachable to community members. When the police are accessible, people are more likely to cooperate with them, to have a reduced fear of crime, and to provide crime-related information.

Some officers walk the beat, while others may ride a horse or a bike. The mode of transportation is not as important as the commitment to ensuring that the officer has the time and opportunity to talk with people formally and informally. The police mode of transportation is merely the vehicle by which officers get into contact with the members of the community.

The Strategic Facet

The police must develop strategies by which to implement the philosophy of community policing. Strategies provide guidelines for the development of specific programs. Community policing has at least three strategic facets. These facets include: (1) geographic focus and ownership, (2) direct, daily, face-to-face contact, and (3) prevention focus. These three parameters should guide operational planning when implementing community policing.

Geographic Focus and Co-ownership

Traditional law enforcement focuses on time, function, and place as opposed to geographies within a community. In terms of time, police departments revolve around shift work. Patrol officers, detectives, and other officers are assigned to shifts. Police effectiveness is measured by activities across time; that is, what occurred on a particular shift. In terms of function, police departments are highly specialized with a number of different units, patrol, criminal investigation, traffic, community relations, etc., responsible for their own unique tasks. Officers assigned to one functional area seldom have the time or inclination to work or worry about activities that fall into another functional area.

In fact, typically only the chief in small and medium departments and precinct commanders in large departments have full responsibility for a given geographical area. Specialization by time and task inhibits the evaluation, or even articulation, of policing at the neighborhood level.

For community policing to be successful, there must be some level of geographical permanence. Officers must work a geographical area on a permanent basis so that they become familiar with residents, activities, and social problems. Geography is not a sole matter of place, territory or location; it is the product of complex human interactions. Furthermore, if police officers are permanently assigned to an area, they hopefully will come to identify with the area and take greater care in safeguarding it and working to solve its problems. While the "territorial imperative" does not end police must begin to understand the human geography of the areas in which they work. Command staff must also come to identify with and take responsibility for "geographical" areas. Once there is a level of geographical accountability within police departments, officers and units will respond more effectively to human and neighborhood needs and demands.

The importance of stationing a CPO permanently in a specific beat rests on allowing the officer to co-own that particular piece of turf and to begin to understand how that space is created and given meaning by human subjects. The optimal size of each beat can differ dramatically from place to place, but it will always involve people and human interactions. The goal is to keep the geographic area small enough so that the officer can get around the entire beat often enough to maintain direct contact with the people who create it. In high-density areas, an officer might only be able to handle a few blocks at most, while in a relatively tranquil residential area of single-family homes, the officer's ability to cover the physical distance might be the primary limiting factor.

Another important consideration in setting up beats is for the department to identify areas of community cohesion. Whenever possible, it pays to not divide a distinct neighborhood so that they fall into two or more beats. Along these same lines, it is not a good idea to have more than one distinct neighborhood group in the same beat. The goal is to decentralize police service by dividing the area into natural and manageable units that are derived from human interactions not maps, so that people can receive quality police service regardless of whether they live in little-town, Texas, or mid-town Manhattan. Beats, where possible, should be as homogeneous and natural as possible.

A major misunderstanding about community policing stems from the misconception that the reward for freeing an officer from the patrol car transforms the officer into a visible deterrent to crime. While that may be seen as a useful by-product of freeing officers from the patrol car or even a specific tactic in a high-crime area, the more important purpose is to involve the officer in the life of the community. This allows officers to integrate into the community. Obviously, the size of the beat significantly affects the quality of this integration process.

Direct, Daily, Face-to-Face Contact

Community policing also rests on maintaining the same officers in the same beat every day. The goal is to involve officers so deeply in the life of the community that the officers feel responsible for what happens in their beats, and the people who live there learn to trust them and work with them, and hold them accountable for their successes and failures. Community officers should not be used as pinch hitters to fill vacancies elsewhere in the department, nor should they be rotated in and out of different beats. The only way that community policing can work is when both the officers and the residents can count on a continued, daily presence. This breeds familiarity on the part of the officers and community members, which is an important ingredient in community policing.

There is considerable debate around the question of whether community officers should be allowed to use cars for at least part of their shifts, simply to get around their beat areas more quickly. The optimal situation allows officers to walk or ride a horse, motor-scooter, or bicycle around the beat area, at least some of the time. These modes of transportation make it easy to stop and chat and to reassure people that the officer is concerned with them and their problems. Freeing officers from patrol cars altogether may be an essential step in reversing the pitfalls of traditional policing.

The danger in the traditional system's reliance on the patrol car is that the patrol car becomes a barrier to communication with people in the community. Officers trapped inside cars are segregated from the public. They become slaves to the police radio, which serves less as a link to people in the community and more as a means for the department to control the officers' behavior and activities. This is especially true in large cities where officers run from one dispatched call to another. In some cities, officers never have the opportunity to talk with pedestrians or business owners in their beat areas.

Prevention Focus

As previously alluded to, community policing dictates that the police be proactive rather than reactive to problems and situations. A crucial part of proaction is prevention. Prevention is a much more attractive alternative when dealing with crime as compared to enforcement because it reduces the level of victimization in a community. Prevention subsumes a number of operational possibilities. Prevention refers to ferreting out the problems and conditions that cause crime. In essence, the police must examine the conditions surrounding crime in an effort to develop effective measures of eliminating it. This requires think about crime in a very different way. For literally hundreds of years, police have seen crime as a product of the individual actions of "bad" people who make the decision to engage in crime, rather than viewing crime as an act of "agency" (the ability to freely choose) that is carried out under real social conditions "structure" (the social, political and economic conditions that guide a decision) choice. Patrol, criminal investigation, and other operational units must become actively involved in prevention and seeing the structural and social conditions that contribute to individual crimes.

Crime prevention units in police departments must become more involved and broaden their range of activities. Historically, crime prevention in a given police agency has centered on a few activities such as home and business surveys. Crime prevention units must become more active, and in addition to their regular target-hardening activities, they should assist operational units by serving as a resource when dealing with specific crime problems or hot spots, and they should work closely with crime analysis and operational units to identify crime, problems and solutions.

A part of a police department's crime prevention responsibility includes attacking the conditions that contribute to, or result in, crime. Police departments must take the lead in implementing programs that attack causes of crime. Here, the police can assume a number of social welfare roles. Police departments now have programs to assist and refer people in need to appropriate social welfare agencies; they have initiated educational and recreational programs aimed at providing wholesome life skills experiences for underprivileged youth; and in some cases, police departments have begun to provide direct services to the needy. Crime prevention also means helping people at risk attain a minimum standard of living.

The Programmatic Facet

The above philosophy and strategies must be operationalized into specific tactics or programs. For the most part, community policing comes to life through: (1) reoriented police operations, (2) problem-solving and situational crime prevention, and (3) community engagement.

Reoriented Police Operations

The traditional police response to crime primarily consisted of random, routine patrols. It was believed that random patrols would deter crime through a consistent, unpredictable police presence. If patrols were unable to prevent crime, then officers, as a result of their distribution across beats, would be in a good position to observe the criminal activity and apprehend criminals. Finally, if this failed, detectives would be dispatched to investigate the crime and make arrests.

Community policing requires going beyond this reactive strategy. It means not waiting to be called, but instead identifying and targeting problems and implementing solutions. Police operational units must use foot patrols, directed patrols, surveys, and alternatives to random patrol to target community problems. In other words, the police must devise and implement police strategies based on the problems at hand. Community policing requires the police to tailor services to community needs. The police must ensure that they have an intensified police presence through larger numbers of positive community contacts.

Problem-Solving and Situational Crime Prevention

Two primary tactics in community policing include problem-solving (Eck & Spelman, 1987) and situational crime prevention (Clarke, 1992). Problem-oriented policing evolved as a result of the writings of Herman Goldstein and work by the Police Executive Research Forum (PERF). Goldstein (1979; 1990) observed that American police had devolved into call-takers. That is, police officers typically responded rapidly to calls for service, attempted to deal with problems or issues as quickly as possible, and then returned to their cars so as to be available to respond to another call. Goldstein noted that the police did little substantively when responding to calls for service, and if the police were to be effective; officers must devote more time and attention to calls. They must attempt to understand the issue at hand and provide some meaningful, not just short-term, solution. In other words, the police should engage in problem solving, rather than focusing solely on responding. Goldstein's idea evolved into problem solving, which now falls under the umbrella of community policing.

Problem-solving consists of the following four-step process: (1) specific identification of the problem, (2) careful analysis of the problem and its attributes, (3) identification of possible solutions, and (4) implementation of a solution and a subsequent evaluation to measure the effectiveness of the solution. Simple questions such as: What is the problem? What is causing the problem? What can I do to resolve it? These questions should be asked by officers when attempting to solve problems. Effective solutions require comprehensive responses. When effective problem solving occurs, solutions that go beyond traditional police responses become the norm. Such solutions include encouraging the city to demolish an abandoned

building being used as a crack house; strictly enforcing alcohol laws in and around bars and taverns that experience high levels of crime; or encouraging people to construct fences around residential areas to prevent transients from entering the neighborhood and committing property crimes. Problem solving ventures beyond responding to and documenting calls. It represents a sincere attempt by the police to eliminate the conditions and problems that result in community problems and calls to the police.

Situational crime prevention, a form of problem solving, comprises "opportunity-reducing measures that are: (1) directed at highly specific forms of crime, (2) that involve the management, design, or manipulation of the immediate environment in as systematic and permanent a way as possible, and (3) so as to increase the effort and risks of crime and reduce the rewards as perceived by a wide range of offenders" (Clarke, 1992:4). Adherents to situational crime prevention believe that crime is a product of "rational choice" where criminals weigh the likelihood of being discovered with the potential benefits of the act (Cornish & Clarke, 1987). They believe increases in difficulty in committing crime or likelihood of apprehension result in reduced levels of crime. This approach, however, does not really get at the social conditions that general crime. Often it only diverts or displaces crime from one location to another and does not involve community development as a crime prevention effort. While situational crime prevention and problem solving play a role in community policing, they are not by themselves community policing.

In essence, community policing requires that police officers be creative when devising solutions and attacking community problems. Police must think "outside the box" and consider nontraditional solutions to community problems. Too often, police officers restrict their thinking to the same old responses to problems. Problem solving requires a substantial amount of innovativeness, and police managers must give officers the freedom to innovate.

Community Engagement

Community engagement implies that the police must depart from the "Joe Friday" attitude associated with the professional model, and work with individuals and groups. Community policing dictates that the community become involved in protecting itself. People must realize that crime is not the exclusive domain of the police and government. People can become involved in a variety of ways. They can form neighborhood watches or patrols, report criminal or suspicious activities, become involved in sports or educational activities for disadvantaged youth, assist nongovernmental agencies in providing social services to the disadvantaged, or volunteer services. The police must encourage, motivate, or otherwise induce people to become involved in their communities. This is best with police supporting opportunities for involvement. In other words, create a need, and the police and the community will fulfill it with the appropriate amount of effort.

The police must also become involved in community building and empowerment. In some cases, a neighborhood or community will be so disorganized that it does not have the resources to become involved in helping itself. In these instances, the police must engage the community, identify leaders, and begin building the community. The police must work with religious and civic leaders to increase the level of neighborhood governance, and they must work to improve governance even when a neighborhood has a strong infrastructure. There should be a reduction in crime concomitant with increases in local governance. In essence, the police must assist in building a neighborhood's ability to ward off crime.

Community engagement is often best accomplished through the establishment of partnerships. Not only must the police partner with community and neighborhood leaders, the police must also work with other governmental and private agencies. Many governmental agencies have not embraced the concept of community policing. Rather, they still view their roles in the community as bureaucracies whose purpose is to follow bureaucratic rules when serving clients. The police must be leaders in identifying partner agencies and encouraging their involvement in addressing community problems.

The above sections provide a theoretical foundation for community policing. Community policing, as a model, is very complex because it entails implementation throughout a police department, not just selected units or officers. It is complex because it requires that the police department, at a number of levels, be in synchronization with the community it serves. Finally, it is complex because it requires not only that police agencies do different things (i.e., meet with the community, allow the community to decide police operations, or emphasize order maintenance over law enforcement), but it also means that police departments perform many of their old tasks differently.

There is an obvious danger in suggesting that police administrators can consider the elements that make up community policing as a shopping list from which they can pick and choose the things that sound easy to adopt and ignore those that are difficult to implement. We will discuss the consequence and practice of picking and choosing among the various programs and tactics that have become associated with community policing in the concluding chapter of the book. Yet, community policing can and must take different forms in different areas, depending on the internal dynamics of the department and the external situations in the community. Ultimately, the sincerity of the commitment to the philosophy probably matters more than the particular strategies or tactics, and some departments may have good reason to phase in aspects of community policing over time.

WHAT COMMUNITY POLICING DOES NOT CONSTITUTE

The above sections provide a fairly in-depth discussion of the idea of community policing. Community policing is a comprehensive philosophy that affects every person and part of a police department. It is also an overarching philosophy that dictates a department's operational strategies and tactics. To reinforce understanding of what community policing is, it is important to understand what community policing does not constitute. By understanding what does not constitute community policing, we get a better idea of what needs to occur if it is to be implemented correctly.

Community policing is not a technique. Many police departments have moved away from the old quasi-military model, but many others are rapidly embracing

Figure 14.2 Traditional Versus Community Policing Models

QUESTION	TRADITIONAL POLICING (TPM)	COMMUNITY POLICING (CPM)
1. Who are the police?	A *government agency* principally responsible for law enforcement.	*Police are the public* and the public are the police; police officers are those who are paid to give full-time attention to the duties of every citizen.
2. What is the relationship of the police to other public service departments?	*Priorities often conflict.*	The police are *one department among many responsible* for improving the quality of life.
3. What is the role of the police?	Focusing on *solving crimes.*	A broader *problem-solving* approach.
4. How is police efficiency measured?	By detection and *arrest rates.*	By the *absence of crime and disorder.*
5. What are the highest priorities?	*Crimes* that are high value (e.g., bank robberies) and those involving violence.	Whatever *problems* disturb the community most.
6. What specifically do police deal with?	*Incidents.*	Citizens' *problems* and concerns.
7. What determines the effectiveness of police?	*Response times.*	*Public cooperation.*
8. What view do police take of service calls?	Deal with them only if there is no *real police work* to do.	Vital function and great *opportunity.*
9. What is police professionalism?	Swift/effective response to *serious crime.*	Keeping close to the *community.*
10. What kind of intelligence is most important?	*Crime intelligence* (study of particular crimes or series of activities crimes).	Criminal intelligence (*information about* individuals or *groups*).
11. What is the essential nature of police accountability?	*Highly centralized;* governed by rules, regulations, and policy directives; accountable to the law.	Emphasis on *local accountability* to community needs.
12. What is the role of headquarters?	To provide the necessary *rules and policy* directives.	To preach organizational *values.*
13. What is the role of the press liaison department?	To *keep the "heat" off* operational officers so they can get on with the job.	To *coordinate* an essential channel of communication with the community.
14. How do the police regard prosecutions?	As an *important goal.*	As *one tool* among many.

Source: Adapted from M. Sparrow (1988). *Implementing Community Policing.* Perspectives on Policing, pp. 8–9. Washington, DC: National Institute of Justice and Harvard University.

military tactics under the language of community policing (Kappeler & Kraska, 1998; Kraska & Kappeler, 1997). Additional movement and redirection by many departments is required if they are to embrace the spirit of community policing successfully. Regardless, community policing is not a technique that departments can apply to a specific problem, but an entirely new way of thinking about the role of the police in the community. It says that the police must focus on addressing community concerns rather than their own agendas.

Community policing is not public relations. Improved public relations is a welcome by-product of community policing, though not its sole or even primary goal. Public relations units, however, tended not to attempt to help the community or focus on community needs, but rather they were designed to "sell" the police department. The underlying philosophy was that a substantial amount of dissatisfaction with the police was the result of people not understanding the police and the difficulties facing them as they enforce the law (Wintersmith, 1976). Police-community relations programs were seen as vehicles to educate the public and lessen the strains between the police and community. Community policing, on the other hand, enhances the department's image because it is a sincere change in the way the department interacts with people in the community. Police-community relations, by and large, was appearance, while community policing is substantive. It treats people as partners and establishes a new relationship based on mutual trust and shared power. The traditional system often makes people feel that the police do not care about their needs (see, Reisig & Parks, 2000; Sampson & Jeglum-Bartusch, 1998). In traditional departments, officers often see people in the community as "them," those nameless and faceless strangers whose reluctance to cooperate and share what they know makes them indistinguishable from the criminals (see Van Maanen, 2006). Community policing instead treats people in the community as an extension of "us."

Community policing is not soft on crime. Critics suggest that community policing's broad mandate, its focus on the community as opposed to crime, and its use of tactics other than arrest to solve problems detract from a proper focus on serious crime. CPOs often face ridicule from fellow officers who call them "lollicops" or the "grin-and-wave" squad. The reality is that CPOs make arrests just like other officers do, but CPOs deal with a broader variety of community problems in addition to crime, not as a substitute for addressing serious crime. In fact, as Scott and Goldstein (2005:2) observe, "There is growing evidence that by addressing the conditions that underlie crime and disorder problems, rather than merely looking to arrest offenders, police can more effectively prevent and control such problems." The major difference is that CPOs ask themselves whether an arrest will solve the problem, will it make matters worse, and what solutions can prevent this problem from happening again in the future?

Crime analysis routinely shows that the majority of calls for service come from a relatively small number of locations (Sherman, 1987). An important ingredient of community policing is to focus on these "hot spots." But merely focusing on the hot spots fails to recognize that police behavior and programs influence who will and who will not call the police for assistance. Furthermore, applying location-oriented policing based on traditional notions of what calls are worthy of a police response violates the spirit of community policing. If a person calls the police, the problem is important to them and CPOs should see this as an opportunity no matter how trivial the call seems. CPOs must dissect these areas, determine what is occurring in terms of problems, and develop strategies for reducing problems. CPOs must also be mindful that their behaviors, programs, and data collection techniques, at least in part, determine what a "hot spot" is. By way of example, one rarely hears police speak of a concentrated group of drug users as a hot spot for the transmission of HIV, a hotbed of unemployment, or an area in the city with juvenile crime problems as devoid of social activities for youth. Community policing dictates that officers consider strategies and tactics, which include, but are not limited to, arrest and suppression. This does not mean that community policing is soft on crime; it means that community policing is smart about crime and open to suggestions on solving broader social problems that generate crime.

Community policing is not flamboyant. When a SWAT team successfully disarms or kills a sniper or a barricaded person, their work makes the headlines. When police officers engage in high speed pursuits it often makes to nightly news. When a CPO helps organize a summer softball league for idle neighborhood youngsters, the long-term impact may be equally as dramatic, but the effort will not rate a feature on the nightly TV news. It very likely will not be picked up by the media. An officer may not experience the cultural satisfaction associated with the crimefighter image. The media reinforces the image of the macho police officer whose job is glamorous, tough, and often dangerous (Kappeler & Potter, 2005; Kasinsky, 1994). The hero myth and "warrior fantasy" (Kraska, 1996; Crank, 2004), which accounts for a substantial degree of resistance to community policing, also appeals to police officers themselves. Community policing recognizes that the job gets done through steady, hard work, not warrior images and tactical exercises. CPOs must learn to defer traditional-cultural sources of gratification and notoriety and focus on the job and the long-term benefits of community building.

Community policing is not paternalistic. Police departments are organized as a paramilitary hierarchy where those at the top, to some extent, expect to set the department's agenda, based on their experience and expertise. This organizational structure and mentality often extends beyond the police department itself and is manifested in the way officers typically interact with the community (Kappeler, Sluder & Alpert, 1998). In its most extreme form, the message to the average person is that the police think people do not know enough about police work to do much more than pay taxes and respond to officers when questions are asked. The traditional, paternalistic police attitude suggests that crime is so complex and difficult that it must be left in the hands of skilled professionals specifically trained for the job. How many police officers, however, are trained at creating jobs and social activities for youth? How many police officers know the signs of mental and physical health problems? How many police officers know the relationship between crime, mental health, and the provision of meaningful activities for youth? Simply ordering around people and officers does nothing to affect crime. Community policing threatens those who enjoy the traditional system, because it requires that police superiors empower officers and people with the decision-making authority to properly serve communities.

Community policing is not an independent entity within the department. Ultimately, the community policing philosophy must inundate the entire department. There are a number of ways of implementing community policing, including doing so gradually. Piecemeal arrangements include the formation of a special unit or concentration on specific geographical areas. In fact, it is virtually impossible to suddenly and comprehensively implement community policing in all but the smallest departments. When community policing is implemented piecemeal, it can generate tremendous pressure on the CPOs, who are the most visible expression of the new commitment. The challenge is finding ways to demonstrate to noncommitted members of the department how the community policing philosophy works.

Patrol officers in particular must be shown that CPOs not only help them by providing information, but also that they help ease tensions between the police and the community, which can be a particular problem in minority neighborhoods. In the Flint, Michigan, experiment, a foot patrol officer arrived on the scene shortly after patrol officers had responded to a call about a man brandishing a gun. The foot officer was able to tell his motor patrol peers that the man inside was known as a heavy drinker, and that his wife routinely visited her sister when he got drunk. A phone call there confirmed that the wife was safe and had her children with her, and that the man was probably asleep in the back bedroom. When the officers entered, they found the man passed out in bed as predicted. By working together, the motor officers and the CPO solved the problem with the least risk to themselves and others and avoided using a SWAT team. This is quite a different approach to the problem when compared to the use of paramilitary teams using force to extract people from their homes. CPOs are able to assist other officers because of the intimate knowledge they amass as a result of close ties with the community—thus, hopefully reducing the need for force-based actions.

Community policing is not cosmetic. Unlike crime prevention and police-community relations programs, community policing goes beyond providing information and expressing goodwill. Community policing requires that departments make substantive changes in how the department interacts with the public. Community policing broadens the police mandate to focus on proactive efforts to solve problems. CPOs are simply the patrol officers who serve as community outreach specialists, offering direct, decentralized, and personalized police service as part of a full-spectrum community policing approach that involves the entire department in new community-based efforts to solve problems.

Unlike limited proactive or community-relations efforts of the past, community policing not only broadens the agenda to include the entire spectrum of community concerns, but it offers greater continuity, follow-up, and accountability. It is important to understand that community policing goes beyond handing out brochures, making speeches, talking with community leaders, telling people how to guard against crime, and urging fellow officers to treat people with respect. As line officers directly involved in the community, CPOs have the opportunity to make real, substantive changes.

In Florida, a CPO concerned about the poverty and high unemployment in his beat area actively solicited leads on jobs, which he posted in the neighborhood community policing office. Officers in the Jefferson

County, Kentucky, Police Department participated in neighborhood programs in public housing where youths were tutored in reading and mathematics. Community policing's proactive focus goes beyond target hardening, street sweeps of so-called hot spots, and other relatively superficial solutions, to initiating creative efforts that attack the very social fiber of crime problems. Such solutions hold the promise of long-term changes whose full impact may not become fully evident for years.

Community policing is not just another name for social work. The broad constellations of problems that plague society, especially in the inner city, defy simple solutions. Yet critics of community policing think that involving officers in efforts that have not traditionally been viewed as part of the police mandate is not only wasteful, but also silly. Traditionalists insist that the police have their hands full trying to battle serious crime, so efforts that detract from that effort not only waste valuable time and money, but they can erode the credibility and authority of the police. Their attitude is that the police should leave social work to the social workers, so that the police can focus all their energies on their real and important job of fighting crime.

Yet, this position ignores the fact that serious crime constitutes only a very small portion of what the police are called upon to do (Gaines & Kappeler, 2008). Indeed, if the police actually attempted to limit their mandate solely to crime, it would be almost impossible for most departments to justify the bulk of their budgets, especially since crime is declining dramatically (Kappeler & Potter, 2005). The fact is police officers are already involved in many non-law-enforcement activities that have little, if anything, to do with serious crime. These activities include: crowd control at public events, protecting politicians, issuing traffic tickets, providing people with directions, investigating accidents, and helping stranded motorists. The issue is not whether the police should become involved in efforts that do not directly focus on serious crime, but what other kinds of services the police should provide. Is it more effective to have another police officer issuing traffic citations or to have an officer in public schools speaking to youths about the hazards of drinking and driving or the unsafe operations of motor vehicles?

The police officer must be many things, law enforcer and peace officer, armed symbol of authority and part-time social worker. It is this blend of force and compassion that makes the job so potent and unique. No other job in civilian society permits a person to choose from an array of responses that range from flashing a friendly smile to using deadly force.

Community policing is not elitist. One of the biggest difficulties that CPOs often face is that they are heroes in the community, but objects of sarcasm and scorn among their peers. Some of the resentment stems from CPOs receiving seemingly preferential treatment or special consideration by the department. Left unchecked, this friction can erupt into outright hostility. Departments that launch new community policing efforts must pay particular attention to educating everyone in the department about the community policing philosophy, the role of the CPO, and how this new way of policing can benefit everyone in the department directly. It takes constant reinforcement from the top to explain that CPOs are not being treated like an elite corps, but as the department's direct link to the community. It is also important to establish CPO standards and allow everyone the opportunity to become involved. If everyone is given an opportunity to participate, it generally reduces some of the hostility.

Community policing is not designed to favor the rich and powerful. The dramatic surge in drug-related murders in Washington, DC, at the end of the 1980s prompted more than one commentator to suggest that if these murders were occurring in an affluent enclave nearby such as Georgetown, the police would be forced to take more action. That damning indictment that the police pay more attention to the problems of the rich and powerful deserves a closer look because it offers more than a kernel of truth.

The fact is, of course, that the odds are that an upscale community like Georgetown will never suffer a similar spate of drug-related murders. The mistake is to think that this is because most of the residents of Georgetown obey the law, while the majority of those who live in poor neighborhoods in the District of Columbia do not. But what it does mean is that the high price tag required to afford to live in Georgetown means the community does not suffer from poverty, unemployment, illiteracy, over-crowdedness, substandard education, declining health care, or despair, the myriad of social ills that plague many inner-city neighborhoods. Crime clusters in neighborhoods that already suffer from social and economic problems, and these problems can overwhelm the people forced to live there.

Yet there may well be more than a little truth to the persistent allegations that the police often accede to pressures to pay more attention to the wants and needs of the rich and powerful. Though this can include paying attention to even the most serious crime of murder, any gap in the level of service between rich and poor is likely to grow even wider in the level of response for less important calls for service. In fact, one of the most common complaints from inner-city residents is under-enforcement of the law (Walker, 1994). Inner-city residents complain that the police do not give their problems the same consideration that they give to problems in more affluent communities.

It is easy to see why the police might hustle faster to investigate an abandoned car, up on blocks with no wheels, if the call comes from a senator in Georgetown rather than someone from a bad section in the District. The first reason is that the police in Georgetown may well be far less busy, because there are fewer emergency calls demanding an immediate response. Second, that abandoned car would be a relative rarity in Georgetown, which makes it seem more suspicious. And the unfortunate and unavoidable third reason is that a Senator who is unhappy with the police response can do far more to make problems for the department. The Senator may well know the chief personally and would have few qualms about calling at home to complain. Senators also have access to the media, a bully pulpit from which they can denounce the department's inefficiency. Poor people, on the other hand, seldom have any access whatsoever when they feel grieved as a result of government inaction or insufficient action. Community policing is egalitarian in the sense that it says that regardless of whether you have money and power, and despite whether you do or do not vote or pay taxes, all people deserve direct assistance and support from the police. Community policing requires that every area within a city be evaluated and serviced. Community policing mandates that the police not

disregard the needs of the poor, disadvantaged, or least powerful in society (see Bursik, 2000; Taylor, 2001; Velez, 2001). Research shows that officers who value equality are more willing to work with minorities (Zhao, He & Lovrich, 1999). In fact, the police can play an important role in leveling many of the disadvantages created by the political and economic system.

Community policing is not "safe." Allowing officers the freedom to attempt creative solutions to problems carries with it the risk of mistakes that can range from the embarrassing to the disastrous. The traditional system instead focuses on routinizing tasks and codifying procedures as a way to eliminate the potential for mistakes that can threaten the department's reputation.

At issue, of course, is whether police officers are educated professionals who can be trusted to do their jobs. Community policing dictates that police departments must learn to suffer the occasional mistakes, so that officers can bring the full impact of their education, training, experience, professional instincts, and imagination to bear on solving community problems. History shows that the traditional approach is far from being error-free, and that treating personnel as if they cannot be trusted cannot eliminate problems.

The preceding sections have laid out the idea of community policing. Our discussion shows that community policing represents a significant departure from the way policing has been thought about in the past.

Community policing is not a series or bundle of programs. Although many departments have implemented a number of new programs under the rubric of community policing, they have not yet achieved an operational level whereby they should declare themselves a community policing department. Too often, programs are implemented in a vacuum, whereby they have little contact with other units and programs. Administrators fail to recognize that, for most problems, there is no quick fix, and that problems are complex, often requiring substantial effort to solve. Previous sections in this chapter examined community policing's comprehensiveness in terms of philosophy, organization, strategy, and programming. Each of these dimensions must be addressed for a department to truly implement community policing effectively. A series or bundle of programs, although having the appearance of community policing, will not be as effective as a comprehensive approach.

Community policing is not merely problem-oriented policing. Problem-oriented policing emphasizes social problems and holds the police solely accountable and responsible for addressing these concerns. Community policing recognizes that the police alone cannot solve social problems and that the community must be engaged in a meaningful way if change is to occur. Under the problem-oriented policing approach, the community may or may not be engaged in the identification and control of a community problem. Under community policing, there is always a collaborative level of cooperation between the police and the community. In fact under community policing the police mobilize the community for problem solving. Michael Scott (2000:98) summarized the difference in the following passage:

> Community policing strongly emphasizes organizing and mobilizing the community, almost to the point that doing so becomes a central function of the police; problem-oriented policing advocates such efforts only if they are warranted in the specific context of addressing a particular problem. Under community policing, certain features of police organizational structure and policy, like geographic decentralization and continuity in officer assignments to neighborhoods, are deemed essential; under problem-oriented policing, many of these features are seen as helpful, but not essential—problem-oriented policing can be done under a variety of organizational arrangements. Community policing emphasizes that the police share more decision-making authority with the community; problem-oriented policing seeks to preserve more ultimate decision-making authority for the police ...

Problem-oriented policing without community policing retains the traditional authoritarian top-down approach to community problems and does not involve the power sharing necessary to make real changes in the community. If the police are not willing to share power and decision making with the community, there is little chance that the community will embrace the police, the problems the police deem necessary to address, or the solutions they come up with in isolation. Problem-oriented policing without community policing can quickly erode into aggressive law enforcement practices that foster conflict and divide the police from the community. In such a situation police are merely moving crime around like deck chairs on the Titanic, all the while ignoring that they are heading for an iceberg. Problem-oriented policing without community policing is merely the repackaging of traditional policing which has been shown to have devastating social consequences (we trace these consequences in the next chapter).

RECONCILING LAW ENFORCEMENT WITH COMMUNITY POLICING

Community policing represents a departure from traditional reactive law enforcement. It de-emphasizes the law enforcement function, emphasizes order maintenance and community building, as well as the provision of services to the public. Indeed, only a small percentage of police activities and calls for service relate to the law enforcement function (Gaines & Kappeler, 2008). There has been some criticism of community policing and its new direction. For example, Johnson (1997) notes that the community development goals of community policing are noble, but it is questionable whether the police can actually change value systems and cultural norms. He argues that family, peer, and community pressures and influences play a larger role in shaping identities than do surrogate associations with police officers. While there is truth to this assertion, values and culture are expression of the real concrete living conditions of a community—not some ether that magically appears. Regardless, the police must realize that they are confronting a monumental task when attempting to change a community's culture. Some would even argue that this falls outside the scope of law enforcement—but at some point, the scope of policing must be revolutionized.

Figure 14.3 Selected Comparisons Between Problem-Oriented Policing and Community Policing Principles

PRINCIPLE	PROBLEM-ORIENTED POLICING	COMMUNITY POLICING
Primary emphasis	Substantive social problems within police mandate	Engaging the community in the policing process
When police and community collaborate	Determined on a problem-by-problem basis	Always or nearly always
Emphasis on problem analysis	Highest priority given to thorough analysis	Encouraged, but less important than community collaboration
Preference for responses	Strong preference for alternatives to criminal law enforcement be explored	Preference for collaborative responses with community
Role for police in organizing and mobilizing community	Advocated only if warranted within the context of the specific problem being addressed	Emphasizes strong role for police
Importance of geographic decentralization of police and continuity of officer assignment to community	Preferred, but not essential Essential	Essential
Degree to which police share decision-making authority with community	Strongly encourages input from community while preserving ultimate decision-making authority to police	Emphasizes sharing decision-making authority with community
Emphasis on officers' skills	Emphasizes intellectual and analytical skills	Emphasizes interpersonal skills
View of the role or mandate of police	Encourages broad, but not unlimited role for police, stresses limited capacities of police and guards against creating unrealistic expectations of police	Encourages expansive role for police to achieve ambitious social objectives

Source: Scott, M. (2000). *Problem-Oriented Policing: Reflections on the First 20 Years.* Washington, DC: Office of Community-Oriented Policing Services, U.S. Department of Justice, p. 99.

The advent of community policing has witnessed resurgence in focused law enforcement activities. Police departments across the country are using saturation patrols, undercover operations, field interrogations, and other highly visible enforcement tactics (Gaines, 1996). Such tactics are being justified as a part of community policing. Police managers maintain that these tactics are efforts to "take back the streets" or regain control over areas that have been lost to crime. The emergence of this failed philosophy is rooted in Wilson and Kelling's (1982) "Broken Windows" theory and the U.S. Justice Department's funding of "Weed and Seed" programs. Broken Windows postulates that, if unchecked, a neighborhood in decline will continue to decline and the number of disorder and crime problems will increase. Therefore, the police and government must intervene and attempt to reverse neighborhood deterioration. Weed and Seed is an extension of Broken Windows. Under Weed and Seed, police departments across the country were funded to clean up drug-infested neighborhoods, and, once the cleanup was complete, to engage the community and assist in revitalizing it. Decades of using aggressive law enforcement practices where the police wage a war against certain segments of the community have shown this to be a failed practice that only furthers community problems, reinforces the "crime-fighter" orientation of the police, and often times leads to riots and civil unrest. Far too often, after police have aggressively "weeded" communities with law enforcement tactics, political leaders have failed to proved the promised "seed" to revitalized these communities leaving the police with still another community relations nightmare. Worse yet, these tactics have been used in the interests of big

---

Figure 14.4 The Weed and Seed Strategy

In 1991, the U.S. Department of Justice established Operation Weed and Seed—a community-based multi-agency approach to law enforcement, crime prevention, and neighborhood restoration. The Community Capacity Development Office (CCDO), Office of Justice Programs, administers operation Weed and Seed. The goals of Weed and Seed are to control violent crime, drug trafficking, and drug-related crime in designated high-crime neighborhoods and provide a safe environment free of crime and drug use for residents. The Weed and Seed strategy brings together Federal, State, and local crime-fighting agencies, social service providers, representatives of the public and private sectors, prosecutors, business owners, and neighborhood residents under the shared goal of weeding out violent crime and gang activity while seeding in social services and economic revitalization. Weed and Seed began with three pilot sites in 1991 and has spread quickly to more than 300 high-crime neighborhoods across the nation.

The Weed and Seed strategy is a two-pronged approach to crime control and prevention:

+ Law enforcement agencies and prosecutors cooperate in "weeding out" criminals from the designated area.
+ "Seeding" brings prevention, intervention, treatment, and neighborhood revitalization services to the area.

The Weed and Seed approach is unique when compared with traditional crime prevention approaches of the past. The strategy is based on collaboration, coordination, community participation, and leveraging resources. Weed and Seed sites maximize existing programs and resources by coordinating and integrating existing federal, state, local, and private sector initiatives, criminal justice efforts, and social services. The strategy also puts heavy emphasis on community participation. Residents of Weed and Seed neighborhoods are actively involved in problem solving in their community. Neighborhood watches, citizen marches and rallies, cleanup events, drug-free zones, and graffiti removal are some of the common programs that encourage community participation and help prevent crime.

Source: Office of Justice Programs (2004). The Weed and Seed Strategy, pp. 1–2. Washington, DC: U.S. Department of Justice, Office of Justice Programs.

business to displace residents for the purposes of development and gentrification. Unfortunately, a number of police departments see aggressive law enforcement as a potent tool in the policing arsenal. These are, however, tools that are not in keeping with the spirit of community policing and were the hallmarks of the failed traditional model of policing.

Perhaps the best known of these programs is New York City's "zero-tolerance" policing. Here, the police have lowered their tolerance and now enforce many minor infractions that historically were ignored by the police. The idea was that law violations ultimately lead more serious crime, and by attacking minor crime; the police can have an impact on serious crime. At the same time, the department also began to target high-crime areas with highly aggressive law enforcement. The result was large numbers of arrests and a misguided belief that these practices resulted in a decline the rate of serious violent crime. One must remember that almost every American city, even those that have not employed aggressive zero-tolerance practices, has experienced significant reductions in crime during this same period. The aggressive policing also resulted in an increase in complaints against the police. Greene (1999) questions the effectiveness of New York's aggressive policing. She notes that other cities, particularly San Diego, experienced similar drops in crime without aggressive policing. San Diego was able to lower crime statistics while adhering to a brand of community policing that emphasized community partnerships. The research is mixed regarding aggressive patrol's impact on crime. Novak and his colleagues (1999) found that it had no impact, while Sherman and Weisburd (1995) and Weiss and Freels (1996) found a very weak relationship. The research can be only marginally characterized as mixed, the historical result of aggressive policing is clear. These police practices result in alienation of the community (Reisig & Parks, 2000; Sampson & Jeglum-Bartusch, 1998), riots and civil disorder and a distrust of the police.

Law enforcement remains a central part of the police mission. Aggressive policing has become a frequently used tactic by departments that say they adhere to community policing. We would argue that aggressive law enforcement is anti-community policing. Others would argue that the police must take control of "lost" neighborhoods before more positive relationships and actions can develop. Police executive must begin to take a cold, hard, and sober look at the politics underlying policing and crime control. They must ask some hard questions like: What public policies and political decisions led to the creation of communities that needed "weeding"? Did the very people who failed to provide the necessary "seed" to grow healthful communities make these decisions? Whose interests are really being served? Were the police abandoned to deal with the consequences of poor public policy and politically motivated decisions? Is aggressive policing a fix for communities or for political leaders?

SUMMARY

Community policing represents a new, bold approach to law enforcement. Not since the beginning of the 1900s has law enforcement moved back to its social service roots. Community policing represents a comprehensive attack on community problems. It signals a time whereby the police are concerned with people and their problems as opposed to focusing solely on responding to calls for service and making arrests. Community policing truly is a paradigm shift.

It is important for the police administrator to not mistake some strategy or tactic for community policing. While community policing employs a number of strategies and tactics, the essence of community policing (empowerment of the community, community engagement, problem solving, and community partnerships) represents the glue that holds these strategies and tactics together. Community policing requires that police work as closely as possible with people to identify and solve their problems. Under community policing, crime reduction and "crook-catching" are not primary objectives, but represent strategies that are a part of a rich, over-arching philosophy.

REFERENCES

Bayley, D.H. (1994). "International Differences in Community Policing." In D. Rosenbaum (ed.) *The Challenge of Community Policing*, pp. 278–281. Thousand Oaks, CA: Sage.

Bayley, D.H. (1988). "Community Policing: A Report from the Devil's Advocate." In J. Greene & S. Mastrofski (eds.) *Community Policing: Rhetoric or Reality?*, pp. 225–238. New York, NY: Praeger.

Bracey, D. (1992). "Police Corruption and Community Relations: Community Policing." *Police Studies*, 15(4):179–183.

Buerger, M. (1991). *Repeat Call Policing*: The RECAP Casebook. Washington, DC: Crime Control Institute.

Bursik, R.J. (2000). "The Systemic Theory of Neighborhood Crime Rates." In S. S. Simpson (ed.) *Of Crime & Criminality: The Use of Theory in Everyday Life*. Boston, MA: Pine Forge Press.

Campbell, A. & H. Schuman (1972). "A Comparison of Black and White Attitudes and Experience in the City." In C. Harr (ed.) *The End of Innocence: A Suburban Reader*, pp. 97–110. Glenview, IL: Scott Forsman.

Carter, D. (1985). "Hispanic Perception of Police Performance: An Empirical Assessment." *Journal of Criminal Justice*, 13:487–500.

Chermak, S. & A. Weiss (2006). "Community Policing in the News Media." *Police Quarterly*, 9 (2): 135–160.

Clarke, R.V. (1992). *Situational Crime Prevention: Successful Case Studies*. New York, NY: Harrow and Heston.

Colvin, C.A. & A. Goh (2006). "Elements Underlying Community Policing: Validation of the Construct." *Police Practice and Research*, 7(1): 19–33.

Cornish, D.B. & R.V. Clarke (1987). "Understanding Crime Displacement: An Application of Rational Choice Theory." *Criminology*, 25:933–947.

Crank, J.P. (2004). *Understanding Police Culture*, Second Edition. Newark, NJ: LexisNexis Matthew Bender/ Anderson Publishing.

Dietz, S. (1997). "Evaluating Community Policing: Quality Police Services and Fear of Crime." *Policing: An International Journal of Police Strategies and Management*, 20(1):83–100.

Eck, J. & W. Spelman (1987). "Newport News Tests Problem-Oriented Policing." *NIJ Reports*, (Jan.-Feb.):2–8.

Eck, J. & D. Weisburd (1995). *Crime and Places*. Monsey, NY: Willow Tree Press.

Felson, M. (1998). *Crime and Everyday Life: Insights and Implications for Society*, Second Edition. Thousand Oaks, CA: Pine Forge Press.

Felson, M. (1994). *Crime and Everyday Life: Insights and Implications for Society*. Thousand Oaks, CA: Pine Forge Press.

Frank, J., S.G. Brandl & R.C. Watkins (1999). "The Content of Community Policing: A Comparison of the Daily Activities of Community and 'Beat' Officers." *Policing: An International Journal of Police Strategy and Management*, 20(4):716–728.

Gaines, L.K. (1996). "Specialized Patrol." In G. Cordner, L. Gaines & V. Kappeler (eds.) *Police Operations*, pp. 115–130. Cincinnati, OH: Anderson Publishing Co.

Gaines, L.K. & V.E. Kappeler (2008). *Policing in America*, Sixth Edition. Newark, NJ: Lexis-Nexis Matthew Bender/ Anderson Publishing.

Gaines, L.K. & C.R. Swanson (1997). "Empowering Police Officers: A Tarnished Silver Bullet?" *Police Forum*.

Gaines, L.K., J. Worrall, M. Southerland & J. Angell (2003). *Police Administration*. New York, NY: McGraw-Hill.

Gallup (1996). "Community Policing Survey." October.

Goldstein, H. (1990). *Problem-Oriented Policing*. New York, NY: McGraw-Hill.

Goldstein, H. (1979). "Improving Policing: A Problem-Oriented Approach." *Crime & Delinquency*, 25:236–258.

Greene, J. (2000). "Community Policing in America: Changing the Nature, Structure, and Function of the Police." *In Criminal Justice 2000, Volume 3, Policies, Processes, and Decisions of the Criminal Justice System*, pp. 299–370. Washington, DC: National Institute of Justice.

Greene, J. & C. Klockars (1991). "What Police Do." In C. Klockars & S. Mastrofski (eds.) *Thinking About Police: Contemporary Readings*, Second Edition. New York, NY: McGraw-Hill.

Greene, J.A. (1999). "Zero Tolerance: A Case Study of Police Policies and Practices in New York City." *Crime & Delinquency*, 45(2):171–188.

Hale, C. (1996). "Fear of Crime: A Review of the Literature." *International Review of Victimology*, (4):79–150.

Hartmann, F.X. (1988). "Debating the Evolution of American Policing." *Perspectives on Policing*, No. 5. Washington, DC: NIJ and Harvard University.

Johnson, R.A. (1997). "Integrated Patrol: Combining Aggressive Law Enforcement and Community Policing." *FBI Law Enforcement Bulletin*, 66(11):6–11.

Kappeler, V.E. & G.W. Potter (2005). *The Mythology of Crime and Criminal Justice*, Fourth Edition. Prospect Heights, IL: Waveland Press.

Kappeler, V.E. & P.B. Kraska (1998). "Police Adapting to High Modernity: A Textual Critique of Community Policing." *Policing: An International Journal of Police Strategies and Management*, 21(2):293–313.

Kappeler, V.E. & P.B. Kraska (1998a). "Police Modernity: Scientific and Community Based Violence on Symbolic Playing Fields." In S. Henry & D. Milovanovic (eds.) *Constitutive Criminology at Work*. Albany, NY: SUNY Press.

Kappeler, V.E., R.D. Sluder & G.P. Alpert (1998). *Forces of Deviance: Understanding the Dark Side of the Force*, Second Edition. Prospect Heights, IL: Waveland Press.

Kasinsky, R. (1994). "Patrolling the Facts: Media, Cops, and Crime." In G. Barak (ed.) *Media, Process, and the Social Construction of Crime*, pp. 203–234. New York, NY: Garland Publishing, Inc.

Kelling, G., T. Pate, D. Diekman & C.E. Brown (1974). *The Kansas City Preventive Patrol Experiment: A Summary Report.* Washington, DC: The Police Foundation.

Klockars, C.B. (1988). "The Rhetoric of Community Policing." In J. Greene & S. Mastrofski (eds.) *Community Policing: Rhetoric or Reality*, pp. 239–258. New York, NY: Praeger.

Kraska, P.B. (1996). "Enjoying Militarism: Political/ Personal Dilemmas in Studying U.S. Paramilitary Units." *Justice Quarterly*, 13(3):405–429.

Kraska, P.B. & V.E. Kappeler (1997). "Militarizing American Police: The Rise and Normalization of Paramilitary Units." *Social Problems*, 44(1):1–18.

Lord, V. (1996). "An Impact of Community Policing: Reported Stressors, Social Support, and Strain among Police Officers in a Changing Police Department." *Journal of Criminal Justice*, 24(6):503–522.

Manning, P.K. (1997). *Police Work*, Second Edition. Prospect Heights, IL: Waveland Press.

Manning, P.K. (1988). "Community Policing as a Drama of Control." In J. Greene & S. Mastrofski (eds.) *Community Policing: Rhetoric or Reality*, pp. 27–46. New York, NY: Praeger.

Mastrofski, S. (1988). "Community Policing as Reform: A Cautionary Tale." In J. Greene & S. Mastrofski (eds.) *Community Policing: Rhetoric or Reality*. New York, NY: Praeger.

Mastrofski, S. & R.R. Ritti (1999). *Patterns of Community Policing: A View from Newspapers in the United States.* COPS Working Paper. Washington, DC: USDOJ.

McEwen, T. (1994). *National Assessment Program: 1994 Survey Results.* Washington, DC: National Institute of Justice.

National Institute of Justice (1997). "Criminal Justice Research under the Crime Act—1995 to 1996." Washington, DC: U.S. Department of Justice.

Novak, K.J., J.L. Hartman, A.M. Holsinger & M.G. Turner (1999). "The Effects of Aggressive Policing of Disorder on Serious Crime." *Policing: An International Journal of Police Strategies and Management*, 22(2):171–190.

Parks, R.B., S.D. Mastrofski, C. Dejong & M.K. Gray (1999). "How Officers Spend Their Time with the Community." *Justice Quarterly*, 16(3):483–517.

Peak, K.J. & R.W. Glensor (1996). *Community Policing & Problem Solving*: Strategies and Practices. Upper Saddle River, NJ: Prentice-Hall.

Radelet, L. & D. Carter (1994). *The Police and the Community*. New York, NY: Macmillan.

Reisig, M.D. & R.B. Parks (2004). "Can Community Policing Help the Truly Disadvantaged?" *Crime & Delinquency*, 50(2): 139–167.

Reisig, M.D. & R.B. Parks (2000). "Experience, Quality of Life, and Neighborhood Context: A Hierarchical Analysis of Satisfaction with Police." *Justice Quarterly*, 17: 607–630.

Sampson, R.J. & D. Jeglum-Bartusch (1998). "Legal Cynicism and (Subcultural?) Tolerance of Deviance: The Neighborhood Context of Racial Differences." *Law & Society Review*, 32:777–804.

Sampson, R.J., S.W. Raudenbush & F. Earls (1997). "Neighborhoods and Violent Crime: A Multilevel Study of Collective Efficacy." *Science*, 277, 918–924.

Scaglion, R. & R.G. Condon (1980). "Determinants of Attitudes toward City Police." *Criminology*, 17(4):485–494.

Scott, M. (2000). *Problem-Oriented Policing: Reflections on the First 20 Years.* Washington, DC: Office of Community-Oriented Policing Services, U.S. Department of Justice, p. 99.

Scott, M.S. & H. Goldstein (2005). *Shifting and Sharing Responsibility for Public. Safety Problems. Problem-Oriented Guides for Police, Response Guide Series*, 3:1–53.

Sherman, L. (1987). "Repeat Calls for Service: Policing the 'Hot Spots.'" *Crime Control Reports*. Washington, DC: Crime Control Institute.

Sherman, L. & D. Weisburd (1995). "General Deterrent Effects of Police Patrol in Crime "Hot Spots": A Randomized, Controlled Trial." *Justice Quarterly*, 12:625–648.

Skogan, W.G. (1990). *Disorder and Decline: Crime and the Spiral of Decay in American Neighborhoods*. New York, NY: The Free Press.

Skogan, W.G. & S.M. Hartnett (1997). *Community Policing, Chicago Style*. New York, NY: Oxford University Press.

Sparrow, M. (1988). *Implementing Community Policing*. Perspectives on Policing, No. 9. Washington, DC: National Institute of Justice and Harvard University.

Spelman, W. (2004) "Optimal Targeting of Incivility-Reduction Strategies." *Journal of Quantitative Criminology*, 20(1):63–89.

Spelman, W. & J. Eck (1987). "Newport News Tests Problem-Oriented Policing." *National Institute of Justice Reports*, (Jan.-Feb.):2–8.

Stephens, D. (1996). "Community Problem-Oriented Policing: Measuring Impacts." In L. Hoover (ed.) *Quantifying Quality in Policing*. Washington, DC: PERF.

Strecher, V.G. (1997). *Planning Community Policing*. Prospect Heights, IL: Waveland Press.

Suttles, G.D. (1972). *The Social Construction of Communities*. Chicago, IL: University of Chicago Press.

Taylor, R.B. (2001). *Breaking away from Broken Windows*. Boulder, CO: Westview.

Toch, H. (1997). "The Democratization of Policing in the United States: 1895–1973." *Police Forum*, 7(2):1–8.

Van Maanen, J. (2006). "The Asshole." In V. Kappeler (ed.) *The Police & Society: Touch Stone Readings*, Third Edition. Prospect Heights, IL: Waveland Press.

Velez, M.B. (2001). "The Role of Public Social Control in Urban Neighborhoods: A Multi-Level Analysis of Victimization Risk." *Criminology*, 39: 837–864.

Walker, S. (1994). *The Police in America*, Second Edition. New York, NY: McGraw-Hill.

Walker, S. (1993). "Does Anyone Remember Team Policing? Lessons of the Team Policing Experience for Community Policing." *American Journal of Police*, 12(1):33–56.

Weiss, A. & S. Freels (1996). "The Effects of Aggressive Policing: The Dayton Traffic Enforcement Experiment." *American Journal of Police*, 15:45–64.

Wilson, J.Q. (1968). "Dilemmas of Police Administration." *Public Administration Review*, (Sept./Oct.):407–416.

Wilson, J.Q. & G. Kelling (1982). "Police and Neighborhood Safety: Broken Windows." In V. Kappeler (ed.) *The Police & Society: Touch Stone Readings*, Second Edition, pp. 154–168. Prospect Heights, IL: Waveland Press.

Wintersmith, R.F. (1976). "The Police and the Black Community: Strategies for Improvement." In A. Cohn & E. Viano (eds.) *Police Community Relations*, pp. 422–433. Philadelphia, PA: J.B. Lippincott.

Wycoff, M.A. & W.K. Skogan (1993). *Community Policing in Madison: Quality from the Inside Out*. Washington, DC: National Institute of Justice.

Zhao, J., N. He & N.P. Lovrich (1999). "Value Change among Police Officers at a Time of Organizational Reform: A Follow-up Study Using Rokeach Values." *Policing: An International Journal of Police Strategies and Management*, 22(2):152–170.

Zhao, S., M. Scheider & Q. Thurman (2002). "The Effect of Police Presence on Public Fear Reduction and Satisfaction: A Review of the Literature." *The Justice Professional*, 15:273–299.

THE POLICE

Historical and Contemporary Perspectives

*Geoffrey P. Alpert
and Roger G.
Dunham*

The police have been a common feature in American society for more than a century. Today, police officers are seen patrolling streets, directing traffic, and serving the public in a multitude of ways. It has not always been so. Historically, the police were political assets for the power elites and had no pretence of treating everyone equally. The purpose of this chapter is to review briefly the history of the police, discuss the modern-day reality of police work, and assess the future of policing.

BRITISH TRADITION

A great deal of U.S. policing heritage can be linked directly to its British roots. Policing in the community, crime prevention, and elected sheriffs all have origins in English law enforcement. The history of policing in England includes a variety of stories and scenarios that involve radically conservative interpretations of law enforcement and a liberal view of governmental intervention (Reith, 1938). Originally, all security in England was private. Those who could afford the luxury lived in well-built houses that were guarded by servants who acted as bodyguards. The remainder of the population merely hoped that their neighbors and those chosen as "watchmen" would protect them and chase away the criminal element. This system of shared and informal policing was referred to as "kin" policing (Reith, 1956) and the "frankpledge system." It was established to encourage citizens to act as the "eyes and ears" of the authorities, to protect their family and neighbors, and to deliver to the court any member of the group who committed a crime.

The pledge to protect others created a sense of security based on being protected by one's family and neighbors. Communities were organized into *tythings*, or groups of 100 citizens, which were part of larger units called *shires* (similar to counties today). Shires were headed by *shire reeves* (later called "sheriffs"). Shire reeves were appointed by the king, and were primarily responsible for civil duties, such as collecting taxes and ensuring obedience to the authority of the king. From the frankpledge system came the *parish constable system*. In the 13th century, the position of the constable was formalized, thus permitting the appointment of watchmen to assist in their duties (Bayley, 1999). Watchmen had numerous responsibilities, from guarding the gates of town at night to watching for fires, crimes, and suspicious persons. This system of law enforcement continued without much change until the 18th century.

During the 18th century, there was unprecedented population growth and the population of London more than doubled. Accompanying the growth was a more complex and specialized society, resulting in law enforcement problems that challenged the control systems in existence. Rioting in the cities, which the existing system could not control, is one such example. As a result of the changing social climate, a more formal and organized method of law enforcement became necessary. It was around this time that Henry Fielding (author of *Tom Jones*) and his brother, Sir John Fielding, helped improve policing in London and all over England by suggesting changes to the existing system of control that developed into what is known as the modern police department.

THE FIRST MODERN POLICE: LONDON

It was Sir Robert Peel, the British Home Secretary, who created a 3,000-strong police force. Peel drafted and then guided through Parliament the "Act for Improving the Police in and Near the Metropolis," which is better known as the Metropolitan Police Act of 1829. Under the direction of Peel, the police were organized for crime prevention. By 1829, the entire city was patrolled by men assigned specific territories, or beats, on a 24-hour-a-day basis (Reith, 1956). The officers, or "bobbies," wore blue uniforms so that they could be easily recognizable as public servants whose purpose was to deter crime. The leaders of the London police force provided a central administration, strict discipline, and close supervision of the officers. They eventually decided to introduce a military structure to what had been a rather loose organization. Peel and his bobbies were so successful that requests for help from outside areas were received and assistance was sent. This movement set the stage for modern police

departments, which were developed according to the principles of what has become known as "the London model of policing." Thus, the structure and function of current police agencies, as well as their overall mission, are heavily influenced by Sir Robert Peel.

THE MODERN ERA

In fundamental ways, modern police departments remain slaves to their history. In the 1970s, Jonathan Rubinstein (1973) commented that understanding what police do is difficult because they have such a wide variety of tasks. Thirty-six years later, this statement remains as true as it did then. Citizens are split between viewing the police in positive terms, calling them brave "crime fighters" and heroes, and referring to them negatively, as corrupt, heartless, and brutal. Often, these different views are influenced by a citizen's experiences with the police and whether it was a positive or a negative one. Partly because of severe criticisms of the police by citizens, policing has been forced to change and develop into what it is today.

Although much of policing has changed drastically since its initiation into American government, changes in the selection and training of officers have been among the most important. There were few standards when hiring officers during the early years of policing, and practically no training. In fact, positions on the police force often were viewed as a reward for loyalty to political parties who were in power. Newly elected officials often fired existing officers and hired their political supporters. As a result, citizens thought of the police as nothing more than political "hacks," enforcing the interests of those in power. This corrupt system of hiring officers has developed into the very elaborate and professional civil service hiring systems present in most departments today. Further, the practice of virtually no training of officers that existed earlier has progressed into the long and arduous training programs found in most departments today.

Recruitment and Selection of Officers

The importance of recruitment and selection cannot be emphasized enough. As police work is labor-intensive, and a large percentage of an agency's budget is devoted to personnel issues, the officer is the most significant investment a police department can make. Police agencies are always looking for innovative ways to attract and retain good officers. Once an individual decides he or she wants to enter police work, the agency must screen the person for characteristics that make a good police officer. This is known as "selecting in," a strategy that identifies those individuals best suited for police work. The agency must also eliminate or "screen out" those applicants who are unfit for police work. Many tests are available to evaluate someone's psychological and physical characteristics to determine if success in police work is likely. There are multiple hurdles for recruits to pass. Unfortunately, there are no clear and accepted criteria to determine which candidates will make the best police officers. One reason for this uncertainty was suggested by Brenner (1989), who noted that an officer must be able to adapt to various situations and use a variety of styles and approaches, depending on the circumstances. He points out that officers must interact with violent criminals and distressed victims, perhaps during the same interaction, and it is unlikely that an officer's behavior will satisfy all of the stakeholders all of the time. As it is extremely difficult to determine an applicant's fitness for duty, officers must pass the many hurdles. Each decade or era has its own problems associated with the recruitment of police officers. The overall economy plays a role, as does the country's involvement in war and the use of the military. In fact, these and other issues also impact trained police officers when they return from a leave or other assignment. There is enormous variance in the selection procedures and training among agencies, so the following discussion illustrate the options agencies have at their disposal to review and assess candidates.

Traditionally, police departments use standardized written tests to assess basic skills and attitudes. The use of traditional pen-and-pencil tests has been criticized for its lack of predictive ability, which has led many agencies to supplement these tests with a more comprehensive assessment procedure. Departments using this method process applicants through a series of assessments, including simulated and role-play activities. The activities are developed to force a person to respond to situations and individuals who "test" the person's character and ability to negotiate in a specific situation. Common examples of simulations used in assessment centers include a domestic altercation, a routine traffic stop, or a bar fight.

In addition, officers are given medical exams and physical agility tests that involve job task simulations, such as lifting weights through windows, carrying heavy objects, and other tasks that might confront a police officer on the job. Officer candidates are often given a polygraph test to determine if they have told the truth about their backgrounds or past experiences on their application forms and in their interviews. One area that is investigated is prior drug use history.

Further, applicants are often interviewed by an individual or a group of commanders. These interviews are designed to determine a candidate's ability to communicate and to respond to difficult questions. Once an applicant has passed these initial hurdles, he or she is sent to training. This training varies from state to state and agency to agency, but all have some common elements, including preservice, field, and in-service training.

Academy Training

Police academies can be ran by the department or by the state, and they can be independent or connected to community colleges or universities. The average length of academy training is approximately 600 hours, but varies from state to state. Regardless of the total number of hours required at the academy, the training and education is an experience that plays a significant role in shaping the officer's attitudes about policing in general, including ways to address specific tasks, and the role of the police in society.

The building blocks of a good law enforcement training program are anchored to two issues: First, the programs should incorporate the proper statement of mission and ethical considerations, which should be taught in the context of what an officer will do on a daily basis. Second, there must be a balance of time spent on "high-frequency" versus "high-risk" activities in the required training. In the 21st century, it is also necessary to prepare police officers to think, make good decisions, and to respond to a variety of difficult situations.

Recruits must pass the requirements of the academy to graduate. Many academies insist that the recruit pass all courses the first time to graduate, while other academies have built-in provisions for remedial training to help marginal students pass. Academies use a variety of methods to evaluate and grade the progress of their recruits, such as multiple-choice tests, role-play exercises, written answer tests, and oral tests. Once graduated, with newly acquired attitudes and skills, the young officer is often required to enroll in departmental training or could be assigned street work with a field training officer. Unfortunately, others are sent directly to the street, with gun, badge, and vehicle, with no further training.

Field Training

Most departments provide training after completion of the academy through a field training officer (FTO) model. Although recruits should have been exposed to a number of real-life experiences during academy training, those were created for training or role-play scenarios and are conducted in an artificial atmosphere. Field training is meant to bridge the gap between the protected environment of the academy and the isolated, open danger of the street. The new officer, or "rookie," is paired with a more experienced police officer(s) for a period of time, usually several months.

It is the field training officer's job to teach the young rookie how to survive and how to become a good police officer. Field training programs are often divided into several phases. Although agencies vary the length and scope of their field training, all programs should include introductory, training, and evaluation phases. The introductory phase is structured to teach the rookie officer about the agency's policies, procedures, and local laws and ordinances, Departmental customs

and practices are also communicated at this time. During the training and evaluation phases, the young officer is gradually introduced to complex tasks that require involved and complicated decisions. The young officer will have to interpret and translate into action what was learned in the academy and the field. The field training officer then evaluates the decisions and actions made by the recruit. Eventually, the successful trainee will be able to handle calls without assistance from the field training officer.

There exists a long-standing concern in policing that each rookie is told by an experienced officer to forget what was learned at the academy and to just watch and learn how things are done right. As Van Maanen (1978) described, "The newcomer is quickly bombarded with 'street wise' patrolmen assuring him that the police academy was simply an experience that all officers endure and has little, if anything, to do with real police work" (p. 300). This unfortunate message is that the formal training received at the academy is irrelevant or unrealistic. It is hoped that field training officers are selected and trained to make sure these types of counterproductive messages do not occur. After an officer has passed the probationary period, he or she may think training is over. However, most states and many departments require refresher courses, training on new issues, and other sorts of in-service training.

In-Service Training

Many states have now mandated in-service training for police in the same way lawyers and teachers must continue their education. In-service training is designed to provide officers with new skills and changes in laws, policies, or procedures. Also, since many skills learned at the academy or while in field training are perishable, in-service training can restore an officer's skills. Some agencies send officers to lengthy management schools or specialized trainings. It is hard to believe that some agencies still do not train veteran officers aggressively. Police work is constantly changing, and remaining a good police officer is different from the process of becoming one.

If conducted properly, in-service training can provide a critical component to the agency's training scheme. There must be training for supervisors and managers, communication specialists and investigators, as well as street officers. In other words, patrol officers need certain skills and those on specialized assignments need others. Some skills, such as those used in the control of persons, emergency vehicle operations, and other high-risk activities, need more frequent and in-depth training than those engaged in more routine tasks. Officers must not only be provided with proper information, but they must also be given the opportunity to ask "What if" questions of the instructor. Further, officers must pass an examination before it can be assumed that they know the information and are competent to put it into practice in real-world situations.

The Internet is providing a new forum for training police officers. Many departments are creating home pages that provide information about the agency and the community served. There are also many police "chat rooms" which allow officers to share information and have discussions about many topics and issues. Innovative trainers can take advantage of these technological advancements for the improvement of their officers' knowledge and experience.

The expense of training is one of the important issues many departments must consider. Not only is it costly to evaluate needs, to plan and to provide for training, but it is also very expensive to remove officers from the streets to be trained. In the short term, the expenses are great, but in the long term, the framing and its related costs will pay off.

Once selected and trained, there are many recruits who enter into police work only to realize that the work, schedule, and rewards are not what they anticipated. In addition, administrators will learn that some of the citizens they recruit and even train are not able to perform the required task appropriately. Other reasons officers do not make careers in policing include family influences, "burn out," and better-paying job offers.

After officers have negotiated successfully their initial training, most are assigned to the patrol function and, as a result, have the most contact with the public. There are multiple methods of patrol, including automobile, foot, horse, motorcycle, bicycle, and boat. Each type serves a different function, promotes different relationships, and creates different problems. In any case, these officers are now prepared to police independently and to interact with citizens on their own.

POLICE OPERATIONS

Police Patrol

Patrol has long been considered the "backbone" of policing, as this is where almost every police officer gets his or her "street experience." This experience on the street with citizens is vital in shaping the outlooks and views of the police officer. While many patrol officers will go on to supervisory or investigative positions, this starting point creates shared experiences and facilitates socialization with fellow officers. An important question is, what are the major factors that influence a patrol officer's behavior?

Although officers experience similar situations, their responses may differ due to the complexities and special circumstances of interactions. They soon learn that they cannot enforce all laws, and as Kenneth Culp Davis (1975) observed, the police must use discretion and selective enforcement.

Written guidelines or policies direct police officers' activities, reactions, and behavior. Policies are based on relevant laws and presumably best practices. They are directives that provide members of the organization with sufficient information so that they can successfully perform their day-to-day operations. Some agencies provide their officers with very detailed policies, while others have promulgated more general policies but have supplemented those with detailed in-service training. While officers are allowed discretion with specified boundaries, it is an important research question to determine what factors explain why police officers respond differently to the same conditions.

For example, the process of forming suspicion has been a topic that has received relatively little attention in the research literature. Jonathan Rubinstein (1973) was one of the first scholars to thoroughly discuss the formation of suspicion. He notes the following:

> Many of the things the officer is looking for are a product of prior situations, a consequence of events about which he knows nothing, although he often makes assumptions about some of them. ... While the patrolman is looking for substantive cues indicating flight, fear, concealment, and illegal possession, he is also making judgments based on his perception of the people and places he polices, (pp. 255, 257)

After an exhaustive review of the literature, the National Research Council (2003) concluded that a suspect's social class, gender, as well as other social factors do not explain variance in behavior in police–citizen interactions.

An important area of police behavior to address is the foot pursuit. Similar to vehicular pursuits, these activities were not regulated until the 1990s. Around that time, it became apparent that officers and suspects were unnecessarily injured or put in situations that resulted in unnecessary force and deadly force because they abandoned proper practices and went on foot pursuits alone, or were separated from other officers in an attempt to corner or head off a fleeing suspect. Without proper communication, or a plan, officers put themselves in dangerous situations, which can result in crossfires and unnecessary force.

It appears that officers' beliefs and prior experiences strongly influence their responses to citizens. Perhaps the cognitive theorists are correct in arguing that officers learn by experience, and that the relative power of that learning is influenced by one's degree of familiarity and repeated associations in a fashion similar to the theory of differential association. In other words, these developed schemas form a mental model and illusory correlation that strongly influence a person's responses to people and places in future encounters (Alpert, MacDonald, & Dunham, 2005). This is all extremely important because officers' behavior creates an image for a police department, and supervisors must manage how the officers act and respond to situations. While the patrol function forms what has been called the backbone of policing, perhaps it is the first-line supervisors who form the nervous system of the agency. The patrol officers are the ones closest to the community and know the most about the people and places they police. It is they who are crime fighters, community policing officers, and problem solvers—all at the same time. It is the supervisor who directs and manages their activities.

The Crime Control Function

What are the major operations by which the police set out to control crime? The crime control function of the police relies on four primary tactics: (1) randomized and directed patrol (preventative patrol), (2) problem identification and solving, (3) response to calls for service by citizens, and (4) criminal investigation.

Preventive patrol is largely based on the assumption that it serves as a deterrent effect on crime. Although this assumption was questioned in the Kansas City Preventive Patrol Experiment, other studies have indicated that citizens' attitudes and beliefs are impacted by seeing officers on motorized and foot patrols. Problem identification involves the identification of specific locations and times wherein crime is most likely to occur or that are otherwise deemed most problematic.

The effectiveness of rapid responses to calls has been examined over the years. The initial rationale behind a speedy response is that it will improve the likelihood that police will apprehend a suspect. Unfortunately, citizens often report crimes after the fact, and a few seconds shaved by the police responding at breakneck speeds to a call for service does not make much difference in the officer's likelihood of affecting an arrest. Interestingly, whether or not the initial officer responding to a scene can identify a suspect may make a difference in whether the case is resolved, but the time differential is measured in minutes, not seconds.

Finally, the work of detectives and the criminal investigation process have been studied in a variety of ways. The RAND Corporation study provides an important benchmark for establishing what is known about the effectiveness of retrospective investigation of crimes (Greenwood & Petersilia, 1975). There are several important findings in this report that merit discussion. First, detectives spend very little of their time (less than 10%) on activities that directly lead to solving crime. A large proportion of the time they do spend on casework is often used on cases after they have been solved (e.g., preparing a case for court). Second, solving crimes has little to do with any special activities performed by investigators. Instead, the most important factor affecting case clearance (e.g., whether a suspect can be identified) is the behavior of the initial responding officer and members of the public. As noted above, clearance rates are related to whether either the initial responding officer (or a victim or witness on the scene) was able to identify a suspect. It is usually a civilian and not the officer who can make an identification, thereby reducing the need for officers to risk the safety of civilians on the streets by driving at high speeds to get to a call.

While patrol is an important aspect of policing, police departments and their officers perform functions other than crime fighting. Order maintenance, rather than law enforcement, may be a better approach in certain places and with certain people. As police officers are available 24/7, they are called on to provide emergency aid, information, and animal control and to make referrals to other human welfare agencies, among other responsibilities. The time spent on these services can be significant and can be seen as taking away from routine crime-fighting activities. Even some terrorist threats that require attention can be seen as taking away resources from immediate community-level crimes and problems.

Several issues that require time and effort are gangs and weapons. Although these concerns are neither new nor novel, the police response must change continually to be effective. Taking guns off the street and reducing gang violence must be goals of every police department. As new strategies are developed, new techniques by gang members are discovered.

IMPORTANT INFLUENCES ON OFFICERS' BEHAVIOR

A considerable amount of research has been conducted on the influences on officers' behavior while on the job. Policing is an occupation for which the behavior of the incumbent can have very serious implications for those they police. Few occupations give individuals as much power over others as the police position. In exercising their discretionary power over others, officers may severely injure citizens; end their lives; destroy their reputations; or send them to jail or prison, among many other very severe penalties. Thus, it is important to monitor how officers make such decisions and try to understand which factors influence them.

THE CULTURE OF THE POLICE

The nature of police work is different from that of work performed in most other occupations. As has been noted, the police are among the few professionals that are required to be available 24 hours a day, 7 days a week, 52 weeks a year. Furthermore, the police deal with social problems and societal ills that extend beyond simply fighting crime. The police are also unique in terms of the persons with whom they most routinely interact. While police officers deal with the entire spectrum of humanity, they spend the majority of their time dealing with the seamier side of society. The central features of the police culture may be categorized according to the way officers relate to the unique nature of the job, the special category of persons with whom they come into contact, and the environment in which they work. In other words, the unique aspects of the police role, such as being given tremendous authority, and the corresponding right to use force on citizens; morality issues related to the police being the enforcers of right over wrong; and danger, or the threat of danger, shape the nature of the police and their work.

Research indicates that the environment in which police do their work is shaped by their isolation from citizens, their solidarity within the police subculture, their loyalty to each other, and their desire for autonomy in carrying out policing duties. These conditions all contribute to the character of the police subculture, which has been characterized by extreme loyalty to one's coworkers, particularly one's partner. However, the police operate in a bureaucracy that is based on a paramilitary model with many guidelines or policies, rigid lines of authority, and communication that is authoritative and clear. These also make important contributions to the police culture and have an important impact on how the police do their work.

Police Bureaucracy

Police departments are organized in a manner similar to the military, using ranks to designate authority (captain, lieutenant, sergeant, etc.). True to the bureaucratic form of organization, the larger police departments are divided into special divisions and units with lines of authority leading from the chief to the line officers. Police department hierarchies of authority vary in respect to how tasks are divided and which divisions report to which supervisors.

The traditional hierarchy is represented by a pyramid-type structure. On the top, to set and enforce policies and to provide overall leadership, is the chief. Other divisions include at least internal affairs, communication, and patrol. Smaller agencies may combine different elements into one division, but all agencies must perform the same basic duties.

For example, internal affairs or professional compliance bureaus investigate all allegations of police misconduct. These concerns can be initiated by civilian complaints or by fellow police officers. This division or section is of paramount importance to the operations of any law enforcement agency and must receive support from the chief administrators. Most Internal Affairs Division managers report directly to the chief of police to avoid any question of prominence or importance.

One of the most critical elements of police work is its system of communication. It is this "heart line" that receives calls for service and forwards information to officers in the field. The communication process forms the link between the community and the police. The information provided to officers is the basis on which they prepare and respond. In other words, if the police department is told about a particular situation, officers

and supervisors must recognize how many officers are needed, how quickly they need to respond, and where they need to be sent.

The degree of centralization in the organization is one of the most critical decisions an administrator must make. A centralized structure, with a dominant supervisor, will have strong controls and may be cost effective. A decentralized structure will have flexibility and will be cost efficient as it emphasizes team building as a mode of problem solving. As each structure has positive and negative characteristics, the goals of the organization, with input from the community, should serve to design the structure. Certainly, large departments can centralize administrative and certain investigative functions while they decentralize patrol and other activities. The trend has been to decentralize many police functions and to be more responsive to the unique characteristics of communities. Regardless of the type of organization, there are always going to be critical concerns and high-risk activities performed by the police. The next section looks at these activities and places them in their proper perspective.

CRITICAL ISSUES AND HIGH-RISK ACTIVITIES

Given the large number of issues that exist in policing today, this discussion must be limited to the most important ones. The approach here is therefore selective and focuses on a limited number of critical issues: minority hiring and promotion, women in policing, the use of force, and pursuit driving.

Minorities in Policing

Tremendous strides have been made in hiring minorities in recent years. Since the mid-1990s, police agencies have increased significantly the hiring and promoting of minority officers.

Advocates for the hiring and promoting of minorities argue that if minorities are adequately represented in police departments, departments become representative of the communities they serve. Police departments that reflect the racial and ethnic characteristics of the communities they serve may increase the respect of community residents and thereby increase the flow of information concerning crime and the identification of criminals. Similar to ethnic minorities, females have not played an important role in law enforcement until relatively recently.

Until the early 1980s, the few females who were involved in police work were often assigned to clerical duties or restricted to work with either female or juvenile offenders. The reasons for this exclusion were many: First, male officers did not want to put up with the social inhibitions placed on them by the presence of women; second, they did not want to be overshadowed by or even to take orders from women; finally, most men did not want to be supported by a female in the performance of potentially dangerous work (Caiden, 1977; Martin, 2001). The common belief was that females would not function to the level of their male counterparts—specifically, that they would react improperly and would not be able to apprehend suspects in violent or dangerous situations. Recently, the myths about women in the police world have been debunked, and benefits connected with recruiting more female officers have been stressed. For example, female officers are often better than male officers at avoiding violence and de-escalating potentially violent situations. Moreover, while women currently represent approximately 13% of all sworn personnel, they are responsible for only 5% of citizen complaints, 2% of sustained allegations of excessive use of force, and 6% of the dollars paid out in judgments and settlements for excessive use of force (National Center for Women in Policing, 2002).

The next issue is the use of force by police officers, which often is handled more appropriately by female officers than by their male counterparts. The use of force is a highly controversial issue, and this examination will look at both the problems connected to it and some of the potential solutions that can prevent the abuse of this most necessary of police powers.

Use of Non-Deadly Force

The use of force, particularly deadly force, has traditionally been one of the most controversial aspects of police work. Clearly, a distinction must be made between appropriate police use of force and excessive force. While some level of force is legitimate and necessary to control suspects and protect innocent citizens, the use of excessive force is unacceptable and is one of the most troubling forms of police misconduct. New technologies, such as the Electronic Control Device or the Conducted Energy Device, provide police officers with alternatives to traditional batons, fists, and fights. While these technologies can lead to fewer injuries than traditional uses of force, they also create their own issues, such as device malfunctions that have been linked to several deaths. Although a disproportionate amount of media attention is given to the use of force by the police, it is a rare event considering the numerous times police officers have encounters with citizens.

To understand police use of force, it is important to examine the sequence of events as they unfold in police–citizen interactions. The way to accomplish this task is to understand how the levels of force and resistance, and the sequence in which they take place, affect the outcome of the encounter. This effort requires using detailed information on the sequence of actions and reactions to make sense of the interaction process of the encounter (Alpert & Dunham, 2004).

Alpert and Dunham (2004) have formulated an interaction theory to help understand police use of force and the overall interaction processes between officers and citizens that lead to using force. The *authority maintenance theory* depicts the police–citizen encounter as an interaction process that is somewhat unique because authority dominates the process and it is more asymmetrical than in most other interactions. Another aspect of police–citizen interactions, according to the theory, is that the expectations and behaviors of these actors are more likely to violate the principle of reciprocity, an important function of human interactions. Officers are more likely to resort to using force when suspects block the officers from reaching their goals concerning the outcome of the encounter. Likewise, citizens respond to the blockage of their goals with varying degrees of resistance. The resistance/force sequence typically escalates until one party changes the other's expected goals voluntarily or involuntarily.

Use of Deadly Force

Since police use of force is often measured by its severity, deadly force is often analyzed as a separate category. It is estimated that each year, approximately 400 persons are killed by the police, and the issue becomes particularly problematic due to the widespread perception that minorities are more likely than white subjects to be killed by the police. Regardless of the research evidence that shows the threatening behavior of the suspect is the strongest indicator of police use of deadly force, the perception of racially biased or motivated killings by the police remains.

The authority to use deadly force can be traced to English common law, when police officers had the authority to use deadly force to apprehend any suspected fleeing felon (the "fleeing felon" doctrine). During this time period, the fleeing-felon doctrine was considered reasonable. First, all felonies were punishable by death in England, and second, defendants did not possess the lights or the presumption of innocence that they enjoy today. In 1985, the U.S. Supreme Court modified the fleeing-felon doctrine in the *Tennessee v. Garner* (1985) decision.

The landmark case of *Tennessee v. Garner* (1985) involved the use of deadly force against a fleeing felon: At approximately 10:45 on the night of October 3, 1974, a slightly built eighth grader, Edward Garner, unarmed and alone, broke a window and entered an unoccupied house in suburban Memphis with the intent of stealing money and property. Two police officers, Elton Hymon and Leslie Wright, responded to a call from a neighbor concerning a prowler. While Wright radioed dispatch, Hymon intercepted the youth as he ran from the back of the house to a 6-foot cyclone fence. After shining a flashlight on the youth who was crouched by the fence, Hymon identified himself and yelled at Garner to stop. Hymon observed that the youth was unarmed. As the boy jumped to get over the fence, the officer fired his service revolver at the youth, as he was trained to do.

Edward Gamer was shot because the police officers had been trained under Tennessee law that it was proper to kill a fleeing felon rather than run the risk of allowing him to escape.

A lawsuit filed by the family ended up reaching the U.S. Supreme Court. The underlying issue being decided by the Court was when and under what circumstances police officers can use deadly force. The Court held that the Tennessee statute was "unconstitutional insofar as it authorizes the use of deadly force against ... unarmed, nondangerous suspect[s]" (*Tennessee v. Garner*, 1985, p. 11). The Court cited with approval the Model Penal Code:

> The use of deadly force is not justifiable ... unless (i) the arrest is for a felony; and (ii) the person effecting the arrest is authorized to act as a police officer ...; and (iii) the actor believes that the force employed creates no substantial risk of injury to innocent persons; and (iv) the actor believes that (1) the crime for which the arrest is made involved conduct including the use or threatened use of deadly force; or (2) there is a substantial risk that a person to be arrested will cause death or serious bodily harm if his apprehension is delayed, (cited in *Tennessee v. Garner*, 1985, pp. 6–7, note 7)

In the final analysis, the Court ruled that "where the suspect poses no immediate threat to the officer and no threat to others, the harm resulting from failing to apprehend him does not justify the use of deadly force to do so" (*Tennessee v. Garner*, 1985, p. 11). The nature of this threat is also clear: "a significant threat of death or serious physical injury" (p. 11). In other words, the Garner decision created a modified "defense of life" standard. It is significant that this pronouncement can be reduced to a moral judgment. This was made clear when the Court noted, "It is not better that, all felony suspects die than that they escape" (p. 11).

Police Pursuits

The use of deadly force by the police, involving the use and abuse of firearms, has been under scrutiny for a long time by police administrators, by the public, as well as by the courts. Another use of potentially deadly force that has only recently attracted significant attention is the police pursuit (see Alpert, Kenney, Dunham, & Smith, 2000). The purpose of a pursuit is to apprehend a suspect following a refusal to stop. When an officer engages in a chase in a high-powered motor vehicle, that vehicle becomes a potentially dangerous weapon. As the training guide for the California Peace Officer Standards and Training (CPOST) explains, firearms and vehicles are instruments of deadly force and the kinetic energy or kill power of a vehicle is far greater than that of a firearm.

Considered in this light, it is not surprising that there is such great concern over police pursuits. Each year, the National Highway Traffic Safety Administration (NHTSA) collects data on police-pursuit-related fatalities. The data are collected as part of the Fatality Analysis Reporting System (FARS); however, they do not capture all of the pursuit-related deaths. For example, many law enforcement officers are not trained to check the "pursuit related" box when a fatality occurs. Similarly, if the police vehicle is not involved in the crash, officers don't always report a death on the form. Nonetheless, the NHTSA data show that at least one person will die every day of the year in a police pursuit, with approximately one third of those deaths being innocent bystanders.

While the costs of pursuits are high, the benefits should not be discounted. On the one hand, it is the mission of the police to protect lives and, clearly, pursuits are inherently dangerous to all involved. On the other hand, there is an ongoing need to immediately apprehend some law violators. Determining how to balance these two competing goals will shape the future of police pursuits. Depending on the reason for the chase and the risk factor to the public, abandonment or termination of a pursuit may be the best choice in the interests of public safety. The critical question in a pursuit is what benefit will be derived from a chase compared to the risk of a crash, injury, or death, whether to officers, suspects, or the public. In other words, a pursuit must be evaluated by weighing the risk to the public against the need to immediately apprehend a suspect.

There are two myths that are commonly stated by proponents of aggressive pursuit policies. The first myth is that suspects who do not stop for the police "have a dead body in the trunk." The thinking behind this statement is that people who flee from the police are serious criminals who have something to hide. While the empirical truth is that many who flee from the police are "guilty" of offenses other than the known reason for their flight, the offense is most often minor, such as a suspended driver's license (Alpert et al., 2000). The second myth is that if the police restrict their pursuits, crime will increase and a significantly greater number of citizens will flee from the police. While this myth helps justify aggressive pursuit policies, it is not substantiated by empirical data. In fact, agencies that have restricted pursuits do not report any increase in fleeing suspects.

Police pursuits are dangerous activities involving risk to all persons involved, and even to those innocent bystanders who might be in harm's way. Research shows that approximately 40% of pursuits result in a crash, 20% result in an injury, and 1% result in a death (Alpert & Dunham, 2004). It is very difficult to force a vehicle to stop without the use of a deadly force tactic, such as ramming or shooting at a vehicle. As these tactics are also very dangerous, it becomes important to develop technologies to get vehicles to stop without risking lives. These technologies are being developed, and military technology is being declassified and used to assist law enforcement officers in stopping vehicles and avoiding unnecessary high-speed pursuits.

THE FUTURE OF POLICING

Although this chapter has presented only a snapshot of policing issues and research, a number of areas have had an increasing influence on policing and will guide policing in the future: (a) continued and concerted attempts by the police to be more attentive to the needs of citizens and solving the underlying problems that contribute to crime (e.g., community policing and problem-oriented policing); (b) responses by the police to demands for greater accountability from citizens, policymakers, and police administrators (e.g., Early Warning or Identification Systems, COMPSTAT, and citizen review boards); and (c) the application of new technologies to help officers and administrators accomplish these goals, including face recognition software and other computer applications.

Community and Problem-Solving Policing

One of the most important factors that moved policing strategies in new directions was the body of research indicating that traditional methods of policing (e.g., rapid response to citizen calls for service, preventive patrol, and the criminal investigation process) were not as efficient as expected in combating crime. The results of this research, and anecdotal information, highlighted the central role that the community played in the detection and prevention of crime. It is clear that without the cooperation of the community, very little crime would be solved at all, and public attitudes concerning the police would be very unfavorable. The argument that traditional policing is reactive rather than preventative, and treats the symptoms of crime rather than broaching the fundamental problems themselves, forced policing specialists to become proactive and to solve problems rather than simply respond to them after the fact. As these techniques improve and sufficient resources are allocated to proactive strategies, there may be a reduction in crime and a corresponding improvement in public perceptions of the police.

Responding to Demands for Greater Accountability

An integral part of community policing is greater accountability on the part of the police for their actions. In recent years, departments have adopted several strategies to facilitate an increase in officer accountability, both internally to superiors and externally to the citizens they serve. In order to promote accountability within police departments, police organizations across the United States are experimenting with COMPSTAT and other programs that develop, gather, and disseminate information on crime problems and hold police managers accountable to reduce the problems. Another innovation in accountability is the early identification of potentially problem officers. The Early Identification System (EIS) includes three basic elements: identification and selection of officers, intervention, and post-intervention monitoring. Each element selects a variety of performance indicators that capture officers' behavior or compare officers in similar situations. The goal is to identify and intervene with officers whose behavior may be problematic.

New Technology

The improvement and application of technology is perhaps most likely to influence policing in the future. Implicit in this discussion of the implementation of community- or problem-oriented policing and the concomitant and innovative methods of enhancing police accountability has been the advent of technology. Perhaps the most important technological advancements inside a police department are crime analysis, computerized reports, GPS systems and car locators, and crime mapping. In the community, the use of cameras may result in crime deterrence or displacement and the enhanced ability to solve crimes.

Crime analysis has three primary functions. These include assessing the nature, extent, and distribution of crime for the purpose of allocating resources. The second primary function is to identify suspects to assist in investigations. The final function of crime analysis is to identify the conditions that facilitate crime and incivility and to direct approaches to crime prevention. The ability of law enforcement agencies to engage in crime analysis and fulfill these three primary functions has been greatly enhanced by advancements in information technology (IT). For example, computer-aided dispatch (CAD) systems have had a tremendous impact on the ability of the police to analyze and prioritize calls for service. CAD systems automatically collect and organize certain information from every call including the type of call, the location, the time, and the date. When these data sources are linked to others, crime analysts are capable of identifying "hot spots" of crime, detecting patterns of crime and disorder, and identifying factors or conditions that may be contributing to crime.

Most police officers complete handwritten reports on paper. New technology now permits many functions to be completed on computers in vehicles and automatically uploaded to agency computers as the vehicles drive by radio towers. Computerized reports can also permit key words, names, and specific information to be searched among all reports, and similarities can be flagged for further investigation of people and places.

New technologies installed in vehicles allow officers to access maps and allow managers to see where officers are located, at what speed they are driving, and where they have been. These new systems can assist the police function, protect officers, and serve as an accountability feature at the same time. In addition, experiments with license plate and face recognition software are taking place that allow officers while driving to be notified when a person or vehicle license of interest is observed.

The origin of crime mapping goes back to crude statistical analysis: a series of color-coded "push pins" in maps displayed on precinct station walls. Today, the police are able to use geographic information systems (GIS) technology to create maps that show the type of crime, victim information, location, time, and a variety of other criteria, all of which can be compared to census information or other databases containing what would otherwise be unconnected information. These data can be analyzed over time and space for trends or similarities, which can subsequently assist a department with crime detection, crime prediction, and resource analysis, among other things.

CONCLUSION

Increased interaction with the community, greater accountability within the police force and to the public, as well as technological advances will all increase and will ultimately have an effect on the police function and how it is carried out. As officers are provided with more time and resources, allowing them to interact more positively with citizens, the police will likely recognize the constructive results of these contacts. Innovative approaches to community mobilization should be designed to empower citizens and build trust in the government. Clearly, the application of technology will provide unique and innovative means of identifying, creating, and updating blueprints for resolving the many problems faced by the police.

REFERENCES AND FURTHER READINGS

Alpert, G., & Dunham, R. (2004). *Understanding police use of force: Officers, suspects, and reciprocity*. New York: Cambridge University Press.

Alpert, G., Kenney, D., Dunham, R., & Smith, W. (2000). *Police pursuits: What we know*. Washington, DC: Police Executive Research Forum.

Alpert, G., MacDonald, J., & Dunham, R. (2005). Police suspicion and discretionary decision making during citizen stops. *Criminology, 43*, 407–434.

Bayley, D. H. (1998). *Policing in America: Assessments and prospects*. Washington, DC: Police Foundation.

Bayley, D. H. (1999). Policing: The world stage. In R. Mawby (Ed.), *Policing across the world: Issues for the twenty-first century* (pp. 3–22). London: UCL Press.

Brenner, A. (1989). Psychological screening of police applicants. In R. G. Dunham & G. P. Alpert (Eds.), *Critical issues in policing: Contemporary readings* (pp. 72–86). Prospect Heights, IL: Waveland Press.

Caiden, G. (1977). *Police revitalization*. Lexington, MA: Lexington Books.

Davis, K. C. (1975). *Police discretion*. St. Paul, MN: West Publishing.

Greenwood, P. W., & Petersilia, J. (1975). *The criminal investigation process: Summary and policy implications*. Santa Monica, CA: RAND.

Langworthy, R. H., & Travis, L. F. (2002). *Policing in America: A balance of forces* (3rd ed.). Upper Saddle River, NJ: Prentice Hall.

Martin, S. (2001). Female officers on the move? A status report of women in policing. In R. G. Dunham & G. P. Alpert (Eds.), *Critical issues in policing: Contemporaiy readings* (4th ed., pp. 401–422). Prospect Heights, IL: Waveland Press.

Miller, W. R. (1977). *Cops and bobbies: Police authority in New York and London, 1830–1870.* Chicago: University of Chicago Press.

National Center for Women in Policing. (2002). *Men, women, and police excessive force: A tale of two genders. A content analysis of civil liability cases, sustained allegations, and citizen complaints.* Los Angeles: Author.

National Research Council. (2003). *Fairness and effectiveness in policing: The evidence.* Washington, DC: National Academies Press.

Reith, C. (1938). *The police idea: Its history and evolution in England in the eighteenth century and after.* London: Oxford University Press.

Reith, C. (1956). *A new study of police history.* Edinburgh, Scotland: Oliver & Boyd.

Rubinstein, J. (1973). *City police.* New York: Farrar, Straus & Giroux.

Stead, P. (1985). *The police of Britain.* London: Macmillan.

Tennessee v. Garner, 471 U.S. 1 (1985).

Uchida, C. D. (1997). The development of the American police: An historical overview. In R. G. Dunham & G. P. Alpert (Eds.), *Critical issues in policing: Contemporaiy readings* (3rd ed., pp. 18–35). Prospect Heights, IL: Waveland Press.

Van Maanen, J. (1978). Observations on the making of policemen. In P. K. Manning & J. Van Maanen (Eds.), *Policing: A view from the street* (pp. 292–308). Santa Monica, CA: Goodyear.

Walker, S. (1983). *The police in America: An introduction.* New York: McGraw-Hill.

Wilson, J. Q. (1968). *Varieties of police behavior: The management of law and order in eight communities.* Cambridge, MA: Harvard University Press.

ETHICS AND POLICE IN A TIME OF CHANGE

*John P. Crank
and Michael A.
Caldero*

R arely in our history have Americans invested their internal security so completely to the trust of the police, and never before has so much been at stake. The legal authority of the police to intervene in citizens' affairs is increasingly relaxed by a congress and court system panic-stricken over media-amplified images of terrorism, crime, and social decay. Police expansion of legal and extralegal authority is supported by a crime-fearing public and academics who champion innovative police strategies.

The early twenty-first century is a time in which the social fabric of the country is in the midst of dramatic change. The age of Anglo-Saxon demographic dominance is giving way to a polyglot society, for better or for worse. Urban and rural spaces are increasingly characterized by different kinds of groups sharing the same local geography. Ethnic, religious, cultural, and age-based conflicts are possible. These conflicts and their resolutions will define the "order" that the police must deal with in our emerging future. On the one hand, public order problems are increasingly defined in terms of relations among diverse groups. On the other, large numbers of immigrants live in the United States, and approximately 30 million alien visitors travel to the United States on visas yearly. The notion of a core ethnicity, characterized as Anglo-Saxon or put simply, white, is dissipating into a polyglot of ethnic variety. We are, like it or not, a true world civilization. What kind of police organization does this civilization need?

The police, Mike has argued, are authorized representatives of a moral standard and use the law to advance that standard. The standard is the noble cause. How will this moral authority mix with the needs of policing in a polyglot society? Asserting their own brand of noble cause morality, they may lose legitimacy in those same communities they try to protect.

We will describe a different way of thinking about public order. In a society marked by diversity and conflict, successful maintenance of public order will require powerful skills in negotiating order among contending groups. Police will be prepared for the future if they possess the skills, and morality, and the patience to weave threads of order together from differing racial, ethnic, and religious accounts. In other words, they must negotiate order rather than assert it.

We believe that policing in the U.S. is at a crossroads. The second half of the twentieth century was what we call the era of citizen based policing. By citizen-based policing, we mean that police officers saw their primary role in citizen protection terms, and their work was organized around responding to citizen calls for assistance, rapid response, random preventive patrol, and protecting the public generally. The height of the citizen-based policing era is the first half or "velvet glove" period of the community policing movement, from its incipient form as team based policing in the early 1970s to the early 1980s. It was characterized by colourful strategies, such as "police community reciprocity," which promoted a notion of the police and public working as equal partners for community self-protection.

The second half of the community based policing movement, from Wilson and Kelling's "broken window's article in 1983 until 2000, is probably better characterized as a victim-based policing movement, with hardening responses to criminals, dramatic expansion of penal sanctions for drug and alcohol offences, lowered concerns about the impact of aggressive practices on minority groups, and sharp expansion of prison populations, with its inevitable consequences—large numbers of offenders returned to the streets with no employable skills, overburdened parole and probation and increasingly economically burdened minority communities. In this era, police justified their work in terms of victims concerns and tended to take a very hard or "iron fist" attitude toward criminals. This response has continued into the early twenty-second century, amplified by technological developments of real-time intelligence through COMPSTAT and crime mapping technologies.

The community policing movement, never particularly popular among the police, collapsed with the presidency of Bush in 2000 and the consequent sharp disinvestment in federal community policing grants. Today, we are increasingly moving into what we call "neo-professionalism" with three elements. The tactical and strategic purposes of the police are increasingly focused on aggressive law enforcement.

The purposes of policing are couched in and justified in terms of a "security" rhetoric, and police work is about protecting government at all levels from disruption, be it in the form of crime, disorder, external threat, or fiscal emergency brought about by natural causes. A "broken windows" philosophy permeates this approach because it resonates with ideas of police response to external threats. Practices such as intelligence-led policing, COMPSTAT (with its focus on real-time crime intelligence), and a blended intelligence-investigation function justified in terms of "connecting the dots" are important elements of this policing.

Chapter 9 looks at the notion that police work is citizen-based. It argues that the citizen basis for policing is important for police work, but has lost much of its viability in the early part of the twenty-second century. Chapter 10 looks at where police work is going. A section called the "Noble Cause Ascendant" is a cautionary tale to managers about what can happen when the law can be justified in terms of the noble cause. This is followed by a review of the most popular police operational tactics in the current era, which focus heavily on aggressive enforcement practices.

SECTION
V

Courts and
Judicial Process

OVERVIEW OF COURTS AND JUDICIAL PROCESS IN THE UNITED STATES

Douglas Klutz and
Mark M. Lanier

Take a second and think about your favorite courtroom drama on television. Think about the heated courtroom battles that regularly ensue between the prosecution and the defense. Despite the intense drama these shows provide, the reality is the courtroom is more of a collaborative effort than an adversarial showdown. Unfortunately, Jack Nicholson's "You can't handle the truth!" moments are far and few between. In reality, over 90 percent of cases in the state and federal court systems result in plea bargaining. That is, securing a guilty plea in exchange for a lighter sentence or a reduction in the severity or amount of criminal charges. Plea bargaining does not make for great television drama, but it does serve to expedite cases in a court system already mired in red tape and backlogged cases. It also highlights the collaborative effort in the courtroom between prosecutors and defense attorneys.

Due to the strained resources in the criminal justice system, our court system in the United States operates largely on the crime-control model of justice. The crime-control model emphasizes speed and efficiency in processing cases. Plea bargaining is a central tenet of the crime-control model of justice. Cases enter the system and are processed as quickly as possible in order to make room for more cases. Think of the crime-control model as an assembly line. In fact, the crime-control model is commonly referred to as "assembly-line justice." In direct contrast to the crime-control model is the due-process model of justice. Under the due-process model, the adversarial process using the courtroom is underscored. Instead of an assembly line, the due-process model of justice can be thought of as an obstacle course. While the due-process model would be ideal, where every individual case is able to go to trial, the reality is the court system has limited resources. Even with over 90 percent of cases ending in a plea bargain, the court system is still heavily overloaded.

DUE PROCESS OF LAW

*Bruce E.
Altschuler, Celia
A. Sgroi, and
Margaret Ryniker*

INTRODUCTION

The Fifth Amendment prohibits the federal government from depriving anyone of life, liberty, or property without due process of law, a protection the Fourteenth Amendment extended to apply to the states. The familiarity of the phrase "due process," however, can hide its complexity. As Justice Felix Frankfurter put it in the case of *Joint Anti-Fascist Refugee Committee v. McGrath*, 341 U.S. 123 (1951), "'Due process,' unlike some legal rules, is not a technical conception with a fixed content unrelated to time, place, and circumstances. ... Due process is not a mechanical instrument. It is not a yardstick. It is a delicate process of adjustment inescapably involving the exercise of judgment by those whom the Constitution entrusted with the unfolding of the process."

How can we understand a concept without a fixed meaning? Fortunately, that concept is so fundamental to our freedom and its history so rich with detail that we can set out standards for judgment even if exact definition is impossible.

The Limits of Due Process

Due process is basically a guarantee of government fairness. Government cannot take our lives, liberty, or property unless it provides us with the chance to protect our interests that is called due process. In other words, the due process clauses protect us from arbitrary and unreasonable actions by government. This sets out the first limit of the concept. It applies to government actions, not private ones. When the Fifth Amendment was ratified, government played a relatively small role in the lives of most citizens, so the distinction was clear and cases few. Between the adoption of the Constitution and the end of the Civil War, the Supreme Court decided only one case based on due process! One of the major changes in our society since then, however, has been the growth of government into virtually all areas of life. This has often created situations intertwining public and private action, making the boundary between the two more difficult to draw.

Thus, the actions of a public college are covered by due process, but what about a private college that gets a substantial amount of government funding? What if the government outsources what had previously always been a public function? For example, private companies now operate prisons under contracts with the government. Do their prisoners have the same rights to due process as those in government-run prisons? In one of the cases presented in this chapter, a court has to determine whether an employee of a privately run but largely publicly funded library has the same due process rights as a public employee. Such examples can be easily multiplied.

The second limit is that due process applies only to something—life, liberty, or property (not the pursuit of happiness, which is in the Declaration of Independence but was replaced by property in the Constitution)—that belongs to the person alleging its deprivation. If there is no such entitlement, there can be no deprivation, hence no requirement of due process. Thus, the government cannot execute you, incarcerate you, or take something you own unless it acts within the guidelines of due process. However, a public hospital could ban smoking without violating due process because there is no right to smoke. Even though smokers may be significantly inconvenienced, they are not being denied life, liberty, or property. Although cases in this chapter discuss what constitutes a liberty interest, chapter 6, on property, examines in far greater detail what is or is not property subject to the protection of the due process guarantee.

Procedural and Substantive Due Process

Traditionally, due process has been divided into two areas: procedural and substantive. Originally, due process referred to the procedures by which laws were carried out. Procedural due process requires that before any deprivation there must be notice and opportunity for a fair hearing before someone neutral and competent. In the mid-nineteenth century the concept was expanded to include substantive due process, which requires that laws be reasonable attempts to achieve legitimate governmental goals while putting the least burden on people's

rights. It also requires laws to be clear enough so that citizens know what is allowed and what is not. Under the doctrine of substantive due process, the courts examine the content of laws to ensure that they do not violate traditional notions of fairness. This may require courts to protect rights that are not explicitly stated in the Constitution, giving judges significant discretion in determining what these rights are. Today, most legal scholars agree that the Supreme Court went overboard during the early twentieth century, using substantive due process to overturn economic reforms that the justices disagreed with. These decisions so discredited the concept that it nearly disappeared for a time. That is why Justice Douglas included language specifically refusing to base his decision in *Griswold v. Connecticut* (see p. 62 in chap. 2) on substantive due process.

This caution has not prevented courts from continuing to use substantive due process, but the major change has been that it is now used more to protect civil rights than economic ones. During the first decades of the twentieth century, the Supreme Court invalidated minimum wage, maximum hour, and child labor laws on the basis of "rights," such as that of entering into a contract. Today society's values have changed so much that these decisions appear mistaken to most people. Courts are more likely to use such civil rights as the right to privacy to limit what government can do. The concept of substantive due process is one of the clearest examples of how such changes in society result in changes in the meaning and application of legal doctrines.

Procedural due process is the more frequently invoked and more familiar of the two types of due process. It requires fair procedures before government can deprive someone of life, liberty, or property; however, the Constitution makes little attempt to define these procedures except in criminal cases for which the Bill of Rights provides specific guarantees, such as the rights to counsel, to confront witnesses, and to avoid compelled self-incrimination. As indicated by the quote from Justice Frankfurter at the beginning of this chapter, the courts have held that the procedural requirements of due process vary with the situation. In general, the person being deprived must be given adequate notice and a fair hearing at which to present his or her side to a disinterested party. In general, the greater the deprivation, the more formal the hearing, with criminal trials providing the greatest protection and minor deprivations the least. Conversely, emergency situations can justify more expedited procedures. As of this writing the courts are wrestling with the issue of what procedures to require for those captured in Afghanistan and subsequently held in Guantanamo Bay who are challenging their detention as what the Bush administration has termed "illegal combatants." The materials in this chapter help clarify what procedural process is required in a variety of circumstances by looking at specific issues.

This introduction provides a basic understanding of the main points of due process. Although it cannot be defined with precision, it is a basic guarantee requiring that when government deprives someone of life, liberty, or property, it must do so in a manner that both is and appears to be fair. This may give courts considerable discretion, but it also provides the flexibility necessary to avoid injustice.

THE MEANING OF DUE PROCESS

In the first reading, Judge Edward D. Re explains the role of courts in protecting the due process rights of individuals. In doing this he stresses both the importance and flexibility of due process. Note that the lack of a specific definition of due process has not prevented courts from providing guidelines to help apply the concept. Also, pay close attention to his discussion of Section 1983 of the 1871 Civil Rights Act, which is frequently used to authorize lawsuits seeking to protect individual rights threatened by government action.

Due Process, Judicial Review, and the Rights of the Individual *Edward D. Re*

In Anglo-American law probably no concept is more important than that of due process of law. It is from the guarantee of due process that all of the substantive and procedural rights embodied in the Constitution

and laws acquire meaning and vitality. Indeed, it is at the heart of the common law system of jurisprudence.

The phrase "due process of law" implies that a person will receive fair treatment, and a procedure designed to achieve just result. In the judicial context, it connotes an opportunity to be heard before a decision is made that will affect one's rights or legally protected interests. It applies both to personal rights, sometimes termed "liberty interests," and to property rights. The type or nature of the hearing to which one will be entitled and when it will be granted, will depend upon the nature of the interest affected and the degree or severity of the deprivation that may be imposed. To say that a person has been deprived of due process of law implies that the person has not been granted or has not received those protections or safeguards that are guaranteed to all persons under the law.

The guarantees of due process of law are specifically set forth in the Fifth and Fourteenth Amendments to the Constitution. The Fifth Amendment provides that "No person shall be … deprived of life, liberty, or property without due process of law. …"

The Fifth Amendment, adopted as part of the Bill of Rights, was originally interpreted to serve as a check upon the acts of the federal government only. The Fourteenth Amendment, adopted over three-quarters of a century later in the aftermath of the Civil War, applies expressly to the state government. In more recent years, in a series of landmark decisions, the Supreme Court has held that most of the protections contained in the Bill of Rights have been incorporated into the Fourteenth Amendment and, therefore, are also binding upon the states. In addition to these constitutional provisions, there are specific statutory enactments that are designed to promote the enforcement of these constitutional guarantees.

In the American constitutional system, the judiciary plays a unique role in interpreting and applying the guarantees and freedoms enumerated in the Constitution. On judicial review, it is the role of the courts to determine whether the enactments of the legislature, or the actions of an administrative or executive agency, comport with requirements of due process of law. If the challenged government actions do not meet the constitutional standards of due process, the courts will overturn those actions in order to ensure that the aggrieved party receives the "due process" to which that party is entitled.

The courts have developed a body of case law that embodies the standards of due process that must be followed in particular cases. This body of case law, developed over time, provides guidance not only for all of the courts of the land, but also for all branches of government in defining and applying due process in different situations and cases.

The basic premise of due process of law is that all persons are entitled to the benefits, protections, and privileges of the law of the land. As Chief Justice John Marshall stated in the landmark case of *Marbury v. Madison*: "the very essence of civil liberty certainly consists in the right of every individual to claim the protection of the laws ..." However, while it is clear that everyone is entitled to the protections of due process of law, the difficulty arises in the application of due process of law in the particular case or circumstance. It is therefore difficult, if not impossible, adequately and accurately to define due process because the concept is elastic and flexible, and must be adaptable to countless different contexts.

There is a reluctance to define due process for fear that the definition may be interpreted in a way that would limit or restrict its application in a particular case.

The guarantees and protections of due process apply to both criminal and civil cases, as well as the countless civil matters in which a person comes into contact with administrative agencies and government officials. In criminal cases, what is termed a "liberty interest" is usually at stake. In civil matters, a liberty interest or a property right may be at issue. Although due process applies in all cases, the specific degree of protection may vary depending on the nature of the interest threatened, and the competing governmental or other interests that must also be considered.

In our constitutional system, it is fundamental that persons are entitled to due process of law before they are deprived of a liberty interest or a property right. Property rights can take on many forms, from tangible things such as land or money to intangible interests such as the right to a public education or an interest in continued employment. In order to pursue a claim

based on a deprivation of a property right without adequate due process, a person must show a "legitimate claim of entitlement" to the interest affected by governmental action. It is important to remember, however, that generally "[p]roperty interests are not created by the Constitution, 'they are created and their dimensions are defined by existing rules or understandings that stem from an independent source such as state law'" *Cleveland Board of Education v. Loudermill*, 470 U.S. 532 (1985).

Since the due process clauses of the Fifth and Fourteenth Amendments govern only the federal and state governments, respectively, there must be some type of "state action" for a court to grant relief. Hence, the actions of a private party acting in a purely personal capacity are generally not restricted or restrained by the requirements of due process. The Supreme Court has held that, for the purposes of determining whether an action is subject to the due process requirements of the Constitution, "a State normally can be held responsible only when it has exercised coercive power or has provided such significant encouragement, either over or covert, that the choice must in law be deemed to be that of the State" *Blum v. Yaretsky*, 457 U.S. 991 (1982).

A federal court of appeals has stated that, "[w]henever a governmental body acts so as to injure an individual, the Constitution requires that the act be consonant with due process of law" *Dixon v. Alabama State Board of Education*, 294 F.2d 150, 5th Cir., cert. denied 368 U.S. 930 (1961). Thus, courts have found state action and property interests sufficient to activate or require due process in situations such as the firing of a government employee, the termination of welfare benefits, and the suspension of a student from a public school or state university.

After a court has decided that there has been a deprivation of life, liberty, or property interest, and sufficient state or official government action to invoke the due process clause, the court must determine whether the person has been denied or deprived of due process of law. At a minimum, a deprivation of life, liberty, or property must be accompanied by "notice and opportunity for hearing appropriate to the nature of the case" *Mullane v. Central Hanover Bank & Trust Co.*, 339 U.S. 306 (1950). Usually, the hearing must be held prior to the deprivation because it should occur "at a time when the deprivation can still be prevented" *Fuentes v. Shevin*, 407 U.S. 67 (1972). When there is a significant government interest in postponing a hearing, a post-deprivation hearing may be sufficient to satisfy due process requirements, although at some point the delay may be considered a constitutional violation.

A hearing serves several purposes. First, the opportunity for the aggrieved or threatened party "to present his side of the case is recurringly of obvious value in reaching an accurate decision" (*Loudermill* at 543). Thus, by allowing or requiring both sides to present their cases, the risk of factual error or mistake is reduced. Second, even when no facts are in dispute, allowing the affected party to respond or explain permits the responsible administrator or official to make a more informed decision, and permits a sounder exercise of discretion.

Whether the hearing or procedure involved was fair depends upon the nature of the interest affected and all of the other facts and circumstances of the particular case. In *Mathews v. Eldridge*, 424 U.S. 319 (1976), the Supreme Court identified three factors that a court must balance or consider in evaluating a due process claim:

"First, the private interest that will be affected by the official action; second, the risk of an erroneous deprivation of such interest through the procedures used; and the probable value, if any, of additional or substitute procedural safeguards; and finally, the [state] interest, including the function involved and the fiscal and administrative burdens that the additional or substitute procedural requirement would entail."

These formulations reflect the efforts of the courts to ensure the fairness of any government action while recognizing, at the same time, the need for a governmental body to function efficiently and economically. Thus, a student faced with disciplinary action by a public university would not be entitled as a matter of due process to the full panoply of procedural protections afforded a criminal defendant. Similarly, a government employee who has been discharged for cause has a right to be informed of the nature of the charges and to respond to the charges. Normally, however, the employee would not be entitled to a full-blown adversary hearing conducted under strict rules of evidence and procedures appropriate for the trial of criminal cases.

A crucial function of the due process clauses is to give full force and effect to the ideal of fairness enshrined in the Constitution. In attempting to effectuate and implement the ideals of equal justice and non-discrimination, Congress has enacted certain civil rights statutes prohibiting discrimination in voting, education, housing, employment, and other areas on the basis of race, color, religion, national origin, gender, age, or handicap. These statutes are specific and go beyond the constitutional protections in that they have a broad application to the discriminatory actions of private individuals, as well as governmental agencies and officials.

An enforcement mechanism is the Civil Rights Act of 1871, 42 U.S.C. Section 1983. This act, which was passed in response to post-Civil War racial abuses and terrorism, "provides for a broad and comprehensive civil rights jurisdiction, and was intended 'to ensure that individuals whose federal constitutional or statutory rights are abridged may recover damages or secure injunctive relief'" *Freeman v. Rideout*, 808 F.2d 949 (2d Cir. 1986).

In essence, section 1983 provides jurisdiction and a right of action in a federal court for a person whose constitutional rights have been abridged or denied under the color of state law. It is not limited to constitutional violations involving racial discrimination, but functions as a source of relief for persons who have been deprived of a host of constitutional rights under color of state law.

Section 1983 provides a right of action, for example, for someone whose home, in an outrageous manner, has been illegally searched in violation of the Fourth Amendment by police officers acting under color of state law.

In a federal system founded upon the separation of powers and the role of law, all branches of government perform indispensable functions. Nevertheless, without the beneficial scrutiny of judicial review, government officials may on occasion forget that all public servants are duty bound to obey the law, and protect the rights of the persons whom they are to serve.

The guarantee of due process of law, as embodied in the Fifth and Fourteenth Amendments to the Constitution, and, as interpreted by the courts, provides for fair treatment for all who are affected by government action. It implies that a person will receive fairness of treatment, and a procedure designed to achieve a just and equitable result. The guarantee of due process serves to check or control the misuses of abuse of power, and ensures that other rights and privileges protected by the Constitution and laws are given force and effect. By confining the agents of government to their properly delegated authority under the Constitution and laws, due process of law provides a fundamental cornerstone for a free and lawful society.

NOTE

1. Chief Judge Emeritus, U.S. Court of International Trade; Distinguished Professor of Law, St. John's University School of Law. Originally published in *Cleveland State Law Review* 39 (1991): 5–13. Reprinted by permission.

FOR DISCUSSION

1. Judge Re states that in our law, "no concept is more important than that of due process of law." Why does he believe it is so significant? Do you agree or is there another concept that you think is more important?
2. The courts have deliberately chosen not to define due process. Explain why. What are the advantages and disadvantages of this lack of a specific definition?
3. What is a "liberty interest"? Why is it important?
4. Explain the steps taken by a court in determining whether or not procedural due process has been violated.
5. How does Section 1983 of the 1871 Civil Rights Act help to enforce the due process guarantee?
6. According to Judge Re, in due process cases, "the specific degree of protection may vary depending upon the nature of the interest threatened, and the competing governmental or other interests that must also be considered." Why should there be such variations in due process protection? Would you prefer a single standard for every case?

GOVERNMENT ACTION

When an employee of a privately run library is fired, she files a Section 1983 lawsuit, claiming that the fact that more than 85 percent of the library's funding comes from government makes her a public employee protected by due process. By examining past cases, the court determines which factors can convert the actions of a private entity into state action. Note how they apply these factors to the Westport Library Association.

Horvath v. Westport Library Association U.S. Court of Appeals, Second Circuit (2004) 362 F.3d 147

POOLER, Circuit Judge: Horvath began working for the Westport Library Association ("the Library"), located in Westport, Connecticut ("the Town"), in October 1989 as a "business manager assistant." She was discharged on December 29, 2000. The Library contends that Horvath was terminated because of her resistance to the implementation of new payroll technology and because of general incompetence.

Horvath's Section 1983 claim is based upon her contention that the Library violated her right to due process by not affording her notice and an opportunity to be heard prior to termination. The district court, however, rejected Horvath's Section 1983 claim because the Library was not a state actor, and was therefore not charged with affording its employees due process before terminating them. Because Horvath has dropped her ADEA [Age Discrimination in Employment Act] claim, the only facts germane to this appeal are those that are relevant to the Library's status as a state actor.

We note at the outset that both parties rely heavily upon factual findings contained in two written decisions of the Connecticut State Board of Labor Relations ("the Board"), one from 1977 and one from

1989, issued in cases in which the Library was a party. Both of these cases involved disputes between the Library and the labor union representing its staff members regarding whether the Library was a "municipal employer" within the meaning of Connecticut law. The Library states in its brief on this appeal that these factual findings are "consistent with the Library's current status," except to the extent set forth in an affidavit filed in the district court by the Library's current Director.

We emphasize, however, that, although both the 1977 and 1989 Board opinions concluded that the Library was not a "municipal employer" under Connecticut law, these conclusions are clearly irrelevant to our consideration of whether Horvath should have been afforded the due process protections available to public employees under federal law. As the magistrate judge correctly noted, the Library "cannot transform the legal conclusions reached in 1977 and 1989 into facts by reiterating them ... as if they were facts." Thus, while the paucity of the record gives us no alternative to relying upon the factual findings set forth in the Board decisions, we emphasize that our legal conclusions regarding Horvath's Section 1983 claim are independently derived.

The 1977 Board decision contains the following factual findings that we believe are relevant to the instant appeal:

1. The Westport Library Association is a non-stock corporation created by a special act of the [Connecticut] General Assembly in 1907 with the right to acquire, hold, and manage such property as may be necessary for establishing and maintaining a public library in the Town of Westport, and to "make such by-laws, rules, and regulations ... as it shall deem best for the management of the property and affairs of said Association."

* * *

3. Under the Library by-laws the Library director is appointed by its board of trustees and has charge of the administration of its affairs under the direction and review of a board of trustees. This includes the responsibility for the care of the building and equipment; the hiring, disciplining, and promotion of employees, and the supervision of their duties; responsibility for the service to the public and the operation of the library under the financial conditions set forth in the budget.

* * *

5. One half of the trustees of [the] Library are designated by the Town.

6. [The] Library has some income from investments, gifts, and fines and rentals, but the bulk of its annual income comes from an appropriation from the general funds of the Town. The operating budget for 1976–7 was $545,210 of which the Town appropriation was $489,345.

* * *

12. None of the current trustees of [the] Library is an employee or official of the Town. The 1989 Board decision contains the following additional relevant findings of fact:

2. The Library is governed by a Board of Trustees composed of 14 voting members.

3. Seven (7) members of the Library's Board of Trustees are appointed by the Representative Town Meeting of the Town of Westport. ... The other seven (7) Trustees are appointed by the Board of Trustees themselves.

* * *

4. None of the current seven (7) Trustees who were appointed by the Representative Town Meeting are elected or appointed officials of the Town of Westport.

5. The Director of the Library is appointed by the full Board of Trustees. The Director is responsible for hiring the Library's Department Heads who in turn hire the members of the staff.

6. The operations of the Westport Public Library are funded by a budget (1988–89) that is composed of (1) grants from the Town of Westport, (2) gifts, (3) investments, (4) fines, and (5) rentals. 88% of the budget is composed of grants from the Town of Westport.

7. The Library's budget process entails creation of a preliminary budget request by the Library staff which is presented to the Board of Trustees for their approval. If approved, the Library staff and Board of Trustees present the budget request to and participate in meetings with the Town's Board of Finance. The Town's Board of Finance ultimately

recommends a budget to the Representative Town Meeting for final approval. The final budget allocation is in a lump sum and is without restriction as to expenditure by the Library.

As already noted, the 1977 and 1989 Board decisions have been supplemented by an affidavit of the Library's current Director. The affidavit contains the following information concerning the Library's budget: The Library's budget for FY 2000–2001 was $3,187,644 with 86.5% of $2,777,494 coming from the Town of Westport. The remainder of the Library's funding comes from private fund-raising, fines, late fees and profits derived from a cafe, which it owns and runs on premises.

In her own affidavit, Horvath discloses that she, along with the rest of the Library's staff, is a member of a union which is only identified in the record as the Brotherhood of Municipal Employees ("the Union"). Also in the record is a copy of the collective bargaining agreement between the Library and the Union in force at the time of Horvath's discharge. The agreement provides that a staff member may only be discharged "for just cause" and that, if discharged, the staff member "shall be given the reason therefore, in writing, within three (3) days with a copy to the Union President." The agreement also provides for a three-stage grievance procedure for "any grievance or dispute which may arise between the parties concerning the interpretation or application of any provision" of the collective bargaining agreement. The first two stages involve internal dispute resolution procedures and the third is an appeal to the Board. We also note that the agreement enrolls Library staff members in the Town's municipal employee pension plan.

It is unclear whether Horvath followed the first two stages of the collective bargaining agreement's grievance procedure, but she did appeal her discharge to the Board. A three-member panel of the Board—composed of a "Public Member," a "Management Member," and a "Labor Member"—held a hearing on the matter on January 8, 2001. Horvath was represented at the hearing by the President of the Union, and a decision was issued on February 15, 2001. The decision states that "the ultimate issue" for the panel's consideration is whether Horvath was discharged

for just cause, but that "a threshold question [was] whether the Westport Public Library [was] a municipal employer and thus subject to the due process requirement of the Fourteenth Amendment of the U.S. Constitution." As to the latter issue, the panel majority summarily reaffirmed the 1977 and 1989 Board decisions holding that the Library was not a municipal employer. The majority also found that the evidence of Horvath's "shortcomings" was so extensive as to make it "self-evident" that she was discharged for just cause.

The "Labor Member" of the panel issued a dissenting opinion. In his view, the Library qualified as a municipal employer because "it [was] clear that a symbiotic relationship existed between the Westport Public Library and the State of Connecticut, because the Library received appropriations from the Town and the State." In addition, he believed that the evidence demonstrated that Horvath was "a loyal employee with twelve years of service [who] was given a constructed [sic] termination."

Again, the substance of Horvath's § 1983 claim is that the Library violated her right to due process when it terminated her without prior notice and an opportunity to be heard. There is no question that "[a] public employee who has a right not to be fired without 'just cause' ... has a property interest in her employment that qualifies for these protections of procedural due process." *Otero v. Bridgeport Hous. Auth.*, 297 F.3d 142, 151 (2d Cir. 2002) (internal quotations and brackets omitted). As already noted, the collective bargaining agreement between the Library and the union representing Horvath provides that members of the Library staff can be fired only for just cause.

The issue that remains for us is whether Horvath was a public employee when she worked for the Library. The right to due process established by the Fourteenth Amendment applies only to government entities, and an attempt to vindicate that right through a Section 1983 claim can be lodged only against a government entity. Accordingly, "the ultimate issue in determining whether a person [may bring] suit under § 1983 is the same question posed in cases arising under the Fourteenth Amendment: is the alleged infringement of federal rights 'fairly attributable to the State?'" *Rendell-Baker v. Kohn*, 457 U.S. 830 (1982). The magistrate judge answered this question in the negative, although it noted that "the question appears closer than defendants allow." We believe that the question must be decided in Horvath's favor.

As a general matter, defining the limits of the State's presence tends to be a difficult endeavor because of the protean character of contemporary government activity. The Supreme Court has noted something like this in its most recent substantial statement on state action doctrine:

> What is fairly attributable [to the government] is a matter of normative judgment, and the criteria lack rigid simplicity. From the range of circumstances that could point toward the State behind an individual face, no one fact can function as a necessary condition across the board for finding state action; nor is any set of circumstances absolutely sufficient, for there may be some countervailing reason against attributing activity to the government. *Brentwood Academy v. Tennessee School Athletic Ass'n.*, 531 U.S. 288 (2001) ("Brentwood Academy").

Not surprisingly, therefore, "there is no single test to identify state actions and state actors." Rather, there are "a host of facts that can bear on the fairness of ... an attribution" of a challenged action to the State.

State action may be found in situations where an activity that traditionally has been the exclusive, or near exclusive, function of the State has been contracted out to a private entity. For example, only the State may legitimately imprison individuals as punishment for the commission of crimes. Acts of prison employees will therefore almost certainly be considered acts of the State whatever the terms of their employment. But it can hardly be said that the provision of library services is similarly a "traditionally exclusive public function." *American Mfrs. Mutual Ins. Co. v. Sullivan*, 526 U.S. 40 (1999). On the contrary, a private individual or enterprise certainly could provide library services to the citizens of the Town in just the same manner as Benjamin Franklin provided library services to the citizens of Philadelphia two hundred and fifty years ago. It cannot be said "that the operation of a library constitutes ... a function traditionally associated with

sovereignty." *Hollenbaugh v. Carnegie Free Library, of Connellsville, Pa.*, 545 F.2d 382 (3rd. Cir. 1976).

Further, Horvath's argument in favor of a finding of state action focuses most heavily on the fact that the Library's budget is almost exclusively composed of public funds. It is almost self-evident that this weighs in favor of Horvath's claim, but the Supreme Court has cautioned that it is far from the case that a predominance of public funding is conclusive evidence of state action. In *Rendell-Baker v. Kohn*, a privately operated school for students with disciplinary problems was sued by various former employees over the circumstances of their discharges. Most of the school's students had their tuition paid by public school districts, and the school also received aid from various federal and state education agencies. For several years, therefore, public funds accounted for more than ninety percent of the school's operating budget. In short, public entities were by far the school's biggest customer and source of funds.

The Supreme Court held, however, that the school was not a state actor, at least for the purposes of the petitioners' claims. The decisive factor in the Court's view was that the school's personnel decisions were uninfluenced by public officials and that "the decisions to discharge the petitioners were not compelled or even influenced by any state regulation." In light of the autonomy with which it made its decisions as to whom to hire and fire, the school was not "fundamentally different from many private corporations whose business depends primarily on contracts to build roads, bridges, dams, ships, or submarines for the government. Acts of such private contractors do not become acts of the government by reason of their significant or even total engagement in performing public contracts."

Thus, it is plain that the Library is not a state actor by virtue of public funding alone. But we do not believe that *Rendell-Baker* controls this case, because it is also plain that the Library is not merely a private contractor whose internal management decisions are beyond state regulation. Nor is the Library merely an entity that has the State for its biggest customer. Rather, as noted above, the Library is governed by a Board of Trustees, half of whose members are appointed by the Town. The significance of this fact in the state action inquiry is most extensively set forth in *Lebron v. National*

Railroad Passenger Corp., 513 U.S. 374 (1999), a case not cited by either of the parties.

In *Lebron*, the Supreme Court considered the state actor status of the National Railroad Passenger Corporation, commonly known as Amtrak. Amtrak was established by a Congressional statute, which explicitly states that it "'will not be an agency or establishment of the United States Government.'" This designation, however, was held to be anything but conclusive because "it is not for Congress to make the final determination of Amtrak's status as a Government entity for purposes of determining the constitutional rights of citizens affected by its actions." Rather, the Court looked to the fact that the statute creating Amtrak also "provided for a board of nine members, six of whom [were] appointed directly by the President of the United States." Two other members of the board are appointed by Amtrak's preferred shareholders, and the final member was appointed by the other eight members. The Court concluded that "where ... the Government creates a corporation by special law, for the furtherance of government objectives, and retains for itself permanent authority to appoint a majority of the directors of that corporation," the corporation would be considered a state actor.

Following *Lebron*, we have utilized the following standard to determine whether or not a corporate entity qualifies as a state actor: "only if (1) the government created the corporate entity by special law, (2) the government created the entity to further governmental objectives, and (3) the government retains 'permanent authority to appoint a majority [of] the directors of the corporation' will the corporation be deemed a government entity for the purpose of the state action requirement." *Hack v. President & Fellows of Yale Coll.*, 237 F.3d 81, 84 (2d Cir. 2000) (quoting *Lebron*). In *Hack*, we considered whether Yale qualified as a state actor. Although we found that the first two elements of the *Lebron* standard were "easily satisfied," the fact that the State of Connecticut retained the right to appoint only two of Yale's nineteen board members meant that the school was "a long way from [being] controlled" by the state.

Here we believe that the *Lebron* standard has been satisfied. It is plain that the first two elements are present; as noted above, the Library was created by a special act of the Connecticut State legislature and there is no doubt that the provision of library services is a legitimate statutory objective. As to the third element, it is correct that only one-half, and not a majority, of the Library's trustees are appointed by the Town. However, we do not believe that this precludes a finding that the third element of Lebron has been satisfied. The additional fact that only a little more than a tenth of the Library's funding comes from sources other than the Town convinces us that the Town maintains sufficient control over the Library to qualify it as a state actor for the purposes of Horvath's claim. Thus, we conclude that the argument that the Library is a private entity "is overborne by the pervasive entwinement of public institutions and public officials in its composition and workings, and there is no substantial reason to claim unfairness in applying constitutional standards to it." *Brentwood Academy*, 531 U.S. at 289.

Two arguments to the contrary do not persuade us. The Library urges that the decision to terminate Horvath was made solely by the Library's Director who, although appointed by the trustees, is not herself a public official. This is significant because a finding of state action must be premised upon the fact that "the State is *responsible* for the *specific conduct* of which the plaintiff complains." *Blum v. Yaretsky*, 457 U.S. 991 (1982) (first emphasis in original; second emphasis added). In *Brentwood Academy*, however, the Supreme Court has cautioned that the concept of responsibility is not to be read narrowly in the context of the state action inquiry. That is, the State need not have coerced or even encouraged the events at issue in the plaintiff's complaint if "the relevant facts show pervasive entwinement to the point of largely overlapping identity" between the State and the entity that the plaintiff contends is a state actor. The combination of pervasive public funding of the Library and control of one-half of its governing board persuade us that such "pervasive entwinement" is present here.

We also note that none of the trustees appointed by the Town to the Library's board at the time of Horvath's discharge were themselves public officials. But this fact certainly does not preclude a finding of state action because, pursuant to *Lebron*, it is the Town's "authority to appoint" trustees, and not the identity of the trustees appointed, that is relevant to the state action inquiry.

For the forgoing reasons, we reverse the district court's grant of summary judgment. We note that the district court's holding was limited to a finding that the Library was not a state actor for the purposes of Horvath's Section 1983 claim, and that the court made no factual findings regarding Horvath's assertion that she was denied notice and an opportunity to be heard prior to her discharge. Our decision is similarly limited to the question of the Library's status as a state actor, and we express no opinion as to whether the Library satisfied the requirements of due process when it terminated Horvath.

FOR DISCUSSION

1. Why is it so important to determine whether or not the library is a "state actor"?
2. What is Horvath's basis for concluding that even though it is a private entity the library is really a state actor? How does the library reply?
3. In 1977 and 1989 the State Board of Labor Relations ruled that the library was not a "municipal employer." How did these rulings affect Judge Pooler's decision?
4. Judge Pooler compares the library to Amtrak and to Yale University. Explain how she uses these comparisons in her decision.
5. What are the crucial factors in determining whether the library's actions are subject to due process?
6. What happens next? What do you think the likely outcome of the case will be?

PROPERTY RIGHTS AND LIBERTY INTERESTS

In his essay, Judge Re wrote that "persons are entitled to due process of law before they are deprived of a liberty interest or a property right." In the next case, Michael Winbush was relieved of his duties as assistant football coach and head women's softball coach, denied a promised raise, and reassigned as intramural coordinator without change to his existing paygrade.

The Court of Appeals of North Carolina has to decide whether he has been deprived of property. If he has, he can challenge the dismissal on due process grounds. If you are wondering why, despite overturning the trial

You Be the Judge

Margaret Apao obtained a $280,000 mortgage on her Honolulu home from San Diego Home Loans, Inc. After three years she notified the bank that she intended to cancel the mortgage and make no further payments because of her belief that the mortgage violated the federal Truth in Lending Act. The bank moved to foreclose based on provisions of the mortgage contract and a Hawaii statute that authorized a private nonjudicial foreclosure sale provided the borrower is notified through publication in a widely read newspaper over three weeks and posting notice on the premises three weeks before the property is sold. Copies of this notice must also be filed with the state director of taxation. The provisions of this law and the mortgage contract were followed, resulting in a foreclosure sale of the property.

Apao sued under the Fourteenth Amendment, arguing that the sale deprived her of her property without due process of law as she had no opportunity to challenge the provisions of the contract. She noted that the sale was authorized by statute, that it was conducted by a self-interested lender, and that the mortgage business is regulated by both state and federal law. Was the sale of her property state action that she can challenge in court as a violation of her due process rights?

For the decision of the U.S. Court of Appeals, see *Apao v. The Bank of New York* in the You Be the Judge Key at the end of the chapter.

court order to reinstate Winbush, the appellate court affirmed in part and reversed in part, that is because it agreed that the Office of Administrative Hearings and State Personnel Commission did have jurisdiction.

Winbush v. Winston-Salem State University
Court of Appeals of North Carolina (2004)
598 S.E.2d 619

BRYANT, Judge. Winston-Salem State University (respondent) appeals a superior court order filed 17 March 2003 reversing an order by the State Personnel Commission (SPC) and ordering the reinstatement of Michael T. Winbush (petitioner) to his duties as Assistant Football Coach and Head Women's Softball Coach.

On 2 October 2000, petitioner filed a petition for a contested case hearing with the Office of Administrative Hearings (OAH). The petition alleged petitioner had been discharged or reassigned from his coaching duties without just cause. Attached to the petition was a statement by petitioner that he had been "relieved of [his] athletic duties and privileges effective June 30, 2000" by respondent's Athletics Director. In a recommended decision, the administrative law judge (ALJ) who initially heard the case concluded: (1) the OAH had "jurisdiction over this contested matter" and (2) petitioner was demoted without just cause. The SPC, however, rejected the ALJ's findings of fact and conclusions of law as "erroneous as a matter of law." In rejecting the ALJ's recommended decision in its entirety, the SPC stated: "The Commission finds that neither the ALJ nor the Commission have jurisdiction under Chapter 126 over petitioner's complaint, as an employee subject to the State Personnel Act, that he was not assigned the job duties of his choice, i.e. specifically certain coaching duties and responsibilities." Petitioner appealed the SPC ruling to the superior court.

In an order filed 17 March 2003, the superior court in turn reversed the SPC decision, finding jurisdiction and making the following pertinent findings of fact:

> 33. As a result of the disciplinary action … , [petitioner] did not receive the 10%

raise in salary in July[] 2000, which he had been told that he would receive for his coaching accomplishments.

***

> 35. [Petitioner] is still employed at WSSU as a recreation worker, and his pay grade has not changed. [Petitioner] was hired as a coach, has excelled as a coach and has developed a reputation as an excellent coach; however, he has not been allowed to coach at WSSU since June 30, 2000.

The superior court concluded petitioner had been demoted or discharged for disciplinary reasons without just cause from his position as coach. The superior court also concluded that petitioner had been denied a 10% pay raise for his coaching responsibilities.

The issues are whether: (I) the allegations in the petition invoked the jurisdiction of the OAH and SPC and (II) the superior court erred in concluding petitioner had been demoted or discharged from his coaching duties in violation of N.C. Gen. Stat. § 126–34.1(a)(1).

The rights of university employees to challenge any employment action in the OAH arise solely from the State Personnel Act (SPA). Thus, the OAH's jurisdiction over appeals of university employee grievances is confined to the limits established by the SPA. In 1995, N.C. Gen. Stat. § 126–34.1 was enacted to specifically define the types of employee appeals that constitute contested case issues of which the OAH may hear. N.C. Gen. Stat. § 126–34.1 provides in pertinent part that a State employee or former State employee has the right to challenge his "dismissal, demotion, or suspension without pay based upon an alleged violation of G.S. 126–35, if the employee is a career State employee." Pursuant to N.C. Gen. Stat. § 126–35, "no career State employee subject to the [SPA] shall be discharged, suspended, or demoted for disciplinary reasons, except for just cause." Therefore, an employee petition filed with the OAH that alleges the employee has been dismissed, demoted, or suspended without just cause is sufficient to invoke the jurisdiction of the OAH and SPC.

In this case, the petition filed by petitioner alleged he had been discharged without just cause or reassigned without just cause when he was "relieved of [his] athletic duties and privileges effective June 30, 2000" by respondent's Athletics Director. Under our liberal rules of construction for allegations raised in a party's pleading, the petition thus alleges either a discharge or demotion. Accordingly, the superior court properly concluded that the OAH and SPC had jurisdiction to hear the petition.

We next consider whether the superior court erred in concluding that petitioner had been demoted or discharged from his coaching duties in violation of N.C. Gen. Stat. § 126–34.1(a)(1).

The evidence establishes that petitioner was neither dismissed nor demoted from his respondent employment. In 1994, respondent's Student Affairs Department hired petitioner to fill the position of "Recreation Worker II." Petitioner's annual salary was $22,557.00, which was equivalent to a "paygrade 64" on the N.C. State Salary Schedule. As a respondent employee, petitioner's primary responsibility was to coach football and women's softball. In April 2000, petitioner was commended for his coaching accomplishments and told he would receive an additional 10% raise in salary effective 1 July 2000.

In June 2000, a dispute arose over petitioner's coaching performance: Petitioner had organized a youth football camp to occur on 18 and 19 June 2000. After having scheduled the football camp, petitioner learned he was required to attend a respondent staff retreat on 17 and 18 June 2000. Petitioner made arrangements for his staff to operate the football camp while he attended the required respondent staff retreat. However, against the instructions of his supervisor, petitioner failed to obtain prior, written approval to conduct the football camp. Consequently, effective 1 July 2000 petitioner was removed from his coaching duties and began serving as intramural coordinator, without change to his paygrade or Recreation Worker II status. In addition, he failed to receive the promised raise in salary for his coaching accomplishments.

This evidence shows petitioner was neither dismissed nor demoted in his Recreation Worker II position at respondent. At most, the evidence speaks to a reassignment, as petitioner claims to have lost his more significant coaching responsibilities. "Because petitioner [is] a permanent State employee, it is well-settled that he [has] a 'property interest of continued employment created by state law and protected by the Due Process Clause.'" *Nix v. Dep't of Administration*, 417 S.E.2d 823, 825 (1992). That interest "does not extend to the right to possess or retain a particular job or to perform particular services." *Fields v. Durham*, 909 F.2d 94, 98 (4th Cir. 1990), cert. denied, 498 U.S. 1068, (1991).

As previously stated, a demotion is defined as a "lowering in rank, position, or pay," Black's Law Dictionary 444. Rank is defined as "relative standing or position" within a group. *Webster's Third New International Dictionary* 1881 (3d ed. 1966). A reduction in position under the SPA has been construed by this Court to mean the placement of an employee "in a lower paygrade." *Gibbs v. Dept. of Human Resources*, 335 S.E.2d 924, 927 (1985) (rejecting a petitioner's contention that she had been demoted under the SPA when she was reassigned to a position with fewer responsibilities but which was subject to the same paygrade). In the instant case, petitioner's paygrade remained the same. Furthermore, as the promised raise in salary had not yet come into effect at the time of his reassignment, petitioner has also failed to show a demotion through a decrease in pay. As such, petitioner was neither discharged nor demoted and is not entitled to relief under the SPA. Accordingly, the superior court erred in concluding that petitioner had been discharged without just cause.

Affirmed in part, reversed in part.

FOR DISCUSSION

1. In order to invoke his due process right, Winbush must show that he has been deprived of something he is entitled to. What does he claim he was deprived of? What did the Office of Administrative Hearings rule? On what basis? Why did the State Personnel Commission overturn that ruling?

2. The trial court ordered Winbush reinstated as assistant football coach and head women's softball coach. What was the basis for that decision?
3. Why does the Court of Appeals of North Carolina overturn the lower court order reinstating Winbush? Why is his failure to receive the promised 10 percent increase not a loss of property?
4. If you were deciding this case, how would you rule?
5. Why does the court never evaluate the reasons for Winbush's reassignment? Does that seem fair to you?

SUBSTANTIVE DUE PROCESS

Unlike procedural due process, substantive due process looks at the content of the law. One of the most common uses of substantive due process is to protect against vagueness. A law must define what conduct is required or prohibited clearly enough so that people know how to conform their conduct to it. Laws that fail to do so violate substantive due process. The next case shows how courts evaluate claims that laws are unconstitutionally vague.

Bell v. Arlington County, Virginia U.S. District Court, E.D. Virginia, Alexandria Division (1987) 673 F. Supp. 767

CACHERIS, District Judge The issue in this case is the constitutionality of the Arlington County Code Sections which prohibit cross-sexual massages.

Both plaintiff and defendant Arlington County, Virginia, moved for summary judgment on the constitutionality of Arlington County Code Chapter 49. The court finds that the statute is unconstitutionally vague and grants plaintiff's Motion for Summary Judgment.

Plaintiff Gail Bell has brought suit under 42 U.S.C. § 1983, alleging a violation of her Fourth Amendment right to be free from unreasonable search and seizure, defamation, intentional infliction of emotional distress, false arrest and imprisonment, negligence and malicious prosecution.

Plaintiff is a trained masseuse who has all the necessary business licenses and permits to provide massage services as a massage therapist. In May, 1986, the defendants began an investigation of plaintiff's massage therapy practice. Despite her status as a licensed massage therapist, plaintiff was arrested under Chapter 49 of the Arlington County Code and charged with violating the Code section which prohibits a massage technician from giving a massage to a member of the opposite sex.

On October 1, 1986, the Arlington County Commonwealth's Attorney dismissed the charge against the plaintiff. On November 14, 1986, the Arlington County Circuit Court expunged all police and court records relating to the criminal charge filed against Bell.

Plaintiff has moved for summary judgment on her claim for declaratory injunctive relief relative to Chapter 49 of the Arlington County Code, requesting the court to declare that the Code Section is unconstitutionally vague. The defendant Arlington County has opposed the motion and asked for summary judgment on the grounds that the statute is not unconstitutionally vague.

The court recognizes that when a statute is fairly susceptible to more than one interpretation, the interpretation most consistent with constitutionality should be adopted. The court should determine whether a constitutional construction of the ordinance is possible in order to avoid a question of an unconstitutional construction.

In Arlington County's Motion, the County argues that the ordinance sets up two distinct categories, massage therapist and massage technician. The former could perform a cross-sexual massage, while the latter was prohibited. However, prior to Bell's arrest, the Police Department operated on the understanding, given to them by Henry Hudson, Arlington County Commonwealth's Attorney, that neither massage therapists nor massage technicians could give cross-sexual massages.

As the basis for Bell's arrest, the police department had interpreted the ordinance to state that massage therapists were a subclass of massage technicians, and therefore, were prohibited from giving cross-sexual massages.[1]

Police Chief Stover, who was charged with the responsibility of enforcing the ordinance, had several problems understanding the statute. Stover believed the ordinance was "too vague," could only be understood by a lawyer, "unfair" to Ms. Bell, unclear "to a reasonably ordinary intelligent person of what is and what is not permissible," and that "it fails to give reasonable notice to a lay person as to what is lawful and what is not lawful for a massage therapist."

Lt. John Karinshak, who was in charge of the Police's vice-control section, was under the belief that until last year all cross-sexual massages were illegal under the Arlington County Code. Karinshak thought that, based on his interpretation of law, the statute had problems and that it was vague. He felt it was not clear as to who could or could not give cross-sexual massages. As a result of problems with the Bell case, he found it necessary to draft a policy statement for the vice-squad in 1986 to prevent a repetition of an arrest similar to the one that occurred in this case. Karinshak's memorandum indicated that massage technicians could not engage in cross-sexual massages, however, massage therapists could. Nevertheless, even after the County clarified its policy, Detective Kozich was still unclear as to whether Bell was entitled to massage men under the current ordinance.

The standard for determining whether the ordinance is unconstitutionally vague is where "its prohibitions are not clearly defined" and where a "person of ordinary intelligence" is not given a "reasonable opportunity to know what is prohibited so that he may act accordingly." *Grayned v. City of Rockford*, 408 U.S. 104 (1972). The court continued in *Rockford* to state:

> [A] vague law impermissibly delegates basic policy matters to ... [officials charged with enforcement] for resolution on an ad hoc and subjective basis, with attendant dangers of arbitrary and discriminatory applications.

It is quite obvious that the statute is unconstitutionally vague. The County's argument that the statute sets up one standard for massage technicians and another for massage therapists fails because the police officers who were charged with the responsibility of enforcing the ordinance have found that they themselves have difficulty in interpreting it. Reading § 49–2's definition of massage technician together with § 49–7(2)'s prohibitions against cross-sexual massages, the statutes appear to

say that any person who receives money from massages cannot give cross-sexual massages. This interpretation would include licensed massage therapists who receive money for massages. Yet, the Chapter appears to contemplate that massage therapists can give cross-sexual massages. Obviously the ordinance is confusing because the officers who were charged with the responsibility for enforcement are confused over its interpretation. If the officers are confused, it is too much to ask the citizenry to know what is prohibited. Therefore, the court finds that § 49–7(2) is unconstitutionally vague. Plaintiff's Motion for Summary Judgment is GRANTED and defendants' Motion for Summary Judgment is DENIED.

FOR DISCUSSION

1. The Court never discusses the purpose of this law. What do you think it is? If you need some help, review the *Stidwell* case in the You Be the Judge section of chapter 2 (p. 86).
2. Judge Cacheris gives a great deal of weight to the confusion of the police about the meaning of the law. If all of the police officers who had testified in this case had agreed on the law's meaning, do you think it would have changed the result?
3. Can you articulate a standard for deciding when a law is too vague to meet the test of substantive due process?
4. Can you write a law that would accomplish the goals of Arlington County Code Chapter 49 and not be unconstitutionally vague? Examine Judge Cacheris's footnote to see the definition used in the statute being challenged.
5. Could your law be challenged as discriminating on the basis of gender?

Substantive due process also requires that laws not be arbitrary. This case is a good example of how courts are generally reluctant to overturn legislation as arbitrary as long as it can be argued that the law is a reasonable, even if not necessarily the best, method of achieving a legitimate goal of government. At the time of this decision, Donna Shalala was the Secretary of Health and

Human Services, the cabinet department that oversees Social Security.

Muriel Lauger on Behalf of John Lauger v. Shalala U.S. District Court, S.D. California (1993) 820 F.Supp. 1239

HUFF, District Judge.

The plaintiff appeals the Secretary's denial of her application for disability benefits. Both the plaintiff and the defendant move for summary judgment. Because the court finds the denial of benefits did not violate substantive or procedural due process, the court grants the defendant's cross-motion for summary judgment.

The plaintiff's husband died on August 8, 1990. At the time of his death, the plaintiff was suffering from neck pain and was recovering from a hysterectomy performed in April 1990. In December 1990, she learned of social security burial benefits and contacted the social security office. An interview was arranged with the social security office in Oceanside for February 20, 1991. Prior to that time, a social security employee contacted the plaintiff and informed her that, in addition to burial benefits, she may be entitled to Title II social security disability benefits. On February 15, 1991, she submitted an application for the disability benefits, but her application was denied on February 20, 1991, due to untimeliness.

The plaintiff seeks reconsideration of the denial of disability benefits. After a hearing, an ALJ [Administrative Law Judge] reaffirmed the denial of benefits, and the Appeals Council affirmed the decision. The plaintiff now seeks judicial review from this court. 42 U.S.C. § 423(a)(1) provides for the payment of disability benefits if an application is filed within three months from the date of death. The section makes no exceptions for late filings. The plaintiff argues this time limitation is arbitrary and, thus, unconstitutional. Specifically, the plaintiff argues there is no rational basis for refusing to excuse late filings based on good cause.

The court must uphold economic regulations against constitutional challenge if the statute "has a rational relationship to a legitimate goal of government." *Price v. Heckler*, 733 F.2d 699, 701 (9th Cir. 1984). Courts generally must be deferential to the government's determination of preferable means of regulation and will overturn such a determination only if it is "wholly arbitrary." *City of New Orleans v. Dukes*, 427 U.S. 297 (1976). The Supreme Court has granted a strong presumption of constitutionality to legislation conferring monetary benefits because the Court believes that Congress should have discretion in deciding how to expend necessarily limited resources.

The court cannot hold that Congress's imposition of a time limit upon the receipt of benefits is arbitrary. The imposition of a time limitation ensures that the Social Security Administration will know with certainty the demands made upon a particular fund. The amount necessary to pay disability benefits would become substantially less certain if a good cause exception was allowed. Section 423(a)(1) does not become arbitrary merely because Congress has allowed longer time limitations in other sections governing the receipt of social security benefits. 42 U.S.C. § 402 provides for a "lump-sum death payment" if an application is filed within two years after the date of death. This longer time limitation does not necessarily render more restrictive time limitations irrational. For example, the payment under section 402 is limited to $255 per person. Disability benefits, however, are determined according to a complex formula set forth in 42 U.S.C. § 415. These payments could substantially exceed $255 per person. Thus, Congress may have determined a more restrictive time limitation is necessary in order to budget for larger expenditures. The court, therefore, finds the three-month time limitation is not arbitrary.

The court also finds the statutory section comports with procedural due process. To determine the procedures needed to comply with due process, the court must consider (1) the private interest affected by the governmental action, (2) the risk of an erroneous deprivation of such interest through the procedures used, and (3) the government's interest, including the fiscal and administrative burdens, that the additional procedure would entail.

The plaintiff has received full hearings on whether she in entitled to disability benefits and, specifically, the constitutionality of section 423 before an ALJ and this court. Contrary to the plaintiff's allegation, due process does not require the Social Security Administration to provide notice to all individuals who may be entitled to some payment of social security benefits.

First, it is the plaintiff's burden to demonstrate eligibility for benefits. Further, the cost in terms of resources and money to the Administration would be astronomical. This cost would substantially reduce the amount of benefits available for disabled individuals. Although the court is sensitive to the plaintiff's situation, the court finds procedural due process has been satisfied in this case.

Accordingly, the court grants the defendant's cross-motion for summary judgment and denies the plaintiff's motion for summary judgment.

FOR DISCUSSION

1. What provision of law is Muriel Lauger challenging? How does she believe it hinders her right to substantive due process?
2. What governmental interest does the law further? Is this a legitimate interest of government?
3. The time limit in the law provides for no exceptions. What reasons might Ms. Lauger have for filing late? Does the court find this particular time limit a due process violation as applied to this case? Explain whether you agree.
4. Congress has allowed more time to file for other types of Social Security benefits. Does that affect this case? Evaluate Judge Huff's reasoning on this point.
5. Can you think of a situation where a time limit would be so arbitrary as to violate due process?
6. Why do you think courts are so reluctant to overturn laws as arbitrary? Reviewing some of the material in chapter 2 may be helpful in answering this question.

PROCEDURAL DUE PROCESS

A good way to understand the concept of procedural due process is to look at a specific area familiar to most readers, due process in schools. In the following essay, Donald Gehring describes and criticizes current student disciplinary procedures. He argues for a less legalistic and adversarial process that would be more educational for those students involved. Because he is discussing due process rights, it is important to remember that the court decisions he refers to are for public schools. Private colleges and universities are not legally bound to follow due process, although most do, mainly because any that arbitrarily disciplined students would likely see a decline in student applications.

READING

The Objectives of Student Discipline and the Process That's Due: Are They Compatible? Donald D. Gehring

PURPOSE

How can campus judicial officers teach while ensuring enforcement of campus rules? Are the two tasks compatible? What does the law have to say about what public institutions need to do in order to discipline students? The purpose of this article is to burn off the blanket of legal ground fog by exposing it to the light of judicial opinion, which not only finds the teaching function compatible with the law, but also actually encourages it. It is the intention of this article to use the actual words of the courts to dispel the need for formalism and to illustrate how a simpler process can rise to the level of what is constitutionally due while meeting our objective of enhancing development.

The Process That's Due

The best place to begin is with the opinion of the Fifth Circuit Court of Appeals in *Dixon v. Alabama State Board of Education* (294 F.2d 150, 5th Cir. 1961; cert. den. 386 U.S. 930, 1961). The court was considering the expulsion of students who had been denied both a notice of the reason they were expelled and an opportunity to speak in their own defense. While the court said the students were entitled under the Constitution to "...notice and some opportunity for hearing before ... [being] expelled for misconduct" it also made it clear that " This does not imply that a full-dress judicial hearing with the right to cross-examine witnesses is required." The Supreme Court denied certiorari. Normally the denial of certiorari does not tell us whether the Court agreed or disagreed with the opinion. However, in a subsequent case considering the 10-day suspension of school children, the Supreme Court referred to *Dixon* as the "landmark case" in the area of student discipline. Dixon has since been cited by two U.S. Courts of Appeals as "the pathbreaking decision recognizing the due process rights of students at a state university" (*Blanton v. State University of New York*, 489 F.2d 377, 2d Cir. 1973) and "The classic starting point for an inquiry into the rights of students at state educational institutions" (*Jenkins v. Louisiana State Board of Education*, 506 F.2d 992, 5th Cir. 1975). Thus, it seems that *Dixon* is good law and a standard to be followed.

To say that due process is required in student disciplinary cases is only the beginning of the inquiry. However, due process is not well defined, but is a flexible concept.

Justice Holmes referred to the process as "... the rudiments of fair play ..." (*Chicago, Milwaukee & St. Paul R.R. Co. v. Polt*, 235 U.S. 165, 1914). The Supreme Court has provided further guidance when it told us that:

> Considerations of what procedures due process may require under any given set of circumstances must begin with a determination of the precise nature of the government function involved as well as the private interest that has been affected by governmental action (*Cafeteria & Restaurant Workers Union v. McElroy*, 367 U.S. 886, 1961).

The Nature of the Government Function in Student Discipline

What is the "precise nature of the government function involved" in student discipline? There are those who would analogize the "nature of the government function involved" in student disciplinary situations to the prosecution of crimes.

Recently, the federal Congress passed the Higher Education Amendments of 1998 mandating that institutions keep statistics on students "referred for campus disciplinary action for liquor law violations ..." Other federal legislation equally confuses violations of law (criminal behavior) with violations of campus community standards. Those who confuse crimes and campus rule violations fail to understand that to be considered a violation of law, specific elements must be proven beyond a reasonable doubt whereas a violation of a community standard only requires that it be shown the person more likely than not engaged in the prohibited behavior. While a crime may be a violation of campus rules, a violation of campus rules is not necessarily a crime. It is often the case that students found responsible for violating campus rules are not prosecuted and are never convicted of a violation of law, thus, they are not guilty of a crime.

When care is not taken to separate legalistic language from campus codes confusion arises, and there is a misunderstanding on the part of students, attorneys and others. While it is true that one infraction, such as a rape, may be a violation of the law (a crime), and also a violation of campus regulations, only the local prosecutor has the authority to prosecute the crime. Colleges and universities do not prosecute crimes, but simply discipline students who violate their rules. Any analogy of criminal prosecution and crimes to campus proceedings and violations of campus rules is simply not valid.

The courts have consistently reiterated that they "... do not believe there is a good analogy between student discipline and criminal procedure" (*Norton v. Discipline Committee, East Tennessee State University*, 419 F.2d 195, 6th Cir. 1969). Four other United States Courts of Appeals have echoed this sentiment.

Essential Elements of Due Process

If criminal procedures are not the model to follow in student disciplinary actions where the individual could be suspended or expelled ("the private interest affected ..."), then what standards of process are due? Again, the 1961 "landmark case" of *Dixon* provides counsel and it is instructive to revisit the court's words.

> For the guidance of the parties in the event of further proceedings, we state our views on the nature of the notice and hearing required by due process prior to expulsion from a state college or university. ... The notice should contain a statement of the specific charges and grounds which, if proven, would justify expulsion under the regulations ... a hearing which gives the Board or the administrative authorities of the college an opportunity to hear both sides in considerable detail. ... [T] he student should be given the names of the witnesses against him and an oral or written report on the facts to which each witness testifies. He should be given an opportunity to present to the Board or the administrative official of the college his own defense against the charges and to produce either oral testimony or written affidavits in his behalf.

In this case when the court referred to the "Board," it meant the Board of Education and not a campus judicial board. It is interesting to note that the *Dixon* court said that if these procedures were followed, "... the rudiments of an adversary proceeding may be preserved without encroaching upon the interests of the college." Note first that the court spoke of the "rudiments of an adversary proceeding" not an adversarial environment like a criminal trial which is confrontational and contentious. Thus, a hearing before an administrative official would preserve the elements of an adversary proceeding (one against the other) but would not necessarily create an adversarial environment (permeated with confrontation and contentiousness) in which the educational value of the experience might be lost. It is also of consequence to observe that the court specifically pointed to the college's interests and said those could be preserved. In other words the court is saying that even in an expulsion hearing, following the procedures it has outlined would allow the institution to take advantage of an opportunity to teach valuable lessons.

As noted in the facts of the case and the court's language, these procedures were confined to expulsions and allowed for an administrative official of the college to hear the student's defense.

While allowing an administrator to hear the student's defense is legally defensible, including students on a hearing panel has certain educational benefits. However, excluding the maturity and wisdom administrative officials bring to the hearing can preclude taking advantage of a "teachable moment" for the student accused of violating community standards.

The Process That's Not Due

These "essential elements of due process" are those noted in *Dixon*, and do not include a right to be represented by counsel, to cross-examine witnesses, or even, in some cases, to confront them physically, nor to appeal the decision. Although there is no general right to counsel, when the college or university is represented by counsel it is only "fair" to allow the student the same right. But, there is no legal or other reason for the institution to use counsel, thereby complicating the procedures and moving to an adversarial rather than a teaching mode, and thus giving up the opportunity for a positive learning experience to take place. However, students who are also charged with criminal conduct arising from the same set of facts should be allowed to have counsel advise, but not represent them at the hearing. This would not necessarily create an adversarial environment since counsel would have a limited role "... only to safeguard appellee's rights at the criminal proceeding, not to affect the outcome of the disciplinary hearing" (*Gabrilowitz v. Newman*, 582 F.2d 100, 1st Cir. 1978).

Cross-examination of witnesses by accused students can turn disciplinary hearings into invective proceedings that are ill suited to teaching or even to civility. Often students accused of violating campus rules who appear before judicial boards to claim their innocence are angry and are certainly not trained to cross-examine witnesses who may be reluctant to testify in the first place. In most student disciplinary actions there is generally no legal or other reason for accused students to engage in cross-examination of witnesses since the judicial board can ask questions of anyone giving testimony in order to get at the truth. Even where the consequence of the hearing may be expulsion, the courts, beginning with *Dixon* have said there is no right to cross-examine witnesses. Two disciplinary hearings contested in court because of the failure to allow the accused student to directly cross-examine adverse witnesses were resolved in favor of the institution. Once case dealt with an act of academic dishonesty (*Nash v. Auburn University*, 812 F.2d 655, 11th Cir. 1987) and the other a date rape (*Donohue v. Baker*, 976 F. Supp. 136, N.D. NY 1997). The Eleventh Circuit Court of Appeals said in the academic dishonesty case that there was "... no denial of applicant's constitutional rights to due process by their inability to question the adverse witnesses in the usual adversarial manner." In the situation involving a date rape where credibility was an issue and the facts were disputed, the federal district court said due process was satisfied if the student was allowed to question his accuser through the disciplinary panel.

There are also institutions that permit multiple levels of appeals beyond the original decision. While it may be reasonable to have an expulsion or long-term suspension reviewed by an administrative official to ensure that the institution followed its own procedures and the violation merited the sanction, there is no legal basis for an appeal. The Supreme Court has made it clear that "Due process does not comprehend the right of appeal" (*District of Columbia v. Clawans*, 300 U.S. 617, 1936). The Court's logic in stating that due process does not include the right of appeal was explained in one of its earliest cases when it said "If a single hearing is not due process doubling it will not make it so" (*Reetz v. Michigan*, 188 U.S. 505, 1903).

The Process That's Due for Lesser Offenses

In instances where students are not in jeopardy of being expelled or suspended for a long period of time, "the private interest that has been affected by government action" (*McElroy*) is minimal and thus the requirements of due process are lower. The Supreme Court has said that even in the case of a student suspended for 10 days there

was only required "some kind of notice and ... some kind of hearing." The Court characterized this as an "... informal give-and-take between student and disciplinarian ..." (*Goss v. Lopez*, 419 U.S. 565, 1975).

The Supreme Court also recognized that "the educational process is not by nature adversarial, instead it centers around a continuing relationship between faculty and students, 'one in which the teacher must occupy many roles—educator, advisor and at times parent-substitute'" (*Board of Curators of University of Missouri v. Horowitz*, 435 U.S. 78, 1978). The Court has thus even permitted school administrators to suspend students for short periods if they engage in a "give-and-take" conversation, which would allow for taking advantage of the teachable moment a disciplinary hearing presents.

The "essential elements of due process" as the Supreme Court pointed out, are "some kind of notice and ... some kind of hearing." These two essential aspects of due process need not be overly formalized in lesser disciplinary sanctions but are amenable to a simple and straightforward administrative notice and hearing in which the student and the administration engage in a "give-and-take" discussion.

Discussion

The "creeping legalism" described by Dannells[2] has gone far beyond what the courts have actually required in order to provide students with due process. Institutions have unnecessarily formalized their procedures to incorporate the right to counsel, confrontation and cross-examination of witnesses and multiple appeals. These types of procedures are confusing to students, preclude the "opportunity for development efforts" (Dannells 1997: 79) and even "... create an adversarial atmosphere likely to produce harsher, not more lenient results."[3]

Whether the relationship between a student and an institution is characterized as one of contract or association, the institution must substantially follow its own rules. Thus, the more straightforward and clear the disciplinary procedures are, the easier they will be for students to understand and for the institution to follow. Adversarial procedures that pit one antagonist against another, like criminal procedures, are complex but even worse, do not provide the support necessary for personal and social development.

Institutions would be well served by a comprehensive review of their disciplinary procedures. Legalistic language and structure should be eliminated and procedures streamlined. Hearings should be designed as fact-finding procedures and a time to raise ethical questions. Minor offenses, which could result in less than a suspension, should be dealt with at the lowest level possible and provide the student with an oral or written notice and an opportunity to present his or her side of the story. Decisions about responsibility for violating rules of conduct can be based on whether it is more likely than not that the student engaged in the behavior. There would be no need for confrontation or cross-examination of witnesses or representation or advice of counsel (unless there is a pending criminal charge). A letter to the student should state the outcome of the hearing and the basis for the findings. One level of review of the decision could be provided if requested and justified.

Major offenses where the result could be suspension or expulsion could be handled in a similar procedural manner, since the essential elements of due process are present. Of course, if there is a question of credibility of a witness, cross-examination should be allowed, and even then this can be accomplished by having questions directed through the hearing officer or panel. If criminal charges are pending as a result of the same incident, the students should have counsel to advise them. Even where the outcome is expulsion, there is no need for more than one level of appeal and it should be granted only where it can be shown either that there is new evidence which clearly was not available at the time of the hearing, that there has been a substantial and prejudicial departure from the procedures, or that the student's rights were in some way violated. These added measures would be called into play only in unusual circumstances. For most cases a one-on-one dialogue can take place which allows the administrator to hear both sides in considerable detail and make a decision of responsibility. This type of dialogue may also permit the administrator to assess the individual's level of development and ask questions that require the student to reflect on a higher level. Finally, administrators may also want to include students as members of hearing panels for the educational benefits such service provides. While this is an excellent educational opportunity, it requires a great deal of preparation and training and should not be undertaken unless appropriate resources are available to provide the support required.

If institutions review their disciplinary procedures with the objective of providing a system that both aides in the development of students and meets what the courts have defined as due process in student discipline without excessive formalism, then everyone involved will benefit.

Note

1. Originally published in *NASPA Journal* 38 (Summer 2001): 466–81. Reprinted by permission.
2. § 49–2 defines massage technician as "any person who administers a massage to another person for pay," and a massage therapist is defined as a massage technician with certain specified training.
3. M. Dannells, *From Discipline to Development: Rethinking Student Conduct in Higher Education* (Washington, DC: Association for the Study of Higher Education, 1997).
4. G. Pavella, "Due Process at Private Colleges," *Synfax Weekly Report*, Oct. 18, 1999, 906.

For Discussion

1. Gehring is particularly critical of "those who confuse crimes and campus rule violations." Explain his criticisms and whether you agree.
2. What should be the goals of student disciplinary hearings? How, if at all, do they differ from the goals of a criminal trial?
3. What procedures have the courts required colleges to use in student disciplinary hearings to meet the requirements of due process? What procedures that are required in criminal trials are not required for disciplinary hearings? Explain the reasoning behind this and whether you agree.

4. According to Gehring many colleges have "gone far beyond what the courts have actually required." Why do you think they have done so? Do you agree with Gehring that this is not a good thing? Explain.

5. How does Gehring think disciplinary hearings should be conducted? If you were charged with violating your college's disciplinary code would you find these procedures fair? Would you feel differently if you were bringing a complaint against someone?

6. Compare your college's disciplinary rules with those advocated by Gehring. Explain which you prefer.

The next case presents an example of what happens when a university disciplinary hearing is challenged in court as violating due process. Note the standards that the court uses to determine whether the school's actions met the minimum requirements of due process.

Osteen v. Henley U.S. Court of Appeals, Seventh Circuit (1993) 13 F.3d 221

POSNER, Chief Judge. Late one night, as Thomas Osteen, an undergraduate at Northern Illinois University, was leaving a bar in the company of two male friends and the girlfriend of one of them, the girlfriend began "mouthing off to a male [another student] who was outside of a bar who decided to mouth off to her and the two of them mouthed out to each other and he didn't realize she was with three football players so when he realized that he was mouthing off to a young lady that was being accompanied by three football players one of which was her boyfriend, it was a little bit too late for him." (We are quoting, not Gertrude Stein, but one of the defendants, university judicial officer Larry Bolles.) "I'm told without one word, Mr. Osteen, not one word out of his mouth he stomps this guy in the head with some cowboy boots. This is what the guy said, he had on some boots and he stomped him." Osteen's kick or stomp broke the other student's nose. Another student, apparently a friend of the one whom Osteen had just assaulted, approached

Osteen, who again without a word "broke his face with one punch." Osteen had broken his second nose for the night. The incident, aggravated in Bolles's mind by the fact that the woman whose honor Osteen was defending in this violent manner was not even Osteen's own girlfriend, led to Osteen's expulsion for two years and to this lawsuit (dismissed by the district court), in which Osteen challenges the expulsion as a deprivation of property without due process of law, in violation of the Fourteenth Amendment.

Bolles mailed Osteen a notice of charges and a copy of the university's student judicial code, thus initiating disciplinary proceedings. According to the code, Bolles's function as university judicial officer was to meet with Osteen and attempt to resolve the matter without a hearing, but if this failed he was to present the case against Osteen at a hearing. The two met and in Bolles's presence Osteen signed a form in which he pleaded guilty to the charges but requested a hearing on Bolles's proposed sanction, which was a two-year expulsion. The hearing was held before an appeals board consisting of the university's assistant judicial officer (i.e., assistant to Bolles) presiding and in addition one faculty member and two students. The case against Osteen was presented by Bolles, Osteen being represented by a student advocate. Osteen, his advocate, and Bolles addressed the board (we quoted part of Bolles's statement earlier), which in addition considered character references and other documents and concluded that the two-year expulsion was the proper sanction. Osteen attempted to appeal to the university's vice-president for student affairs but was told that the vice-president's authority under the judicial code had been delegated to an associate vice-president. After considering Osteen's appeal that officer upheld the expulsion but postponed it to the end of the semester.

The suit attacks a number of features of the disciplinary proceeding. Bolles had played a dual role as judge and prosecutor. The presiding officer of the appellate tribunal was Bolles's assistant. She cut off Osteen's advocate on the ground that the issue of guilt was not before the board, just the issue of sanction, when the advocate was trying to give Osteen's version of the assaults. Osteen was not allowed to cross-examine.

His lawyer (his real lawyer, not the student advocate) was not permitted to participate in the proceedings. At the oral argument before us Osteen's counsel repeated, what had been in his complaint but not in his briefs, the alarming further charge that Bolles had induced Osteen to plead guilty on the representation that on appeal the two-year expulsion would be rescinded—then (as we know) turned around and argued passionately to the appeals board for expulsion.

In his opening brief in this court Osteen raised just three issues; the others are therefore waived, and we will not consider them. The issues he raised are the defendants' failure to comply with all the requirements of the student judicial code, the interruption of himself and his advocate by the appeals board, and the denial of a right to counsel. The first point has no possible merit. As we tirelessly but unavailingly remind counsel in this court, a violation of state law (for purposes of this case the student judicial code may be treated as a state law) is not a denial of due process, even if the state law confers a procedural right. The standard of due process is federal. *Cleveland Board of Education v. Loudermill*, 470 U.S. 532 (1985).

As for the interruption of his student advocate, Osteen had by pleading guilty to the charges against him conceded his guilt, so the presiding officer was entitled to cut off what appeared to be an attempt to reopen the issue. Osteen was allowed to make a statement in mitigation; his advocate was interrupted only when it appeared that she was trying to revisit the issue of guilt. The interruption, designed to confine the proceeding to relevant matters, was well within the outer bounds of the presiding officer's discretionary authority over the scope of the hearing—and it is the outer bounds that the due process clause patrols.

The most interesting question is whether there is a right to counsel, somehow derived from the due process clause of the Fourteenth Amendment, in student disciplinary proceedings. An oldish case (by the standards of constitutional law at any rate) says yes, *Black Coalition v. Portland School District No. 1*, 484 F.2d 1040 (9th Cir. 1973), but the newer cases say no, at most the student has a right to get the advice of a lawyer; the lawyer need not be allowed to participate in the proceeding in the usual way of trial counsel, as by examining and cross-examining witnesses and addressing the tribunal. E.g., *Gorman v. University of Rhode Island*, 837 F.2d 7, 16 (1st Cir. 1988). Especially when the student faces potential criminal charges (Osteen was charged with two counts of aggravated battery; the record is silent on the disposition of the charges), it is at least arguable that the due process clause entitles him to consult a lawyer, who might for example advise him to take the Fifth Amendment. In fact *Gabrilowitz v. Newman*, 582 F.2d 100 (1st Cir. 1978), so holds, though over a dissent which points out that the Supreme Court had rejected the same argument in the parallel context of prison disciplinary proceedings. *Baxter v. Palmigiano*, 425 U.S. 308 (1976).

Even if a student has a constitutional right to consult counsel—an issue not foreclosed by *Baxter*, as we shall see—we don't think he is entitled to be represented in the sense of having a lawyer who is permitted to examine or cross-examine witnesses, to submit and object to documents, to address the tribunal, and otherwise to perform the traditional function of a trial lawyer. To recognize such a right would force student disciplinary proceedings into the mold of adversary litigation. The university would have to hire its own lawyer to prosecute these cases and no doubt lawyers would also be dragged in—from the law faculty or elsewhere—to serve as judges. The cost and complexity of such proceedings would be increased, to the detriment of discipline as well as of the university's fisc [budget]. Concern is frequently voiced about the bureaucratization of education, reflected for example in the high ratio of administrative personnel to faculty at all levels of American education today. We are reluctant to encourage further bureaucratization by judicializing university disciplinary proceedings, mindful also that one dimension of academic freedom is the right of academic institutions to operate free of heavy-handed governmental, including judicial, interference. The danger that without the procedural safeguards deemed appropriate in civil and criminal litigation public universities will engage in an orgy of expulsions is slight. The relation of students to universities is, after all, essentially that of customer to seller. That is true even in the case of public universities, though they are much less dependent upon the academic marketplace than private universities are. Northern Illinois University can't have been happy to lose a student whom it had wanted so much that it had given him a football scholarship, and who had made the team to the greater glory of the institution.

The canonical test for how much process is due, laid down by the Supreme Court in *Mathews v. Eldridge*, 424 U.S. 319 (1976) requires consideration of the cost of the additional procedure sought, the risk of error if it is withheld, and the consequences of error to the person seeking the procedure. The cost of judicializing disciplinary proceedings by recognizing a right to counsel is nontrivial, while the risk of an error—specifically the risk that Osteen was unjustly "sentenced"—is rather trivial. Not only has the university, as we have said, no incentive to jerry-rig its proceedings against the student—and there is no indication of that here, for even permanent expulsion would not have been an excessive sanction for Osteen's brutal and gratuitous misuse of his football player's strength. In addition the issue of the proper sanction generally and here involves no subtleties of law or fact, being judgmental

rather than rule-guided, like federal sentencing before the Sentencing Guidelines. Finally, the consequence for Osteen—a nonpermanent expulsion that did not prevent him from enrolling in another college—is not so grave as to entitle him to the procedural protections thought necessary in litigation because large interests of liberty or property may be at stake.

The last point gives us the most pause, as we suspect, though the record is barren on the point, that the expulsion cost Osteen scholarship assistance that he or his family needed. But when we consider all the factors bearing on his claim to a right of counsel, we conclude that the Constitution did not confer such a right on him. We doubt that it does in any student disciplinary proceeding. After *Walters v. National Association of Radiation Survivors*, 473 U.S. 305 (1985), the scope of the due process right to counsel seems excruciatingly narrow. *Gabrilowitz v. Newman* may survive, because "right to counsel" is rather a misnomer for the far more limited, and hence less costly and disruptive, right of consultation recognized there and not at issue in *Baxter v. Palmigiano*, where the prisoners were seeking

Update

Before his appointment to the U.S. Court of Appeals in 1981, Richard A. Posner was a longtime professor at the University of Chicago law school. During that time, he wrote extensively, especially concerning the application of economics to the law. He served as chief judge of the Seventh Circuit from 1993 to 2000. While serving as a judge he has continued his prolific writing with more than thirty books and three hundred articles and book reviews to his credit.

One of his recent books, *An Affair of State: The Investigation, Impeachment, and Trial of President Clinton*, raises the question of the boundaries of sitting judges writing about contemporary legal and political controversies. Writing in the *New York Review of Books* (vol. 47, March 9, 2000), Ronald Dworkin claims that Posner's ethics "are open to question because judges are not meant to enter political controversies." He is particularly critical of Posner's assertion that "it is clear Clinton perjured himself."

In the book's introduction, Posner points out that except for the Chief Justice of the Supreme Court, the judiciary is excluded from the impeachment process. Because no cases involving impeachment were pending when the book was written, he does not believe he has violated the rules of ethics of the federal judiciary. He writes that he is "unapologetic ... about my decision to write about the struggle to impeach and remove Clinton, despite its partisan overtones and its origins in a sexual relationship widely regarded as tawdry."

What do you think? Is it appropriate for a federal judge to weigh in with his opinions on matters as controversial as the Clinton impeachment?

the full right of counsel. But Osteen was not denied the right to consult counsel; and he had no greater right.

We do not condone trickery and coercion, alleged by Osteen but abandoned in this court. And we are sensible of the anomaly of having one's own assistant (Bolles's) sitting in judgment on one's case (Bolles was the "presenter"—in effect the prosecutor), although this kind of conflict of interest has not been thought in the previous cases involving school disciplinary action to violate due process. We need not decide today at what point informality of disciplinary procedures crosses the line drawn by due process. It is enough for the decision of this case that none of Osteen's nonwaived complaints about the procedure to which he was subject, signally including the limitations on the participation of counsel, crosses it. AFFIRMED.

For Discussion

1. Osteen has a number of complaints about the process, yet his appeal raises just three. What were the other issues, and why do you think he failed to raise them? Was the court correct in not considering these other matters, one of which Judge Posner calls "an alarming further charge"?

2. Judge Posner rejects the argument that the university's failure to comply with its own rules violated due process as having "no possible merit." Why does he dismiss it so quickly?

3. What does the court have to say about the interruption of Osteen's student advocate? Explain what Judge Posner means when he states that "it is the outer bounds [of the presiding officer's discretionary authority] that the due process clause patrols."

4. The most difficult issue for the court is whether Osteen had a right to counsel, especially considering that he was also facing criminal charges for the incident. What right to counsel does the court believe the due process clause requires for student disciplinary hearings? How does that apply in this case?

5. How do you think Gehring would react to this decision? Explain your answer.

Of course student disciplinary hearings are not the only situations in which procedural due process must be followed. Any time the state seeks to take away someone's life, liberty, or property, it can only do so in accord with due process. Taking custody of a child from a parent is a deprivation that requires due process. In the next case, the Court of Appeals of Kentucky rules that when a court orders a significant change in child custody arrangements, the appearance of fairness can be as important as the correctness of the decision.

Sherryl Frey Lynch v. Boyd Lee Lynch Court of Appeals of Kentucky (1987) 737 S.W.2d 184

REYNOLDS, Judge. This appeal arises from an order of the Fayette Circuit Court which changed appellant's sole custody of the parties' two minor children into a "joint reciprocal custody" arrangement in favor of both parents. Appellant maintains she was denied due process of law and a fair trial. We reverse as the record reflects, at a minimum, the appearance of a denial of due process.

Both parties are aware of the underlying facts behind this long-running dispute, and we therefore find it unnecessary to provide more than a brief recitation of the background. Sherryl Frey Lynch (appellant) and Boyd Lee Lynch (appellee) were married on August 4, 1973. Two children were born of this marriage, John (approximately 13 years old), and Leanne (approximately 8 years old). On October 13, 1982, appellee filed a petition for divorce. A decree of dissolution was entered by the Fayette Circuit Court on May 13, 1983. This decree, pursuant to a separation agreement, gave custody of the two children to appellant and provided appellee with open visitation.

However, this policy of open visitation was not successful and, within four months, appellee made his first motion for specific visitation. The parties' inability to reach any sort of understanding on visitation is amply illustrated in the over 400 pages of record which accompanied this action. The current dispute began on April 21, 1986, when appellee filed a motion for a change of custody.

A hearing on this motion began on September 2, 1986, and continued into the next day. During these two days, appellee presented most of his case-in-chief. By agreement, one of appellant's witnesses, a licensed psychologist, testified out of order. The hearing was then continued to October 3, 1986.

Appellee concluded his case-in-chief on that day. Appellant then began her argument and completed all of her evidence, except for one witness who the trial court deemed unnecessary. It was at this point in time that the court presented each party with a 16-page document explaining:

> I have heard all of this testimony and I strongly believe that the decision should be made immediately in this case. I have undertaken to draw up Findings of Fact and Conclusions of Law and an Order in anticipation of not learning anything new today. I will give you copies of it, copies so that you and your clients may read it. ...

Over appellant's objection, this order was subsequently entered.

The order, citing the inability of the parties to work out their visitation disagreements, set up a system known as "joint reciprocal alternating custody." Briefly, this procedure divides the year into four three-month periods. During the first three months, one party (in this situation appellant) would have custody for three weeks, followed by one week in which the other party (appellee) would have custody, followed by three weeks for appellant, followed by one week for appellee, and so on. At the end of the first three-month period the times switch, giving appellee custody for three weeks, followed by appellant for one week, and so on. The sequence continues to reverse with each quarter.

It is not necessary for this Court to decide the appropriateness of such a system at this time. Appellant's primary argument is concerned with the manner in which this order was entered.

It is clear from the record that the trial court had prepared its findings, conclusions and order prior to the final day of testimony. Except for one witness, previously taken out of order, appellant had not presented any evidence until after the document had been prepared. Due process requires, at the minimum, that each party be given a meaningful opportunity to be heard. Hearings should be conducted in a manner which leaves no question to their regularity. Although the trial court retained the option of not releasing its previously prepared order, its action in this situation creates the appearance that it had made up its mind before it had all of the evidence.

The record does contain information which might explain the trial court's desire for a quick solution. The two children had been in a state of uncertainty, because of their parent's inability to work together, since the divorce. We understandingly sympathize with the trial court's attempt to bring this matter to an equitable solution as soon as possible, but due process cannot be ignored.

Appellant has directed us to a recent criminal case which somewhat parallels our situation. In that action, the trial court had prepared the final judgment prior to a sentencing hearing. The Kentucky Supreme Court held that this was an abuse of discretion, even though the trial court retained the option of changing the judgment if the defendant produced some compelling evidence. *Edmonson v. Commonwealth*, Ky., 725 S.W.2d 595 (1987). The trial court's discretion "must be exercised only after the defendant has had a fair opportunity to present evidence at a meaningful hearing ..."

In *Edmonson*, the Kentucky Supreme Court vacated the judgment and returned the case for action by a different circuit judge. We conclude that this would also be the correct procedure in this situation. There is a complete record, including video transcripts of the hearing, making additional testimony unnecessary.

Although we decline to discuss the merits of the trial court's decision, two of appellant's other points merit a brief discussion. Appellant claims that the trial court considered material outside the evidence. It is well settled that extra-judicial evidence, not part of the record, cannot form the basis of a decision. Appellant also contends that the trial court erred in not making the specific findings required by KRS 403.340. We agree. While this Court has concluded that such findings are unnecessary when changing from joint custody to sole custody, such findings are always required when changing single custody into another arrangement.

You Be the Judge

Shortly after their child was born, father O.A.H. was divorced from mother E.P.A. Since that time, the father has had little contact with his child. The parents dispute whether the child was abandoned by its father or concealed by its mother, who is now remarried. E.P.A. went to court seeking termination of O.A.H.'s parental rights and adoption by the child's stepfather. O.A.H., who is incarcerated and indigent, requested that counsel be appointed to represent him. The trial judge refused. After a hearing that O.A.H. was unable to attend in person, separate orders were entered terminating his parental rights and granting the stepfather's adoption of the child.

The statute involved does not require appointment of counsel for those unable to afford it. Does procedural due process require that indigents like O.A.H. be furnished with counsel at court proceedings to terminate parental rights? For the appellate court ruling, see *O.A.H. v. R.L.A.* in the You Be the Judge Key at the end of the chapter.

For the foregoing reasons, the order of the Fayette Circuit Court is vacated and this action is remanded with directions that it be assigned to a different circuit judge for new findings and conclusions, based on the present record.

For Discussion

1. Does the Court of Appeals conclude that there is anything wrong with the order of the trial court?
2. Is there any evidence that the trial court judge was concerned with anything other than the welfare of the Lynch children? If not, why does Judge Reynolds conclude that Sherryl Frey Lynch's due process rights were violated?
3. According to Judge Reynolds, procedural due process requires "that each party be given a meaningful opportunity to be heard." Since Ms. Lynch presented her case before the trial court, how were her rights violated?
4. The trial judge could have changed his opinion if Ms. Lynch had presented strong arguments. Does this repair any due process violations?
5. If the trial judge had waited a day or two before releasing his decision, would there have been any violation of Ms. Lynch's procedural due process rights?

6. When a court order is vacated, the case is often returned to the original trial judge who is likely to be the most familiar with the case. Why does the Court of Appeals direct that this case be assigned to a different judge who will have to rely on a videotaped transcript of the original hearing?

Legal Terms to Know

liberty interest
procedural due process
Section 1983
substantive due process
state action

For Further Reading

Bach, Jason. "Students Have Rights Too: The Drafting of Student Conduct Codes." *Brigham Young University Education and Law Journal* 2003 (2003): 1–35.

Berger, Curtis, and Vivian Berger. "Academic Discipline: A Guide to Fair Process for the University Student." *Columbia Law Review* 99 (March 1999): 289–362.

Metzger, Gillian. "Privatization as Delegation." *Columbia Law Review* 103 (October 2003): 1367–502.

Orth, John V. *Due Process of Law: A Brief History.* Lawrence: University of Kansas Press, 2003.

Rubin, Peter. "Square Pegs and Round Holes: Substantive Due Process, Procedural Due Process, and the Bill of Rights." *Columbia Law Review* 103 (May 2003): 833–927.

Vance, Virginia T. "Applications for Benefits: Due Process, Equal Protection, and the Right to Be Free From Arbitrary Procedures." *Washington and Lee Law Review* 61 (Spring 2004): 883–927.

YOU BE THE JUDGE KEY

1. In *Apao v. The Bank of New York*, 324 F.3d 1091 (9th Cir. 2003), the U.S. Court of Appeals upheld the trial court's dismissal of Apao's lawsuit on the grounds that the foreclosure sale did not involve state action. Merely because a business is subject to government regulation does not convert its actions into the state action required to invoke due process. So much of business is regulated by government in some fashion that accepting Apao's argument would nearly destroy the distinction between government and private action. The foreclosure sale was a purely private remedy for a contract violation. Without "overt official involvement" in the foreclosure, there was no state action.

2. The Court of Appeal of Florida, Second District overturned the trial judge's denial of counsel in *O.A.H. v. R.L.A.*, 712 So.2d 4 (1998). It noted that there had been a trend in other states in favor of appointing counsel, with a majority of states now requiring it in parental termination proceedings. Because this proceeding ends all legal relationships between the adopted person and his birth father, it is such a severe deprivation as to require counsel to protect the fundamental rights of the parent.

Justice Delayed or Justice Denied?

A Contemporary Review of Capital Habeas Corpus

Jon B. Gould

In the last year, researchers released two reports about capital cases and habeas corpus. Together, these studies offer a contemporary snapshot of postconviction review and illustrate the influence of state collateral processes on capital habeas litigation in the federal courts. This essay examines those new findings, seeking to pair the studies to understand how the processing of capital habeas petitions has changed since the last wave of national reform and to explain why the courts differ in the time and attention they give these cases. Although capital habeas-corpus petitions now take twice as long to complete in the federal courts as they did over a decade ago, the new studies report considerable geographic disparities in the processing of capital habeas petitions and also point to sources that lie in state, not federal, litigation. The federal courts must not only pick up the pieces when states fail at collateral review, but also, in occasionally taking their time to review habeas matters more thoroughly, ensure that due process means as much in practice as it does in theory.

Death is different," Justice Thurgood Marshall reminded us in the case of *Ford v. Wainwright* (1986, at 411). Given the stakes at issue in capital prosecutions, courts and commentators have devoted extra attention to the procedures and processes used to try, convict, and sentence defendants to death. Much of that review has been accomplished by the writ of habeas corpus, a right protected under the U.S. Constitution that permits prisoners to challenge the constitutionality of their convictions and sentences. Habeas corpus has long been a subject of controversy, as partisans have simultaneously questioned the efficiency and effectiveness of the habeas process.

In the last year, researchers released two reports about capital cases and habeas corpus. The first, by Judge Arthur Alarcón of the U.S. Court of Appeals for the Ninth Circuit, concerns the processing of capital cases in California. The second, funded largely by the National Institute of Justice and conducted by Professor Nancy King of Vanderbilt Law School and Fred Cheesman and Brian Ostrom of the National Center for State Courts, examines federal habeas-corpus processing nationwide and the handling of capital habeas cases in thirteen federal district courts. Together, these studies offer a contemporary and complementary snapshot of postconviction review and illustrate the influence of state collateral processes on capital habeas litigation in the federal courts.

The picture that emerges is unlikely to satisfy critics, for capital habeas petitions now take twice as long to complete in the federal courts as they did at the time of the last national reform in 1996. Indeed, not one of the federal courts studied has been able to complete habeas review in less than an average of 500 days, well above the limits that prior legislation established for states that sought a fast-track option. Lest these studies generate additional proposals by Congress to limit habeas review, critics would do well to consider *why* habeas cases take as long as they do, for the new studies report considerable geographic disparities in the processing of capital habeas petitions and also point to sources that lie in state, not federal, litigation.

This essay examines those new findings, seeking to pair the studies to understand how the processing of capital habeas petitions has changed since the last wave of national reform and to explain where possible why the courts differ in the time and attention they give these cases. In doing so, the article provides a recent history of habeas reform, summarizes the recent research on capital habeas, and challenges the critics of collateral review to address the likely sources behind the problems they so casually condemn.

Readers should understand that this article is addressed to the processing of capital habeas petitions, not necessarily to their results. To be sure, who wins and why are essential questions, some of which have been taken up in the recent research. Case processing is addressed here because the critics of capital habeas corpus have focused so heavily on "delay" in collateral litigation, making an argument that at times seems to forswear even modest judicial review of capital habeas petitions. Justice delayed may be justice denied, but speed for speed's sake threatens to weaken the very purpose of habeas corpus.

RECENT HISTORY OF HABEAS CORPUS

Since the days of ancient England, common-law judicial systems have maintained the writ of habeas corpus, granting individuals held by the state the right to assert that their custody is unconstitutional. In the United States, Article I, Section 9 of the Constitution makes clear that habeas corpus is guaranteed except, when in times of rebellion or invasion, public safety necessitates its suspension.

The last two decades have seen several changes to habeas corpus in the United States. In 1988, the Judicial Conference of the United States convened an ad hoc committee to consider existing problems in the administration of habeas corpus and to recommend changes in its operation. Popularly known as the Powell Committee in honor of the committee's chair, Associate Justice of the Supreme Court Lewis Powell, the committee released a report a year later concluding that the system of habeas corpus was plagued by "unnecessary delay and repetition" (Ad Hoc Committee, 1989). In response, the committee recommended a series of stepped-up deadlines in capital habeas cases, provided that the states agreed to appoint competent postconviction counsel for petitioners and allocated adequate resources to investigate and litigate these cases fairly. The committee also recommended changes that would limit the number of claims and resulting litigation that the federal courts would be required to consider in favor of resolving more of these matters in the state courts where collateral review originated.

ANTITERRORISM AND EFFECTIVE DEATH PENALTY ACT

Congress took up many of the Powell Committee's recommendations a few years later when, in 1996, it passed, and President Clinton signed, the inelegantly named Antiterrorism and Effective Death Penalty Act (AEDPA), which changed the administration of habeas corpus in the federal courts. Under AEDPA:

- State prisoners now face a one-year statute of limitations from the denial of their direct appeal in state court to the filing of their habeas-corpus petition in federal court. The statute is tolled during the pendancy of the petitioner's collateral claims in state court, but in practice a defendant who has not sought collateral review of his conviction within a year of sentencing faces a time bar on habeas consideration.

+ Petitioners must exhaust all state remedies before a federal court will entertain a habeas claim. This requirement has been softened subsequently by the U.S. Supreme Court's decision in *Rhines v. Weber* (2005), which permitted federal courts to stay federal habeas cases while a petitioner returns to state court to complete the litigation of some claims. Nevertheless, this right is limited to so- called mixed petitions, in which the majority of habeas claims already have been considered during state collateral review.

+ Federal courts are now directed to defer to the judgment of state courts on matters related to the habeas claim. Unless the state court's decision is either "contrary to" or an "unreasonable application of' clearly established federal law, it carries precedential weight in federal habeas proceedings. For that matter, petitioners who defaulted on their cases in state court are barred from an evidentiary hearing in federal court unless the district judge determines there is "cause" and "prejudice" or the petitioner can establish his factual innocence.

+ Finally, AEDPA gives the federal courts of appeal greater supervisory powers for habeas corpus. The federal courts may not hear a claimant's second or subsequent habeas petition unless a panel of the relevant court of appeals approves. Moreover, decisions of the federal district courts are final in habeas cases unless either the trial judge or a panel of the court of appeals grants a certificate of appealability.

OPT-IN PROVISIONS

Perhaps one of the most striking changes embedded in AEDPA—and a measure recommended by the Powell Committee—was the creation of new, faster deadlines for capital habeas cases in those states that agree to provide better resources for collateral review. Such states, which are said to "opt-in" to AEDPA's optional standards, must a) provide and reasonably compensate attorneys for indigent capital defendants in state postconviction proceedings, b) maintain standards of competency for appointment of these attorneys, and c) ensure that a petitioner's postconviction attorney is not also his counsel from trial or direct appeal unless both consent.

In exchange for meeting these requirements, AEDPA grants opt-in states shorter deadlines for consideration of the federal habeas cases. Petitioners must file their federal habeas claims within six months of the denial of their direct appeals in state court; federal district courts must resolve these claims within 180 days of their filing; and the federal appellate courts have 120 days to complete their consideration once the parties have filed their briefs. Under the USA Patriot Improvement and Reauthorization Act of 2005, the federal district courts' deadline has been extended from 180 to 450 days in capital habeas cases brought from opt-in states. Should the courts fail to meet these deadlines, AEDPA allows the states a writ of mandamus to the next higher federal court.

Interestingly, of the thirty-eight states that had the death penalty at the time of AEDPA, not one has been permitted to avail itself of the faster opt-in schedules. AEDPA placed authority with the federal courts to determine whether a state qualified for the opt-in rules. In *Spears v. Stewart* (2001), the Ninth Circuit concluded that Arizona had met the requirements laid out under AEDPA, but the court refused to allow Arizona to apply the expedited deadlines to the *Spears* case "because it did not comply with the timeliness requirement of its own system with respect to [the] petitioner" (at 992). No other state has successfully managed to qualify for AEDPA's opt-in deadlines.

Aware of this phenomenon, and presumably intending to qualify more states, Congress in 2005 transferred authority from the federal courts to the attorney general to decide which states qualify under AEDPA's fast-track option. In June 2007, the U.S. Department of Justice under then Attorney General Alberto Gonzalez released a draft of its proposed opt-in requirements. Under the draft proposal (Office of the Attorney General, 2007), a state would be permitted to utilize the faster deadlines if it has:

+ "established a mechanism for the appointment of counsel for indigent prisoners under sentence of death in state postconviction proceedings"
+ "established a mechanism for compensation of appointed counsel in state postconviction proceedings"
+ "established a mechanism for the payment of reasonable litigation expenses"
+ provided "competency standards for the appointment of counsel representing indigent prisoners in capital cases in state postconviction proceedings"

The Department of Justice sought public comment for its proposal and, in fact, extended the deadline for further submissions to September 24, 2007. As of this writing, the department had not issued a final rule, in part because of the transition from Attorney General Gonzales to Attorney General Michael Mukasey. Nonetheless, as is described later in this article, an expansion of "opt-in" habeas cases will likely clog and delay the disposition of cases in the federal courts.

THE CRITICS

Notwithstanding the changes wrought by AEDPA, critics still contend that the writ of habeas corpus moves too slowly, that capital cases in particular grind their way through the courts at an unacceptable, glacial pace. There has been no greater critic of capital habeas practice than Senator John Kyl (R-Ariz.), who in 2005 introduced the Streamlined Procedures Act (SPA), which proposed to limit the federal courts' consideration of capital habeas matters, required the dismissal of claims unexhausted in state court, limited claimants' ability to amend their habeas petitions, and tightened the counting of deadlines for AEDPA's statutes of limitations, among other provisions (Congressional Research Service, 2005).

SPA came in for considerable opposition, its critics including not only the U.S. Conference of Bishops but also the federal courts themselves. Kyl eventually abandoned SPA but not before he succeeded in placing authority for opt-in decisions with the attorney general, a change ratified by the USA Patriot Improvement and Reauthorization Act of 2005. Still, even this change

saw testimony in opposition from the federal judiciary. Appearing before the Senate Judiciary Committee, Senior Judge Howard McKibben (D. Nev.), chairman of the Judicial Conference Committee on Federal-State Jurisdiction, said, "There are no empirical data to indicate the courts have not properly determined opt-in requests." Indeed, he "repeatedly urged the committee to gather data to determine whether there is a systemic problem of delay in habeas review or just isolated cases in certain circuits before approving the comprehensive overhaul" advanced in SPA (Coyle, 2005).

NEW RESEARCH

Judge McKibben's testimony was prescient, for 2007 saw the publication of two important reports that provide a new look at the processing of capital habeas-corpus petitions from state prisoners in federal courts. The first report, by Judge Arthur Alarcín, concerns the processing of capital cases in California. The second, conducted by King, Cheesman, and Ostrom, examines federal habeas-corpus processing nationwide and the handling of capital habeas cases in thirteen federal district courts.

Judge Alarcón's piece is a normative and empirical inquiry, offering his explanations for the time taken to hear capital cases on both direct and collateral appeal in California, as well as providing a review of processing times for cases before the California Supreme Court and the federal courts with jurisdiction over California. By contrast, the King, Cheesman, and Ostrom report is entirely an empirical study. As the authors explain, they and their research assistants examined 2,384 randomly selected cases from among the 27,000 noncapital habeas cases filed by state prisoners in federal district court during 2003 and 2004. Simultaneously, they reviewed capital habeas cases filed in 2000, 2001, and 2002 in the thirteen federal districts with the highest volume of capital habeas filings. Researchers coded more than twenty variables on each of these cases. The courts included all four districts in Texas, as well as the U.S. district courts in Eastern Pennsylvania, Northern and Southern Ohio, Central California, Arizona, Nevada, Northern Alabama, Middle Florida, and Western Oklahoma.

Reviewing the two studies side by side, it is immediately apparent that habeas-corpus cases now take longer to litigate than they did at the time AEDPA was passed. As King, Cheesman, and Ostrom report, capital habeas cases that terminated in federal district court lasted an average 29 months, almost twice the 15 months they took before AEDPA. But this hardly tells the full story about case-processing time, for as the authors note, one in four federal capital habeas cases filed in 2000–02 were still pending as of November 2006 and had been pending an average of 5.3 years. Taking account of pending cases, they say, the average time to disposition for federal capital habeas cases was 3.1 years, or 1,152 days (King, Cheesman, and Ostrom, 2007:7). Given the paucity of past research on habeas case-processing times, their study is a significant contribution in this respect alone. Indeed, as the authors note, the benchmark for their findings is a decade-old report on habeas corpus (Hanson and Daley, 1995), which while useful, makes it impossible to provide tabular summaries of annual case-processing times.

NEW TIME PRESSURES

A disposition time of 1,152 days quite clearly exceeds the 450-day limit slated under AEDPA for states that manage to opt-in to the shorter deadline. Interestingly, not one of the thirteen districts examined by King, Cheesman, and Ostrom concluded its hearing of capital habeas petitions in shorter than an average of 500 days, even excluding the time that petitions were stayed for state court proceedings. Put another way, should the Department of Justice issue its final regulations, and should states successfully opt-in under AEDPA, the federal courts would face a serious problem in meeting the 450-day deadline.

It is not difficult to imagine this scenario. The criteria laid out by the Justice Department in its proposed rulemaking are relatively simple for most interested states to satisfy. With the exception of requiring states to pay "reasonable litigation expenses," not one of the standards set out by the attorney general demands more than a bare-bones system of

appointment. States must offer counsel to indigent defendants in postconviction proceedings, use some unspecified criteria to measure the attorneys' competency, and pay them some unspecified amount for their work. Missing in the proposed rule are standards to ensure that lawyers pass the constitutional standard for competency set in *Strickland v. Washington* (1984) and that the compensation offered by the states is sufficient for counsel to provide adequate representation.

It is difficult to say how many states would seek opt-in status after the Department of Justice finalizes its proposed rule. As of February 2008, thirty-six states had the death penalty (Death Penalty Information Center, 2008), but not all of these would immediately seek to opt-in to AEDPA's shorter deadlines. Some, like Alabama, would not qualify because they fail to provide postconviction counsel to the indigent (Freedman, 2006). Others may be wary of the increased pressure that the opt-in provision would place on staff within their attorney general's offices, which would be called to litigate capital habeas petitions at a faster pace. Indeed, informal conversations I have had with several federal defenders suggest that as few as seventeen states may seek opt-in status once the Department of Justice releases its final rule.[1]

Still, an increase of seventeen states would put a heavy burden on the federal courts to reconfigure their caseloads to accommodate a substantially shorter deadline for capital habeas petitions. In 2000 alone, the Case Management/Electronic Case Filing System (i.e., PACER) reports that more than 200 state prisoners filed habeas-corpus petitions in the federal courts challenging their death sentences, which were considered by forty-seven different district courts. Of these forty-seven districts, thirty-six courts received more than one petition. Civil cases and even some criminal matters will have to be put to the side if the federal courts are expected to devote compressed attention to the considerable litigation involved in capital habeas-corpus petitions. The federal courts, and anyone who appears before them, should be fearful of this prospect, for it likely means that some groups of cases will be delayed to accommodate the rising tide of "opt-in" habeas cases.

WHAT EXPLAINS CASE-PROCESSING TIMES?

Before requiring breakneck changes from the federal courts, Congress and the Justice Department would do well to consider what forces explain case-processing time in capital habeas petitions. King, Cheesman, and Ostrom offer several reasons. First, they say habeas caseloads affect case-processing times; holding other forces constant, the more habeas petitions a judge must consider, the longer it takes him or her to complete a habeas case. Second, a number of capital habeas cases have been stayed in federal court under *Rhines v. Weber* (2005) to permit petitioners to return to state court to litigate their unexhausted claims. In the King, Cheesman, and Ostrom sample, 17 percent of capital habeas cases had at least one stay, which averaged almost two years (2007:6). It makes intuitive sense that a stayed case would take longer to conclude than other cases. Yet stays are not uniform across the federal courts. Of the thirteen districts examined by King, Cheesman, and Ostrom, four are in Texas; these courts are among the least likely districts to issue stays, and their stays are also among the shortest in the sample. Contrast these districts with those in California, where the average stay to return to state court lasted 2.8 years (Alarcón, 2007:749). The King et al. study includes only one California district in its sample—Central California, based in Los Angeles—while excluding Northern California (San Francisco), Eastern California (Sacramento), and Southern California (San Diego).

King, Cheesman, and Ostrom do an admirable job of anticipating and testing a number of hypotheses that may explain the time it takes for federal courts to consider capital habeas petitions. They include such factors as whether the claimant filed an amended petition, how many claims were raised in the petition, and what substantive issues were claimed. Some of these factors are shown to have an influence. For example, cases take longer when a petition is amended or when the petitioner asserts a claim under *Roper v. Simmons* (2005), *Atkins v. Virginia* (2002), or *Ring v. Arizona* (2002) challenging the constitutionality of his capital conviction and sentence. But the greatest influence on case processing is the location of the court hearing the capital habeas petition. As the authors explain, "even

after controlling for other factors, one of the factors with the most powerful associate with processing time for both capital and non-capital cases was the identity of the circuit, district, or state in which the case was filed" (King, Cheesman, and Ostrom, 2007:9).

GEOGRAPHIC EFFECTS

It is difficult to say what forces explain these geographic differences. It cannot be regional disparities in compensation rates, as attorneys who represent indigent defendants in federal capital habeas cases are paid a common rate across the country, $125/hour for lead counsel through 2004 and $160/hour or more since then. A more likely factor—and one that King, Cheesman, and Ostrom did not estimate—is a state's "capital culture." This construct represents a state's historical attachment to the death penalty and posits that capital habeas cases are litigated more strenuously and considered at greater length when arising from states that do not have as strong an attachment to the death penalty as do others.[1] For example, although both Alabama and Illinois have the death penalty, Alabama's death-row population is significantly larger than that in Illinois (Death Penalty Information Center, 2008), especially if one controls for state population. In these circumstances, one can imagine a capital habeas petition taking longer in Chicago as judges and lawyers expend great care to scrutinize the state legal processes that sent a convicted defendant to death row than in, say, Montgomery, where capital convictions are a more common occurrence and where citizens, lawyers, and the judiciary may have grown accustomed to an "assembly-line justice" process (Bright, 2004).

The geographic differences may also reflect the varying cultures of the local legal markets and the professional backgrounds of the lawyers appointed to the federal bench there. Major cities like New York and Los Angeles are legal markets often dominated by large, commercial law firms, which create a culture in which lengthy, meticulous, and often expensive litigation is not only accepted but also at times expected. By contrast, the legal markets in smaller cities like Little Rock, Arkansas, or Cheyenne, Wyoming, may not support such painstaking litigation, in part because a different client base—one with more individuals and smaller companies—may not be able to afford extravagant legal bills or tolerate the longer wait for litigation to resolve.

There are well-documented differences in "local legal culture" (Church, 1985; Gallas, 2005; Ostrom et al., 2007), in which common experiences of litigation become shared norms of "court culture." Indeed, "the concept 'local legal culture' was developed from research findings that participants in the federal and state courts in the same locale had relatively consensual views of the appropriate length of time to disposition for cases, although there was considerable variation among different locales" (Wasby, 2007:131). Whether a local legal culture, which includes the expectations of judges and lawyers, or a more narrow notion of court culture, which reflects the views of judges and court administrators, better explains geographic differences in disposition times, both constructs illustrate how the lawyers who litigate habeas-corpus claims in a given jurisdiction and the judges who hear these petitions can become accustomed to an acceptable range of time and effort for the litigation.

Some might say capital habeas should be immune to such differences in local legal culture, that because so few lawyers handle these cases, and because the death penalty is an issue of national salience, the lawyers who litigate capital habeas create their own niche and subculture of litigation norms. Those norms are shared, in turn, with the federal judges who hear such matters, who may also take their cues from the small cadre of other federal judges with experience in capital habeas matters. Although the argument has merit—especially in explaining aspects of a defense culture that is led by the national Capital Defense Network—the data instead suggest that local differences are more powerful than national norms. Recall that King, Cheesman, and Ostrom examined only thirteen federal districts. Of these, the four Texas districts accounted for half of the 368 cases studied (King, Cheesman, and Ostrom, 2007:50). By contrast, a PACER search shows that in several other districts, including Southern New York, Western Missouri, Western Tennessee, and Southern Georgia, only a single state prisoner filed a capital habeas petition

in each during the same time. Thus, the case data actually suggest that capital habeas-corpus petitions are an occasional or even rare occurrence for many federal district courts. When these courts are called upon to hear these cases, they may bring their own idiosyncratic perspectives—perhaps gleaned from their experience with the local legal culture—to the litigation of capital habeas petitions.

Geographic effects may, of course, have other explanations. One is ambiguous or changing precedent. King, Cheesman, and Ostrom report that the District of Arizona "had the lowest percentage of terminated [capital habeas] cases" of the thirteen federal district courts they sampled (2007:9). This finding is understandable when one considers that the sample was drawn from 2000-02, when judges in Arizona were aware that the U.S. Supreme Court had taken certiorari in *Ring v. Arizona* (2002), which threatened to—and did—change the law on the death penalty in Arizona. Observing the considerable litigation about the decision's retroactivity that followed, a federal judge in Arizona might very well have waited on any habeas petitions until the law became more settled. Of course, *Ring* had national significance, but the most likely site to litigate its implementation would have been Arizona, where the case originated.

The same period saw the federal and state courts spar over a rule of Arizona criminal procedure that barred a defendant from raising a claim of ineffective assistance of counsel in a federal habeas petition. By 2002, the U.S. Supreme Court finally ruled, having first certified a question to the Arizona Supreme Court. But in remanding the case to the Ninth Circuit (*Stewart v. Smith*, 2002), the Supreme Court may well have signaled to the Arizona federal judges that further litigation would be required to interpret and apply the Court's holding. Against this backdrop, it is understandable that the U.S. District Court in Arizona completed a smaller percentage of capital habeas petitions during the study period than did other federal courts examined.

State law and practice likely have a strong influence on the processing of federal capital habeas petitions as well. Texas, for example, has strict default rules, which require defendants to raise certain issues on direct appeal and others during a simultaneous collateral-review process. Issues not litigated in the correct proceeding are lost and may not be raised again in the Texas courts. Nor will the federal courts step in, the U.S. Supreme Court having ruled that state procedural default is a bar to federal consideration under habeas corpus unless there is a finding of cause (*Coleman v. Thompson*, 1991) or, now under AEDPA, innocence. As a result, the unfortunate defendant who is confused by the Texas appellate process may unwittingly default on an issue and lose the claim forever. Faced with fewer claims that he can raise in a federal habeas petition, the federal court in Texas may then dispose of his case more swiftly than in other jurisdictions. Indeed, as King, Cheesman, and Ostrom (2007:9) have found, "capital petitions filed in the four districts in Texas were more likely to be concluded, and concluded sooner, than cases filed in any of the other nine districts in the study."

CALIFORNIA AS A MICROCOSM

It is also important to remember that the progress of federal habeas cases depends to some extent on the quality of state court litigation that precedes them, whether on direct appeal or collateral proceedings. Judge Alarcón (2007:748) issues a stark reminder: habeas-corpus cases take an average 6.2 years in the California federal courts, he reports, largely because 75 percent of the cases must return to state court where they spend an average 2.8 years litigating the petitioners' unexhausted claims.

Judge Alarcín is too polite to say it directly, but California's system of postconviction review seems designed to have the state punt its responsibility for constitutional review to the federal courts. As he explains, "lawyers who file state habeas corpus petitions on behalf of death row inmates in California currently do not receive sufficient funds for investigation of their clients' claims" (Alarcón, 2007:748). Whether because the hourly rate for attorney compensation is too low—$140, compared to the $287 rate permitted under the "lodestar" method in federal civil cases[3]—or because California caps habeas expenditures for investigators and experts at $25,000 over three years, capital

defendants are not getting a fair opportunity to challenge their convictions and sentences in the California courts. As a result, "lawyers appointed to represent death row inmates in federal habeas proceedings are forced to conduct an investigation at federal government expense to determine all the facts necessary to support exhausted federal constitutional claims and to discover facts necessary to prove unexhausted claims" (Alarcín, 2007:748).

For that matter, the California Supreme Court seems unwilling to provide a complete record that would permit the federal courts to identify—and thus give proper deference under AEDPA to—the findings made in state habeas proceedings. To be sure, the California Supreme Court receives many petitions for habeas corpus; in the years 1978–2005, the number reached as high as 689 habeas petitions. However, the court decided 632 of these cases on the petition and response alone, ordering further proceedings in just 47 matters and an evidentiary hearing only 31 times (Alarcín, 2007:741). The result is that, in many cases, the court offers a scant record to justify its rulings. In 92 percent of the 689 habeas-corpus petitions on which it has ruled, the California Supreme Court has issued nothing more than a summary report to announce its decision. Sometimes called "postcard denials," these summary dispositions provide no explanation or details for the court's holding, thus giving the federal courts virtually nothing to consider besides the decision itself in weighing the constitutional merit of the defendant's later federal petition.

California chief justice Ronald George has not been shy in explaining his court's reluctance to offer guidance for its habeas decisions. Responding to questions from Senator Dianne Feinstein (D-Cal), George said "that drafting and reviewing an order containing more information than the basic ground for denying relief consumes far more time on the part of both staff and the justices, to the detriment of the court's performance of its responsibilities in noncapital cases" (quoted in Alarcín, 2007:742). However, as Senator Feinstein correctly notes, the California Supreme Court's failure to spell about the reasons for its habeas decisions "often requires federal courts to essentially start each federal habeas death penalty [case] from scratch, wasting enormous time and resources" (quoted in Alarcin, 2007:743). This would seem to turn AEDPA on its head. Passed largely to speed up the consideration of postconviction claims by condemned prisoners, AEDPA requires federal courts to defer to state court decisions that are neither "contrary to" nor an "unreasonable application of" clearly established federal law. Yet without an opinion that explains the basis for its decision, one can hardly understand how the California Supreme Court has applied federal law in its state habeas cases. If anything, California's actions seem determined to thwart the intentions of AEDPA and shift costs to the federal government by requiring the federal courts of California to do the work that its state system should complete.

"DELAY"

The result of California's actions, Judge Alarcin concludes, is "delay." Referring to state habeas review, he says:

> The average delay between the filing of the responsive brief by the attorney general and the prisoner's reply brief was 6.5 months. The average delay between the filing of the reply brief and oral argument before the California Supreme Court was 18.5 months. The average delay between oral argument and the filing of the California Supreme Court's opinion between 1978 and January 19, 2004 was 6.2 months (Alarcón, 2007:722).

Yet Judge Alarcin's use of delay is imprecise, for the term fails to distinguish between those points in the collateral process that take *some* amount of time and those that may take *too much* time. Moreover, the word has a pejorative meaning, implying that habeas-corpus claims take too long to process when, in fact, there may be some courts that do not give these matters sufficient consideration. To be sure, many would agree with Judge Alarcin that a gap of twenty-four years between sentencing and execution, as happened in the case of Clarence Allen, is unacceptable. Whether one supports the death penalty and seeks swift

administration of justice or opposes capital punishment and believes that a two-decade wait on death row constitutes cruel and unusual punishment, the state and federal courts ought to be able to complete their postconviction review within a shorter amount of time. The gap is all the more troubling when the petitioner is actually innocent, or when his sentence is disproportionally high, and he must keep time on death row until he wins eventual reprieve.

These exceptional cases do not mean, however, that every gap in litigation constitutes illegitimate delay. Indeed, at a most basic level, meritorious cases are likely to take longer to litigate than those habeas petitions that are dismissed, for as King, Cheesman, and Ostrom demonstrate, the federal courts are more likely to hold evidentiary hearings for habeas petitions they eventually grant. Hearings, and the motions and submissions that go with them, often extend the life of a habeas petition. Would Alarcin or others include such time in delay? Likely not, yet the loose use of the term when describing case processing only reinforces the notion advanced by others that collateral review in capital cases is itself an unnecessary delay. One need only consider the remarks of California governor Arnold Schwarzenegger, who "in a strongly worded statement" criticized the federal court in San Francisco for "interject[ing] itself into the details of the state's execution process" when it halted the execution of Michael Morales out of concern that the state's method of execution would violate the Eighth Amendment (CNN, 2006). Such sentiments are understandable if they come from relatives of the victim, who in this case decried "the entire process [as] a mockery" (CNN, 2006), but those sworn to uphold the Constitution should not consider federal review of a state's execution process to be an unacceptable delay.

Defining an appropriate length for collateral review is beyond the scope of this article, for, of course, each case is unique and warrants individual attention. Nonetheless, it is troubling that so much of the debate over capital habeas corpus has focused on how long the federal courts take rather than whether some of those courts, not to mention their state cousins, fail to give habeas petitions appropriate consideration. Why, for example, do we focus on states like California, asking, as I have heard in hushed conversations, whether anti-death penalty judges are "putting these cases in drawers"? Why not address the cases King uncovered in Texas, where habeas review takes place more quickly than anywhere in the nation? Why is it that the U.S. District Court for Southern Texas, which completed an astonishing 92 percent of the eighty-seven capital habeas petitions it received from state prisoners in 2000–01, granted only 7 percent of the petitions, whereas the Eastern District of Pennsylvania was still considering eleven of the nineteen petitions it received in the same period and had granted relief in 75 percent of the terminated cases (King, Cheesman, and Ostrom, 2007:11)? Do we explain these differences by variations in state law and practice, local legal culture, or quality of postconviction counsel, or is this evidence of "activist" judges imposing their ideology on capital habeas cases, whether for or against the death penalty? The short answer is that we do not know exactly, but the question deserves more reasoned attention than it has received so far.

LESSONS

Both the King, Cheesman, and Ostrom and Alarcín studies are excellent steps through which to bring empirical evidence and informed debate to the question of postconviction review in capital cases. Perhaps others will add to these data. As reported in the March 2007 minutes of the Judicial Conference of the United States (Proceedings, 2007:16), the Administrative Office of the U.S. Courts and the Federal Judicial Center were undertaking a "capital habeas corpus study." At the time of this writing, there was no information available on the status or findings of that review. Were this information to be forthcoming, it presumably would add much to the body of new data that are now being generated on the processing of capital habeas corpus-petitions.

Regardless of whether additional reports will be forthcoming, the studies by Alarcín and King, Cheesman, and Ostrom present three important lessons. First, not only does capital habeas corpus take longer now than it did before AEDPA, but there is also tremendous variation in the time and treatment that federal courts give to these petitions. Second, even if we account for the many variables that King, Cheesman,

and Ostrom test, the strongest explanation for case processing is geography; state, circuit, and district effects overwhelm other potential explanations for case-processing times and outcomes. Third, and perhaps most important, these geographic differences compel us to dig deeper into qualitative research and case studies to better understand why the federal courts treat similar constitutional claims differently. This essay has suggested several potential reasons, from varying local legal cultures to differences in state law and practice, to the failure of certain states to carry out their responsibilities in postconviction review.

If there is one "takeaway lesson" from this research, it is the folly of branding the federal courts scapegoats for other deficiencies in the intergovernmental system of collateral review. Habeas corpus may take longer than many of us would prefer, but this does not mean that the federal courts are dragging their heels, resistant to rule on claims that may send the losing party to the death chamber. To the contrary, not only must the federal courts pick up the pieces when states fail at collateral review, but in occasionally taking their time to review habeas matters more thoroughly, the federal courts are also ensuring that due process means as much in practice as it does in theory.

REFERENCES

Ad Hoc Committee on Federal Habeas Corpus in Capital Cases, Judicial Conference of the United States (1989). Committee report and proposal.

Alarcón, A. (2007). "Remedies for California's Death Row Deadlock," 80 *Southern California Law Review* 697.

Antiterrorism and Effective Death Penalty Act, 28 U.S.C. §2241–2266 (1996).

Bright, S. (2004). Interview with PBS *Frontline*, http://www.pbs.org/wgbh/pages/frontline/shows/plea/interviews/bright.html (last accessed March 10, 2008).

Church, T. W., Jr. (1985). "Examining Local Legal Culture," 10 *Law and Social Inquiry* 449.

CNN (2006). "Victim's Family 'Devastated' by Execution Delay." http://www.cnn.com/2006/LAW/02/22/ morales.execution/index.html (last accessed March 11, 2008).

Congressional Research Service (2005). Review of S1088. http://thomas.loc.gov/cgi-bin/bdquery/ z?dl09:SN01088:@@@D&summ2=m& (last accessed March 7, 2008).

Coyle, M. (2005). "Congress Moves to Limit Prisoner Habeas," *National Law Journal*, November 23. http:// www.law.com/jsp/article.jsp?id=1132580126812 (last accessed March 7, 2008).

Death Penalty Information Center (2008). "Facts About the Death Penalty." http://www.deathpenaltyinfo. org/ FactSheet.pdf (last accessed March 9, 2008).

Freedman, E. M. (2006). "Giarranto is a Scarecrow: The Right to Counsel in State Capital Postconviction Proceedings," 91 *Cornell Law Review* 1079.

Gallas, G. (2005). "Local Legal Culture: More Than Court Culture," 20 *Court Manager* 23.

Hanson, R. A., and H. W. K. Daley (1995). *Federal Habeas Corpus Review: Challenging State Court Criminal Convictions*. Washington, DC: Bureau of Justice Statistics.

King, N. J., F. L. Cheesman II, and B. J. Ostrom (2007). *Habeas Litigation in the U.S. District Courts: An Empirical Study of Habeas Corpus Cases Filed by State Prisoners Under the Antiterrorism and Effective Death Penalty Act of 1996*. Nashville, TN: Vanderbilt University Law School.

Office of the Attorney General, Department of Justice (2007). "Notice of Proposed Rulemaking: Certification Process for State Capital Counsel Systems," *Federal Register* 72(108): 31217–220.

Ostrom, B. J., C. W. Ostrom, R. A. Hanson, and M. Kleiman (2007). *Trial Courts as Organizations*. Philadelphia: Temple University Press.

Proceedings of the Judicial Conference of the United States (2007). Minutes, March 13. http://www. uscourts.gov/judconf/07MarchProceedings.pdf (last accessed March 10, 2008).

Wasby, S. L. (2007). "Of Note." Review of Gallas, "Local Legal Culture," 21 *Justice System Journal* 131.

NOTES

1. The Office of Defender Services, a branch of the Administrative Office of the U.S. Courts, has several staff members who follow developments with AEDPA.

2. There are several ways of modeling this construct, including the per-capita size of a state's death-row population or the number of convicts it has executed in the modern era, again on a per-capita basis.

3. "Under the typical federal fee-shifting statute, the court will arrive at an attorney's fee by first determining the 'lodestar' amount, which is calculated by 'multiplying the attorney's reasonable hourly rate by the number of hours reasonably expended.'" *Grant v. George Schumann Tire & Battery Company*, 1990, at 879.

CASES CITED

Atkins v. Virginia, 536 U.S. 304 (2002).

Coleman v. Thompson, 501 U.S. 722 (1991).

Ford v. Wainwright, 477 U.S. 399 (1986).

Grant v. George Schumann Tire & Battery Company, 908 F.2d 874 (11th Cir. 1990).

Rhines v. Weber, 544 U.S. 269 (2005).

Ring v. Arizona, 536 U.S. 584 (2002).

Roper v. Simmons, 543 U.S. 551 (2005).

Spears v. Stewart, 283 F.3d 992 (9th Cir. 2001).

Stewart v. Smith, 536 U.S. 856 (2002).

Strickland v. Washington, 466 U.S. 668 (1984).

Section
VI

Corrections

Overview of Corrections in the United States

Douglas Klutz and
Mark M. Lanier

Corrections is the piece of the criminal justice system that is most removed from the public eye. Ironically, it is also the piece of the puzzle that most American citizens are likely to be involved with. A record number of American citizens are under correctional supervision. Approximately 1 out of every 31 Americans are involved in the correctional system in some capacity. This includes forms of community corrections such as probation and parole.

The history of "corrections," much like the history of criminal justice (as understood to be a system), itself has a sordid record. The pendulum has swung from punishment to treatment and back to punishment several times. Increasingly, however, court mandates, often rendered on the behalf of complaining inmates, require certain minimum levels of both physical and mental care of inmates. Court mandates do not always translate into practice, however. Budgetary issues, philosophical beliefs, and prison realities that take precedence over courtroom legislation often supersede judicial decrees and edicts. Even when well-intended, correctional staff often place custody and order maintenance over legally mandated health (physical and mental) care concerns of inmates. This prison reality is well documented, defended, and rationalized as being inevitable.

In this section the readings outline these, and more, issues related to incarceration and correctional practice. The section begins with a historical overview; this is followed by a paper on "special needs" incarcerated populations (females, elderly, juveniles, et al.) and the final piece addresses the scale of imprisonment in the United States in the twenty-first century.

Historical Overview

Dobash, Dobash, and Gutteridge (1986) provided a critical, compelling, and historically accurate portrayal of the development of the women's penal system in Great Britain. While focused on one country, one gender, and one system, it is still a relevant critique since much of the Anglo, westernized correctional and penal systems emulated the English tradition, if not the exact model. The

225

largest difference is that "prisons in North America are organized and administered on a number of different levels, unlike British prisons which are centrally administered" (p. 3) according to Dobash et al. (1986). However, we suggest that some American states, such as Texas, greatly surpass the whole of England in land mass, gross national product, and population. This discrepancy may be a moot point anyway since the defining characteristics are identical. Consider just one accepted and rarely questioned (yet perhaps detrimental) example: to this day men and women are segregated in correctional settings. This practice itself may be pathological and lead to serious health consequences like same-sex rape, increased depression, and "prison homosexuality." Clearly, having co-ed prisons would also create tensions and problems, but that type of custodial setting would better reflect "real world" experiences and prior socialization, thus better equipping inmates for their eventual release.

The first type of correctional practice was public punishment and what we would consider torture by today's standards. According to Schmalleger and Smykla (2011) the ancient Greek city-states were the first to document public punishment. The city-state of Athens provided the best historical documentation with "execution, banishment, or exile. Greek poets described stoning the condemned to death, throwing them from high cliffs, binding them to stakes (similar to crucifixion) and cursing them ritually" (2011: 35). Mutilation was also commonly used in ancient and medieval societies. This form or punishment, or retaliation, was called "Lex talionis" and mirrored the Biblical philosophy of "an eye for an eye and a tooth for a tooth" (Schmalleger and Smykla 2011: 39). In medieval Europe, floggings, stocks, and even execution were the means to both punish criminals and to deter others from committing crimes. According to Dobash et al., "physical and symbolic punishments, such as whipping, hanging and public ridicule, were the main methods used in pre-industrial societies" (1986: 15). Such disciplinary avenues did in fact have an immediate deterrent effect, leaving both the offender scarred and others assuredly threatened with the price of retribution. However, while the purpose of public punishment was to demean the criminal, the ultimate outcome was

barbaric and eventually proved counterproductive to deterring criminals, as it neglected several of what are recognized today as the goals of sentencing.

Following the era of public punishment, even including the death penalty, came the emergence of incarceration as punishment (Schmalleger and Smykla 2011: 44). The first "house of corrections" was established in the 1550s by Edward VI, the son of Henry the VIII, and was named "Bridewell," after the Bridewell Palace, a former royal mansion (Roth 2005: 40). Soon thereafter, the term Bridewell was coined as a term for workhouses as they expanded and multiplied across the land (Schmalleger and Smykla 2011: 45). During this time there was a major economic shift from an agrarian community to an industrial one, leaving many individuals displaced and resulting in growing poverty, as well as a surplus of beggars and vagrants. As the number of vagrants increased, vagrancy became criminalized, and those unable to provide proof of some means of support were imprisoned in a Bridewell (Schmalleger and Smykla 2011: 45). In the beginning, prisoners were paid for the work they did; however, as the number of prisoners grew, the workhouse system deteriorated. These workhouses were essentially the transition between the brutal corporal punishments of ancient Greece and what we find today in modern imprisonment.

From the seventeenth century to the dawn of the nineteenth century, growing intellectualism in Europe and America, also known as the Age of Enlightenment, became the driving force behind a shift toward a more humane system of punishment. As a reaction to the savagery of corporal punishment, prisons were implemented for the lengthy incarceration of convicted offenders. Two main elements are believed to have fueled the development of the prison system we see today. The first of these being a philosophical shift away from the punishment of the body and toward the punishment of the human spirit or soul, and the second being the passage of laws preventing the imprisonment of anyone except criminals (Schmalleger and Smykla 2011: 45–46).

Today, though we have come a long way from flogging and branding (we only water board now), our correctional system still struggles to adhere to and achieve fundamental goals. One perpetual issue that has yet to receive adequate attention is the issue of corrections and indigenous populations. Research provides that there is an enormous overrepresentation of indigenous populations within the correctional system worldwide.

Specifically looking at Canada, Australia, and South Africa, we find that indigenous populations are overrepresented at nearly every stage of the criminal justice system. Following global colonization, there was a collision of two worlds. The result of this collision established one powerful population and one subordinate. Unfortunately, it was the indigenous, native people who suffered, and still suffer, disproportionally. The inability or lack of desire from the indigenous population to adhere to the unfamiliar governing of the colonialist is what cultivated the misrepresentation of such people within the correctional system.

Imprisonment rates of native peoples in Western Australia are currently more than 4.4 percent of the adult population and are among the highest rates recorded worldwide (Cunneen 2011: 309). According to Chris Cunneen, in Canada as well, native people compose only 3 percent of the general population while at the same time native offenders compose nearly 17 percent of inmates in the federal penitentiary system (2011: 310). Research provides that this overrepresentation is due largely to the criminal justice system essentially failing such indigenous populations (Martel, Brassard, and Jaccoud 2011: 236).

In South Africa we find yet another overrepresentation of the aboriginal population; however, the typical pattern of corrections in general is much different here than among European countries, the United States, and other Western democracies. According to Gail Super, the correctional pattern in South Africa is essentially the reverse pattern of what we consider the norm; having two or three people under community sanctions for every one person confined (2011: 201). In South Africa we find there are approximately ten people incarcerated for every one person on probation; the people in custody outnumber those in the community by more than three to one (Super 2011: 201).

Currently, women represent the fastest-growing segment of prison and jail populations, even though their crime rate is not increasing dramatically. Among women ages 35–39 years, one in 265 is incarcerated. The racial breakdown in that age group shows that one in 355 is white, one in 297 is Hispanic, and one in 100 is black (Pew 2008). As Franklin et al. noted, incarcerated women are characteristically women of color, poor, unemployed, and single mothers of young children (2005). Imprisoned women tend to have fragmented families, other family members involved with the criminal justice system, significant substance abuse issues, and multiple physical and mental health problems (Bloom, Owen, and Covington 2003). Since 1995, the number of women being held in the nation's prisons has increased 50% and at year-end 2007, 115,779 women were imprisoned in state or federal prisons—6.9% of the total prison population (Bureau of Justice Statistics 2008).

Nearly half of all Americans in prison are currently serving a sentence for a non-violent crime. The increased incarceration of so many people appears to be the outcome of U.S. crime policy over the past two decades: government policies prescribing simplistic, punitive enforcement responses for complex social problems; federal and state mandatory-sentencing laws; and the public's fear of crime (even though crime in this country has been on the decline for nearly a decade). "Get tough" policies intended to target drug dealers and so-called kingpins have resulted not only in more men and women being imprisoned, but also in their serving longer sentences.

The history of "corrections," much like the history of criminal justice (as understood to be a system), itself has a sordid record. The pendulum has swung from punishment to treatment and back to punishment several times. Increasingly, however, court mandates, often rendered on the behalf of complaining inmates, require base levels of both physical and mental health care of inmates. Court mandates do not always translate into practice, however. Budgetary issues, philosophical beliefs, and prison realities that take precedence over courtroom legislation often supersede judicial decrees and edicts. Even when well-intended, correctional staff often place custody and order maintenance over legally mandated health (physical and mental) care concerns of inmates. This prison reality is well documented, defended, and rationalized as being inevitable. Scholars have been deficient in bridging this seemingly insurmountable tension between custody and health care. Hopefully some of you reading this can start working to correct that.

One current trend in corrections deals with the expansion of private prisons. A private prison can be defined as a prison that is operated by a nongovernmental outfit, but is also working contractually on behalf of the state.[1] The privatization of prisons across the United States has turned out to be a lucrative business model. An example of the booming private prison business is Corrections Corporation of America (CCA), an owner and operator of privatized correctional facilities in the United States. CCA recently hit a 10-year high on the stock market, and has also been busy receiving contracts to operate or continue operating correctional facilities in Texas, Hawaii, California, and Georgia, to name just a few states.

The growing private-prison enterprise does not impact only state correctional systems, either. Even the federal government has started contracting out correctional services to private prisons. For example, in September of 2010, Corrections Corporation of America announced they would manage federal prisoners in the state of California.[2]

The prison population in the United States has continued to expand since the early 1980s, as a product of the war on drugs. Mandatory drug sentencing laws, coupled with the saturation of the crack cocaine trade, gave rise to more prisoners entering the system throughout the 1980s. The private-prison industry soon learned that building prisons and contracting out correctional services made for a lucrative business. The term "prison industrial complex" brings to light new controversies over the ethical nature of having our correctional system driven by corporate profits.

Criminologists have formulated important theories in an attempt to illuminate the trend in the corporatization of the prison industry. The prison industrial complex can best be explained as a merger between political ambitions and economic interests.[3] Corporate profit margins in the private-prison industry are assisted by the recycled political rhetoric concerning the fight against crime. In order to help secure votes, politicians will implement new laws in order to appear tough on crime, even if this means criminalizing a greater amount of minor offenses. More laws means more violators of laws, which in turn means more business for the private-prison industry.

It is easy to see why corporations investing in the business of corrections have a vested interest in keeping privately owned prisons at full inmate capacity. Inmates produce goods and services that can be sold for a profit and the private-prison industry can undercut the costs associated with government-run correctional facilities. However, cost-cutting does not always equate to overall success from an operational standpoint. Privatized prisons have significant problems maintaining secure prisons facilities and research shows that inmate-on-guard and inmate-on-inmate assaults occur at a higher frequency in private prisons.[4]

As the private-prison industry continues to expand, should our correctional system be driven by corporate profits? In order to answer this question successfully, you must identify what the primary goal of a corrections should be. In the case of private prisons, corporations work in the interest of shareholders, not necessarily in the best interest of the inmates themselves. Growing quarterly revenues, shoring up additional contracts, and keeping existing facilities at full capacity are what is ultimately good for business and growth in the private-prison industry. However, these corporate goals run contrary to the concept of rehabilitation as a product of corrections. What incentive would a privately owned prison have for inmates to be released early? These conflicting goals in corrections will continue to be discussed as cash-strapped governments across the country look to private prisons to provide lower-cost services in correctional settings.

NOTES

1. Harding, Richard. "Private Prisons." *Crime and Justice.* Vol. 28, (2001), pp. 265–346. The University of Chicago Press.
2. Corrections Corporation of America Announces New Management Contract at California City Correctional Center to House Federal Prisoner and Detainee. Reuters. September 27, 2010.
3. Chang T. F. H. and Thompkins D. E. "Corporations Go to Prisons: The Expansion of Corporate Power in the Correctional Industry." (2002) *Labor Studies Journal*, 27 (1), pp. 45–69.
4. Camp, S. D. and Gaes, G. G. (2002), "Growth and Quality of U.S. Private Prisons: Evidence from a National Survey." *Criminology & Public Policy*, 1: 427–450.

THE SCALE OF IMPRISONMENT IN THE UNITED STATES

Twentieth Century Patterns and Twenty-First Century Prospects

Franklin E. Zimring

INTRODUCTION

The prison has been far more important to criminal justice practice than to academic theory in the century examined by this Symposium. Imprisonment is the dominant severe criminal sanction worldwide and there is no evidence that its hegemony at the deep end of crime control will change. But the study of imprisonment has not been a major feature of criminal law theory at any time, while some aspects of prisons have commanded attention in the literature of criminology. So imprisonment has played a dominant role in American criminal justice but a minor role in the discourse about criminal law. The *Harvard Law Review*, for example, listed twenty-seven articles with "prison" or "imprisonment" in the title in one hundred years of publication beginning in 1910.

The interdisciplinary character of the *Journal of Criminal Law and Criminology* and its crime focus made it into the leading forum in law-related scholarship covering issues of prison operation and function. No fewer than 155 main articles were published with "prisons" or "imprisonment" in their titles in a century of publications, by far the largest concentration one would find in any scholarly journal closely linked to legal education.[1] And prisons played a prominent part in the scholarly portfolio of the *Journal* from the very beginning, with slightly more articles on prisons in the first half of its volumes than in the second. The range of prison-related topics covered from the beginning—including comparative and empirical work—was impressive.

But little of the first half-century of the *Journal* touched on the central issue in this analysis—what I shall call *the scale of imprisonment*. Zimring and Hawkins define the issue of scale as analysis of the appropriate "size of a society's prison enterprise in relation to other criminal sanctions and to the general population. How many prisoners? How many prisons? What criteria should govern decisions about how large a prison enterprise should be constructed and maintained?"[2]

Only one of the more than seventy articles with prison in its title that appeared in the *Journal* in its first half-century was principally concerned with rates of imprisonment: an article by Edwin Sutherland describing the decline in rates of imprisonment in England.[3] One important reason for the lack of scholarly attention to variation in the rate of imprisonment in the United States is that there was not a great deal of variation over time in the rate of imprisonment.

Indeed, the lack of dramatic variation in rates of imprisonment inspired Alfred Blumstein and Jacqueline Cohen to construct what they called "A Theory of the Stability of Punishment"[4] in the *Journal* in 1973, probably the most important and certainly the most ironically timed article on imprisonment in the *Journal*'s first century. Blumstein and Cohen posit that levels of severe criminal punishment trend toward stability over time and they offered as evidence of this phenomenon the rather stable rates of imprisonment in the national aggregate over the years 1930–1970. The interpretation of this data was straightforward:

> It can be seen from Figure 2 that over that period the imprisonment rate was reasonably constant, having an average value of 110.2 prisoners per 100,000 population and a standard deviation during that time … of 8.9 prisoners per 100,000 population. … The stability of the time series is especially noteworthy when it is considered that the

population of the United States increased by over 50 percent in the same period.[5]

Twice more in the 1970s, Blumstein and his associates would produce data and analysis to augment their stability of punishment theory,[6] but then their entire theoretical structure was overtaken by events. From its low point in 1972, U.S. prison populations had begun a consistent and unprecedented climb. Figure 21.1, taken from U.S. Bureau of Justice Statistics data, shows an uninterrupted increase in aggregate imprisonment rates that lasted the full generation after 1972.

The contrast between the four decades after 1930 and the three and a half decades after 1972 is stark. The highest annual imprisonment rate in the 1930–1970 period was 38% above the lowest (131.5 versus 95.5 per 100,000) and there was no clear trend over time. In the thirty years after 1972, the rate of imprisonment grew every year and the rate of imprisonment by 2007 was five times greater than at the beginning.

The first impact on scholarship of this unprecedented increase in the use of prisons in the United States was to end any serious discussion of "stability of punishment." That theory was produced by flat trends over time in the United States after 1925 and was destroyed by the imprisonment boom that followed 1972.

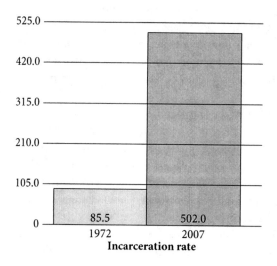

Figure 21.1   Imprisonment in 1972 and 2007, U.S. Rates per 100,000.

Source: Bureau of Census and Bureau of Justice Statistics

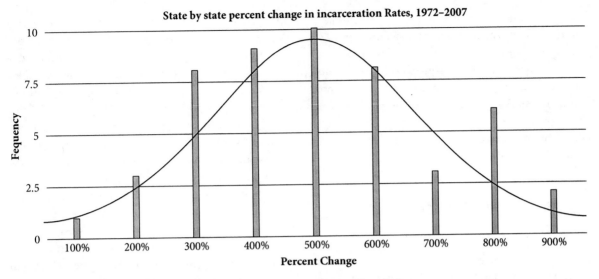

Figure 21.2   The Almost Bell Curve Distribution of State Imprisonment Growth Rates

The second product of the sharp increase in American prison population was academic interest in what features of society and government might influence rates of imprisonment over time. Once the dynamic and non-homeostatic qualities of imprisonment rates were established by the history of imprisonment after 1975, the causes of variation in imprisonment over time and cross-sectionally became an important topic for empirical analysis. The same upward march in prison population that ended interest in stability of punishment generated curiosity about the scale of imprisonment as a variable in crime policy and governance.

There are two parallels between the "stability of punishment" exercises of the 1970s and the more recent efforts to comprehend and measure what determines the scale of imprisonment in the United States. The first important shared characteristic of these two lines of inquiry is that each theory was derived from and driven by empirical data. For all its Durkheimian analysis, the inspiration for Blumstein and Cohen's stability of punishment insight was the fiat distribution of imprisonment rates over time in the United States, a pattern that invited speculation about its potential causes. In that sense, the stability pattern was a practice in search of a theory before any explanation was produced. The more recent work

on the scale of imprisonment was also provoked by the changing trends that demanded explanation and analysis. All of the recent studies of imprisonment scale have been inspired by these sharp increases, so here again the data to be explained arrive prior to the theories to be tested.

The second parallel is an unjustified assumption of temporal normality. Despite the fact that theories of stability and then of variability were inspired by provocative empirical trends, the analysis of historical data testing these theories has assumed that the periods to be analyzed are normal and typical. In the earlier work, the observed stability was assumed to be representative of other periods as well, so that the generality of patterns observed could be expected. Again, in the statistical explanations of the period after 1972, the empirical analysis has been assuming that the prison trends of the thirty years after 1972 are representative of other periods and public moods so that the statistical relationship and magnitude of effects noted in this period will hold for other times and conditions.

This Article focuses on three aspects of the prison trends in the United States since 1975. First, I discuss the size and generality of the increase in prison population with special emphasis on the features of government that make the pattern of growth so surprising.

Second, I identify and discuss two central empirical questions about the imprisonment boom after 1972. Part IV explores the effects of the analysis in Part III on the proper method of testing whether crime rates are important in predicting imprisonment. The final section of this Article asks whether and to what extent the volatility in the growth of prison populations might also signal that major drops in the scale of imprisonment might happen soon.

THE MAGNITUDE OF PRISON GROWTH

The thirty-five years after 1972 produced a growth in rates of imprisonment that has never been recorded in the history of developed nations. Figure 21.1 compares the rate of imprisonment in 1972 with the rate in 2007.

The 502 per 100,000 rate of state and federal imprisonment is not only five times the rate of imprisonment in the base year of 1972 but also almost four times the highest level of imprisonment in the four decades prior to 1970. By the early 1980s, the U.S. prison population passed its previous high rate and continued a sharp increase without any pause for more than two additional decades. In the generation after 1970, the rate of imprisonment in the United States doubled (between 1972 and 1988) and then doubled *again*.

When this growth began in the 1970s, the rate of imprisonment in the United States was on the high end of western democracies but not what statisticians would call an "outlier" totally apart from the other nations in the G7.[7] But the rate of imprisonment achieved by 2007 in the United States was three times that of any fully developed nation at any point in the post World War II era. So the extent of growth experienced by the United States in the thirty-five years after 1970 would be remarkable for any nation in any era. But there are three aspects of the governmental and legal structure of the United Slates that make the uninterrupted upward march of prisoners nothing short of astonishing.

The first distinct feature of U.S. government that should even out variations in prison population over time is the decentralized structure of criminal law and criminal punishment. The national government is responsible for less than 10% of the persons incarcerated in the United States, with the fifty states each responsible for determining definitions of crimes and schedules of punishment and typically administering and funding prison systems. This decentralized punishment policy means that the aggregate "rates of imprisonment" in Figure 21.1 and Figure 21.2 of this article are really an aggregate average from fifty-one different systems, each of which has responsibility and power to set autonomous policy for prisons. These multiple decision points should moderate the extreme values of individual states and produce modest aggregate changes over time. Except that the moderating influence of aggregating fifty-one different systems was not very substantial in the generation after 1970. While there was some variation in rates of growth from state to state, the overpowering trend was toward sustained high rates of growth. Zimring and Hawkins identify the 1980s as the period when the push toward and beyond historically high rates of imprisonment became clear:

> As of 1980 only eleven slates reported rates of imprisonment higher than al any previous point in the century. But a cyclical hypothesis has been decisively disproved by prison population trends since 1980. Forty-six of the fifty states report rates of imprisonment between 1985 and 1987 which are the highest they have experienced in a century.[8]

The near unanimity of century-high imprisonment mentioned in the previous paragraph was noted in the mid-1980s, when the aggregate rate of imprisonment had only come near to completing its first doubling. By the early 1990s the journey of slate governments into unprecedented high rates of imprisonment had become universal if not uniform. So decentralized power and multiple autonomous centers of policy power became the first structural feature of the American system that should have moderated the expansion of rates of imprisonment but didn't to any significant degree.

The second element of the U.S. system in the 1970s and 1980s that one would expect to moderate the growth of imprisonment was the absence of significant change in penal legislation during the first two decades of the great American prison expansion. There was no general trend toward either increasing the number of crimes or escalating either minimum or maximum terms of imprisonment during the period from 1970 to 1985. A few states shifted from indeterminate to determinant sentencing systems (including California and Illinois) in the 1970s, but there is no evidence that these structural changes had any significant impact on the growth of imprisonment during the period.[9]

The wide discretion in determining punishments in the prosecution and sentencing systems of the United States mean that substantial changes in aggregate punishment policy can take place without any substantial change in the legislation governing the levels of punishment available or the choice of punishments in individual cases. The first doubling of the U.S. prison population after 1972 is decisive evidence that the extraordinary latitude for exercise of discretion in American systems of criminal justice can produce very large changes in rates of imprisonment with no important changes in the legal framework of criminal punishment. Because there are so few restrictions on discretionary choices in individual cases, a substantial shift in the choices made by prosecutors and judges and police can produce very sharp shifts in policy. Certainly for the first fifteen years of the prison population expansion, this model of collective change in discretionary decisions is a much better model for explaining increases that any pattern of significant legal change. The legal structures in place in the United States when it had a state prison population of 205,000 in 1972 were not greatly different from the legal structures that were responsible for 800,000 prisoners in 1991.

The third systemic element that might be expected to moderate the rate of prison growth in the United States is the relatively fixed number of prisons and space for prisoners in the United States. Prisons are capital goods with high fixed costs, long useful lives, and substantial lead times between authorization and completion. By the mid-1980s, over 90% of all the states in the United States were at the high point of the century for rates of imprisonment so that the relatively fixed resources in these places to house inmates were presumably close to their usual capacities. Under these circumstances, the crowding of existing prison facilities

would he expected to restrain the rate at which still more prisoners were sent to penal facilities. The highly discretionary processes that produce commitments to prison should be sensitive to population pressure without delay.

So the rate of prison population growth should have moderated alter the first doubling of rates in the 1970s and 1980s as crowding pressures restrained prosecutors and judges from unlimited expansion policies, but this did not happen. Even with the population of prisoners swelling to unprecedented numbers in the 1990s, the expansion of incarceration continued, new facilities were constructed, and old prisons were retrofitted to accommodate larger populations. The single cell became the double cell and, not infrequently, the triple cell. So inertial forces which would ordinarily be expected to substantially slow the expansion of prison populations were overwhelmed by whatever systemic and political forces were driving prison expansion.

Perhaps the continual expansion of prisons tells us that capacity restraints and decentralized punishment power were overestimated as moderating forces on prison growth. But the unrestrained momentum of prison population growth after 1970 shows also that the political forces which drove the penal expansion were substantial and had substantial impact. This may be of some importance in predicting the size and speed of any future downward pressure on imprisonment.

TWO FUNDAMENTAL QUESTIONS

The thirty-five annual entries in the national portrait of rates of imprisonment after 1972 in Figure 21.2 give the impression of a single national pattern and a continuous upward trajectory. But looks can be deceiving. This section addresses two fundamental questions about the character of the thirty-five-year growth in rates of imprisonment. The first part of this section discusses whether the aggregate growth of imprisonment in the fifty states and the federal system is best viewed as (a) a single process with fifty-one different levels of government participating in essentially similar transformations of policy or (b) an aggregation of different levels or types of policy change. The second part of the section addresses whether the thirty-five years of increase are a single era of growth or are composed of two or three distinct and discrete eras with different causes and magnitudes.

One Process or Many?

The aggregate growth rates portrayed in Figure 21.2 are the sum of data from fifty-one different governmental systems. As a matter of political science and perhaps of logic, it is inaccurate to speak of the rate of imprisonment in the United States as a single measure or to speak of the growth rate of imprisonment in the United States as a unitary phenomenon.

But noting the multiplicity of different components of policy in American penality is the beginning, rather than the end, of the analysis that I am suggesting is required. Despite the large number of states and the diversity of their social and demographic composition, it is not unusual for nationwide trends to be evident in matters relating to crime and punishment. One recent example of a plenary national trend was the sharp decline in reported serious crime in the United States during the 1990s.[10] Zimring and Hawkins noted in 1991, "one of the most puzzling features of recent decades is the way in which the many political units that share power in the American criminal justice system altered their policies in a way that increased prison populations at the same time and with similar intensity."[11]

The fourfold increase in the imprisonment rate in the United States obviously must be a broad trend to produce an aggregate impact that large. But there are two rather different patterns that can produce large growth in the aggregate. The large growth numbers can mask very large differences between highest growth and lowest growth jurisdictions where there are significant differences between one cluster of jurisdictions and another. In that case, aggregate growth levels are not the best way to study the causes of differential growth. The differences between states will be at least as important as national trends over time.

But the large number of states might all be more or less evenly participating in a national trend, in which case studying the factors associated with different rates of growth in different states will not provide an obvious key to the states' shared characteristics that are the main causes of growth in all states. This methodological point was argued by Zimring and Hawkins:

> At stake ... is the appropriate unit of analysis for imprisonment policy. To the extent that the United States is a single social system, approaches that view variations in imprisonment as an outgrowth of social and economic processes would emphasize the national scale as a unit of analysis ... [t]o the extent that prison population is best viewed as an outcome of conscious governmental choice ... the most significant political power over imprisonment is exercised at the state level and the state should be the significant unit of analysis.[12]

While Zimring and Hawkins spotted an important issue, their analysis jumps to premature conclusions about the appropriate level of government for studies of the scale of imprisonment. Even if the major influences on rates of imprisonment are political, the mechanisms that produce political change at the state level may be national in scope and might best be studied at the national aggregate level. If most states respond in relatively uniform ways to a national-level stimulus, interstate variation should not be the central focus of the search for causal factors.

The pattern of state rate growth most consistent with a unitary national trend over the time period would show the largest concentration of states in the middle of the distribution with very few states at both extremes. The model for this type of pattern is a normal distribution around a mean value. To the extent that extreme values are found, they should tend to be in smaller states, and there should not be any clear pattern of regional clustering in one part of the distribution. That pattern would be a distribution consistent with a unitary national trend.

A pluralistic distribution would not concentrate in the center of the growth rate scale, would have clusters of cases at some distance from the mean, and would produce clusters of cases with apparent similarities in

Table 1   The Probable Normality of Distribution of Imprisonment Growth Rates of Fifty U.S. States

Test	Obs.	W	V	Z	Probability > Z
Shapiro-Wilk	50	0.97322	1.259	0.492	0.31151
Shapiro-Francia	50	0.97985	1.045	0.085	0.46612

geography, crime, or politics and different characteristic growth rates. To the extent that a distribution suggests a unitary pattern, the appropriate level of analysis is the national aggregate. To the extent that plural clustering is evident in the distribution, the explanation of patterns of state variation becomes an important focus of inquiry.

A formal statistical analysis confirms the visual impression that the pattern of state growth rates over 1972–2007 is consistent with a normal distribution. We use the fifty state growth rates as our sample set because they were produced in the same fashion. The federal data are excluded from this analysis. Two statistical tests analyze how often a distribution of fifty outcomes (in this case percent growth in state imprisonment rate) would be likely to occur as chance variations from a normal distribution. They are the Shapiro-Wilk and Shapiro-Francia tests each named after its creators.[13] Table 1 shows the fifty state results for the growth rates reported.[14]

The smaller the probability that this is a fifty-case sample from a normal distribution, the more likely the pattern of difference observed is not normal, with a probability of 0.05 or less a usual benchmark for strong statistical evidence of non-normal distribution. But using a Shapiro-Wilk test produces a probability of normal distribution of 0.31151 and the Shapiro-Francia test probability is 0.46612. The question these tests address is "how likely'" it is that a distribution like the one being tested could be the outcome of sampling fifty readings from a normal distribution. The answer is "pretty likely." There are thus no indications in these analyses of anything other than fifty different outcomes of a uniform process.

One Policy Era or Three?

When trends in national rates of imprisonment are charted over time in Figure 21.2, the visual image is of two discrete trends—a flat and relatively stable period from 1930 to about 1970 and a second continuously upward period of uninterrupted growth. While the upward trajectory of increased rates of imprisonment moderates as the base rate of prison population increased in the 1980s and early 1990s, the number of prisoners added to the U.S. population remained between 300,000 and 437.000 for each five year period between 1985 and 2000.[15] So the visual temptation in a graph like Figure 21.2 is bifurcation into a single era of stability and a single era of growth.

It is however one thing to note that a growth rate has been constant over a long period of time and quite another to assume that the substantive influences that were driving increases in prison population in the late 1970s are the same that were operating in the 1980s and remained stable in the 1990s. There are some indications that policy emphasis changed over the generation of growing rates with higher rates of commitment for a wide range of felonies being more important in the period prior to 1986, greater proportionate growth in drug and sex crimes being of greater significance from the mid 1980s to the mid-1990s, and with legislative increases in prison terms and longer prison sentences showing a more important role in the decade after 1995.[16]

Without a doubt the changes in emphasis and priority over time during the different eras turn generalization over the entire growth period about causes of imprisonment growth into a hazardous occupation. The sharp growth not only in drug prisoners, but in the percentage of state prisoners sentenced for drug crime between 1987 and 1991[17] suggest different causal paradigms for earlier prison growth than during the drug war's peak years.

But there may be more unity in the process of prison growth than preoccupation with the changing characteristics of crimes and sentences would allow. To the extent that a relatively fixed expansion of imprisonment might be either desired or tolerated in the years after 1972, the crimes or sentence lengths that are added to reach that level may not be an important influence on the motivation or tolerance for prison growth. To the extent, then, that the relatively constant growth of imprisonment before and after the peak emphasis on the war on drugs indicates that drug offenders simply crowded out marginal property offenders or restrained longer prison sentences for street criminals when they took priority in the late 1980s, the drug panic was not itself a primary cause of change in the growth rate of imprisonment. To the unknown extent that the pace of national prison expansion operated independently of the categories of cases that were given emphasis in filling the new space, the conception of the post-1972 growth of imprisonment as a unitary trend across thirty-five years is plausible.

DOES CRIME MATTER?

Of the potential hypotheses to use in applying analytic tools for study of the scale of imprisonment, the link between variations in crime and variations in imprisonment is a natural priority for two reasons. The link between crime volume and imprisonment volume should be a fundamental one, because criminal conviction is a necessary condition for eligibility for prison. All prisoners at any time are convicted criminals so that variations in the supply of crime and presumably criminals is one obvious source of variation in the amount imprisonment is used or demanded. This essential linkage has produced a second condition that recommends the crime/imprisonment issue as a demonstration example—the relatively large number of empirical studies published in this and other journals that have explored the topic and reported significant findings when crime rates are tested as an influence on relative growth of imprisonment in the era of prison expansion. There have not been many published studies on the scale of imprisonment nor have a wide variety of different analytic strategies been used, but the crime/imprisonment relationship has still received as much attention as any other potential cause.

Since criminal convictions are necessary (but not sufficient) conditions for imprisonment, an increase in convictions is one obvious reason why more people would be sent to prison, and one natural influence on the volume of convicted offenders is the volume of reported crimes. Several published studies have found that variation in crime at the state level predict variations in the growth of imprisonment at the state level. But a detailed comparison of the data analyzed suggests several limits to existing studies of the crime versus rates of imprisonment relationship.

One limit of the current studies is that the time periods studied were during the post-1972 uninterrupted growth in rates of imprisonment. Does growth in crime predict growth in imprisonment during periods with less growth to explain? If not, the relationship of crime trends and prison trends may be much weaker in more "normal" periods of relative stability in imprisonment rates in which variations in rates of many crimes are not predictive of differential imprisonment growth.

And even in periods of high growth in imprisonment, the type of growth most clearly associated with increasing prison numbers may have a large effect on the impact of crime rates on prison growth. In the first era of growth from 1974 to 1987, the most prominent cause of incarceration growth was the increasing rate of imprisonment for high volume felonies at the margin between prison and lesser sanctions—burglary, auto theft, unarmed robbery, assault.[18] Variations in crime rates might have a strong influence on prison use by increasing the number of such offenses just when the prison risk for such crimes was going up—the two forces might interact to redouble the risk increase that was occurring independently. But variations in reported part I or index crime (property crimes with victims and violent crimes of some seriousness) levels would not have as strong an influence during an imprisonment policy focus driven by increases in sentenced drug offenders and non-rape sex offenders—the special features of the increase in imprisonment over the period 1987–1995, because there is no count of drug offenses or of non-rape sex offenses that would measure variations in the rate of these types of offenders. So the relationship of variations in official crime rates to differential growth rates of state imprisonment should be much weaker in an era of special emphasis on these non-index crimes. In fact, many of the studies that find strong crime/imprisonment links involved data from

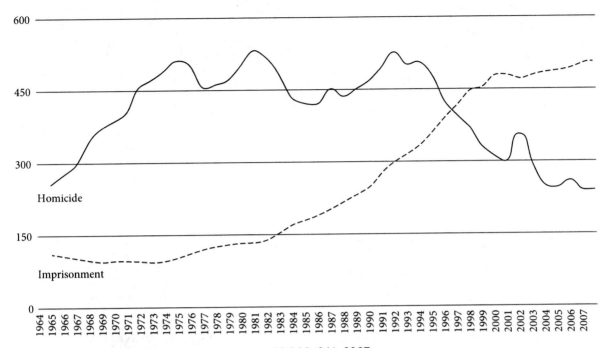

Figure 21.3   Homicide (x50) and Imprisonment per 100,000 1964–2007

Imprisonment: Figure 1 from Zimring supra note 18; Robbery Figure 1 from Zimring, supra note 12

the first period of increasing prison risk for marginally serious index crimes (e.g., Table 1 in Pfaff).[19] For this reason, such studies probably overestimate the impact on official rates of index crime and prison population even for the entire set of high growth eras.

And because these studies were only attempting to access the role of differential crime growth in explaining state-to-state differences in growth of imprisonment, the studies that were conducted produce no direct evidence on the question of how much of the growth in imprisonment at the national level was driven by the growth of crime. The greater the likelihood that a single national-level process was taking place during the period beginning in the 1970s, the more appropriate it becomes to explore the relationships between crime and imprisonment over time at the national level.

Figure 21.3 uses homicide rates over time as a proxy for crime trends nationally and compares temporal trends for homicide and imprisonment rate per 100,000 for the United States as a whole.

Homicide is selected as one proxy for serious crime because it is reliably reported and a good index of

variation in rates of life threatening violence.[20] Over the forty-three years after 1964, the observed rates of homicide and imprisonment are on very different trend lines. Homicide rates double between 1964 and 1974 in the United States, while imprisonment rates continue to decline until 1973. When imprisonment rates begin to rise over the late 1970s, homicide rates first fall then increase back to just above the 1974 high in 1980, then drop substantially until 1984, increase from 1986 to 1991, then drop steadily throughout the 1990s and level off in the years after 2000.

The temporal pattern for imprisonment shows little of the cyclical variations of homicide. Imprisonment drifts downward for eight years and then turns up for thirty-five years. One might argue that the increase in homicide in the late 1960s starts to drive imprisonment upward after a long lag, but an eight-year gap between the increase in killings and the increase in imprisonment would be much larger than any standard economic or policy lags. And the shape of the patterns for homicide and imprisonment are very different for the entire period rather than revealing similarities when

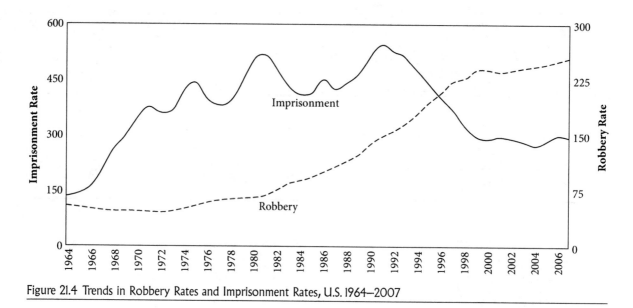

Figure 21.4 Trends in Robbery Rates and Imprisonment Rates, U.S. 1964–2007

lags are introduced. There is a significant relationship between homicide and incarceration trends, but it is negative, (-0.53) over the period 1964–2007. This might be good news for those who suggest that imprisonment reduces crime, but it is bad news for advocates that crime rates drive imprisonment rates.

Figure 21.4 shows trends in robbery and imprisonment to parallel the homicide story.

This time, the overall relationship between robbery and imprisonment is nonexistent (-0.08), consistent with the two trends operating independently of any systematic interaction.

Of course adding time lags and other statistical bells and whistles will produce variation in statistical outcomes. But the central point of these exercises seems secure: the notion that variations in crime in the period after 1964 are driving imprisonment rates, which is clear in the study of interstate variations, is not well supported once attention shifts to the national aggregate. So if that is the appropriate level of analysis (a plausible implication of a normal distribution of growth rates at the state level), it's back to the drawing board.

IS VOLATILITY A ONE-WAY STREET?

In retrospect, the mid-1970s witnessed a transition between relatively stable imprisonment trends to sharp upward variation in incarceration rates. But the description of prison population trends as "volatile" in this period may be inaccurate if that term is intended in its ordinary economic or linguistic sense of changeable or "tending to fluctuate sharply and regularly." The recent history of imprisonment in the United States has established that populations tend to fluctuate sharply and regularly, but only in an upward direction. The "average" increase in incarceration rate per 100,000 population has been about fourfold, a very substantial variation indeed. And there is strong evidence in recent years that growth rates have declined and increases in aggregate population levels are, by recent standards, quite small. Some state systems have declining rates of imprisonment already, and there is reason to believe that stability and decline may touch many systems in the near future.

So declining rates of imprisonment are a likelihood at some point in the American near term. What is not known is the *scale* of decline that might follow the increases of recent history. Are the large increases of recent history indications that the downward variations in incarceration rates might approach the scale of the post-1973 increases? Or are there inertial forces in the politics or governance of imprisonment that can be expected to restrain the downward variation of prison population so that cyclical movements appear non-symmetrical? Illustrations of the contrasting arithmetic of symmetrical versus asymmetrical downward variation are not difficult to construct. The equivalent of a 400% increase in prison population rate is an 80% decrease in rate per 100.000 from the inflated base rate of imprisonment back to break even. Is downward variation of that magnitude either possible or likely in a thirty-year frame of the twenty-first century?

There are no *downward* variations in prison population of that scale in the history of any developed nation on earth, just as there were no precedents for the statistical growth documented in figure 2 until it happened. The number of significant decreases in prison populations in U.S. history is rather small, and the size of recorded declines to date are far less than half the 80% decline that would constitute statistical symmetry with the late twentieth-century increase. California produced a decline in rates of imprisonment in the early 1970s of approximately 30%.[21] and the New York State system, dominated by New York City prisoners, has dropped in the wake of the city's 80% drop in most forms of serious crime.[22] The early California experience lasted just under a decade before it was overtaken by increases in the 1980s.

The extent to which the scale of current imprisonment is reversible is a question not of statistics but of the political economy of imprisonment. There are a variety of institutional and political reasons why prison population rates might be stickier on the way down than they proved to be on the way up. Once the physical capacity to imprison has been expanded, there *may* be inertial forces or economies of scale that bias systems to continue to use them. The expanded scale of prison capacity may also reflect changing public preferences for imprisonment and these preferences may endure independent of any real economies in the variable costs of incarceration. And while public preferences and values may not have strong independent influence on rates of imprisonment, this attitudinal software might interact with changes in both crime rates and public fear of crime to create political pressures for penal expansion or limits on contraction.

Of all the modern historical trends in imprisonment, the period after 1994 presents the most impressive evidence of asymmetrical volatility for American imprisonment. This was the era when imprisonment rates in the United States defied gravity, when incarceration rates increased while crime rates decreased. To the extent that the attitudes and political circumstances of the middle and late 1990s hold in the future, the case for volatility as a one-way street is quite strong. But there are two reasons to suspect that the conditions that obtained in the late 1990s will vary. The first issue is that longer exposure to stable or declining crime rates might reduce fear and soften public hostility. There may be time lags of some size before declining crime and violence is transformed into assumptions of social safely. The slowing of growth in incarceration rates seven and eight years after the crime decline started may be a typical lag between statistics and perception in public safety.

There is a second respect in which the 1990s may not be representative of future attitudes toward crime and punishment. The mid-1990s was an era of punitive hostility unparalleled in modern U.S. history and this may not have been closely linked to crime rates. The era of three strikes and truth in sentencing may have been driven by unsustainable levels of fear and hostility rather than a continuing chronic condition. What we know for sure after the mid-1990s is that the software of public fear and concern is more predictive of policy than any trends in crime or drug use. What is not known is the variability of public attitudes in the second and third decade of the twenty-first century. Stay tuned!

CONCLUSION

Just as theories of stability of punishment followed sustained periods of little change in prison population, a concern with explaining wide variations in rates of imprisonment grew out of the fourfold expansion of rates of imprisonment in the United States in the generation after 1970. Among the long list of unanswered questions about the determinants of rates of imprisonment is whether the dramatic rise in prison population over the past decades is a new norm for the scale of imprisonment or a precursor to significant declines in the rates of imprisonment in the early decades of a new century.

NOTES

1. The *Journal of Criminal Law and Criminology* search was conducted by *Journal* staff while the Harvard search was conducted on January 22. 2010, by Ellen Gilmore, a reference librarian at the University of California. Berkeley Law Library

2. Franklin E. Zimring & Gordon Hawkins, *The Scale of Imprisonment* xi (1991).

3. Edwin H. Sutherland. *The Decreasing Prison Population of England*, 24 J. Crim. L. & Criminology 880 (1934).

4. Alfred Blumstein & Jacqueline Cohen. *A Theory of the Stability of Punishment*, 64 J. Crim. L. & Criminology 198 (1973).

5. *Id.* at 201.

6. Alfred Blumstein, Jacqueline Cohen & Daniel Nagin, *The Dynamics of a Homeostatic Punishment Process.* 67 J. Crim. L. & Criminology 317 (1977); Alfred Blumstein & Souniyo Moitra, *An Analysis of the Time Series of the Imprisonment Rate in the States of the United States: A Further Test of the Stability of Punishment Hypothesis.* 70 J. Crim. L. & Criminology 376 (1979).

7. Zimring & Hawkins, *supra* note 2. at 150 tbl. 6.6; see also Franklin E. Zimring & Gordon Hawkins, *Crime Is Not the Problem* 31 tbl. 2.2 (1997).

8. Zimring &. Hawkins, *supra* note 2, at 152.

9. *Research on Sentencing: The Search for Reform* 206 (Alfred Blumstein et al. eds., 1983).

10. Franklin E. Zimring, *The Great American Crime Decline;* 3–24 (2007).

11. Zimring & Hawkins, *supra* note 2, at 137. 12 *Id.* at 137–38.

12. *Id.* at 137–38.

13. J.P. Royston, *A Simple Method fur Evaluating the Shapiro-Francia W' Text of Non-Normality*, 32 Statistician 297 (1983); Patrick Royston, *Estimating Departure from Normality*, 10 Stat. Med. 1283 (1991); S.S. Shapiro & M.B. Wilk. *An Analysis of Variance Test for Normality (Complete Samples)*, 52 Biometrika 591 (1965); S.S. Shapiro & R.S. Francia. *An Approximate Analysis of Variance Test for Normality*, 67 J. Am. Stat. Ass'n 215 (1972).

14. Bureau of Justice Statistics, Key Facts, http://bjs.ojp.usdoj.gov/indcx.cfm?ty=tp&tid=13#key_facts; Nat'l Criminal Justice Reference Serv., http://www.ncjrs.gov/App/Topics/Topic.aspx?TopicID-l.

15. See the comparison of growth rates and numbers in Zimring, *supra* note 12, at 50 fig. 3.5.

16. Franklin E. Zimring, *Penal Policy and Penal Legislation in Recent American Experience*, 58 Stan. L. Rev. 323, 329–34 (2005).

17. See Franklin E. Zimring & Behnard E. Harcourt, *Criminal Law and the Regulation of Vice* 219 fig. 3 (2007).

18. See, e.g.. Franklin E. Zimring & Gordon Hawkins, *Prison Population and Criminal Justice Policy in California* 14 (1992).

19. John F. Pfaff. *The Empirics of Prison Growth: A Critical Review and Path Forward*, 98 J. Crim. L. & Criminology 547 (2008).

20. Zimring & Hawkins, *supra* note 9, at 67–71.

21. Rosemary Gartner, Anthony Doob & Franklin Zimring, *The Past Is Prologue? Decarceration in California: Then and Now*, Criminology & Pub. Policy (forthcoming 2011).

22. Franklin E. Zimring, *The City that Became: Safe!, New York and the Future of Crime Control* ch. 8 (forthcoming 2011).

Prison

Peter B. Wood

In 21st-century America, imprisonment has become a $60+ billion per year industry, and will continue to increase in scope in the coming decades. The "prison industrial complex" includes not only those agencies directly involved in delivering punishment (courts, corrections, parole and probation agencies, etc), but also a widening array of vested interests that depend for their political and economic well-being on an ever-increasing supply of inmates. This new constellation of interests includes financial institutions that bankroll and finance construction and management of correctional institutions; political action committees that lobby for new prisons; politicians who run on law-and-order platforms that emphasize punishment for criminal offenders; local development authorities that compete for prisons, believing they will be economic development catalysts for their communities; the many for-profit firms engaged in prison privatization; architectural and construction firms that specialize in large institutions; and a broad range of service providers that seek to secure long-term contracts to provide telecommunications, transport, correctional technologies, food and beverage, clothing, computers, and personal hygiene products to the 2.4 million inmates that currently reside in American prisons and jails.

Beyond the tremendous recent growth in the number of inmates and facilities associated with imprisonment, several developments unique to this new era of punishment deserve notice. But before they are introduced, it is instructive to provide some information about how the scope of imprisonment has changed in the last 30 years.

The Transition From 20th- to 21st-Century Imprisonment

For several decades prior to the 1970s, what was most notable was the remarkable stability of the incarceration rate, averaging about 110 per 100,000 (excluding jail populations). While there were minor fluctuations in this period, the rate remained very stable, which led some criminologists to hypothesize a "theory of the stability of punishment," suggesting that a given society develops a certain culture regarding the level of punishment with which it is comfortable, and then, consciously or not, adjusts its policies and practices to meet this desired outcome. In 1972, federal and state prisons held 196,000 inmates for a prison incarceration rate of 93 per 100,000. In addition, about 130,000 inmates were held in jails, resulting in about 1 out of every 625 adults serving time in jails or prisons.

At the time, this level of imprisonment was viewed as egregiously high among those supporting a moratorium on prison construction, and in 1972, the National Council on Crime and Delinquency passed a policy statement calling for a halt to prison construction in the United States. In 1973, the National Advisory Commission on Criminal Justice Standards and Goals recommended that "no new institutions for adults should be built and existing institutions for juveniles should be closed," and concluded that "the prison, the reformatory, and the jail have achieved only a shocking record of failure. There is overwhelming evidence that these institutions create crime rather than prevent it" (National Advisory Commission on Criminal Justice Standards and Goals, 1973, p. 1).

Despite these sentiments, a prison expansion unprecedented in human history was about to take place. No one would have predicted that a large-scale imprisonment binge would characterize the next three decades. Many scholars point to the 1974 "Martinson report" (known for finding that "nothing works" to rehabilitate criminals) as signaling the death knell of the rehabilitation ideal in the United States, and since the late 1970s policy and public opinion has shifted toward more certain and severe punishment characterized by longer prison terms for an ever-increasing number of offense types.

The imprisonment binge over the past 30 years has resulted in a 700% increase in the U.S. incarceration rate to 762 per 100,000 and approximately 2.3 million in prisons (1.5 million) and jails (800,000) in 2007 (The Sentencing Project). With 1 out of every 100 adults incarcerated, the United States boasts the world's highest incarceration rate (well ahead of the Russian rate of 635 per 100,000) and accounts for about 25% of the entire world's imprisoned population. At present, this trend shows no sign of reversing.

In addition, nearly 800,000 prisoners per year are now being released from prisons and jails into communities across the United States—the majority of whom will be readmitted within 3 years. The staggering growth in imprisonment in the United States and its scope compared to the past has generated several unique situations and circumstances not previously seen or anticipated. These include but are not limited to prison hosting, coercive mobility and its effects, issues associated with prisoner reentry, a host of "invisible punishments" and their consequences, and tire impact of mass imprisonment on minority groups—particularly African Americans.

PRISON HOSTING IN THE 21ST CENTURY

In the past, prisons have been viewed as undesirable, and communities have traditionally lobbied against the placement of correctional facilities in their midst. Such institutions were regularly a focus of the NIMBY (Not In My Back Yard) and LULU (Locally Unwanted Land Uses) literatures, along with community mental health centers, mental institutions, free health and methadone clinics, homeless shelters, and other agencies or institutions that residents viewed with concern and even fear.

Such concerns have faded as communities now lobby fiercely for the opportunity to host prisons. Particularly for counties and communities that have fallen on hard economic times, a new prison offers the prospect of a new industry, new jobs, and a potential economic catalyst that will spark community growth and development. Most new prisons in the past 20 years have been built in rural communities characterized by high unemployment and low wages, as local development agencies and authorities are lobbied by correctional firms and interests with the promise of higher wages, job opportunities, and so-called "multiplier effects" that are presumed to enhance quality of life for local residents (Wood & Dunaway, 2003).

Over 1,000 new correctional facilities were built in the United States in the last two decades of the 20th century—most in poor rural communities. Between 1980 and 2003, over 350 rural counties built prisons, and some counties boasted several. Nearly 250 prisons opened in 212 of the nation's 2,290 rural counties in the 10-year period between 1991 and 2001 alone (Beale, 2001). In short, one (or more) prison(s) opened in approximately 10% of all rural counties in the United States in just those 10 years. Currently, nearly 60% of prisoners residing in prisons live in facilities built since 1980 in rural areas, and the average of 25 new rural prisons opening each year in the 1990s (in 1998, a total of 38 new rural prisons opened, the peak year for new rural prisons) is a significant departure from a yearly mean of 16 in the 1980s and 4 in the 1970s.

Correctional facilities are particularly attractive to local legislators and development authorities who seek to "bring home the bacon" to their constituents and hopefully promote economic development in their communities. In addition to the hope that jobs will be created during construction as well as service and supply jobs once the facility is in operation, counties typically charge the state for each inmate/day that a state inmate is housed at the county-level facility. Further, rural counties use minimum-security inmates for municipal and public works. For many rural counties, the majority of municipal and public work is conducted by state inmate road crews. The expense of local municipal services (trash and debris removal, construction work, road maintenance, etc.) is significant, and can be offset by requiring that inmates perform these services as part of their sentence—at no cost to the county. Thus, counties anticipate several payoffs; a new facility may serve as an economic catalyst, counties charge the state to house inmates, and counties use inmates to perform municipal services. In addition to publicly funded facilities, private prisons are increasingly likely to be located in economically distressed rural areas. Prison expansion has spawned a new and powerful coalition of vested interests with stakes in keeping prisons full and building more of them. The result has been a financial and political bazaar with prisoners as the prize.

Any new prison is likely to remain operating in place for at least 50 years, which appeals to communities as a secure source of employment. But there is little evidence that prison hosting stimulates economic development at the local level (Herival & Wright, 2007). Several national and regional studies have demonstrated that rural counties that host prisons typically show no positive benefits in per capita income or reduced unemployment compared to non-prison areas. Why is this the case?

While prisons create jobs, they don't usually go to people in those communities, who don't have the skills or civil service rating to become a correctional officer. And in rural communities, people are used to commuting long distances to work, so guards at nearby prisons may choose to transfer to the new ones. Also, aggressive pursuit of new prisons can create an imbalance in a county's economic development strategy. Energies devoted to prison lobbying can detract from other pursuits that might create more jobs. In addition, there is a stigma attached to becoming viewed as a prison town. How many people think of a family trip to Attica as a summer vacation option?

The prison-building binge may have slowed in recent years, but given the projected increases in national prison populations, other states may soon follow the lead of California, which recently established a plan to add another 53,000 prison, jail, and juvenile detention beds for an estimated cost of $7.9 billion. Though current economic woes have caused federal and state governments to reduce their investments in punishment, the expected fixture increase in the number of inmates, correctional institutions, and costs associated with the decades-long expansion has enough momentum to carry well into the mid-21st century.

COERCIVE MOBILITY IN THE 21ST CENTURY

The aim of get-tough sentencing policies was to reduce crime and improve community life, but neither policymakers nor the public anticipated how putting so many people in prison would damage the communities from which they were removed. While mass imprisonment has indeed incapacitated many who would otherwise have an overall negative effect on community life, it has also removed thousands of people who had a net positive effect on the economy, families, and the community as a whole. Many communities now face economic hardship, family disruption, and more crime due to high levels of incarceration.

A growing literature has begun to document the effects on community life of America's 30-year incarceration binge, but only a few studies have analyzed the complex relationship between incarceration and crime. Most scholarship that examines the incarceration-crime relationship has applied a social disorganization framework. In their seminal Chicago Area Project, Shaw and McKay (1942) found that the highest crime rates were in neighborhoods marked by social disorganization: dilapidated housing and infrastructure; unemployment; poverty; and most important, high residential mobility—people moving in and out of the neighborhood at a high rate. Much subsequent research confirms that crime is disproportionately concentrated in these types of neighborhoods. Because of conditions in these neighborhoods, those who "make it" move out, eroding a community's ability to maintain primary institutions like schools, churches, and neighborhood associations. Social disorganization theorists argue that high residential mobility limits the formation of strong social networks essential in controlling crime, undermining the stability necessary to establish the elements of social capital (i.e., trust, empowerment, norms, and reciprocity) that serve as the backbone of effective mechanisms of informal social control.

Coercive mobility (incarceration and prisoner reentry) is concentrated in poor, urban, and predominantly minority neighborhoods and is an important source of residential mobility that leads to social disorganization and crime. But unlike voluntary mobility, coercive mobility has profound negative effects on other aspects of social life such as labor market participation, family functioning, and political participation. While not all coercive mobility results in social disorganization, at some level (a "tipping point") the benefit of removing those disruptive to the community (criminals) is outweighed by the costs of removing parents, workers, and family members who provide a net positive effect on social capital and informal social control. When the tipping point is reached, too much incarceration can weaken community economies, family relationships, and overall social capital and lead to higher crime rates.

Clear, Rose, Waring, and Scully (2003) collected community-level data regarding prison admission rates, prison release rates, and crime rates for several neighborhoods in Tallahassee, Florida, and Renauer, Cunningham, Feyerherm, O'Connor, and Bellatty (2006) collected similar data on 95 communities in the Portland, Oregon, area. Both research efforts found coercive mobility concentrated in poor communities with large minority populations, and communities with extremely high coercive mobility had higher subsequent crime rates even when controlling for other indicators of social disorganization. As expected, the relationship between coercive mobility and crime was curvilinear—incarceration reduced crime at moderate levels, but began to increase crime rates when they reached a tipping point of about 1.7 per 100 people in Tallahassee and about 2.75 per 100 in Portland.

High levels of incarceration may not lead to less crime because communities with the highest levels of incarceration (poor, predominantly minority ones) are actually weakened by the very thing that is supposed to make them safer. Research described above supports the idea that, at the community level, low and moderate levels of incarceration can reduce crime, but high levels of incarceration can increase it by reducing social and neighborhood capital.

Coercive Mobility and Counting Prisoners

In 21st-century America, imprisonment typically moves people out of large urban centers and into rural communities. This has major implications for electoral apportionment and financial distributions. The census general rule is to count people in their usual residence, "the place where they live and sleep most of the time." The usual residence need not be the same as a person's legal or voting residence, and a person need not be there at the time of the literal census. The person can take a vacation and still count at home, or even work overseas and still count at home.

The Census Bureau counts prisoners as residents of the town that contains the prison in which they are housed. This practice reduces the population of communities where most prisoners originate (usually urban, low-income, minority communities) and swells the population of rural communities that host prisons. When prisoners are counted as residents of the prison town, it leads to misleading portrayals of which counties are growing or declining. Urban and black communities are the losers in the census count, since congressional apportionment of services, grants, funds, poverty relief, welfare, and so forth are based on census figures.

An accurate count of the population is used to apportion voting representation, draw political boundaries, and allocate state and federal funds among local and state governments. Mass incarceration distorts this fundamental tool of representative democracy. In the 1990s, 30% of new residents in upstate New York were prisoners. About 200 counties in the United States have more than 5% of the population in prison. Many have more than 20% of their population in prison. (In at least 21 Texas counties, inmates account for over 20% of the local population.) But when released, prisoners usually return to the community they call home. Whatever benefits accrue to a jurisdiction by virtue of its population, urban communities with high incarceration rates are losing. Conversely, rural counties with prisons are getting more than their fair share.

The official constitutional purpose of the census is political apportionment. About 12% of all African American men live in prison. Most of them are apportioned to districts that do not reflect the interests of their home communities or their personal political concerns. Significant densities of prisoners in state legislative districts are important because most criminal justice policy is made at the state level. Each free resident of a rural district with prisons gets a larger voice in the state capital than free residents in urban districts that have high numbers of residents in prisons. Prisons inflate the political clout of every real rural constituent. And at the state level, counting urban residents as rural residents dilutes urban voting strength and increases the weight of a vote in rural districts.

Larger places (those with larger populations) receive a correspondingly larger share of government resources. The primary measure of size for determining resource distribution is the official census count. The coercive mobility of offenders creates a consistent distortion in funding formulas such that rural counties come out ahead of urban counties that send them prisoners. For example, the U.S. Department of

Agriculture (USDA) distributes some $60–70 million annually to poor Appalachian communities via the Appalachian Regional Commission, and population is a distribution factor—so rural communities with prisons have an advantage over those without prisons. The USDA does not intend to reward prison construction, but that is the result.

It is estimated that the total cost of counting prisoners in their prison communities rather than their home communities runs between $50 and $250 per person, and averages about $100 or more per prisoner for the local community where they are housed. When a jurisdiction plans to open a new 1,000-bed prison, it can generate at least $100,000 in new "unearned" revenues that accrue simply from counting the prisoners. That $100,000 doesn't sound like much, but it can mean a new fire truck, a renovation for a youth center, or a computer upgrade for a municipality. In sparsely populated areas, large prisons in small towns can result in significant distortions of the local population. A new 500-bed prison can yield $50,000 in new revenue. The most dramatic impact can be seen in towns like Florence, Arizona, with a free population of about 5,000 and another 12,000 in at least three prisons. State and federal funds specifically linked to the prison population are estimated at $4 million annually. This has tempted other towns to follow the path toward prison hosting.

Another effect of coercive mobility and counting prisoners where they are held is on the calculation of per capita income, which is figured by dividing the total community income by the total population. When prisoners account for a substantial proportion of the population, the apparently low per capita income makes that community more competitive for U.S. Housing and Urban Development (HUD) grants aimed at low-income areas. The appearance of greater need results in those communities getting more than their fair share. For example, in Virginia, distribution of K–12 education aid uses a formula based on county population. Several years ago, according to the Census Bureau, Rural Sussex County, which has a population that is 19% inmates, received $115,000 extra as a result of the imprisoned population. Henrico County (Richmond) loses roughly $200,000 as a result of the "exported" prisoner population. And because Latinos and blacks are imprisoned at 4–8 times the rate of whites, where incarcerated people are counted has significant implications for how black and Latino populations are reflected in the census.

Prison towns gain political clout through enhanced population, while the urban areas from which they come are further deprived through the loss of political influence and resources. When prison communities are credited with large, externally sourced populations of prisoners—who are not local residents—it turns the "one person, one vote" principle on its head. Prison towns do not share a "community of interest" with urban prisoners or their loved ones or neighborhoods. This phenomenon is unique to the new landscape of 21st-century corrections.

PRISONER REENTRY IN THE 21ST CENTURY

Over the past 15 to 20 years, a significant body of scholarship has addressed the issue of prisoner reentry into society, a focus that evolved due to the rapidly increasing number of prisoners being released—now nearly 800,000 per year—as well as the high rate of recidivism. (About two thirds of prisoners are readmitted to prison within 3 years of release.) This issue has become a major concern among those who study issues associated with reentry, deterrence, rehabilitation, and the possible criminogenic effects of imprisonment. Some scholars are convinced that the return of so many offenders—many who are committed to a criminal lifestyle—has a significant independent effect on crime rates.

In 2000, researchers at the Urban Institute launched an ongoing inquiry into prisoner reentry research to better understand the pathways to successful reintegration; the social and fiscal costs of current policies; and the impacts of incarceration and reentry on individuals, families, and communities. Their findings focus on several key dimensions of reentry.

Housing and Reentry

Perhaps the most immediate challenge facing returning prisoners is to secure housing. Many plan to stay with families, but those who don't face limited options. The process is complicated by scarcity of affordable and available housing, legal barriers and regulations, prejudices that restrict housing options, and strict eligibility requirements for federally subsidized housing. Research shows that those without stable housing are more likely to return to prison, and the majority of released prisoners themselves believe that having stable housing is important for successful reentry.

The majority of returning prisoners live with family members or intimate partners after release. Three months after release, 60% to 85% of returning prisoners live with families or partners. Many return home to living arrangements that are only temporary, and 6 to 8 months after release about one third had lived at more than one address. More than half of returning prisoners in Illinois thought they would not be staying in their current neighborhood for long, and in Maryland over half expected to be moving within weeks or months (Lynch & Sabol, 2001). Those who do not stay with family face limited options—many of which are unavailable to formerly incarcerated people. The shortage of affordable and available housing is a serious problem for returning prisoners.

Employment and Reentry

Finding and maintaining employment is critical to successful prisoner reentry. Employment is associated with lower rates of reoffending, and higher wages are associated with lower rates of criminal activity. But prisoners face enormous challenges in finding and maintaining legitimate job opportunities—including low levels of education, limited work experience, and limited vocational skills. This is further compounded by the incarceration period during which they forfeit the opportunity to gain marketable work experience and sever professional connections and social contacts that might lead to employment on release. In addition, the general reluctance of employers to hire former prisoners serves as a barrier to job placement.

While prisoners believe that having a job would help them stay out of prison, on average only about 1 in 5 reported that they had a job lined up immediately after release. Moreover, despite the need for employment assistance, few prisoners receive employment-related training in prison. Even ex-cons who do find work do not necessarily have full-time or consistent work. At 4 to 8 months after release, 44% of Illinois respondents reported having worked for at least 1 week since their release. But less than one third were employed at the time of the interview, and only 24% of all respondents were employed full-time. At their first post-release interview, nearly 60% of ex-cons in Maryland were either unemployed or working less than 40 hours per week (Lynch & Sabol, 2001). Making things more difficult, transportation is a significant barrier to employment. More than one third of released prisoners had problems obtaining a car for work, and nearly one quarter reported problems accessing public transportation. It is widely accepted that finding and maintaining employment reduces recidivism, and an increase in levels of employment serves to reduce drug dealing, violent crime, and property crime.

Health and Reentry

Released prisoners have an extremely high prevalence of mental disorders and chronic and infectious diseases—much higher than in the general population. Ex-cons face limited and insufficient access to community-based health care upon release. Further, incarceration disqualifies inmates from Medicaid eligibility, and restoring eligibility can take several months—interrupting access to prescription drugs and health care. Between 30 and 40% of released prisoners reported having a chronic physical or mental health condition—most commonly depression, asthma, and high blood pressure. In New Jersey, one-third of those released in 2002 had at least one chronic or communicable medical condition. Many more released offenders report being diagnosed with a medical condition compared to those who received medication or treatment for the condition while incarcerated. Only 12% report having taken medication regularly in prison. In Ohio, over half reported depression, but only 35% reported receiving treatment or medication. While 27% reported having asthma, less than 14% received treatment for it (Lynch & Sabol, 2001).

Corrections agencies often lack discharge planning and preparation for health care needs upon release. Less than 10% of Illinois ex-cons received referrals to services in the community. Securing health care is a major concern for many released prisoners. At least 75% of those interviewed said they needed help getting health care after release. As might be expected, the vast majority of returning prisoners have no medical insurance—only 10% to 20% reported having private insurance.

Substance Use and Reentry

Research shows that while 83% of state prisoners have a history of drug use, only about 15% of this group receives treatment in prison, and even fewer continue to receive appropriate treatment once released. The majority of those released have extensive substance use histories. In Maryland, in the 6 months before entering prison, over 40% of offenders reported daily heroin use, while nearly 60% of returning prisoners in Texas reported daily cocaine use. Prisoners identify drug use as the primary cause of their past and current problems, but few prisoners receive drug treatment while incarcerated. In New Jersey, though 81% of inmates had drug or alcohol problems, program capacities were limited to only 6% of the state prison population. In Texas, substance abuse program capacity can only serve 5% of the potential population in need (Lynch & Sabol, 2001).

Researchers agree that in-prison treatment is much more likely to effectively sustain a decline in substance use if it is tailored to an individual's need and level of risk, and if it is linked to drug treatment aftercare in the community. Those with substance use histories and who engage in substance use after release are very likely to reoffend.

Families and Reentry

Well over half of U.S. prisoners are parents of minor children, and up to 75% of incarcerated women are mothers of minors. Nearly 3% of all minor children in the United States, and nearly 10% of children of color, have a parent in prison. When a parent is sent to prison, the family structure, financial responsibilities, emotional support systems, and living arrangements are all affected. Incarceration can drastically disrupt spousal relations, parent–child relations, and family networks. There are significant challenges to maintaining family contact while in prison, including visiting regulations, transportation costs to distant facilities, other financial barriers, and emotional strains. More than half of incarcerated parents report never having received a visit from their children.

Nearly 75% of returning prisoners in Illinois and Maryland felt that family support had been important in helping them to avoid prison after release, and strong family support before prison may also reduce likelihood of recidivism. Those who reported positive family relations were less likely to be reconvicted, while those who reported negative family relations were more likely to be reconvicted and reincarcerated. Those with closer family relations and strong family support were less likely to have used drugs since release. Most prisoners have contact with family and children, but it is usually through phone and mail. In Illinois, only 13% of returning prisoners had had in-person contact with family members or children; 29% had visits from spouses/partners.

Distance to the correctional facility is one of the greatest challenges to maintaining contact. Three quarters of family members surveyed said the distance to the facility was the main problem with visitation. For the two-thirds who did not visit family in prison, the median estimated travel time to the prison was 4 hours longer than those who did visit. This issue of distance and visitation is exacerbated in the context of coercive mobility. The 500 Hawaiian prisoners housed in Mississippi are unlikely to receive any visitation during their prison stay, and neither are the 1,500 Californian prisoners due there. States routinely exchange hundreds and thousands of prisoners in order to minimize the cost of housing them in-state.

Close family relationships can improve employment outcomes for returning prisoners, and closer family and partner relations and stronger family support result in more employment after release—likely because many releasees are hired by family members. But it has become increasingly common to export and import prisoners across state lines in order to save money, and more difficult for prisoners to maintain family ties and support systems while incarcerated.

Communities and Reentry

Released prisoners are returning in high concentrations to a small number of communities in urban areas—having a profound and disproportionate effect on community life, family networks, and social capital in these neighborhoods. These places are characterized by social and economic disadvantage, which compounds the problems associated with reentry. In addition, research shows that high rates of incarceration and reentry may destabilize these communities and result in higher crime rates.

A relatively large number of prisoners return to a small number of cities in each state. For example, recent data show that Chicago and Baltimore received more than half of all prisoners returning to Illinois and Maryland, respectively. Houston received one quarter of all prisoners returning to Texas. Two of New Jersey's 21 counties accounted for one-third of all returning prisoners. Nearly 49% of prisoners returning to Massachusetts returned to just two counties. Five of Idaho's 44 counties accounted for three quarters of returning prisoners. Returning prisoners are often clustered in a few neighborhoods in these cities. For instance, 8% of Chicago communities accounted for over one third of all prisoners returning to Chicago; 7% of the zip codes in Wayne County, Michigan (8 of 115)—all of which are in Detroit—accounted for over 40% of all prisoners being released in that state.

High levels of social and economic disadvantage characterize communities to which prisoners return. These communities have above-average rates of unemployment, female-headed households, and families living below the federal poverty level. Former prisoners who relocate tend to move to neighborhoods similar to the ones they left, with similar disadvantages, and prisoners returning to neighborhoods that are unsafe and lacking in social capital are at greater risk of recidivism and reincarceration.

Public Safety and Reentry

Over two-thirds of released prisoners are arrested for a new crime within 3 years of release—many within the first year. Released prisoners make a substantial contribution to new crimes. Most returning prisoners have extensive criminal histories. Most returning prisoners (80%–90%) had at least one prior conviction, and at least two-thirds have previously served time in prison. In Massachusetts, 99% of those released in 2002 had been previously incarcerated in a state or county facility. About 80% of those released from the Philadelphia prison system had been previously incarcerated there.

Many released prisoners are reconvicted or rearrested for new crimes—many within the first year of release. About one third are reconvicted or reincarcerated within 1 year. In Maryland, about one third had been rearrested for at least one new crime within 6 months of release, 10% had been reconvicted, and 16% had been returned to prison/jail for a new crime conviction or parole/probation violation. Releasees with substance use histories and who use substances after release are at high risk to recidivate.

Community Supervision and Reentry

The vast majority of released prisoners (over 80%) are subject to a period of community supervision. There are now over 800,000 parolees in the United States, up from about 200,000 in 1980. And there are many more offenders under probation or some other community-based sanction—of the 8 million under correctional supervision, about 70% are in the community. Resources have not kept up with the increase. Most probation and parole officers average 70 or more cases—about twice the recommended number. Persons on community supervision account for nearly 40% of new prison admissions nationally. Parole and probation violations have increased significantly over the past 25 years, and the number of persons returning to prison for a violation increased 1,000% between 1980 and 2000. About 40% of prisoners in state prison/jail are serving time for a probation and parole violation. Probation and parole officers appear to have little effect on rearrest rates of released prisoners. Findings show that prisoners who are released under supervision fare no better than those without supervision—their rearrest and reconviction rates are not significantly different.

What does all this tell us? Prisoner reentry is fraught with problems, the numbers are increasing rapidly, and not enough resources are being put into the process—particularly given the increase in the number of returning prisoners. This is a growing and difficult problem that has no easy solution and that requires significant investment in time and energy to address.

INVISIBLE PUNISHMENTS IN THE 21ST CENTURY

Entering the 21st century, a new set of dynamics has come into play that calls for an understanding of the ways in which the effects of prison on society are both quantitatively and qualitatively different from previous times. These effects have been conceptualized as collateral consequences of imprisonment and have been dubbed "invisible punishments" by scholars (see Mauer & Chesney-Lind, 2002, for an overview). They are invisible in that they are rarely acknowledged in the courtroom when they are imposed, and equally rarely assessed in public policy discussions. These themes, and their impact on individuals and communities, should be the subject of careful scrutiny by those who study prison dynamics in the 21st century. While prison has always affected the individuals who are imprisoned and their families, the scale of imprisonment now magnifies these effects and expands their scope. Further, the racial dynamics of imprisonment have become a central component of this social policy.

Barriers to Reintegration Among Released Offenders

Once a prison term is completed, the transition back into the community is almost always difficult. Having limited connections with the world of work, for example, becomes even more problematic with the stigma of imprisonment attached to former offenders. In an economy increasingly characterized by a division between high skills/high technology and a low-skill service economy, few offenders have promising prospects for advancing up the job ladder—or even finding a spot at the bottom of it.

Over the past 30 years, policymakers have expanded the reach of punishments beyond sentencing enhancements, and have enacted a new generation of collateral sanctions that impose serious obstacles to a person's life chances long after a sentence has been completed. Many of these obstacles are related to the war on drugs, and include a seemingly endless series of restrictions placed on those convicted of a drug offense. Depending on the state, an 18-year-old with a first-time conviction for felony drug possession now may be barred from receiving welfare benefits for life, prohibited from living in public housing, denied student loans to attend college, permanently excluded from voting, and may be deported if not a U.S. citizen. Ironically, many of these sanctions pertain only to drug offenders, not those convicted of murder, rape, and other serious violent offenses.

Impact on Families and Communities

A growing number of children have a parent in prison, and current estimates place this number at well over 1.5 million. But the racial dynamics of imprisonment produce a figure of between 7% and 10% or up to 1 in 10 for black children. Since this reflects a 1-day count, the proportion of black children who have experienced parental incarceration at some point in their childhood is considerably greater. Being the child of a criminal is not a status worth boasting about; shame and stigma are still the norm. One common consequence of this stigma is the severance of social ties to family and friends, which low-income families rely upon to cope with poverty and other hardships. The impact of parental incarceration will vary depending on which parent is imprisoned. Mothers in prison are far more likely to have been primary caretakers of children prior to imprisonment and were often single parents, and this dramatically impacts the children they leave behind.

In addition to the experience and stigma of parental incarceration, children in low-income minority communities now grow up with a strong likelihood of spending time in prison themselves. An estimated 1 in 3 black males born today can expect to go to prison. While they may not know these odds, their life experiences communicate this reality as they witness older brothers, cousins, parents, and neighbors cycling in and out of prison. Some contend that prison has become a "rite of passage" for young black men today and is almost welcomed as a badge of honor in certain communities. Prison is increasingly viewed as an inevitable part of the maturation process for many low-income minority children—in the same way that going to college is the norm in many middle- and upper-class communities. When there is little chance of traditional success (schools, college, jobs, marriage, etc), the often-taught value of hard work leading to success may seem unrealistic to many children in these communities.

Mass Imprisonment and Voter Disenfranchisement

When the nation was founded in the late 1700s, the vast majority of people in the United States were ineligible to participate in democratic life. Excluded were women, blacks, Native Americans, and other minorities, as well as illiterates, poor people, and felons. Only white males were "citizens" with the right to vote. Over the course of 200 years, restrictions for all these categories have been lifted—save for those with felony convictions.

Today, some 5 million Americans are ineligible to vote as a result of a felony conviction in the 48 states and D.C. that employ disenfranchisement policies for varying degrees of felons and ex-felons. If there was any doubt about the effect of these laws, consider the 2000 presidential election in Florida. That election was decided by less than 1,000 votes in favor of George W. Bush, while an estimated 600,000 former offenders—people who had already completed their sentences—were ineligible to vote due to that state's restrictive policies. One wonders who most former inmates would have supported.

While an estimated 2% to 3% of the national population is disenfranchised, the rate for black men is 13%, and in some states is well over 20%. When such high numbers of men in urban communities can't vote, the voting power/efficacy of that whole community is reduced in relation to communities with low rates of incarceration. New evidence indicates that disenfranchisement effects go well beyond the legally disenfranchised population. Studies of voter turnout show that in the most restrictive states, voter turnout is lower, particularly among African Americans, and even among persons who themselves are not disenfranchised as a result of a felony conviction. Voting is a civic duty, and a process engaged in with families and communities. Family members talk about elections at home, drive to polls together, and see their neighbors there. When a substantial number of people in a community are legally unable to vote, it is likely to dampen enthusiasm and attention among others as well. Forty years after the Voting Rights Act was passed, mass imprisonment and disenfranchisement results in a greater proportion of African American and other minority communities losing the right to vote each year.

Mass Imprisonment and State Budgets

Regarding the impact of mass imprisonment on state economies, specifically higher education, a recent report by Grassroots Leadership shows how massive spending on Mississippi prisons has siphoned funds from classrooms and students, leaving higher education appropriations stagnant and African Americans shouldering the burden. The report documents a startling shift in Mississippi budget priorities. In 1992, the state spent most of the discretionary portion of its budget on higher education. By 2002, the majority of

discretionary funds went to build and operate prisons. Between 1989 and 1999, Mississippi saw per capita state corrections appropriations rise by 115%, while per capita state higher education appropriations increased by less than 1%. Mississippi built 17 new prisons between 1997 and 2005, but not one new state college or university. And several more Mississippi prisons are under construction or consideration. There are now almost twice as many African American men in Mississippi prisons as in colleges and universities, and the state spends nearly twice as much to incarcerate an inmate as it takes to send someone to college. Moreover, due to new drug laws and a "truth-in-sentencing" bill passed in the mid-1990s, nearly 70% of those imprisoned in the state are nonviolent offenders. Mississippi is not unique in this situation—most states have followed this path and are facing serious budget shortages due to multiyear commitments to expand their correctional systems.

These and other dynamics of mass imprisonment make up what are called invisible punishments or collateral consequences. Changing the trends noted here are difficult for several reasons. First, it is very difficult to alter prevailing sentencing policies and practices, which can be legislated in a matter of hours but take years to undo. In a broader sense, the national commitment to mass imprisonment is deeply embedded in a punitive and individualistic approach to social policy. This has not always been the case in the United States, and is certainly not the style adopted in many other countries. Changing this political and social environment remains the real obstacle to a more effective and humane crime policy.

RACE AND IMPRISONMENT IN THE 21ST CENTURY

In the 50-plus years since the historic *Brown v. Board of Education* decision that ordered desegregation of public education, no American institution has changed more than the criminal justice system, and in ways that have profound effects on the African American community. Mass imprisonment has produced record numbers of Americans in prison and jail (now approaching 2.5 million) and has had a disproportionate effect on

African Americans. There are now about 10 times as many African Americans in prison/jail as on the day of the *Brown* decision (98,000 in 1954; nearly 1,000,000 in 2007).

Today, 1 out of every 21 black men is incarcerated on any given day. For black men in their twenties, the figure is 1 in 8. Given current trends, 1 of every 3 (32%) black males born today can expect to go to prison in his lifetime (U.S. Bureau of Justice Statistics [BJS] Web site). More than half of black men in their early 30s who are high school dropouts have a prison record. With regard to black women, 1 of every 18 black females born today can expect to go to prison—6 times the rate for white women. Moreover, black women born today are 5 times more likely to go to prison in their lifetimes than black women born 30 years ago.

Factors contributing to the dramatic increase in the number of African Americans in prison/jail are complex, and involve dynamics both within and outside the criminal justice system. Incarceration rates are about 8 times higher for blacks overall than for whites, and high school dropouts are more than twice as likely to end up in prison than are high school graduates. Consequently, much of the growth in imprisonment has been concentrated among minority young men with little education. By the late 1990s, two-thirds of all prison inmates were black or Hispanic, and about half of all minority inmates had less than 12 years of schooling.

Imprisonment has become so pervasive among young black men that it is now viewed as a common stage in the life course by some researchers (Pettit & Western, 2004). Among all men born between 1965 and 1969, an estimated 3% of whites and 20% of blacks had served time in prison by their early thirties. Among black men born during this period, 30% of those without a college education and nearly 60% of high school dropouts went to prison by 1999. For black men in their mid-30s at the start of the 21st century, prison records were nearly twice as common as bachelor's degrees, and imprisonment was more than twice as common as military service. Imprisonment has become a common life event for black men that sharply distinguishes their transition to adulthood from that of white men.

Black/white inequality is obscured by using employment and wage figures that fail to include inmates. From a life course perspective, the earnings of ex-convicts diverge from the earnings of non-convicts as men get older. By their late 20s, non-convicts have usually settled into a stable path of earnings growth, while ex-convicts follow an unstable trajectory of irregular/transitory employment and low earnings. Research notes that white offenders tend to age out of crime earlier than do black offenders, suggesting that employment and wage earning deficits experienced by black ex-convicts may endure for a longer period of time than for white ex-convicts.

Changes in the criminal justice system over the past 25 years have been wide-ranging, affecting policing, sentencing, prison construction, postrelease supervision, and a variety of other policy areas at the state and federal levels. The sheer magnitude of the commitment of public resources is comparable to that expended in the social welfare efforts of the 1960s and 1970s. Unlike antipoverty policy, however, the punitive trend in criminal justice policy serves to conceal and deepen economic inequality between blacks and whites. Whereas it has often been considered how welfare, employment, and education policy affects inequality, it is now known that criminal justice policy over the past 25 years has impacted racial economic inequality in a significant way, to the point where inequality can be seen as a product of the expansion of mass imprisonment.

CONCLUSION

Over the past 30 years, a complex set of social and political developments has produced a wave of building and filling prisons unprecedented in human history. Beginning with less than 200,000 in 1972, the number of inmates in U.S. prisons has increased to over 1.5 million today. Add to this the over 800,000 inmates in local and regional jails either awaiting trial or serving sentences, and a remarkable 2.4 million (and counting) Americans are behind bars as of 2008.

These figures take on more meaning in comparison with other nations. The United States locks up offenders at a rate 6 to 10 times that of other industrialized nations. The next-closest nation to ours in incarceration rates is Russia—which has been de-incarcerating for several years now. The nature and meaning of incarceration in the United States have changed in a variety of profound ways with far-reaching implications.

Among these is the institutionalization of a societal commitment to the use and expansion of a massive prison system. Nearly two-thirds of prisons today have been built in the past 20 years. These prisons are expected to hold offenders for at least the next 50 years, guaranteeing a national commitment to a high rate of incarceration. The growth of the system has spawned a set of vested interests and lobbying forces that perpetuate a societal commitment to imprisonment. The nearly 1,000,000 prison and jail guards, administrators, service workers, and other personnel represent a potentially powerful political opposition to any scaling down of the system.

The idea of prisons as sources of economic growth appeals to many communities that have lost jobs in recent years. Communities that once organized against the location of prisons now beg state officials and private prison companies to construct new prisons in their backyards. But the scarce research available questions the promise of prisons as economic development catalysts. There is also a rapidly expanding prison privatization movement focused on the bottom line of profiting from imprisonment. Privatization has produced a new dynamic in mass imprisonment that encourages the production of more inmates—which means more money and more profits.

The near permanent status of mass imprisonment is evidenced despite expressed concerns that often focus on the problem of funding for an expanding prison system that diverts resources from other public spending. Vast expenditures on corrections systems are now considered the norm, and represent the largest growth area in most state budgets. Virtually every state has engaged in a significant if not massive prison construction program over the past 20 years, financed through general funds; bonds; and more recently, public-private venture arrangements, which put communities into further long-term debt.

The impact of incarceration on individuals can be understood to some degree, but the effect of mass imprisonment on African American communities is a phenomenon that has only recently been investigated.

Marc Mauer (Mauer & Chesney-Lind, 2002) of The Sentencing Project has asked what it means to a community to know that 4 out of 10 boys growing up will spend time in prison; what it does to family and community to have such a substantial proportion of its young men enmeshed in the criminal justice system; what images and values are communicated to young people who see the prisoner as the most prominent or pervasive role model in the community; and what the effect is on a community's political influence when one quarter of black men cannot vote as a result of a felony conviction.

New prison cells are increasingly being used for drug and nonviolent offenders. About 3 of every 5 (61%) new inmates added to the system in the 1990s were incarcerated for a nonviolent drug or property offense. In the federal system, three quarters (74%) of the increase in the inmate population are attributed to drug offenses alone. Incarcerating ever-increasing numbers of nonviolent property and drug offenders is not the only option open to policymakers, nor is it the most cost-effective. A large proportion of these offenders would be appropriate candidates for diversion to community-based programs—if policy could be diverted away from imprisonment.

Direct consequences of the wars on drugs and crime include the imprisonment of literally millions of people, most of whom are guilty of relatively petty crimes; their lengthy and debilitating incarceration; and their ejection (reentry) back into society—ill-prepared and handicapped by their stigmatized social status. The direct financial cost of the imprisonment binge has been well publicized, and exceeds $60 billion per year. What has not been emphasized enough are the invisible or collateral damages of mass imprisonment, including the harm done to other social programs because so much money has been siphoned off into corrections, the diminution of civil rights of many lands, the erosion of traditional values of fairness and tolerance, the damage done to families and communities, and the creation of new and powerful lobbying groups with vested interests in more imprisonment. Imprisonment in the 21st century has generated far-reaching consequences that touch virtually every aspect of life, for prisoners and non-prisoners alike, and will continue to do so into the foreseeable future.

REFERENCES AND FURTHER READINGS

Beale, C. (2001, August). *Cellular rural development: New prisons in rural and small town areas in the 1990s.* Paper presented at the Annual Meeting of the Rural Sociological Society, Albuquerque, New Mexico.

Clear, T. R., Rose, D. R., Waring, E., & Scully, K. (2003). Coercive mobility and crime: A preliminary examination of concentrated incarceration and social disorganization. *Justice Quarterly, 20*(1), 33–64.

Herival, T., & Wright, P. (2007). *Prison profiteers: Who makes money from mass incarceration?* New York: The New Press.

Hooks, G., Mosher, C., Rotolo, T., & Lobao, L. (2004). The prison industry: Carceral expansion and employment in U.S. counties, 1969–1994. *Social Science Quarterly, 85,* 37–57.

Justice Policy Institute: http://www.justicepolicy.org

Lotke, E., & Wagner, P. (2004). Prisoners of the census: Electoral and financial consequences of counting prisoners where they go, not where they come from. *Pace Law Review, 24,* 587–607.

Lotke, E., & Ziedenberg, J. (2005, March). *Tipping point: Maryland's overuse of incarceration and the impact on public safety* [Policy brief]. Washington, DC: Justice Policy Institute.

Lynch, J. P., & Sabol, W. J. (2001, September). *Prisoner reentry in perspective* (NCJ 191685). Washington, DC: Urban Institute.

Mauer, M., & Chesney-Lind, M. (Eds.). (2002). *Invisible punishment: The collateral consequences of mass imprisonment.* New York: The New Press.

National Advisory Commission on Criminal Justice Standards and Goals. (1973). *Corrections.* Washington, DC: U.S. Government Printing Office.

National Criminal Justice Reference Service: http://www.ncjrs.gov

Pettit, B., & Western, B. (2004). Mass imprisonment and the life course: Race and class inequality in U.S. incarceration. *American Sociological Review, 69,* 151–169.

Prison Policy Initiative: www.prisonpolicy.org

Renauer, B. C., Cunningham, W. S., Feyerherm, B., O'Connor, T., & Bellatty, P. (2006). Tipping the scales of justice: The effect of overincarceration on neighborhood violence. *Criminal Justice Policy Review, 77*(3), 362–379.

Rothfield, M. (2008, May 7). Foes sue over prison bond sale. *Los Angeles Times.* Retrieved April 1, 2008, from http://www.latimes.com

Seiter, R., & Kadela, K. (2003). Prisoner reentry: What works, what does not, and what is promising. *Crime & Delinquency, 49,* 360–388.

Sentencing Project, The: http://www.sentencingproject.org

Shaw, C., & McKay, H. (1942). *Juvenile delinquency and urban areas.* Chicago: University of Chicago Press.

Uggen, C., & Manza, J. (2002). Democratic contraction? Political consequences of felon disenfranchisement in the United States. *American Sociological Review, 67,* 777–803.

Uggen, C., Manza, J., & Thompson, M. (2006). Citizenship, democracy, and the civic reintegration of criminal offenders. *Annals of the American Academy of Political and Social Sciences, 605,* 281–310.

Urban Institute: http://www.urbaninstitute.org

U.S. Bureau of Justice Statistics (BJS): http://www.ojp.usdoj.gov/bjs

Western, B. (2002). The impact of incarceration on wage mobility arid inequality. *American Sociological Review, 67,* 526–546.

Western, B., Kling, J., & Weiman, D. (2001). The labor market consequences of incarceration. *Crime & Delinquency, 47,* 410–427.

Wood, P., & Dunaway, R. G. (2003). Consequences of truth-in-sentencing: The Mississippi case. *Punishment & Society, 5,* 139–154.

COMMUNITY CORRECTIONS

Leanne Fiftal Alarid

Out of the nearly 7 million people currently on correctional supervision in the United States, only 30% of them are incarcerated in jail or prison. The remaining 70% of persons who have had contact with the criminal justice system are supervised within the community (Alarid, Cromwell, & del Carmen, 2008). This entry discusses community corrections, which is defined as a court-ordered sanction in which offenders serve at least some of their sentence in the community.

Three assumptions rest behind the idea of community corrections. First, most people who break the law are not dangerous or violent. The vast majority of offenders have violated a law that requires that they be held responsible through some sort of injunction or punishment, but most do not need to be locked away from the community. Keeping the offender in the community can be effective if the offender is able to maintain employment obligations and family relationships and to attempt to repair harm he or she caused the community or an identified victim—all of this at a reduced cost to taxpayers.

Second, a community sentence seeks to treat behaviors that are directly related to why the offender got into trouble in the first place, so that the risk of future reoffending is significantly reduced. The assumption here is that treatment programs are more numerous and accessible in the community than in jail and prison. This makes it easier for offenders to get the help they need while in the community and subsidize the cost with their own funds. A final assumption is that people who have been incarcerated in jail and prison transition better when they are released with some supervision than without any supervision (Petersilia, 2001).

Understanding the concept of community corrections will be accomplished through a discussion of five main areas:

- ♦ Goals of a community sentence
- ♦ Types of community corrections programs
- ♦ Advantages and disadvantages of community corrections programs
- ♦ Cost of community corrections programs
- ♦ Do community corrections programs work?

GOALS OF A COMMUNITY SENTENCE

Community corrections programs attempt to accomplish many goals. These goals include easing institutional crowding and cost; preventing future criminal behavior through surveillance, rehabilitation, and community reintegration; and addressing victims' needs through restorative justice. Each of these goals is discussed below.

Easing Institutional Crowding and Cost

Two things are abundantly clear. First, building jails and prisons is a costly endeavor. Second, there are legal limits that define how many prisoners a single correctional institution can hold. Correctional institutions that exceed their capacity may incur civil lawsuits and fines. Therefore, one goal of community corrections programs is to ease institutional crowding in jails and prisons by drawing from the population of convicted offenders who are predicted to be less risky to the outside community. Given that there are far fewer beds available than the number of people arrested, community corrections programs control crowding by separating out the people who need to be in jail from the people who pose less risk (Harris, 1999).

Another way of controlling prison populations historically has been to allow prisoners who have served the minimum amount of time on their sentence the opportunity for early release on parole. Parole is the privileged and discretionary release from prison on community supervision until the remaining time on one's sentence has expired. Parole has thus been used to make room for incoming prisoners.

Surveillance

Safety of the public is an important concern for any offender supervision program. To maintain public safety, offenders under supervision should be assessed to determine the degree of risk posed by their participation in community programs. Offenders who pose a serious danger to society or to themselves should not be in a community corrections program. Instead, these offenders should be incarcerated in jail or prison until they are no longer dangerous to themselves or others. For those on community supervision, compliance with court-ordered sanctions is carefully monitored by trained community officers. Finally, violations of supervised conditions are taken seriously for those who cannot or will not comply with the conditions.

Addressing Problems Related to Criminal Behavior

Correcting some of the problems that are directly linked to criminal behavior and continued involvement in the criminal justice system is another goal. Some of these problems include drug or alcohol addiction, lack of emotional control, inadequate education or vocational training, parenting problems, and mental illness or developmental disability (Alarid & Reichel, 2008). The offender attends classes to address these issues while on supervision with greater access to treatment programs than the individual would have had in jail or prison. The basis of effective rehabilitation is the use of cognitive-behavioral techniques and selecting offenders who have the desire to change.

Community Reentry

Community reintegration is an important goal for offenders released from jail or prison to gradually ease their reentry into society. Community-based correctional programs help in this endeavor with a minimal level of supervision while simultaneously allowing the offender to assume responsibilities and parental roles. In this way, getting released from prison is not such a culture shock, and this will hopefully decrease the probability of recidivism (Austin, 2001).

Restorative Justice

Restorative justice assumes that a crime harms the community and that sometimes there are individual victims involved. Often, victims of property crimes just want to be paid back or have things restored to their former condition—something that may not be possible if the offender goes to jail or prison. Restorative justice emphasizes offender responsibility to repair the injustice that offenders have caused their victims. Through victim and community involvement, such as face-to-face mediation sessions, victim impact panels, and volunteer mentoring, the offender remains in the community, completes community service, and pays victim restitution. Restorative justice is most effective for property crimes, particularly those committed by juveniles or first-time adult felony offenders (Bazemore & Stinchcomb, 2004).

Community-based programs are available at three decision points in the criminal justice process: at pretrial release before a defendant is convicted, after an offender is sentenced as an alternative to incarceration, and as an aid in reentering the community following a prison sentence (Alarid et al., 2008). Within these decision points, a wide variety of community programs are available, including residential halfway houses; nonresidential options such as probation, parole, and electronic monitoring; and economic sanctions such as restitution, fines, and forfeitures.

COMMUNITY CORRECTIONS PROGRAMS BEFORE CONVICTION

After the police arrest a suspect, the prosecutor's office decides whether to charge the suspect with a crime. If the prosecutor decides not to charge for lack of evidence, the suspect is automatically released. If the suspect will be charged with a crime, he or she becomes a "pretrial defendant" and appears before a judge to determine whether the defendant is eligible for release from jail. Although most defendants are released on their own recognizance with the promise to appear at their next court date, some defendants must be released on pretrial supervision, which is a form of correctional supervision of a defendant who has not yet been convicted.

Pretrial Supervision

The pretrial release decision is one of the first decisions judges make following an arrest so that some defendants can be released with supervision prior to their next court date. Pretrial release allows defendants who have not yet been convicted the opportunity to live and work as productive citizens until their next scheduled court date. Defendants can support their families and assist their attorneys in case preparation. In turn, the courts can be assured that the defendant will be more likely to appear. Pretrial supervision involves compliance with court-ordered conditions for a specified time period. Examples of court-ordered conditions include calling in or reporting for appointments, obtaining a substance abuse or mental health evaluation, maintaining employment, and avoiding contact with victims. The court can issue a warning, or modify or add more conditions for noncompliance. Continued noncompliance or committing a new crime can result in the court removing the defendant from pretrial supervision and incarcerating him or her in jail until the case has been processed.

Another form of community supervision without a conviction is diversion. Defendants are technically not convicted—rather, they enter into an agreement with the court to complete various conditions of probation, with the understanding that *successfully* completing these conditions will result in having the charges completely dismissed without a conviction. If a defendant does not succeed or commits a new crime during supervision, the courts will change the paperwork so that the defendant's conviction will become a permanent part of the record (Ulrich, 2002). Forms of pretrial supervision and diversion may include house arrest and electronic monitoring.

Electronic Monitoring and House Arrest

Electronic monitoring (EM) is a technology used to aid in the community-based supervision either before or after conviction. Monitoring electronically has a variety of levels, ranging from a basic unsophisticated phone line system that monitors offenders very infrequently to a continuous Global Positioning System (GPS) that can pinpoint the offender's exact location at all times.

House arrest requires a defendant to remain at his or her residence for a portion of the day. House arrest is often used in conjunction with electronic monitoring because the technology can enforce the curfew conditions, which can range from nighttime hours through any nonworking hours. This practice is also known as *home confinement*, which refers to the same program for convicted offenders.

The rest of this section will be devoted to discussing the various types of electronic monitoring, beginning with the earliest phone line systems. All monitoring devices consist of a transmitter that is attached to the offender's ankle, a receiver, and a pager. The less sophisticated versions have a transmitter that emits a continuous signal up to a 500-foot radius, and the signal is picked up by a receiver, usually attached to the offender's home telephone. The receiver is programmed to expect the transmitter's signal during those hours of the day that the offender is supposed to be at home. If the signal is not received when it should be, a computer sends a report of the violation to a central computer. These systems are not able to track offenders' whereabouts once they leave home. Given the drawbacks with the early systems and the increased need to track offenders away from home, a variety of other means of offender tracking have become available, including remote monitoring and global positioning satellite devices (Greek, 2002).

Remote location monitoring systems provide offenders with a special pager that can only receive incoming calls from the probation officer. When the pager beeps, the offender must call a central number within a designated period of time (e.g., 15 minutes). Voice verification ensures a positive match between the voice template and the voice on the phone. The computer records whether or not the voice matched and the phone number where the call originated. Some remote location monitors that offenders carry emit signals that may be intercepted only by the probation officers who carry the matching portable receiving unit. This enables officers to drive by a residence or workplace without the offender's knowledge to verify his or her whereabouts.

When the military allowed Global Positioning Systems (GPS) to be available for civilian use, it became the tracking method of choice for offenders that posed a higher risk to public safety. Offenders carry a transmitter that picks up the offender's location via satellite and a receiver that records and transmits data via a phone and a computer. This allows law enforcement to know an offender's whereabouts at all times (Greek, 2002).

TYPES OF COMMUNITY CORRECTIONS PROGRAMS AT THE SENTENCING DECISION

Probation Supervision

Probation supervision is the most frequently used community sentence for convicted offenders. Probation is defined as the community supervision of an offender under court-imposed conditions for a specified time period during which the court can modify conditions for noncompliance. Probation is credited to Boston shoemaker John Augustus, who devoted his life to helping offenders who had been arrested. Beginning in 1841, using his own money, Augustus assured the court that the defendant would return if the court released the defendant to his care. Probation became a formalized practice in 1878, three decades after Augustus began his work. By 1900, probation spread to other states as a discretionary sentence for persons charged with any level of offense (Panzarella, 2002).

Probation continues to serve as the primary sanction for criminal offenders. Nearly 60% (4 million) of the almost 7 million adults currently under correctional supervision are on probation.

The duties of probation officers have changed very little since the practice began. Probation officers are involved in information gathering for the court to determine the offender's suitability for probation. The probation officer monitors the whereabouts of the probationer and ensures that the conditions of probation are being followed. Officers have a predefined number of times they must contact offenders that they supervise; contacts consist of face-to-face meetings, telephone calls, and home visits. The officer refers offenders out to specialists who provide individual and group counseling to clients in areas such as drug and alcohol education, relapse prevention, and parenting education (Czuchry, Sia, & Dansereau, 2006).

Probation supervision includes standard conditions that every probationer agrees to abide by in return for remaining at liberty in the community. These conditions include full-time employment or attendance at school, obtaining permission before leaving the jurisdiction, submitting to searches without a warrant, avoiding association with persons having a criminal record, meeting with the probation officer on a regular basis, and paying monthly supervision fees. In addition, other more special conditions are ordered that relate directly to the crime or an identified victim. The offender may be required to repay the victim a specified sum of money or to perform a certain number of community service hours. The offender may also be required to pay for and participate in counseling, substance abuse treatment, or parenting classes.

Individuals on probation supervision serve 1 to 3 years, with an average of 2 years. An estimated 8 out of 10 people on probation successfully complete the supervision without any trouble. The remaining 2 people who do not complete their original probation sentence have either committed a new criminal act or have repeatedly failed to abide by multiple conditions of probation. When this happens, probation officers report the infractions to the judge. The judge makes the final decision, choosing either to modify existing probation conditions while the offender remains in the community or to revoke probation completely, which means that the offender is resentenced to jail or prison (Gray, Fields, & Maxwell, 2001).

Day Reporting Centers

Day reporting centers are a more intensive form of community supervision that occurs simultaneously with probation. Whereas probationers on regular supervision may be required to check in monthly or only every 3 months, day reporting centers require probationers to visit a specific center 3 to 6 days each week for an average duration of 5 months. Some visits may be merely checking in, and other visits require participation in classes or outpatient treatment. Day reporting centers aim to provide offenders with access to treatment or services, and they typically supervise offenders who have previously violated probation conditions, such as those who continue to abuse drugs. Therefore, day reporting centers serve as a sanction between probation and jail (Bahn & Davis, 1998).

Day reporting centers operate on a behavior modification model of levels or phases, with the beginning phase being the strictest, with the least amount of freedom. For example, offenders are tested for drug use at random, five times each month during the most intensive phase. As offenders successfully work the program, the freedom gradually increases and the supervision decreases. Day reporting centers also have partnerships with local businesses and treatment facilities to provide numerous on-site services to address employment, education, and counseling.

Community Drug Treatment Programs

For offenders who have problems with drugs or alcohol, community-based treatment programs offer meetings between 1 and 3 times per week for a designated period of time while the offenders live and work independently. It is estimated that drug or alcohol use or abuse affects about 7 out of 10 people who get into legal trouble. Outpatient treatment may be used during transition from inpatient drug treatment, transition from prison, or solely as a part of probation conditions. Several options are available depending on the extent of the problem. Some programs are tailored to chronic abusers, while others are for occasional users (Alarid & Reichel, 2008).

Outpatient treatment for more chronic abusers typically includes a combination of medication and counseling. Some medication is designed to react negatively with alcohol, creating severe nausea and vomiting whenever alcohol is ingested. Other medications ease the discomfort of withdrawal from substances like heroin and cocaine (similar to the way nicotine patches and gum work to help people stop smoking cigarettes). Forms of therapy include relapse prevention that continues to enforce sobriety and ways of dealing with cravings and stress, and Alcoholics or Narcotics Anonymous, based on a support system of recovery using a designated sponsor within a 12-step program. A third method includes involving the family as a social support system in the defendant's drug treatment. Often, family members are not aware of how they subtly contribute to their loved one's habit or how they neglect to provide healthy outlets for sobriety.

Community Service

Community service is a court-ordered requirement that offenders labor in unpaid work for the general good of the community. The appeal of community service is that it benefits the community through the offender's expenditure of time and effort in less-than-desirable jobs. Community service dates back to the Middle Ages when small towns in Germany allowed offenders to clean the town canal and pick up refuse for an unpaid fine. Community service was first used in the United States in the mid-1960s as punishment for juvenile delinquents, traffic offenders, white-collar criminals, and substance-abusing celebrities. Community service may be used in a variety of ways, such as with diversion or with probation. It provides an alternative sanction for poor offenders who are unable to afford monetary sanctions and is also appropriate for wealthy persons whose financial resources are so great that monetary restitution has no punitive effect.

Faith-based organizations, homeless shelters, and other nonprofit organizations have benefited from the community service labor. Offenders must labor between 40 and 1,000 hours before their service is considered complete. Community service ironically remains an underused sanction. Nationwide, only 1 out of 4 felons on probation is required to perform community service hours. Among the reasons behind this underutilization are the lack of coordination with documenting the hours, the difficulty of enforcing compliance during the work, and the need to provide evidence of completion for the court.

Restitution

Restitution is court-ordered payment that an offender makes to the victim to offset some of the losses incurred from the crime. Victim compensation for harm caused is one of the oldest principles of justice, dating back to the Old Testament and to other early legal codes. Restitution is an essential means of repaying the victim and is a step toward offender rehabilitation (Ruback & Bergstrom, 2006).

In the past, restitution payments were cancelled if offenders went to prison. As a result of the victims' rights movement in the 1980s, victims demanded that offenders pay restitution and back child support regardless of their sentence. Restitution is now mandatory in some states for violent crimes such as sexual abuse, domestic violence, and property offenses. However, there are still areas of the country that do not require prisoners to pay restitution if incarcerated, paroled, or released from probation.

The other problem with restitution is its lack of enforcement, leading to low collection rates. Collection of restitution is enforced by probation and parole officers who collect the payment. The court mandates it as a condition of a sentence, but collection rates are surprisingly low. One reason for this is that offenders tend to be employed in low-paying jobs and have other financial obligations such as monthly probation fees and treatment costs. These obligations seem to take precedence over restitution, which is of lower priority. Research shows that offenders who were most likely to make full payments were the ones who were employed or had strong ties to their community.

One method of increasing compliance rates is to get the victim actively involved. Victims who attended offender mediation sessions were significantly more likely to receive full restitution payments from youthful offenders than were victims who were uninvolved. A second method of increasing compliance rates is the use of restitution centers—residential facilities that aid in restitution payment collection while an offender resides there (Outlaw & Ruback, 1999).

Fines

A fine is a fixed amount imposed by the judge, defined by the severity of the crime. In the United States, fines are typically used for traffic offenses, misdemeanors, and ordinance violations, where the average fine is $100. Because traffic and misdemeanor violations are so numerous throughout the United States, fines are actually the most frequently used sanction of all. Fines are used more frequently in smaller jurisdictions than in larger urban counties.

If fines are used for felony crimes that are punishable by one year or more in prison, fines are typically in addition to probation or parole. An average fine for a felony case is $1,000 and could go as high as $10,000. The only exception here is organizational or corporate defendants involved in corporate crime. Fines amounting to hundreds of thousands of dollars are routinely used in lieu of imprisonment for the vast majority of white-collar crimes. In other countries, fines are used for a wider variety of street crimes as standalone punishments—meaning a fine is used as a substitute for incarceration (Ruback & Bergstrom, 2006).

Correctional Boot Camps

Correctional boot camps are modeled after the military and target first-time felony offenders between the ages of 17 and 24. These young adults have committed a crime for which going to prison for 1 year or more was a possibility, and boot camp offers them an alternative chance to spend 90 to 180 days in an intense situation before being transferred out to community supervision. The programs use the military's philosophy of breaking down and rebuilding one's character, physical conditioning, labor, and drills to transform an offender into a responsible adult and hopefully to deter them from future law-breaking behavior (Wilson, MacKenzie, & Mitchell, 2005). Work assignments involve clearing land, digging ditches, or draining swamps in addition to facility maintenance and cleaning. Some boot camps involve inmates in projects benefiting the community such as cutting firewood for elderly citizens or separating recyclables. In addition, treatment and educational components enhance the needs of this young population.

Correctional boot camps began in 1983, and within a decade, over 7,000 offenders were in these programs in 30 states. Program participants often showed short-term positive attitude change, increased self-respect, and improved self-confidence after release. But it seemed that the positive attitudes were not sustained for the long term, and the recidivism rates were no different from comparison groups who had not been to boot camp. These were also the most expensive community corrections programs to operate because of the skills and abilities needed for drill instructors to work with each platoon. Over the last 10 years, boot camp programs have decreased in number or completely closed due to a high cost with negligible long-term benefits (Bottcher & Ezell, 2005).

TYPES OF COMMUNITY CORRECTION PROGRAMS AT REENTRY

Community corrections programs assist offenders in community reentry after they have spent time in prison. Two of them are discussed here: a pre-release facility and parole.

Pre-Release Facility

A pre-release program is a minimum-security residential facility where offenders can live and work and be closely supervised by authorities. Pre-release facilities are also known as community centers, halfway houses, and residential community correction facilities. A 6- to 12-month stay in a halfway house allows time for offenders to gradually adjust to freedom, obtain employment, and save money for independent living on parole. Pre-release facilities provide access to various community services that can help offenders with drug and alcohol dependency, job interviewing, or budgeting. Through a semistructured environment, prerelease facilities allow offenders temporary passes to leave the facility for a variety of reasons, including to reestablish family relationships; find affordable housing; secure employment; obtain a bus pass, identification, eye-glasses, or medication; and reconnect with other social service and community agencies. Residents are often expected to pay for treatment services and subsidize their living expenses with money earned from their job. The goal of pre-release facilities is for the offender to receive parole or some form of post-release supervision (Alarid & Reichel, 2008).

Parole and Post-Release Supervision

Parole is defined as the discretionary release of an offender by a parole board of 3–12 people before the expiration of his or her sentence. In deciding whom to release, the parole board considers factors such as the offender's conduct and participation in rehabilitative programs while in prison, the offender's attitude toward the crime, whether there is a solid release plan (housing, work, etc.), the reaction of the victim to the offender's release, and the need to provide space in the prison to receive newly sentenced prisoners (Petersilia, 2001).

A second form of supervision is called *mandatory release*, which is an automatic release to the community when a prisoner has completed a certain percentage of his or her sentence. While a parole board decides whom to release and who will stay in prison longer, mandatory release follows the law established by legislators in each state. Supervised mandatory release is used in states where parole boards have been abolished or where the parole board has limited powers with certain violent crimes. The rate of mandatory releases now outpaces discretionary releases (Petersilia, 2001).

Both forms of supervision involve conditions such as requiring the parolee to report to the parole officer; to get permission to move, change jobs, or leave the area; prohibition from having weapons; and so forth. Many parole or post-release conditions are similar to probation conditions discussed in a previous section. There is also the same possibility of revocation should the offender violate any conditions or commit a new crime. In the supervision of parolees, parole officers perform tasks similar to those done by probation officers. The two positions are enough alike that in the

federal system and in most states, probation and parole departments are combined.

ADVANTAGES AND DISADVANTAGES OF COMMUNITY CORRECTIONS PROGRAMS

Community corrections programs offer some distinct advantages. The first is a cost issue. Compared to jail and prison, most community programs cost less. Offenders live at home, and in the small number of residential programs where the offender lives at the facility, they help subsidize the cost of living. In addition, offenders who remain in the community can continue financially supporting themselves and their family through receiving wages and paying taxes. They are also more likely than incarcerated offenders to compensate their victim through restitution and to complete community service (Petersilia, 2001).

Second, community programs can ease jail and prison crowding by allowing convicted offenders the chance to complete a drug program, boot camp, or other corrections program, and are thus another form of cost savings.

A third aspect to community corrections is the flexibility of the programs in that they can be used at many points in the criminal justice process. Community punishments limit the freedoms of convicted offenders and mandate treatment. They can also be used as a pretrial release option and as a diversion to avoiding a conviction altogether. Community supervision also aids in the reentry process after a period of incarceration.

Finally, community corrections programs avoid exposing offenders to jail and prison conditions that may be unsafe and at times even violent. Some people might be helped more in other ways. For example, community sentences can be beneficial for those needing medical attention, such as terminally ill, physically disabled, or elderly offenders, who may be better suited for a sentence within their own residence. Other offenders such as developmentally disabled or mentally ill individuals experience higher rates of victimization in prison and may be appropriately placed and treated elsewhere. An institutional environment is not for everyone, and may cause more harm than good (Alarid et al., 2008).

Disadvantages

Perhaps the most prominent advantage of community corrections can also be its greatest disadvantage. As previously mentioned, drug programs and boot camps might ease crowding by placing prison-bound offenders in a program that allows them the chance to avoid incarceration, but such programs might also be filled with offenders who actually should have received a less severe sentence. This is a situation known as *net widening*, and it happens when judges and prosecutors fill the program spaces with offenders who do not necessarily require such a high level of care or intervention rather than the ones the program was actually designed for. Not only are prison-bound offenders not getting their chance to be placed in appropriate programs and have access to services, but the cost of punishment actually increases. Officials often feel they must maximize program capacity because it is there (Alarid et al., 2008).

Another disadvantage is that public safety may be compromised. Offenders are more easily able to continue criminal behavior than if they were confined in jail or prison. With funding going to jails and prisons, resources have not kept pace with community corrections growth. With resources spread so thinly, officers now supervise more offenders and are able to spend less time on each person. Technology is slowly replacing human supervision. However, even when home confinement is combined with electronic monitoring technology, authorities cannot be completely assured that offenders will refrain from criminal activity. For example, being that home confinement programs allow offenders to leave their residences for activities such as work and shopping, it is possible that crimes can be committed even when offenders are legitimately away from home.

Many community supervision programs are disconnected from the various treatment services that exist to address the multitude of problems offenders face. This becomes a disadvantage to an offender's success when treatment attendance is lacking because of transportation problems and inability to miss work. Programs like day reporting centers that comprehensively address drug abuse, job training, employment, physical or sexual victimization, parenting education, and anger management all in one location tend to have higher completion rates (Bahn & Davis, 1998).

DAILY COST OF COMMUNITY CORRECTIONS PROGRAMS

A grand total of $62 billion is spent on the punishment and treatment of 7 million offenders every year. Jails and prisons are the most expensive forms of punishment, costing between $50 and $100 per day per person depending on the level of custody and the region of the country (Alarid & Reichel, 2008). Jails and prisons also consume most of the correctional budget. Very little, if any, of that cost is subsidized by the offender.

Most community corrections programs are subsidized in part by the offender and thus are considered more cost-effective. Starting with a base cost for probation supervision at $1 per day for low supervision, probation can range up to $15 per day per person for intense probation supervision. In each case, the offender pays for about 10% of the cost. Pretrial supervision costs are generally lower than probation. Day reporting centers also vary widely, from $10 to $100 per day per person.

Other programs such as electronic monitoring require that additional staff be hired to supervise the technological devices, at an estimated cost of $4 to $20 per day, depending on the amount the offender pays. Typical home-based electronic monitoring supervision costs the offender nearly $10 per day, and GPS monitoring is about $16 per day (Alarid et al., 2008).

Residential community correction programs are significantly higher. A prerelease program may cost $45 to $60 per day, but one third of that cost is subsidized by the offender. A correctional boot camp is by far the most expensive option, costing more than jail or prison, with no financial support from the offender. As a result, the number of correctional boot camps has declined over the years because the benefits were not outweighing the high costs.

DO COMMUNITY CORRECTIONS PROGRAMS WORK?

In the 1970s, sentencing disparity drew attention in the courts and from the parole boards. People were concerned with the fact that some offenders served significantly longer periods of time than others for the same crime. Community treatment programs were also criticized for not being able to do much about preventing future criminal activity while offenders were under supervision. Studies concluded that some strategies worked and other programs did not significantly reduce crime. The lack of confidence in correctional programming sparked a national debate about the efficacy of rehabilitation and influenced treatment offerings within all community-based programs. One positive outcome of this was the increased attention paid to the different types of offenders and situations in which certain treatment modalities will perform better.

Today, with more sophisticated computer technology and statistical tests available, there are more rigorous tests to determine what does and does not work in terms of both treatment and supervision strategies. The most common way of measuring program effectiveness is to determine whether or not offenders return to criminal behavior. This is better known as recidivism and is measured by rearrest, reconviction, or another term of incarceration. Recidivism should be measured during the period of supervision and after supervision ends, for a period of 1 to 5 years. Other outcome data that could be used to measure effectiveness might be specific components unique to that program, such as the collection rate for fines and restitution, the percentage of offenders who remain employed or in school, the number of GED certificates or high school diplomas awarded, and the number of community service hours performed. Since one of the goals mentioned previously is to ease crowding, effectiveness could be measured based on cost savings or whether a new jail or prison had to be built to accommodate the overflow.

To properly evaluate a program, a "treatment" group of offenders could be selected at random to participate in a program, and a "control" group would consist of the offenders who are sentenced to a form of regular probation supervision. However, the political nature of elected judges and appointed prosecutors rarely permits this type of evaluation to occur. Furthermore, many sentencing laws mandate a certain form of punishment for certain crimes, so random selection may be illegal in some cases. The following is a summary list of principles of effectiveness from various community corrections programs (Bottcher & Ezell, 2005; Deschenes, Turner, & Petersilia, 1995; Fischer, 2003; Padgett, Bales, & Blomberg, 2006; Wilson et al., 2005):

- Offenders who are in day reporting centers, boot camps, and halfway houses have more complex problems and a higher risk of recidivism than typical probationers. As a result, offenders in residential facilities are more likely to receive a wider variety of treatment and counseling services than are offenders on traditional probation or parole.
- Surveillance alone will not reduce recidivism. Regardless of the level of supervision or type of community corrections program, offenders need to be participating simultaneously in treatment programs while under supervision.
- The closer the supervision, the more likely the officer will catch the offender in some sort of a rule violation. Treatment options, as opposed to punitive options, are recommended for offenders who violate supervision regulations.
- Community programs that were the most effective tended to be longer in duration, offered treatment during the program, offered convenience to treatment services all in one location, and intertwined an aftercare program that gradually tapered off the supervision over a period of 2 years.
- Programs that have high completion rates are probation and electronic monitoring programs where the supervision term is for less than one year.
- Correctional boot camp participants overall had no difference in recidivism rates from groups of probationers and parolees. Although there may be some studies showing a small difference—particularly those programs with treatment programs—the overall effect is no different in terms of reducing crime in the future.

♦ Paying fines and restitution has little effect on recidivism.

CONCLUSION

Few studies have compared offenders sentenced to jail or prison with those sentenced to a community-based program. Although the rate of reoffending is lower for offenders sentenced in the community, when prior criminal record is controlled, there is little overall difference in recidivism rates between the two sanctions. If that is the case, it seems reasonable to choose the less expensive punishment option and reserve prisons for the select few persons who are true dangers to the rest of society.

REFERENCES AND FURTHER READINGS

Alarid, L. F., Cromwell, P. F., & del Carmen, R. (2008). *Community-based corrections* (7th ed.). Belmont, CA: Wadsworth/Cengage.

Alarid, L. F., & Reichel, P. L. (2008). *Corrections: A contemporary introduction.* Boston: Allyn & Bacon.

Austin, J. (2001). Prisoner reentry: Current trends, practices, and issues. *Crime & Delinquency, 47*(3), 314–334.

Bahn, C.. & Davis, J. R. (1998). Day reporting centers as an alternative to incarceration. *Journal of Offender Rehabilitation, 27,* 139–150.

Bazemore, G., & Stinchcomb, J. (2004). A civic engagement model of reentry: Involving community through service and restorative justice. *Federal Probation, 68*(2), 14–24.

Bottcher, J., & Ezell, M. E. (2005). Examining the effectiveness of boot camps: A randomized experiment with a long-term follow-up. *Journal of Research in Crime and Delinquency, 42*(1), 309–332.

Czuchry, M., Sia, T. L., & Dansereau, D. F. (2006). Improving early engagement and treatment readiness of probationers. *Prison Journal, 56*(1), 56–74.

Deschenes, E. P., Turner, S., & Petersilia, J. (1995). A dual experiment in intensive community supervision: Minnesota's Prison Diversion and Enhanced Supervised Release Programs. *Prison Journal, 75*(3), 330–356.

Fischer, B. (2003). "Doing good with a vengeance": A critical assessment of the practices, effects, and implications of drug treatment courts in North America. *Criminal Justice, 3*(3), 227–248.

Gray, M. K., Fields, M., & Maxwell, S. R. (2001). Examining probation violations: Who, what, and when. *Crime & Delinquency, 47*(4), 537–557.

Greek, C. E. (2002). Tracking probationers in space and time: The convergence of GIS and GPS systems. *Federal Probation, 66*(1), 51–53.

Harris, P. M. (1999). *Research to results: Effective community corrections.* Lanham, MD: American Correctional Association.

Outlaw, M. C., & Ruback, R. B. (1999). Predictors and outcomes of victim restitution orders. *Justice Quarterly, 16,* 847–869.

Padgett, K. G., Bales, W. D., & Blomberg, T. G. (2006). Under surveillance: An empirical test of the effectiveness and consequences of electronic monitoring. *Criminology & Public Policy, 5*(1), 61–92.

Panzarella, R. (2002). Theory and practice of probation on bail in the report of John Augustus. *Federal Probation, 66*(3), 38–42.

Petersilia, J. (2001). *Reforming probation and parole in the 21st century.* Lanham, MD: American Correctional Association.

Ruback, R. B., & Bergstrom, M. H. (2006). Economic sanctions in criminal justice: Purposes, effects, and implications. *Criminal Justice and Behavior, 33*(2), 242–273.

Ulrich, T. E. (2002). Pretrial diversion in the federal court system. *Federal Probation, 66*(3), 30–37.

Wilson, D. B., MacKenzie, D. L., & Mitchell, F. N. (2005). *Effects of correctional boot camps on offending.* A Campbell Collaboration Crime and Justice Group Systematic review. Retrieved February 1, 2009, from http://www.aic.gov.au

CREDITS

Joycelyn M. Pollock, "Crime in Society," *Crime and Justice in America*, pp. 27–52. Copyright © 2008 by Elsevier Science and Technology. Reprinted with permission.

Joycelyn M. Pollock, "Why Do People Commit Crime?," *Crime and Justice in America*, pp. 53–78. Copyright © 2008 by Elsevier Science and Technology. Reprinted with permission.

Cesare Lombroso with Gina Lombroso–Ferrero, "The Criminal Man." Copyright in the Public Domain.

Mark M. Lanier and Stuart Henry, "What is Criminology? The Study of Crime, Criminals, and Victims in a Global Context," *Essential Criminology*, pp. 1–21. Copyright © 2009 by Perseus Books Group. Reprinted with permission.

William G. Doerner and Steven P. Lab, "The Scope of Victimology," *Victimology*, pp. 1–25. Copyright © 2008 by Elsevier Science and Technology. Reprinted with permission.

Doris Layton MacKenzie, Lauren O'Neill, and Wendy Povitsky, "Understanding Criminals and Crime: Theory and Research," *Different Crimes, Different Criminals*, pp. 1–8. Copyright © 2006 by Elsevier Science and Technology. Reprinted with permission.

Michael C. Braswell, Belinda R. McCarthy, and Bernard J. McCarthy, "Ethics and Criminal Justice Research," *Justice, Crime and Ethics*, pp. 393–415. Copyright © 2008 by Elsevier Science and Technology. Reprinted with permission.

Mark Mitchell; ed. Aaron Pycroft, Dennis Gough, and Tom Wengraf, "Diversity and the Policy Agenda in Criminal Justice," *Multi–Agency Working in Criminal Justice*, pp. 51–64. Copyright © 2010 by The Policy Press. Reprinted with permission.

Michael C. Braswell, Belinda R. McCarthy, and Bernard J. McCarthy, "Ethical Issues in Crime Control Policy and Research," *Justice, Crime and Ethics*, pp. 347–348. Copyright © 2008 by Elsevier Science and Technology. Reprinted with permission.

Victor E. Kappeler and Larry K. Gaines, "The Idea of Community Policing," *Community Policing*, pp. 1–38. Copyright © 2009 by Elsevier Science and Technology. Reprinted with permission.

CPSIA information can be obtained
at www.ICGtesting.com
Printed in the USA
FSOW02n0259260115
4782FS

9 781626 617544